INTERNATIONAL LIBRARY OF
AFRO-AMERICAN LIFE AND HISTORY

1. Dr. John V. De Grasse

2. The 1914 editorial staff of NMA *Journal*

3. Mary Eliza Mahoney, nurse

4. Harlem Hospital, 1887

5. Picketing for medical civil

6. Dr. Hubert A. Eaton

INTERNATIONAL LIBRARY OF

AFRO-AMERICAN LIFE

AND HISTORY

THE HISTORY OF
THE AFRO-AMERICAN
IN MEDICINE

BY

HERBERT M. MORAIS

THE PUBLISHERS AGENCY, INC.
CORNWELLS HEIGHTS, PENNSYLVANIA
under the auspices of
THE ASSOCIATION FOR THE STUDY OF AFRO-AMERICAN LIFE AND HISTORY

To ANNE

in gratitude and appreciation

for her invaluable help

Editor-in-Chief, CHARLES H. WESLEY

Research Editor, PATRICIA W. ROMERO

Production Editor, ALLAN S. KULLEN

Art Director, ARCHIE MIDDLETON

Copy Editor, MARY NEELY ELDRIDGE

Editorial Coordinator, ALLAN S. KULLEN

THE EXECUTIVE COUNCIL OF

THE ASSOCIATION FOR THE STUDY OF AFRO-AMERICAN LIFE AND HISTORY

Foreword

THIS book, the story of the Afro-American in medicine, deals with an important but neglected phase of America's past and present. The author trusts that it will provide stimulating reading for Americans in all walks of life. The work contains biographical sketches, personal recollections of participants and authentic accounts which tell of the struggle waged by Afro-Americans for the elimination of racial bias in the field of medicine. Background material, particularly of a socio-economic nature, has been included to give a deeper insight into those problems that currently beset black doctors, nurses and patients. Today, these problems cry out for solution. There is, as the final chapter suggests, "no time for delay."

The story of Jim Crow in medicine is an aspect of American life that must be presented to the public. This book is the first attempt to do so. It does not purport to be a definitive study; it is rather an introduction to a virtually untapped field. Limitations of space have forced the author to restrict his discussion to black doctors, nurses and patients, though he is fully aware of the noteworthy contributions made by black dentists and pharmacists to their professions and to the civil-rights movement.

It is hoped that this preliminary account will stimulate others to further investigation. The book contains a comprehensive bibliography designed to serve as a guide to the literature, and an appendix consisting of original source documents. The author is indebted to those scholars whose spadework in the field was of inestimable aid in writing this account. Their contributions have been duly noted in an introductory annotation to the bibliography. A special word of appreciation is due to Mr. Allan S. Kullen, production editor of the *International Library of Afro-American Life and History,* for his painstaking care in preparing the manuscript for publication and his untiring efforts in assembling photographs to illustrate the text, and documents to give it greater dimension.

HERBERT M. MORAIS

Laguna Hills, California

Foreword to Revised Edition

Since the mid-1960's, significant developments have taken place in the desegregation of the medical profession and the organization and delivery of health services to black ghettos. To describe these developments and to delineate the progress made, a completely new Chapter Ten has been written. Based on official government documents, reports of semi-public investigative agencies, articles in newspapers and magazines, convention proceedings of medical and paramedical bodies and the bulletins and press releases of foundations and civil rights organizations, the newly written chapter brings the history of the Afro-American in medicine up to date. In addition, it fits into the pattern and sequence of the earlier edition of the book by substantially following its main themes.

H. M. M.

Laguna Hills, California

Preface

THE Association for the Study of Afro-American Life and History joins with Pubco Corporation in presenting this new series of volumes which treat in detail the cultural and historical backgrounds of black Americans. This Association, a pioneer in the area of Afro-American History, was founded on September 9, 1915, by Dr. Carter G. Woodson, who remained its director of research and publications until his death in 1950.

In 1916 Dr. Woodson began publishing the quarterly *Journal of Negro History*. In 1926 Negro History Week was launched, and since that time it has been held annually in February, encompassing the birth dates of Abraham Lincoln and Frederick Douglass. The *Negro History Bulletin* was first published in 1937 to serve both schools and families by making available to them little-known facts about black life and history.

During its sixty-one years of existence, the Association for the Study of Afro-American Life and History has supported many publications dealing with the contributions of Afro-Americans to the growth and development of this country. Its activities have contributed to the increasing interest in the dissemination of factual studies which are placing the Afro-American in true perspective in the mainstream of American history.

We gratefully acknowledge the contributions of previous scholars, which have aided us in the preparation of this *International Library of Afro-American Life and History*.

Our grateful acknowledgment is also expressed to Charles W. Lockyer, president of Pubco Corporation, whose challenging approach has made possible this library.

Though each of the volumes in this set can stand as an autonomous unit, and although each author has brought his own interpretation to the area with which he is dealing, together these books form a comprehensive picture of the Afro-American experience in America. The three history volumes give a factual record of a people who were brought from Africa in chains and who today are struggling to cast off the last vestiges of these bonds. The anthologies covering music, art, the theatre and literature provide a detailed account of the black American's contributions to these fields—including those contributions which are largely forgotten today. Achievement in the sports world is covered in another volume. The volume on the Afro-American in medicine is a history of the black American's struggle for equality as a medical practitioner and as a patient. The selected black leaders in the biography book represent the contributions and achievements of many times their number. The documentary history sums up the above-mentioned material in the words of men and women who were themselves a part of black history.

CHARLES H. WESLEY

Washington, D.C.

Table of Contents

APPENDIX

Introduction

THERE is always a great lesson to be learned from history if one is willing to profit by the mistakes of others. This historical account of the story of "Jim Crow" in medicine and health is no exception. However, the tragedy, the misery, the suffering, the frustration and the despair which lie behind these historical facts, so graphically recorded by the author, can never, in reality, be expressed on paper. The struggles of those black men and women against unbelievable and almost insurmountable odds is a chapter in the history of man which must not be repeated; yet it is unfortunately evident that the lessons contained therein have not yet been learned, even as the year 1966 draws to a close.

The Afro-American is impoverished because he has been denied access to his history. The pride which other races have in their histories, and in their ancestral origins, has been denied the Afro-American. According to Congressman Joseph Resnick of New York, the Negro, unlike other immigrants, is one hundred per cent American because he has had to start from "scratch" here in America, his African origins having been obliterated. Dr. Alvin Poussaint, psychiatrist, states that the Afro-American's self-image has been damaged and distorted. He feels that this must be repaired in order for integration to be successful in this country.

The factual accounts of the achievements, in spite of handicaps, of Afro-American men and women presented in this volume are slightly known to some of you and completely unknown to others of you who will read about them for the first time. Always on the American scene, yet almost always separated by a curtain from the main stage, the players in this historical drama have received rave notices in the inadequate and incomplete archives of Afro-American history. Ignored, distorted, deliberately concealed or innocently omitted, the fact remains that by and large most of the information about the Afro-American in medicine remains unknown in the history of the United States. Whatever the reasons for these omissions, the whole of America suffers because of the obscurity of one of its vital cultures. Individually and collectively, we suffer because of this additional illustration of "man's inhumanity to man."

The author of this volume, with compassion, intelligence, objectivity and a genuine desire to right a wrong, has painstakingly researched and recorded these events, which, although tragic, are at the same time glorious and inspirational. All America can take pride in the achievements of the men about whom the author writes. Dr. Herbert M. Morais, the author, has been engaged for many years in comprehensive research in the history of medicine in the United States. His articles have appeared here and abroad. Among the most recent are "The Medical Profession and Workers' Health in Early Industrial America," published in the May, 1965, issue of the *Journal of Occupational Medicine,* and "Doctors and the American Revolution," published in the December, 1965, issue of *NTM (Naturwissenschaften, Technik und*

Medizin), a German publication of international fame. This present book is a logical outgrowth of his research into American medical history.

A multi-talented individual with great insight, Dr. Morais brings two important qualifications to his work: his close association with the medical profession as a former director of scientific communication for a leading pharmaceutical company, and a broad background in the field of American history. A student of the late Evarts Boutell Greene, DeWitt Clinton Professor of American History at Columbia University, he has delivered a paper before the American Historical Association and, together with other distinguished historians, has contributed to a collection of original studies, "The Era of the American Revolution," edited by Richard B. Morris, a book which was first published by the Columbia University Press and reprinted in 1965 as a volume in the Harper Torchbook Series.

Born in New York City, Dr. Morais now resides in California, where he is devoting himself completely to writing. He received his Bachelor of Arts degree from the College of the City of New York and his Master of Arts and Doctor of Philosophy degrees from Columbia University, New York City.

The denial of the right to good health care because of race cannot be justified. It has wasted too many years and has cost too many lives to be permitted to continue. It is a challenge for each and every one of us to correct this injustice. There is an old adage which states that history repeats itself. If America is to survive, this history must not be repeated. No one can be proud of the infamous dealings with human illness and misery in our history. Racism in medicine, rooted in slavery, continued by tradition and always illogical, casts an ominous shadow on our future. No one can justify the bigotry, the ignorance, the hate and the waste of human lives in this "land of the free, and home of the brave."

This book affords a view backward through the veil of misery and tears which shrouds the dark past. Today, the magnificent "freedom fighters," bravely singing "We Shall Overcome," are demanding the unconditional surrender of the forces of racism and reaction; this book should inspire us to join them as we struggle to erase "Jim Crow" from medicine and from the American scene. The late President John F. Kennedy said, "Every man should at some time in his life take a look about him, and try to right the wrongs that he sees. One man can make the difference, and every man should try."

The implementation of the "golden rule," and the translation of the will to do right into the pattern of each of our daily lives, will do much to ensure a bright and glorious new day, when men of all races may live together in peace and enjoy the fundamental human right to good health care.

JOHN L. S. HOLLOMAN, JR.
President,
National Medical Association

New York City

CHAPTER ONE

By Way of Introduction

. . . the problem of the 20th century is the problem of the color line. . . .
Dr. W. E. B. Du Bois as quoted in *The Crisis,*
January 1947.

Of all the forms of inequality, injustice in health is the most shocking and the most inhuman. . . .
The Rev. Martin Luther King at the Second
National Convention of the Medical Committee
for Human Rights, Chicago, March 25, 1966.

IT was early in April, 1963. The First Baptist Church in a fair-sized Southern city was crowded. The congregation, composed of Negroes all dressed in their Sunday best, was listening attentively as the minister, in ecclesiastic garb, began to warm to his sermon. Suddenly he stopped short. A Negro in the rear of the hall, critically ill, had toppled from his seat. Members of his family, sitting nearby, quickly sprang to his side, and when first-aid measures failed, they rushed him to the local hospital.

The hospital, serving the city, two counties and part of a third, had at least three hundred beds. Despite the fact that Negroes constituted more than half of the area's population, only one-fifth of the beds were allocated to them, except for some additional ones in the segregated pediatric and obstetrical rooms on two other floors. Under the circumstances, it was not unusual for the hospital to refuse admission to Negroes on the ground that no beds were available.

This Sunday morning was no exception. When members of the family arrived with the stricken Negro, they were told that there was "no room." The only thing that could be done, said the white admissions clerk, was to put the patient's name on a waiting list. Frantically, a relative of the sick Negro called on the minister of the church for help. Despite the clergyman's protests and pleas, the receptionist remained adamant. The minister, realizing the hopelessness of the situation, walked out of the room. Still in his church robes, he hurried to the "white" section of the hospital, where he soon found an empty bed. When he informed the clerk of this fact, it had no effect. Nothing could change the hospital's "no room" policy.

Two weeks later, in mid-April, a second Negro patient was denied admission to the same hospital for the same reason. The sick man died shortly after, although forty to sixty-five "white" beds were reported as being available during that period.

Like Negro patients, Negro physicians have been victimized by a racist ideology that has plagued the American scene from colonial times to the present. With few exceptions, they have been excluded from the mainstream of American medicine. Their humiliations, heartaches and frustrations have served only to underscore the old Negro folk saying: "If you're white, you're right, if you're brown, stick around, if you're black, get back." From the very beginning, Negro doctors have found themselves professionally isolated, the gates of opportunity padlocked against them and their potentialities for development not fully realized because of built-in color prejudices. That their achievements have been so considerable is a testimonial to their ability and fortitude.

Although far from complete, the following will indicate a few of the contributions made by Negroes to the forward march of American medicine and surgery: Dr. Daniel H. Williams, a charter member of the American College of Surgeons who discovered a way to "sew up" the heart; Dr. Charles R. Drew, who developed the blood plasma theory and the blood bank that saved countless thousands of lives during and after World War II; Dr. William A. Hinton of Harvard and Boston City Dispensary, originator of the delicate Hinton test for syphilis; Dr. Solomon C. Fuller, neuropathologist at Boston University whose published writings on psychiatry opened up new vistas and horizons; Dr. Theodore K. Lawless, innovator of new dermatologic techniques who taught at Northwestern; Dr. William H. Barnes, diplomate of the American Board of Otolaryngology and inventor of a delicate instrument to facilitate the approach to the pituitary glands; Dr. Louis T. Wright, director of surgery at Harlem Hospital under whom the "miracle drug" aureomycin was first tested in man; Dr. Ernest E. Just, a distinguished biologist who, as professor of physiology at the Howard University Medical School, did pioneer work in cell structure; and Dr. W. Montague Cobb, nationally and internationally known anatomist and physical anthropologist who helped perfect the standard color plate of the anatomy of the heart.

For too many years, Negroes have suffered from discriminatory treatment in medicine and health. Despite recent progress, there are still hospitals in the South where "Keep Out" signs are as firmly in place as ever before. There are hospitals, both North and South, that persist in the discriminatory practice of separating Negro and white patients. More often than not, the segregated colored wards are old, dilapidated and overcrowded. Shunted aside, Negro patients are forced to wait until death overtakes them or complications set in that transform minor illnesses and injuries into major ones.

Numerous current studies have established that Negroes do not have available to them the same quality or quantity of medical and hospital care as the rest of the population. Small wonder then that, as compared to whites, Negroes are more likely to die in infancy, lose their mothers in childbirth and live shorter lives. They miss more work days per year than whites and spend more days disabled and bedridden.

The health gap between the two races, although currently much narrower than during the Reconstruction period and the era of slavery, is still largely a product of racial segregation and discrimination on the one hand and widespread poverty on the other. At present, roughly one out of every two nonwhite families has a cash income below that which government agencies have officially established as the poverty line. To the great mass of Negro workers, unemployment and underemployment are constant threats. Their living conditions, particularly in congested slum areas, border on the desperate. Huddled together in ghettos, the Negro poor and near-poor are susceptible to every kind of illness. Who will deny that overcrowded living quarters, unsanitary conditions and lack of money for a balanced diet and proper medical care are the breeding grounds from which come premature deaths and infectious diseases?

Only by raising the living standards of the impoverished Negro masses and furnishing them with adequate medical care can racial disparities in health be sharply reduced in such categories as pulmonary infections, venereal diseases, childhood disorders and maternal complications, where Negro mortality and morbidity rates are much higher than those of whites. The task of providing jobs for the jobless, raising low incomes to higher levels and assuring adequate health and housing facilities for those in need calls for a social undertaking of monumental proportions. The success of such an enterprise will immeasurably improve the health of white and black alike, for who will dispute the fact that poor health in one segment of the population adversely affects the health of all?

The relatively unfavorable health status of the Negro people has been and still is closely related to larger patterns of racial segregation and discrimination. What Federal Security Administrator Oscar R. Ewing said

Because of overcrowded living quarters, unsanitary conditions and lack of a balanced diet and proper medical care, the Negro poor and near-poor are susceptible to every kind of disease.

OSCAR R. EWING

in 1952 concerning the problem of Negro health bears repetition today.

> We all know this problem stems from the inequality of life for the American Negro. It stems from the fact that he is too often compelled to accept the most unpleasant, the most hazardous, the least rewarding jobs. It stems from the fact that his income is lower than that of the rest of the population. It stems from the fact that he is too often forced to live in the crowded, unsanitary, depressing slums of America—the slums of parts of Harlem or the slums of the rural South. . . . It stems from the fact that he may too often find himself unable to get satisfactory hospital care—or, in some cases any hospital care at all. It stems from the fact that we do not have enough doctors to go around and that where this is the case the Negro patient too often is the one who gets no doctor's care at all. It stems from the fact that the Negro patient is too often unable to pay for the high costs of adequate medical and hospital care.

Racial segregation and discrimination, whether *de jure* in the South or *de facto* in the North, have been detrimental not only to the health of Negro Americans but also to the professional development of Negro physicians, nurses and associated personnel. Even today, as the massive Negro civil rights struggle of the past eleven years moves to fulfillment on the legal front, Negro physicians are barred from admission to state and county affiliates of the American Medical Association and to posts of responsibility commensurate with their talents in units where membership is open to them. They are also excluded from staff appointments in many Southern hospitals and in a number of private facilities in the North. In addition, policy-making positions in hospitals are closed to them, and they are frozen out of many research projects, no matter what their capabilities. Negro nurses, too, still have a long way to go before they attain the full racial equality implicit in the integration of their profession by the American Nurses' Association more than a decade and a half ago.

Today young Negroes are being deterred from careers in medicine not only by the persistence of discriminatory practices but also by the virtual impossibility of meeting high admission requirements with inferior, pre-professional Jim Crow schooling. In recent years, fewer and fewer Negro students have enrolled in medical schools, and as a result, those entering the profession have not been able to counterbalance the number of Negro doctors who have died or retired. The same is true with respect to Negro nurses.

This situation presents a particularly serious problem since the nation currently faces an acute shortage of medical, nursing and auxiliary health personnel. All indications point to the fact that the situation will become increasingly critical in the foreseeable future. Under the circumstances, special efforts should be made now to tap one of the greatest pools of unused talent in the country, the Negro population. One way to attract gifted Negro students to medicine is for the medical profession itself to show earnest intentions by surmounting, once and for all, the remaining bastions of resistance still blocking the road to integrationist goals.

The progress made by Negro physicians and nurses toward racial equality has been the result of ceaseless struggle. From Reconstruction days to the current civil rights upheaval, dedicated Negro men and women have used the cutting edge of the sword of freedom to fight for admission to medical and nursing schools, professional societies and hospitals. Generally, they have fought the good fight through organizations of their own making, both inside and outside the medical profession. The battle has been waged from Tuskegee to Harlem, from New Orleans to Chicago, from Atlanta to Los Angeles.

This struggle has been but a continuation of an earlier one. Even when slavery disfigured the American scene, there were individual Negro healers and practitioners who braved abuse of all kinds, and on Southern plantations even death itself, to bring medical aid and comfort to their people. In the pre-Civil War North, where the ideal but not the reality of freedom prevailed, pioneer Negro doctors James McCune Smith of New York, Martin R. Delany of Pittsburgh and Alexander T. Augusta, eventually of Washington, D. C., persevered against overwhelming odds to pursue medical careers. Similarly, such slave-born practitioners as Cesar of South Carolina, James Derham of New Orleans and David K. McDonough of New York were not the kind of men to be turned aside from their objectives.

These Negroes, as well as those who came after them, have left a legacy of struggle upon which the current equal rights movement in medicine and health can draw. Under the impact of the Negro freedom movement of the past decade, Negroes in the medical and allied professions have staged sit-ins, thrown up picket lines and participated in mass demonstrations. Their militancy has had an exhilarating effect upon many white physicians who have joined them in organizing medical committees for civil rights.

White doctors are joining also the National Medical Association, a predominantly Negro professional body which, since its founding in 1895, has fought for better medical care and medical opportunities for all Americans, regardless of race, creed or economic status. In joining hands with Negro doctors in the fight for a better and healthier America, present-day white physicians are taking up and carrying forward the struggle, begun almost a hundred years ago by such white practitioners as Dr. Robert Reyburn and Dr. Silas L. Loomis, to put an end to racial discrimination in medicine.

Negro physicians have become increasingly militant because of the quickening tempo of events on the international as well as domestic scene. Since the close of World

DR. ROBERT REYBURN

War II, hundreds of millions of colored people, first in Asia, then in Africa, have taken the road to freedom. Their success has fired the imagination of a growing number of Negro Americans who have become more determined than ever to break out of the ingenious system of Negro subordination which has been imposed upon them by white racist elements in every field of endeavor, including medicine and health.

The rise of the Negro freedom movement at home and the emergence of the colored people abroad have combined to underscore the truth of an observation made many years ago by the great Negro leader Dr. W. E. B. Du Bois that ". . . the problem of the 20th century is the problem of the color line." The pages that follow will examine one facet of this problem: the color line in medicine and health as it emerged and developed in the United States. The inquiry will show how the taboos, prejudices and myths that have worked against Negroes as doctors, nurses and patients are deeply rooted in the American past. They first appeared during the dark days of slavery and continued after emancipation in the guise of hundreds of racist laws and practices popularly known as Jim Crow.

The interlocking base of economic and racial injustice, which has contributed in no small measure to the relatively high rate of sickness and death among Negroes, is one part of the story. The other is the struggle of Negro doctors and nurses to achieve equal rights and equal opportunities in their respective professions. Although the periods of slavery, the Civil War and Reconstruction are not ignored, the work deals mostly with the past three quarters of a century: the first fifty years of this saw the Jim Crow system in medical care rise and consolidate its position; and the last twenty-five years have seen the weakening of this system under the hammer blows of an aroused people.

Today there is a need, as the Rev. Martin Luther King put it, to rouse "the conscience of the nation" concerning the quality of medical care received by Negroes. "Of all the forms of inequality," he is quoted as saying, "injustice in health is the most shocking and the most inhuman . . .." Thus, the story of Jim Crow in medicine and health is a story worth telling, especially now as a burgeoning and deepening Negro freedom movement focuses attention not only on jobs, votes, schools and housing, but also on medical care and health. It is the story of our shame and our loss, of indignities heaped upon Negro doctors, nurses and patients, of professional talents wasted and of a people's health undermined.

MARTIN LUTHER KING, JR.

CHAPTER TWO

The Long Night of Slavery

Deep Are the Roots

I met with a negro, a very old man, who has performed many wonderful cures of diseases. For the sake of his freedom, he has revealed the medicine. . . . There is no room to doubt of its being a certain remedy here. . . .
Lieutenant-Governor Gooch of Virginia, 1729.

I have conversed with him upon most of the acute and epidemic diseases of the country where he lives. . . . I expected to have suggested some new medicines to him, but he suggested many more to me.
Dr. Benjamin Rush on slave-born Dr. James Derham, November 14, 1788.

He passes for a Doctor among people of his color and it is supposed practices in that capacity about town.
Fugitive slave notice in the Charleston, S. C., *City Gazette and Daily Advertiser*, June 22, 1797.

DR. BENJAMIN RUSH

JANUARY 5, 1789 was an unusually bleak winter day, even for Philadelphia. Dr. Benjamin Rush, a man with a nimble mind and dynamic personality, was on his way to attend a meeting of the Pennsylvania Society for Promoting the Abolition of Slavery. A middle-aged physician of forty-three, he was highly esteemed. His reputation as one of the city's leading citizens was based on a solid record of achievement: his graduation from Princeton at the age of fifteen, his M.D. degree from Edinburgh, his appointment to a professorship at the newly established medical college in Philadelphia, his participation in the revolutionary ferment of the day, his signing of the Declaration of Independence, his war record as deputy director in the Continental Army's medical department, and his recent exertions on behalf of the ratification of the Constitution.

Dr. Rush was greeted warmly when he arrived at the scheduled meeting of the

To the Pennsylvania Abolition Society

Philadelphia, November 14, 1788

There is now in this city a black man of the name of James Derham, a practitioner of physic, belonging to the Spanish settlement of New Orleans on the Mississippi. This man was born in a family in this city in which he was taught to read and write and instructed in the principles of Christianity. When a boy, he was transferred by his master to the late Dr. John Kearsley, Jr., of this city, who employed him occasionally to compound medicines and to perform some of the more humble acts of attention to his patients.

Upon the death of Dr. Kearsley, he became (after passing through several hands) the property of Dr. George West, surgeon to the Sixteenth British regiment, under whom, during the late war in America, he performed many of the menial duties of our profession. At the close of the war he was sold by Dr. West to Dr. Robert Dove, of New Orleans, who employed him as an assistant in his business, in which capacity he gained so much of his confidence and friendship that he consented to liberate him, after two or three years, upon easy terms. From Dr. Derham's numerous opportunities of improving in medicine, he became so well acquainted with the healing art as to commence practitioner at New Orleans under the patronage of his last master. He is now about twenty-six years of age, has a wife but no children, and does business to the amount of three thousand dollars a year.

I have conversed with him upon most of the acute and epidemic diseases of the country where he lives, and was pleased to find him perfectly acquainted with the modern simple mode of practice in those diseases. I expected to have suggested some new medicines to him, but he suggested many more to me. He is very modest and engaging in his manners. He speaks French fluently and has some knowledge of the Spanish language. By some accident, although born in a religious family belonging to the Church of England, he was not baptized in his infancy, in consequence of which he applied a few days ago to Bishop White to be received by that ordinance into the Episcopal Church. The Bishop found him qualified, both by knowledge and moral conduct, to be admitted to baptism, and this day performed the ceremony in one of the churches in this city.

BENJAMIN RUSH

society. Many knew him as a forceful exponent of Negro freedom, the author of a searching abolitionist pamphlet on the subject, and in 1775 one of the organizers of the Philadelphia antislavery society, the first of its kind in America. After exchanging pleasantries, he and his associates turned to the business at hand: a communication from the Abolition Society of London requesting information on the mental improvement of Negroes. On November 14, 1788, he had made a statement to the body which dealt with a fellow practitioner, Dr. James Derham, a former Negro slave who came to be regarded as "one of the most distinguished physicians in New Orleans."

"I have conversed with him," wrote Dr. Rush, "upon most of the acute and epidemic diseases of the country where he lives and was pleased to find him perfectly acquainted with the modern simple mode of practice in those diseases. I expected to have suggested some new medicines to him, but he suggested many more to me." This was no small compliment from a man who was recognized as the most eminent doctor in the United States, the recipient of jewels and medals from the crowned heads of Europe and a member of the Society of Arts and Sciences of Milan, the National Institute of France and the School of Medicine of Paris.

Philadelphia, the city in which Dr. Benjamin Rush lived and practiced, was also the birthplace of slave-born Dr. James Derham. Not much is known about Derham's ancestry or how he came to learn to read and write. Even the exact year of his birth is conjectured, the most educated guess being 1762. However, we do know that, at an early age, Derham's master sold him to Dr. John Kearsley, Jr., a successful Philadelphia practitioner and an authority on sore throat distempers. The physician took a liking to the bright, lively boy. He

decided to teach him medicine and, in line with the medical training of the day, taught him how to mix drugs and handle patients.

All went well until the outbreak of the Revolution. A confirmed Tory, Dr. Kearsley was carted through the streets of Philadelphia by an irate citizenry. When it was subsequently discovered that he was engaged in treasonable activities, he was arrested and imprisoned. During his confinement, he became insane and in 1777 died in jail. After Dr. Kearsley's death, the young slave became the property of Dr. George West, surgeon to the 16th British Regiment. At the close of the Revolution, Derham passed into the hands of Dr. Robert Dove of New Orleans, who was so impressed by Derham's medical competence that he permitted the youngster to purchase his freedom.

The emancipated slave found colorful, flourishing New Orleans, with its thriving

DR. JOHN KEARSLEY, JR.

During the period of slavery, the techniques of some of the early Negro physicians were not much different from the "kitchen physick" which flourished in colonial America.

Negro and mulatto population, a most suitable place for the practice of medicine. Under Dr. Dove's patronage, he soon developed a very successful and lucrative practice, which included patients of both races. He was earning three thousand dollars a year by 1788, when at age twenty-six he went to Philadelphia to be baptized by Bishop White of the Episcopal Church. While in the city, he met Dr. Rush, America's leading physician. Dr. Rush was so impressed by Dr. Derham's modesty, engaging manners and medical knowledge that he continued to correspond with him for more than a decade. He sent the New Orleans physician his own published writings and received in return highly informative medical news items.

Dr. Derham was more than an ordinary physician. A man of liberal education, self-taught for the most part, he became a superb linguist, speaking French and Spanish fluently. Like the vast majority of the estimated 3,500 practitioners of his day, he was apprentice-trained. In 1776, there were 3,100 apprentice-trained practitioners in America and 400 university-educated physicians with M.D. degrees, largely from European institutions. Studying under able preceptors, he acquired a sound grounding in therapeutics and pharmacy. As his knowledge of medicine deepened, he became an authority on the relationship of disease to climate.

At the time of the American Revolution, when James Derham was a slave in Philadelphia, there were approximately 550,000 Negro chattels in the country. These slaves represented a significant part of the American population, about 20 per cent, and a considerable portion of the total national wealth and capital investment, roughly a quarter of a billion dollars. Unlike the European white who came to America to escape his chains, the African Negro was brought here in chains.

In 1619, one year before the Pilgrim Fathers went ashore at Plymouth Rock, the first boatload of Negroes reached America. The number of Africans who arrived in the country during the seventeenth century was not very large; as late as 1700, the entire Negro population was under twenty thousand. But, as English traders established themselves on the Guinea coast and New England merchants engaged in a triangular trade which included West Africa, the supply of slaves became more plentiful. Ship after ship crossed the Atlantic Ocean with huge boatloads of human cargo. More than twenty thousand slaves were transported annually during most of the eighteenth century.

Despite the more than 30 per cent mortality rate, profits derived from this nefarious traffic were fabulous; original investments were doubled or even trebled in one or two voyages. Many a Liverpool and Newport fortune was built on this immensely profitable business. It was not until 1807, more than three decades after the birth of the American Republic, that the importation of slaves into the United States was legally prohibited. Brought here in chains, Negro chattels were put to work on Southern tobacco, rice, indigo, sugar and cotton plantations. There, under the ever-watchful eyes of masters and overseers, they and their descendants labored without monetary compensation to produce profits running into the multi-billions. By 1860, there were approximately four million Negro slaves in the country, whose value as property or "goods" was estimated at four billion dollars.

The Negro people brought with them from Africa a medicine not much different from the "kitchen physick" flourishing in colonial America. Like their white counterparts, they put great stock in the control of disease through charms and conjuration. They had their medicine men and "conjure" women who, like the priest-physicians of the time, believed that demons were the cause of a wide variety of illnesses. Thus, incantations, relics and the "healing touch" were used to exorcise the malignant spirits. But the African Negroes, like the white settlers, also had their own *materia medica,* the product of centuries of practical experience.

They knew the medicinal value of a wide assortment of mineral, plant and herb concoctions, with the result that "root-docterin" occupied a prominent place in the therapeutic arsenal of many a Southern plantation. They even knew of the practice of "buying the smallpox," a method of inoculation designed to prevent the onset of this dread disease by the use of a serum

COTTON MATHER

from human patients having the infection in a mild form. The Reverend Cotton Mather, who was instrumental in introducing this practice into the colonies in the early eighteenth century, learned of its value not only from articles published in scientific European journals but also from a Negro slave. Similarly, there is every reason to believe that Negro midwives brought with them from Africa medical knowledge concerning birth by Caesarian section.

With such a background, Negro slaves took to the healing art. In this under-developed country, particularly in the earlier period, the only license needed to practice medicine was the success a man or woman had in treating patients. As a result, in both Negro and white communities, a host of self-trained healers sprang up. Barbers pulled teeth, set bones and bled patients. "Old wives" dispensed medicines, though their specialty was obstetrics. Druggists prescribed a wide variety of foul-smelling, bad-tasting potions which killed patients almost as often as they cured them.

During the epoch of slavery, Negroes had their quota of self-trained practitioners, male and female. A fugitive slave named Simon, who pretended "to be a doctor among his people," was described in the *Pennsylvania Gazette* of September 11, 1740, as able "to bleed and draw teeth." The Charleston, South Carolina, *City Gazette and Daily Advertiser* of June 22, 1797, carried this notice of a runaway chattel: "He passes for a Doctor among people of his color and it is supposed practices in that capacity about town." A Negro barber, Joseph Ferguson of Richmond, Virginia, was so competent a leecher and cupper that he went on to study and eventually practice medicine.

There were also many Negro "doctoresses," female servants and older plantation hands who were wise in the ways of midwifery and folk cures. Similarly, there

were Negro pharmacists, like Wilcie Elfe of Charleston, South Carolina, whose prescription book, dated 1853, showed him to be the formulator of many drug recipes. Trained by his master, who was a drunkard, Elfe was just the opposite, steady and sober. He became so proficient at filling prescriptions that he actually assumed the management of the drug store. Over the years, he acquired such an uncommon knowledge of medicines that he concocted a number of patent drugs that were sold throughout South Carolina.

Some Negroes became so famous for their remedies that they were granted their freedom because of this skill. In 1729, Lieutenant-Governor Gooch of Virginia reported that he had:

> . . . met with a negro [sic], a very old man, who has performed many wonderful cures of diseases. For the sake of his freedom, he has revealed the medicine, a concoction of roots and bark. . . . There is no room to doubt of its being a certain remedy here, and of singular use [in the treatment of syphilis] among the negroes, it is well worth the price (£60) of the negro's freedom, since it is now known how to cure slaves without mercury.

Another Negro practitioner, Cesar, was given his freedom by the General Assembly of South Carolina for his discovery of a remedy to cure the bite of a rattlesnake. In addition, the colonial legislature granted him an annual stipend of a hundred pounds sterling and ordered the *South Carolina Gazette,* a Charleston newspaper, to publish the prescription for the benefit of the general public. This was done on February 25, 1751. So great was the demand for the newspaper that copies of it were quickly exhausted.

Cesar's cure for poisoning was widely publicized outside of South Carolina. In 1789, it was published by Carey in Philadelphia, and in 1792, it appeared in *The Massachusetts Magazine.* Cesar, an acute observer, described fully the symptoms accompanying poisoning: breast and stomach pain, difficulty in breathing, irregular pulse, restlessness, inclination to vomit, profuse sweating, slimy stools, lack of appetite, and general weakness in the limbs. He also gave a detailed description of how to prepare and administer his antidote for poison and his remedy for the bite of a rattlesnake, a decoction of roots compounded with rum and lye, two doses of which "never hath failed." This presentation of symptoms and treatment was in the grand tradition of Sydenham, the great English clinician of the seventeenth century. Such was the renown of Cesar's cure for the bite of a rattlesnake that reference was made to it in *Domestic Medicine,* a work published in 1799.

Another slave-born Negro, David K. McDonough, achieved notable distinction as a practitioner. His career began as the result of an argument between his master, a Southern ante-bellum slaveholder, and a fellow planter. The dispute revolved about the question of the innate mental capacity of the Negro to improve himself intellectually. Fortunately for McDonough, his master took the affirmative position and, to prove his point, decided to send his chattel north to an institution of higher learning. To Lafayette College in Pennsylvania went young McDonough. Here he did such outstanding work that he was graduated third in his class and awarded the B.A. degree.

After returning to his home, the Negro slave pleaded with his master to permit him to become a doctor. Permission having been granted, McDonough went to New York, where he was placed under the preceptorship of Dr. John K. Rodgers, one of America's most eminent surgeons and then professor of surgery at Columbia. As a result of Dr. Rodgers' influence, the prospective Negro doctor was given the opportunity of attending lectures at the College of Physicians and Surgeons. After Dr. McDonough received his license to practice, his mentor secured an appointment for him at the New York Eye and Ear Infirmary.

There he achieved so excellent a reputation that he was called upon by some of the most distinguished physicians of the city to serve as a consultant. The first private hospital founded by Negroes in New York was named after him.

Although the career of Dr. McDonough disproves the myth of the inherent inferiority of the Negro, that fiction was nevertheless studiously cultivated as the institution of slavery hardened in the South. Created by the enslavers and their propagandists to justify the ownership of one man by another, this cruel hoax made it impossible for most Negro chattels to practice anything but the most primitive kind of medicine. Serving as a justification to deprive Negroes of even the most rudimentary forms of learning, it prevented slave-born practitioners, prospective and actual, from partaking in the rich feast of a rapidly developing body of medical knowledge.

DR. JOHN K. RODGERS

Mistreatment by slave traders and terrible conditions aboard ship led to the deaths of many captured Negroes.

Similarly, the existence of state laws providing capital punishment in cases involving the preparation and administration of medicines by slaves "with intent to poison" tended to act as a brake upon Negro healers and practitioners. Since the fear of being poisoned was an almost universal obsession among planters, it is not at all difficult to understand why large numbers of Negroes hesitated to engage in the practice of "physick."

Like the European whites, the African Negroes brought with them to America a variety of diseases. Some of these diseases, like malaria and hookworm, were indigenous to the west coast of Africa; others, like smallpox and dysentery, were brought to African shores by white slave traders themselves or picked up in the slave ships heading for America. Captured Negroes died by the thousands as terrible epidemics aboard the ships, caused by overcrowding, unsanitary conditions and poor food, took

their frightful toll. Here, during the seasoning period, the mortality rate continued high. It is estimated that as many as 20 to 30 per cent of the slaves died within three to four years after arrival chiefly because of drastic changes in diet, climate and working conditions. This tragic loss of life, as well as the systematic plunder of a continent, constituted the rape of Africa in the first extensive European overseas expansion.

Newly arrived slaves, as well as their descendants, were highly susceptible to a number of illnesses common to their white masters and neighbors: smallpox, measles, dysentery, diphtheria, "pleurisies" and syphilis. These diseases were a source of constant concern to Southern planters, who were faced with the economic imperative of keeping their chattels alive and productive. Crops were merely income, but slaves were capital. And the value of slaves was constantly rising. Expressed in monetary terms, the price of a good field hand rose from two hundred dollars in 1793 (the year the cotton gin was invented) to six hundred dollars in 1836 and one thousand dollars in 1850. Measured in terms of middling cotton, a prime field hand in the upland cotton belt was equal in value to fifteen hundred pounds in 1800, six thousand pounds in 1830 and sixteen thousand pounds in 1860.

It was such skyrocketing values that made many Southern planters of the ante-bellum period most solicitous in respect to the health of their Negro chattels. Particularly were they concerned with the birthrate, hearts overbrimming with joy to hear, as Howell Cobb in Georgia, that the slaves were increasing like "little rabbits." On one Mississippi plantation, the "Prairie," owned by J. W. Fowler, practically all of the adult slaves were paired as husbands and wives except Caroline, who in twenty years gave birth to ten children. Tom and Milly had nine in eighteen years; Harry and Jaimy, seven in twenty-one; Ben and Fanny, five in seventeen; and so on down the line. On a Louisiana plantation, the "Bayou Cotonier," belonging to E. Tannert, the breeding schedule was considerably lighter. The "livres des naissances" showed fifty-six births during a twenty-six-year period distributed among twenty-three females, two of whom were in their teens.

To see these infants through the post-partum period was a matter of grave concern to planters interested in an ever-growing labor supply. Nursing mothers were brought in from the fields three or four times a day to suckle their babies. Before being permitted to proceed, the mothers were obliged to cool off and rest. Using such safeguards, one planter boasted that, although thirty babies had been born on his plantation in a five-year period, he had not lost "a single one from teething, or the ordinary summer complaints so prevalent amongst the children of this climate."

On some larger plantations infants and children were taken care of in nurseries. Overseers were cautioned to look after the youngsters so that, in the words of Richard Corbin, "none of them suffer in time of sickness for want of proper care." Among the criteria Southern planters used to judge the performance of their overseers was the health of the children. For, after all, these youngsters had to be brought as quickly and efficiently as possible into the labor force, representing as they did quite an important part of the planter's capital investment.

Southern slaveholders found it necessary to provide Negro chattels with a modicum of medical care. Plantation hands, suffering from ordinary illnesses, were usually taken care of by slave practitioners, owners or overseers. It was not unusual for neighboring planters to borrow the services of Negro doctors who were well known in the locality for their success as practitioners. William Dawson, a planter on the Potomac River, requested that Robert Carter send

him "Brother Tom" to treat a sick child on his estate since the Negroes had more faith in him as a physician than they had in any white doctor. Another Virginia planter, James Walker, sent one of his hands to "old Man Docr. Lewiss," a slave, to be treated for poisoning. The treatment, a "decoction of herbs," was successful.

Besides Negro male doctors, there were Negro "doctoresses," who usually combined the duties of obstetrician with skill in preparing and dispensing medical herbs. Elsey, a slave on the estate of Alexander Telfair in Georgia, acted as midwife to both Negro and white women in the neighborhood. At Charles Friend's White Hill plantation in Virginia, a slave named Aggy, after some years of training, was in charge of all obstetrical duties on the plantation. Female slaves likewise served as nurses, mixing and administering drugs while taking care of the sick. Plantation manuals indicate that nurses were drawn from servants in the big house or from older field hands no longer able to do productive labor. On one

Many plantation owners took measures to make sure that the Negro children remained healthy because of their extreme value as laborers.

A Negro herb doctor.

Alabama plantation a nurse and "doctoress" called Mary boasted that she had not lost an adult patient in two years. Negro women engaged in the general practice of medicine were frequently listed in plantation inventories as "Doctor."

Southern plantations had their share of Negro conjure men and women who, in the tradition of magico-religious medicine, believed that sickness was the work of evil spirits acting either on their own or on behalf of a living agent or a dead person's soul. To ward off these malignant powers, Negro witch doctors used prayers, incantations, the healing touch and amulets, the same as did their white counterparts in Europe and America. Old Bab, the conjure man, had, according to the recollections of a Tennessee slave, a pocketful of charms wrapped in a rag and tied with hair, "two from a hoss and one from a mare." These he dispensed along with his inarticulate "mumbledy, mumbledy, mumbledy." In addition to chants and charms, Negro medicine men resorted to such procedures as bleeding, sweating and vomiting to expel the evil spirits afflicting the sick.

A free-born Negro, H. B. Holloway, gives us a first-hand account of a conjure practitioner, Cain Robertson of Georgia, at work: "I left him at the house, and when I came back in, he said, 'I looked at your wife and she had one of them spells while I was there. I'm afraid to tackle this thing because she has been poisoned, and it's been going on a long time. And if she dies, they'll say I killed her, and they already don't like me and looking for an excuse to do something to me.' My wife overheard him and says, 'You go on, you got to do something.'" And go on he did, after fortifying himself with almost a pint of corn whiskey.

He examined the woman's stomach. "Then he scratched it, and put three little horns on the place he scratched. Then he took another drink of whiskey and waited about ten minutes. When he took them off her stomach, they were full of blood. He put them in the basin in some water and sprinkled some powder on them, and in about ten minutes more he made me get them and they were full of clear water and there was a lot of little things that looked like wiggle tails swimming around in it." The sick woman apparently recovered from the illness; and on the recommendation of "old Doc Matthews," who was told the above story, Cain Robertson, the "hoodoo doctor," was thereafter permitted to practice in the locality without fear of molestation.

In addition to male and female slave practitioners, planters and their wives took to doctoring, as did overseers on the larger plantations. Planters considered their books on practical medicine among their most prized household possessions. In the eighteenth century, Robert Carter of Nomini Hall had, among others, Quincy's *Dispensatory*, Harrison's *Accomplished Practitioner* and Lynch's *Guide to Health*. In the following century, Dr. James Ewell's *Planter's and Mariner's Medical Companion* was the constant friend of a large number of slave-masters. In emergencies it was not uncommon for planters to sit with book in hand by the bedside of a sick Negro, look up the symptoms, compare the remedies and then administer the drug. Not infrequently their wives would minister to sick slaves.

On the larger plantations they had the additional responsibility of looking after the nursery and hospital or isolation building. One of their number, Mrs. William Byrd, actually practiced medicine and did very well at it. Overseers were provided with a book of medical instructions and a supply of necessary "plantation

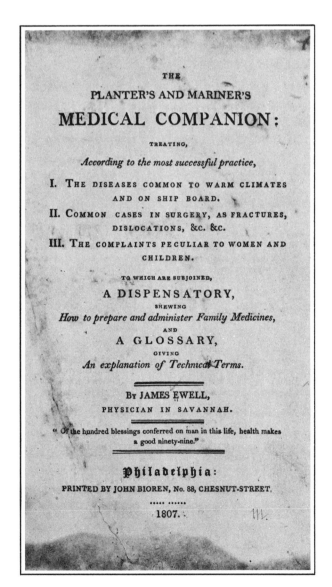

medicines." They were cautioned to give only simple remedies, such as flax-seed tea, mint water and magnesia, and leave to the doctor the prescription of stronger medicines, such as calomel and tartar emetic.

In serious or extraordinary cases, white physicians, retained for the purpose, were called in to treat ailing slaves. The diaries of large and small planters frequently refer to this practice. In eighteenth-century Virginia, George Washington summoned to his Mount Vernon estate such physicians as Drs. Rumney, Laurie, Brown, Craik and Dick. The records of Francis Taylor of Orange County reveal numerous visits by his brother Charles, a physician, to various plantations, including his own. In the nineteenth century, James B. Lamar, who administered a half-dozen estates belonging to himself and to relatives in southern Georgia and northern Florida, tells how he spent half his time rattling over rough roads with doctors and stopping every now and then at farm houses.

During the pre-Civil War years, Southern physicians turned increasingly to the practice of treating slaves. Not only did it consume a large part of their daily work, but it also represented a substantial portion of their income. It was usual for a slavemaster to pay annual doctors' bills averaging one hundred dollars in normal years and five hundred dollars in epidemic years. In cities like Savannah, Charleston, Montgomery, Natchez and New Orleans, physicians supplemented their incomes by running slave hospitals for medical, surgical and obstetrical cases. In line with the then current medical theory of depletion, they were firm believers in purging and bleeding. Thus, they did not hesitate to give their Negro as well as white patients huge doses of castor oil, calomel and salts.

Many a Southern white doctor, tied to the slaveholding classes, mixed medicine with politics. In the ante-bellum period, physi-

DR. SAMUEL A. CARTWRIGHT

cians like Dr. John S. Wilson and Dr. Samuel A. Cartwright developed the thesis that Negroes had to be given different medical treatment from whites because of racial dissimilarities, physical and emotional. Thus, according to Dr. Wilson, only Southern physicians, fully cognizant of these differences, were capable of treating Negroes safely and successfully.

Negro slaves needed constant medical care because of the conditions under which they lived and worked. Even in the high noon of slavery when cotton was king, the health of Negroes was undermined by poor housing facilities, unsanitary conditions and an inadequate diet. Living quarters consisted of wooden huts with leaky roofs and rotting logs. In these broken-down cabins, made up of a single room about twenty feet square, a whole family or several families slept. There was little or no ventilation, and a privy was entirely lacking.

Dietary fare was meager; hominy (corn boiled in water) and bacon were its basis and often its whole content. Clothing was of the cheapest kind, trousers, jackets and dresses being made of the coarsest woolen and cotton cloth. Thus, planters spent as little as possible on the food, shelter and clothing they furnished their slaves. On small plantations the average cost per Negro was thirty to forty dollars a year; and on larger ones, only fifteen dollars. The annual average throughout the cotton belt was about twenty dollars.

Working as well as living conditions tended to affect adversely the health of plantation hands. Slaves began to work at the age of eight or nine; by early youth they reached their maximum efficiency. Up at daybreak, everyone who was able to work, man, woman and child, went to an appointed task. The largest number worked in the fields and never returned to their homes before dark. Breakfast and dinner were given them wherever they were working at the time. There were no holidays except a day or two at Christmas. Thus, they worked year after year from sunup to sundown every day except Sunday. No games or recreation were provided, and even if they had been, there would have been little time to enjoy them. Drudgery, uninterrupted monotony and a deepening sense of futility combined to lower bodily resistance. When illness developed, planters and overseers, interested in extracting the maximum profits from the labor of their slaves, often regarded the sickness as shammed or fancied. In some cases it might well have been so, because pretending to be ill, like work slowdowns, breaking tools and self-mutilation, was a tactic which Negroes employed in their unremitting struggle against slavery.

However, most of the illnesses from which the Negroes suffered were genuine. Smallpox, measles, pleurisies, cholera, whooping cough and other diseases were of such virulence as to cause the loss of a very great number of work days. According to a sick list kept by one large plantation owner, as many as eighty-four days of productive labor were lost by his field hands in a single month, "violent pleurisy" alone accounting for forty of them. Some of these diseases assumed epidemic proportions due in no small measure to crowded and unsanitary living conditions. Such epidemics spread panic in the "big house," for they were costly financial blows. In one cholera epidemic alone, that of 1832 in Louisiana, five to six thousand people died in a two-week period; the monetary loss in slaves was estimated at four million dollars. Such financial losses Southern planters found difficult to

On the plantations, the health of Negroes was undermined by poor housing facilities, unsanitary conditions and an inadequate diet.

bear. It drove some to the very brink of madness. As one of them expressed it in his plantation journal: "Oh! my losses almost make me crazy. God alone can help."

Overcrowded and unsanitary living quarters, a bare subsistence diet, inadequate medical care, arduous and boring work combined to give Negroes on Southern plantations a shorter life expectancy and a higher mortality rate than whites. In this connection, Kenneth M. Stampp, in his authoritative work *The Peculiar Institution: Slavery in the Antebellum South,* presents these census returns on death rates: "The census of 1850 reported average ages of 21.4 for Negroes and 25.5 for whites at time of death. In 1860, 3.5 per cent of the slaves and 4.4 per cent of the whites were over sixty; the death rate was 1.8 per cent for the slaves and 1.2 per cent for the whites." Pre-Civil War mortality figures, he continues, "were not very reliable, but slave deaths were unreported more often than white. If anything, the disparity between slave and white death rates was greater and not less than recorded in the census returns."

Sydnor's statistical study of the "Life Span of Mississippi Slaves" in the *American Historical Review* of April, 1930, reveals that a twenty-year-old Negro in ante-bellum Mississippi could expect to live a somewhat shorter life than a white of the same age. The difference in the latter's favor, he calculated, was about a year and a half, 23.72 for the white and 22.30 for the Negro.

If infant mortality figures were included in the above statistical data, the gap between the life expectancy of Negroes and whites would be widened considerably, not only in Mississippi, but in all Southern states. Although white infant mortality was appallingly high throughout the South, the death rate among Negro babies was even higher. "In Mississippi where the Negro population only slightly exceeded the white, Negro infant deaths," writes Kenneth M. Stampp, "numbered 2,772 and white infant deaths numbered 1,315. . . . Everywhere the Negro infant mortality rate was more than double the white."

Thus, slavery produced significant differences in the health status of Negroes and whites. The health gap, created by "the peculiar institution," continued after emancipation. Although it has narrowed since then, it still persists to the present day.

CHAPTER THREE

Up North

From that moment I was inspired to be a doctor. It took deep root in me, so deep that all the drought of poverty or lack of education could not destroy the desire. From that day I did not want any knowledge save that of the healing art.

Early Recollections and Life of Dr. James Still.

I propose, sir, an army of blacks commanded entirely by black officers, except such whites as may volunteer to serve, this army to penetrate through the heart of the South ... until every slave is free, according to the letter of your proclamation.

Dr. Martin R. Delany, interview with President Abraham Lincoln, February 8, 1865.

WHILE slavery hung like a pall over the whole American Republic, north of the Mason-Dixon line it did not legally exist. One of the great liberating influences of the Revolution of '76 was the gradual emancipation of the approximately 50,000 Negroes then living in the North. By 1860, the free states' colored population reached about a quarter of a million, as against 19 million whites. The vast majority of Northern Negroes were farmers, mechanics and day laborers. Medical practitioners were few in number and generally of lowly origin, with little or no formal learning. In a society where racism encouraged color consciousness, they strove to elevate themselves and their people, the better to disprove the Southern slaveholders' thesis of the inherent inferiority of the Negro.

SELF-TAUGHT HEALERS

The handful of free Negroes who practiced medicine in the ante-bellum North could hardly be described as forming a professional class. Like their white counterparts, they were in the tradition of the time self-taught, apprentice-trained or college-educated. Typical of the first group—which incidentally was the most numerous—was self-instructed James Still of New Jersey, called by his contemporaries the "black doctor" and "doctor of the pines." Born April 9, 1812, at Indian Mill, Burlington County, he was the son of an ex-slave who had purchased his freedom from a Maryland master. While he was still very young, the family moved to the "down Jersey" town of Lumberton, where he lived for the rest of his life. He had two brothers, William and Peter, both destined to be prominent abolitionists, the former as an agent on the Underground Railroad and the latter as the author of *The Kidnapped and the Ransomed*.

The Still family lived in an old, one-story log house without stove, glass windows or

JAMES STILL

I gave her medicine which soon cured her. I thought it no great thing, for it always seemed to me that all diseases were curable, and I wondered why doctors did not cure them.

Industrious, conscientious and able, Dr. Still soon had numerous followers who believed in him. As his practice developed and his reputation grew, charges were brought against him of practicing medicine without a license. Not a man to succumb too easily, he threatened court action. Eventually the charges against him were dropped. Although the medical profession never approved of him, his patients, Negro and white, did, as evidenced by thirty years of a large and successful practice. The sick flocked to his office, and he swung around the circuit in horse and buggy to visit them

any comforts. Life was lonely and drab. James' early childhood was uneventful except for a visit by Dr. Fort to vaccinate the children of the household. "From that moment," he wrote years later, "I was inspired to be a doctor. It took deep root in me, so deep that all the drought of poverty or lack of education could not destroy the desire. From that day I did not want any knowledge save that of the healing art."

The young boy grew to manhood. His formal education consisted of three months' instruction in reading, writing and arithmetic. His life was a hard one—a little farming, work in a glue factory, an early marriage, the death of his wife and child, remarriage—but he never lost the desire to be a doctor. In 1843, at the age of thirty-one, he took the first step. He began to make medicines, which he sold in the neighborhood. Soon he was able to buy some medical books. His first actual practice of medicine was quite by accident. One day, upon request, he examined a neighbor's daughter who was suffering from scrofula.

EARLY   RECOLLECTIONS

AND

LIFE OF DR. JAMES STILL.

PRINTED FOR THE AUTHOR BY
J. B. LIPPINCOTT & CO.
1877.

"deep in the woods." He exuded confidence and believed that all diseases could be cured. As he put it:

> I might fill volumes of [cases] . . . where I have cured patients who have been pronounced incurable in cancers, tumors, white swelling, and almost every kind of disease, which fact led me to believe that all diseases are curable in certain states or conditions. . . .

In his autobiography, Dr. Still cites many cases to reinforce his convictions. One case, that of Mrs. W., gives us an insight into the bedside manner of the horse-and-buggy doctor of a century ago. According to Dr. Still's account, Mrs. W., a woman past sixty, was afflicted with stomach trouble for almost twenty years. Through a series of relevant and penetrating questions, the doctor elicited the response that the sick woman had not perspired for at least ten years. "Well, Mrs. W.," the Negro physician said, "I think I'll make you sweat before I leave. I am going to give you some medicine, and stay to see how it operates."

He proceeded to prepare the drug, and thirty minutes later Mrs. W. was perspiring profusely and vomiting violently. After some time, she calmed down. Before leaving, Dr. Still promised to return in a few days. When he did, he found Mrs. W. "free from pain and vomiting." Within a few weeks, the elderly woman was able to eat and sleep comfortably. "She lived for a number of years after her recovery," he wrote, "and enjoyed good health." In this simple statement, there was justifiable pride, for he had succeeded where other physicians had failed.

As a Negro practitioner, Dr. Still was acutely aware of racial prejudices. Anticipating the present-day movement for racial integration in education, he urged the elimination of separate Negro schools.

> I have been opposed to colored schools wholly because they were against the principles of Christian fellowship. I think that co-education would be beneficial to each race. . . . Separate schools are debasing to the manners of each, whilst it causes the one to imbibe imbecility and the other superiority, thus fixing a great gulf between them, which shall be impassable.

Like James Still, John P. Reynolds, David Ruggles and William Wells Brown were self-taught Negro healers who, without much medical background, apparently helped many and harmed few. Dr. Reynolds, whose knowledge of the healing art was gained in the late 1820's from an "Indian physician," established a thriving practice in Zanesville, Ohio, and later in Vincennes, Indiana. A member of the "eclectic" school of medicine, he was held in high esteem, became quite wealthy and exerted considerable influence in local affairs.*

Similarly, the "water-cure" doctor, David Ruggles, made an enviable reputation for himself. Born of free parents, March 15, 1810, at Norwich, Connecticut, he received his early education in schools founded by emancipationist societies. At the age of seventeen, he came to New York City, where, after a short stint in the grocery business, he devoted himself completely to the cause of abolitionism. He wrote articles for *The Emancipator,* was editor and publisher of *The Mirror of Liberty* and lectured to Negro and white groups in various cities. In 1834, he published his first pamphlet, *The "Extinguisher" Extinguished! Or D. M. Reese, M.D. "Used Up!"* Polemical and trenchant, subtle and ingenious, the forty-eight-page booklet opposed the plan of colonizing American Negroes in Africa and came out for the immediate and universal emancipation of the slave.

So wholeheartedly did Ruggles throw himself into the work of abolitionism that, by the time he was thirty-five, his health began to fail. Seeking a cure, he visited

---

The eclectic school of medicine was composed of a group of physicians in pre-Civil War America who traced their school's origin back to the colonial period and the Indians. They believed in native remedies, particularly in plants and herbs. In 1840 they formed an organization, later known as the Eclectic Medical Association, which remained in existence for about thirty years.

DAVID RUGGLES

German-born Dr. Robert Wesselhoeft of Cambridge, a skilled hydrotherapist. So impressed was he by the German physician's methods that he decided to become a hydropathic doctor himself. In 1846, with the aid of some friends, Ruggles opened a hydrotherapeutic institution in Northampton. Without license or medical degree, he achieved much success in his practice before his untimely death in 1849.

To "Dr. Ruggles' Water-Cure Establishment" in Northampton came doctors, lawyers, clergymen, artisans and abolitionists. On July 17, 1848, the antislavery leader William Lloyd Garrison, dean of them all, arrived to take the cure. He spent the night in the infirmary and the next morning took a refreshing "sitz bath" and a fine ramble. Half an hour later, he was rubbed down with a wet towel. Then he rested and ate, avoiding milk as much as

possible since Dr. Ruggles had told him that milk was not good for his "humor."

Within three months, Garrison's health took a turn for the better. By the end of the year, the grim-faced abolitionist was back in Boston blasting slavery in the press and from the speaker's platform. The Negro abolitionist Frederick Douglass also went to Northampton, but not as a patient. He came as an old friend to visit Ruggles, who, years before as an agent on the Underground Railroad, had helped him escape to freedom. Douglass found the hydropathic practitioner "blind and measurably helpless, but a man of sterling sense and worth."

Another abolitionist-turned-practitioner was courageous and resourceful William Wells Brown. Born of slave parents at Lexington, Kentucky, in 1816, he was taken as a youngster to St. Louis, Missouri. Here he passed through many hands, in-

WILLIAM LLOYD GARRISON

cluding Dr. John Young's, in whose office he was exposed to the rudiments of medicine. At the age of eighteen, he followed the North Star to freedom, traveling by night, hiding in the woods by day, until he arrived safely in Ohio. He immediately threw himself into the abolitionist movement as an agent of the Underground Railroad, a lecturer and a writer. He became so well known that, when he went to England in 1849, he was feted and dined by the country's leading abolitionists. During his five-year stay in Britain, he became friendly with Dr. John Bishop Estlin, the distinguished ophthalmologist and anti-slavery advocate. At Dr. Estlin's urging, Brown decided to resume the study of medicine. Upon his return to Boston, he did so. In 1865, he opened an office and began practice. Described as an "eclectic" doctor in the medical register of the day, he preferred to designate himself a "dermapathic and Practical Physician." Essentially a self-taught healer, his medical background —attendance at some lectures and demonstrations given privately by physicians— was a meager one. He did not seem to have a particularly large or successful practice.

Yet, according to a story told about him, Brown's knowledge of medicine did help him on one occasion to save his own life. During the Reconstruction period, the Boston practitioner was invited to lecture in Louisville, Kentucky. After speaking there, he left for Pleasureville, a nearby town. On the way he was intercepted by a band of Ku Klux Klansmen who carried him off to a house where a man, presumably a member of the organization, was suffering from delirium tremens. Dr. Brown, feeling that he would be lynched before the night was out, decided that he must try to save himself. Announcing that he was a conjure man, he vowed that by means of black magic he could cure the afflicted man. He was given permission to try. Removing a

WILLIAM WELLS BROWN

syringe from his doctor's case, he filled it with a solution of morphine. He concealed the instrument in his vest, went into the next room, made some passes in front of the sick man's eyes, mumbled a few words and then very quickly injected the hypodermic needle. The patient soon quieted down. "Cap," the leader of the band, was so impressed by what he had seen that he took the Negro aside and told him that he was suffering from a pain in his thigh. Dr. Brown invited him into the next room and injected the same solution. "Cap" soon fell asleep. In the meantime, the Klansmen departed one by one. The woman in the house, knowing that Dr. Brown was scheduled to be lynched at dawn, advised him to leave. Needing no further urging, he rushed out of the house and took the first morning train to Louisville.

Brown joined other colored physicians in attacking the pro-slavery thesis that Negroes were racially inferior to whites. In

DR. JOHN S. ROCK

his book, *The Black Man: His Antecedents, His Genius, and His Achievements,* published in 1863, he wrote:

> There is nothing in race or blood, in color or features, that imparts susceptibility of improvement of one race over another. . . . Knowledge is not innate. Development makes the man. . . . The majority of the colored people of the Northern States [are] descended from slaves; many of them were slaves themselves. In education, in morals, and in the development of mechanical genius, the free blacks of the Northern States will compare favorably with any laboring class in the world. And considering the fact that we have been shut out, by a cruel prejudice, from nearly all the mechanical branches, and all the professions, it is marvellous that we have attained the position we now occupy.

TRAINED PHYSICIANS

In addition to the self-taught healers, there were also free Negroes in the North who were trained physicians. In the fashion of the day, they were either apprentice-educated or professionally schooled. In either case, they were few in number because of the prevailing anti-Negro bias. Yet the record clearly indicates that there were some Northern white doctors who were able to overcome the existing climate of opinion to the extent of selecting Negro apprentices for medical training. In New York City, Charles Dunbar studied under Dr. Childs; while in Boston, Daniel Laing, Jr., and Isaac Humphrey Snowden worked under Dr. Clarke. All three were promising young Negro physicians. One of them, Dr. Laing, Jr., went to Paris to supplement the experience he had gained at Boston's famed Massachusetts General Hospital. While abroad, he attended medical lectures and worked in hospitals.

Similarly, Dr. John S. Rock, a native of Salem, New Jersey, studied medicine under Dr. Shaw and Dr. Gibbon. When he tried to enter a medical school in Philadelphia, he was turned down because of his color. He then studied dentistry under Dr. Hubbard, opening an office in 1850 at the age of twenty-five. Some years later, he was admitted to the American Medical College and, upon completing his course of study, practiced both dentistry and medicine. When ill health forced him to give up his practice, he turned to the study of law. In 1861, he passed the bar in Massachusetts and was later appointed a justice of the peace in Boston and Suffolk. One of the best-educated Negroes of his day—he could read and speak both French and German—he developed into so accomplished a lawyer that in 1865 he was the first Negro to be sworn in to argue cases before the Supreme Court.

Dr. Rock was well known in the North for his views on abolitionism and equal rights. A passionate and dedicated advocate of Negro equality, he lent his talents and efforts to destroy the studiously cultivated myth of the racial inferiority of the colored people. In 1860, he declared:

Our enemies have taken every advantage of our unhappy situation, and attempt to prove that, because we are unfortunate, we are necessarily an inferior race. . . . It is not difficult to see that [this idea of Negro inferiority] is a mere subterfuge, which is resorted to to bolster up the infamous treatment which greets the colored man everywhere in this slavery-cursed land, where to us patriotism produces no honor, goodness no merit and intellectual industry no reward. . . . I believe in the equality of my race. . . . We have always proved ourselves your equals, when placed in juxtaposition with you. We are the only oppressed people that advance in the country of their oppression. Look at the sand-hillers of South Carolina, the peasants and mendicants of Ireland, the beggars of the two Sicilies, the gipsy race that infests almost all of Europe, the peasants of Hungary, and the serfs of Russia! These peoples, though possessing superior advantages to the negro [sic], do not advance in the country of their oppression. Not so with the negro [sic]. . . .

Dr. Rock was a vigorous opponent of all plans whose aim was the settlement of Negro Americans abroad. In 1862, addressing himself to various colonizing proposals, he asked: "Why this desire to get rid of us? Can it be possible that because the nation has robbed us for nearly two and a half centuries, and finding that she can do it no longer and preserve her character among nations, now, out of hatred, wishes to banish, because she cannot continue to rob us?" He assured his audience, members of the Massachusetts Anti-Slavery Society, that "Now, when our prospects [for freedom] begin to brighten, we are the more encouraged to stay, pay off the old score, and have a reconstruction of things."

Like Dr. John S. Rock, Dr. Martin R. Delany, whom President Lincoln once described as a "most extraordinary and intelligent black man," was an apprentice-trained physician and fighter for Negro rights. Born May 6, 1812, at Charlestown, Virginia, he moved with his family to Chambersburg, Pennsylvania, where unmolested and unafraid he was able to go to school with other children. At the age of nineteen, he set out for Pittsburgh, moved by the trenchant pen of William Lloyd Garrison and the slave insurrection of Nat Turner, to devote himself to the cause of freedom and the elevation of his people. With unswerving dedication, he became an abolitionist, first as agent on the Underground Railroad and then as editor of *Mystery*. Soon he went into partnership with Frederick Douglass to found and serve as co-editor of the celebrated *North Star*.

In the meantime, young Delany was raising a family and studying medicine. In 1843 he married a bright and attractive young lady, Kate A. Richards, the daughter of a very wealthy and influential property-holder in Pittsburgh. The couple had eleven children, seven of whom survived. In characteristic fashion, Delany named each child after a well-known Negro. In addition to his family duties and abolitionist activities, he found time to study medicine. He served as an apprentice first to Dr.

DR. MARTIN R. DELANY

Andrew N. McDowell and then to Dr. Joseph P. Gazzan and Dr. Francis J. Lemoyne, all distinguished Pittsburgh physicians.

Dr. Delany, seeking to advance himself professionally, applied for admission to medical school. But here he found the doors closed to him because of his color. He sent applications to the University of Pennsylvania, Jefferson Medical College and the medical schools of Albany and Geneva, New York. All four schools turned him down, despite the fact that he had served for several years under qualified preceptors, one of the accepted academic entrance requirements of the day.

Dr. Delany, however, was not one to be easily diverted, particularly when it involved the color of his skin. He applied to the Harvard Medical School for admission and, along with two other Negroes already mentioned, Daniel Laing, Jr., and Isaac H. Snowden, was admitted to the 1850-51 session, notwithstanding a student resolution condemning the "amalgamation" of the races. At Harvard, Delany, Laing and Snowden attended the lectures of such excellent teachers as Walter Channing in obstetrics, Jacob Bigelow in clinical medicine, John B. S. Jackson in pathology, Oliver W. Holmes in anatomy, John Ware in the theory and practice of medicine and Henry J. Bigelow in surgery. Dr. Delany, however, apparently did not remain at Harvard to complete his work for a medical degree. Returning to Pittsburgh, he distinguished himself as a practitioner during the cholera epidemic of 1854. About this time, he was appointed to a subcommittee to furnish the Municipal Board of Charity with medical advice concerning the health needs of indigent Negroes and whites.

His interest in medicine was overshadowed by his intense desire to crush slavery and elevate his people. In 1852, Dr. Delany published at his own expense a book which contained his thoughts on the South's "peculiar institution," in addition to brief sketches of Negro professionals including doctors. In his *Condition, Elevation, Emigration, and Destiny of the Colored People of the United States, Politically Considered,* he joined white abolitionists in castigating the Fugitive Slave Act of 1850, asking:

> What can we do?—What shall we do? This is the great and important question: Shall we submit to be dragged like brutes before heartless men, and sent into degradation and bondage?—Shall we fly or shall we resist?

For him, as well as for his white allies in the abolitionist movement, there could be but one answer: resistance and more resistance.

THE

CONDITION,

ELEVATION, EMIGRATION, AND DESTINY

OF THE

COLORED PEOPLE

OF THE

UNITED STATES.

POLITICALLY CONSIDERED,

BY MARTIN ROBISON DELANY.

PHILADELPHIA:
PUBLISHED BY THE AUTHOR.
1852.

As the antislavery crisis reached a climax during the 1850's, Dr. Delany increasingly turned from the practice of medicine to the emancipation of his people. A short, wiry man, he commanded the respect of friend and foe alike. He was proud to be a Negro. While others expressed their gratitude to God simply for making them men, Delany, according to his friend Frederick Douglass, always thanked God for making him a black man. He traveled extensively in the West, lecturing to audiences on the physiological aspects of racial superiority and inferiority. Like a skillful surgeon, he dissected the fallacies inherent in the Southern argument of white supremacy.

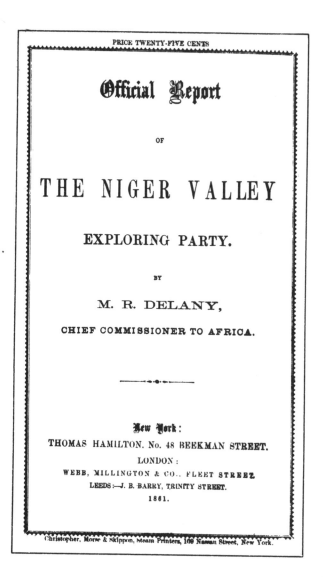

Together with Henry Highland Garnet and Sojourner Truth, Dr. Delany projected the idea of a Negro state, a reflection of the budding consciousness of Negro nationality. He first thought of establishing a Negro republic in Latin America. In the early 1850's, he tried to establish one in Nicaragua with the help of his friend, the Negro practitioner Dr. David J. Peck. When the venture failed, he turned to Africa as a likely site. In 1859, he set sail to explore the Niger valley in the hope of arranging for the settlement of emigrants there. His seventy-five page *Official Report of the Niger Valley Exploring Party* attracted widespread attention. He was elected to membership in the International Statistical Congress and invited to London to deliver a series of lectures.

Even less numerous than apprentice-trained practitioners in the North during the pre-Civil War era were professionally schooled physicians. The reason for this was the reluctance of many Northern white doctors and educators to admit Negro students to medical schools. So strong was the slave power's grip on the country that, even in the free states of the North, Negroes had few or no rights. Under the constant barrage of pro-slavery propaganda, many Northerners were unwilling to accept in their hearts and minds the idea of a democratic society of equal rights and opportunities for all people.

In the 1830's, Alexis de Tocqueville, keen French observer of the American scene, shrewdly noted that slavery had engendered such racial prejudice in the North as to render it "disagreeable to the Negro as a place of residence." Race riots were not uncommon in Northern cities; from 1832 to 1849, Philadelphia alone had five them in the course of which Negro churches, homes and meeting places were destroyed. Many Northern states did not permit Negroes to vote; as late as 1867, New Jersey and Ohio rejected equal suffrage.

York following suit two years later. A number of Northern states denied Negroes the right of trial by jury. Five states prohibited them from testifying against whites in court. Indiana, Illinois, Iowa and Oregon had constitutional or statutory provisions barring their entry.

Even in Massachusetts where Negroes enjoyed the greatest degree of equality, colored people were subjected to discrimination. In 1862, John Rock of Boston, the Negro physician turned lawyer, observed:

> Massachusetts has a great name, and deserves much credit for what she has done, but the position of the colored people in Massachusetts is far from being an enviable one. . . . Some persons think that, because we have the right of suffrage, and enjoy the privilege of riding in the cars, there is less prejudice here than there is farther South. In some respects this is true, and in others it is not true. We are colonized in Boston. It is five times as difficult to get a house in a good location in Boston as it is in Philadelphia, and it is ten times more difficult for a colored mechanic to get employment than in Charleston. Colored men in business in Massachusetts receive more respect and less patronage than in any place that I know of. In Boston we are proscribed in some of the eating-houses, many of the hotels . . . all theatres but one . . . some of the churches, and . . . [even] the grave-yards. This is Boston—by far the best, or at least the most liberal large city in the United States.

Second-class citizenship was accompanied by *de facto* segregation in medicine and health as in other fields. In too many Northern communities, Negroes could not make use of the available health facilities. In New York City, racial discrimination was such that it was not until 1841 that a group of public-spirited citizens succeeded in establishing and subsequently maintaining a few for Negroes at Bellevue Hospital. This neglect of Negro health needs in Northern was in sharp contrast to the way people in the urban centers reacted their white fellow citizens were by disease. During the terrible yellow epidemic of 1793 in Philadelphia, a thousand Negroes worked

through the Free African Society to nurse the afflicted, transport the sick and bury the dead. This was done in the face of a fourfold increase in Negro mortality as the epidemic affected thousands.

In medical education, too, the color bar prevailed north of the Mason-Dixon line. It was not until 1847 that the first Negro student, David J. Peck, was graduated from a Northern medical school, Rush Medical College in Chicago. Two years later, Bowdoin in Maine awarded medical degrees to two Negroes, John V. De Grasse of New York and Thomas J. White of Brooklyn. Peter W. Ray of New York also completed his medical studies at Bowdoin. During the early 1850's, James J. Gould Bias gradu-

THIRTEENTH ANNUAL ANNOUNCEMENT
OF THE
ECLECTIC MEDICAL COLLEGE
OF PENNSYVANIA.

ECLECTIC MEDICAL COLLEGE OF PENNSYLVANIA.

N. E. cor. Sixth & Callowhill Sts. PHILADELPHIA.

COLLEGE BUILDING,
NORTH-EAST COR. OF SIXTH & CALLOWHILL STS.
The only regular Chartered Eclectic Medical College in the State of Pennsylvania.

Holds Two Sessions Annually—Spring Session Commences February 1st, 1864.

ZOPHAR C. HOWELL, Esq., 622 Chestnut Street, President.
JOHN L. SHOEMAKER, Esq., 325 North Sixth St., Secretary.

FACULTY.

THOMAS G. CHASE, M. D., Twenty-Third and Green Streets, Emeritus Professor of Chemistry.
JOHN MINTZER, M. D., Sixth Street above Poplar, Emeritus Professor of Surgery.
JOHN G. RICH, M. D., Emeritus Professor of Anatomy.
JOSEPH SITES, M. D., 892 North Sixth Street, Professor of Obstetrics and Diseases of Women and Children.
HENRY HOLLEMBAEK, M. D., N. E. corner of Sixth and Callowhill Streets, Professor of Materia Medica and Therapeutics.
JOSEPH P. FITLER, M. D., 992 North Second Street, Professor of Chemistry and Toxicology.
JOHN BUCHANAN, M. D., 1809 Callowhill Street, Professor of Surgery and Institutes of Medicine.
M. N. MILLER, M. D., 1133 Race Street, Professor of Anatomy and Physiology.
JAMES MACNICHOL, M. D., 1322 Parrish Street, Professor of Theory and Practice of Medicine and Pathology.
JOHN WATSON, M. D., 413 North Sixth Street, Professor of Operative and Military Surgery.
JOHN L. SHOEMAKER, Esq., 325 N. Sixth St., Professor of Medical Jurisprudence
M. N. MILLER, M. D., 1133 Race Street, Demonstrator of Anatomy.
JOSEPH SITES, M. D., 892 North Sixth Street, Dean of Faculty.

Matriculation Fee, $5, for First Session only. | Diploma, $25.
Course of Lectures, $60. | Demonstrator's Fee, $5.

DR. PETER W. RAY

Because of the color line in medicine, the first few professionally trained Negro physicians received their medical degrees abroad. Of these the most eminent was Dr. James McCune Smith. Born in New York City in 1813, Smith was the son of a merchant of means. He was sent to the New York African Free School, where he was so gifted a student that, when Lafayette visited the United States in 1824, the school authorities called upon the youngster to deliver the welcome address. Unable to matriculate in an American college, Smith went abroad to study and was admitted to the University of Glasgow, where he received the B.A. degree in 1835, M.A. in 1836, and M.D. in 1837. Upon graduation, he returned to New York, where he became a very successful physician with a busy practice and two drug stores.

However, Dr. Smith was not a man to be satisfied with money alone. Devoted to his people, he was ready to give all his time, energy and resources to their emancipation and elevation. So, like his co-worker Dr. Delany, he spent less and less time on medicine and more and more on aboli-

ated from the Eclectic Medical College in Philadelphia; and Robert B. Leach, from the Homeopathic College in Cleveland.

In 1858, the Berkshire Medical School in Massachusetts awarded medical degrees to two Negro students. By 1860, at least nine Northern medical schools had admitted one Negro or more to their lectures. The schools were: Bowdoin; the Medical School of the University of New York; the Caselton Medical School in Vermont; the Berkshire Medical School in Pittsfield, Massachusetts; the Rush Medical School in Chicago; the Eclectic Medical School of Philadelphia; the Homeopathic College of Cleveland; the American Medical College and the Medical School of Harvard University. At that time academic requirements for an M.D. degree consisted of two year's attendance at such lectures, each lasting five or six months.

DR. JAMES McCUNE SMITH

tionism. He was an eloquent speaker, a man of impressive mien, fine head, lofty brow, firm mouth, deep-set eyes, and round, full face. Not only did he breathe fire from the speaker's platform, but he wrote in blood in the columns of the *Colored American,* a newspaper he edited, and the *North Star,* owned by his friend Frederick Douglass.

Dr. Smith used his vast scientific knowledge and great literary skill to defend the Negro people against the racial inferiority myths spouted by pro-slavery apologist Senator John C. Calhoun of South Carolina. During the early 1840's, this "statesman of the Old South" sought to buttress slavery by using the statistics of the United States Census of 1840 and by popularizing the spurious phrenological arguments of Dr. Samuel A. Cartwright of Louisiana. The 1840 Census, the first of its kind on the mentally ill, presented figures indicating that the rate of mental defectiveness among free Negroes was about eleven times higher than among Negro slaves. Accepting these figures at face value—the superintendent of the Census of 1840 was a Southerner, William A. Weaver—the South Carolinian asserted: "The African is incapable of self-care and sinks into lunacy under the burden of freedom. It is a mercy to him to give him guardianship and protection from mental death."

Senator Calhoun also used the ethnological arguments of Dr. Cartwright to justify the existence of Negro slavery. This is how the Louisiana physician in 1843 explained some purported anatomical idiosyncrasies of the Negro:

> ... the brain being ten percent less in volume and weight, he [the Negro] is, from necessity, more under the influence of his instincts and *animality* than other races of men and less under the influence of his reflective facilities. . . . His mind being thus *depressed* . . . nothing but arbitrary power, prescribing and enforcing temperance in all things, can restrain the excesses of his mental nature and restore reason to her throne.

JOHN C. CALHOUN

It fell to the lot of Dr. James McCune Smith to demolish the statistical and pseudo-scientific bases of John C. Calhoun's pro-slavery arguments. In a memorial to the Senate of the United States, approved at a mass meeting of Negroes in New York, May 3, 1844, Dr. Smith punched full of statistical holes the 1840 Census returns as they related to the mental health of the free Negroes of the North. He showed that, in some Northern towns purported to have mentally ill Negroes, there were no Negro residents at all. Concluding that the returns were false as well as self-contradictory, he suggested the Senate "would cause the Census of 1840 to be re-examined, and so far as possible corrected anew. . . ." About four months before the appearance of Dr. Smith's memorial, Dr. Edward Jarvis of Massachusetts, a white physician, statistically disproved the pro-slavery thesis of the 1840 Census in an article entitled "Insanity Among the Coloured Population of the Free States," published in the January, 1844, issue of the *American Journal of the Medical Sciences.*

Similarly, Dr. Smith destroyed another weapon in Senator Calhoun's pro-slavery arsenal. In 1843, he discussed for several evenings the "Comparative Anatomy and Physiology of the Races" before a notable and prominent assembly of New Yorkers. He particularly assailed the "scientific" theory of the "arrested" cranial development of the Negro, the supposed cause of the Negro's inferior intellect. In the estimation of the audience, the speaker had the best of the argument. Three years later, in 1846, the erudite Dr. Smith returned to the attack, contributing to *Hunt's Merchants' Magazine* an article on "The Influence of Climate upon Longevity." This work, a masterpiece of statistical and scientific analysis, was written as a refutation of a physiological disquisition by Senator Calhoun. Sometime after its appearance, a contemporary commentator observed:

> . . . we have heard nothing [more] about Calhoun's learned argument. It may be well to remark, that Senator Calhoun read medicine before he read law, and it would have been well for him if he had left [*sic*] medical subjects remain where *he left* them, for law.

Some years later, another observer, lecturing on the "Claims of the Negro Ethnologically Considered," referred to Dr. Smith as "a gentleman and scholar" and as one who believed that "this, our great nation, so distinguished for industry and enterprise, is largely indebted to its composite character."

Throughout his life, Dr. Smith took a strong stand against the colonization movement, whether backed by Negroes or whites. In 1860, in an open letter, he criticized Henry Highland Garnet for espousing the Haitian emigration movement. He reminded the noted Negro clergyman that, more than a quarter of a century ago, both of them, along with others, had pledged themselves to devote their lives and energies to "the

HENRY HIGHLAND GARNET

elevation and affranchisement of the free colored people on this, the soil which gave them birth, and through their affranchisement, the emancipation of the slaves of the South." Since then the Negro freedom movement had come a long way and now, said Dr. Smith, was near to achievement. This was neither the time to turn back nor the time to pursue "these migrating phantasms." The Negro people, he declared, "want to stay, and will stay, at home: we are in for the fight, and will fight it out here."

In 1860, the Negroes of New York State were in the midst of just such a fight: the right to vote on equal terms with whites. Only in five Northern states (Maine, New Hampshire, Vermont, Massachusetts and Rhode Island)—which contained no more than 7 per cent of the total colored population of the North—did Negroes enjoy equality with respect to suffrage. In New York they were required to own property worth $250, a qualification not imposed upon their white counterparts. As a result, four-fifths of the adult Negro males of the state were disqualified from voting. In 1860, a constitutional amendment eliminating the $250 property qualification for Negroes was submitted for approval in the November elections. To secure adoption of the proposal, Negroes throughout the state organized suffrage committees. In September the New York city and county committee issued a handbill written by James McCune Smith. Urging approval of the amendment, the Negro physician pointed out that "Principles of justice to the individuals who compose the State, and thereby of justice to the State itself, required that the basis of voting should be equal to all." The broadside was distributed in the thousands; but although Lincoln carried the state in November, the voting rights amendment was beaten by a margin of more than three to two.

DOCTORS IN BLUE

To Negro doctors, freedom was a two-way street; like the rest of the Negro people, they gave before receiving. Negro practitioners, like professionally schooled James McCune Smith, apprentice-trained John S. Rock and Martin R. Delany, and the self-taught healers David Ruggles and William Wells Brown, used their considerable talents in opposing slavery. Some served as agents on the Underground Railroad, over which thousands of Negroes, suffering from "drapetomania"—a disorder discovered by pro-slavery Dr. Cartwight and defined by him as "the disease causing Negroes to run away"—took the glory road to freedom. On speakers' platforms and in the press patriotic physicians repeatedly attacked the pseudo-scientific justification for slavery based on the myth of the physical and mental inferiority of the Negro. In this and in other ways, they pushed toward freedom; and in 1860, the six-year-old Republican Party came to power.

With Lincoln's election, the die was cast. One state after another in the deep South seceded from the Union. Contemporary evidence clearly demonstrates that slavery was the fundamental cause of the secessionist movement. In resolutions, speeches and writings, the protagonists of secession mentioned no other cause for their action. According to the distinguished American historians Samuel E. Morison and Henry S. Commager, the resolutions adopted by the state conventions show that "the states of the lower South seceded as the result of a long series of dissatisfactions respecting the Northern attitude toward slavery. There was no mention in their manifestos or in their leaders' writings and speeches of any other cause." And when the Confederacy was launched, the cornerstone of the new state, according to its vice-president, Alexander H. Stephens of Georgia, rested "upon the great truth that the negro [sic] is not equal to the white man. That slavery—subordination to the superior race—is his natural and normal condition." Such naked espousal of slavery and white racial supremacy as the causes of secession was to recede into the background as later historians sought to find more palatable ones, often citing states' rights. As a result, what was officially referred to by the United States Government as the War of the Rebellion has been metamorphosed into the War between the States.

Secession represented the slavocracy's recognition that time was running out. The drive of the slaveholders to destroy the Union was occasioned by the growing Northern threat to their political domination, the accelerated force of the abolitionist movement, and the evergrowing unrest of four million Negro slaves. The bloody war that followed secession by the South caused the deaths of more than 600,000 men and the wounding, burning and crippling of an almost equal, if not greater, number.

From the very beginning of the conflict, militant abolitionists, Negro and white, urged the Lincoln administration to crush the rebellion by adopting such revolutionary measures as the freeing of the slaves and the arming of Negroes. To them, the paramount issue of the War was slavery, and they were appalled by the vacillating policies on this vital question pursued by Lincoln and his advisers during the first eighteen months of the conflict. Even before the fighting began, the Negro physician John S. Rock put his finger on the Achilles heel of the Republican Party when he said in a speech before the Massachusetts Anti-Slavery Society early in 1860: "The idea of 'no more slave States' is good. The fewer the better. But they [the Republicans] do not go far enough. I would have them say 'No more slavery!'" Under the exigencies of the War, Dr. Rock became increasingly critical of President Lincoln's policy of trying to save the Union by avoiding the central issue of the struggle, the abolition of slavery. In August, 1862, he declared:

> . . . I confess I do not understand how it is, that when the national life has been assailed, he [President Lincoln] has not availed himself of all the powers given him; and, more especially why he has not broken every yoke, and let the oppressed go free. . . . We all know that emancipation, if early proclaimed, would not only have saved many precious lives, but the nation itself. Why then delay, when delays are dangerous, and may prove fatal?

One month later, the preliminary emancipation proclamation was issued, with its revolutionary promise that on January 1, 1863, all slaves in the rebellious states would be free.

Similarly, the pressure of events forced the Lincoln administration to adopt the revolutionary idea of arming the Negroes. When war broke out, many Northern Negroes volunteered to serve in the Union army. Among them was Dr. Martin R. Delany, the abolitionist leader. In October,

MAJOR MARTIN R. DELANY

1861, he persuaded President Mahan of Michigan College to apply for a commission to raise a division of Negro troops, to be called the Corps d'Afrique, with himself as divisional medical officer. The Union Government, regarding the conflict solely as a "white man's war," turned down the application. Undeterred, Dr. Delany applied to the War Department for appointment as surgeon to Negro troops in the Union army. Again his request was denied.

Meanwhile, Dr. Delany, Dr. Smith and other Negro abolitionists launched a campaign to build up enough public sentiment in the North to permit Negroes to fight for their freedom. This drive, together with a growing war-weariness and inability to keep up with the necessary manpower needs of the army, led the Lincoln administration in the summer of 1862 to begin arming the Negroes. Black troops were recruited first from among the freedmen of the South and then, early in 1863, from among the free Negroes of the North.

Allowed to fight for their freedom, Negroes responded to the call to arms. Under the slogan "Union and Emancipation," they marched off to battle. In the North, they came from all walks of life—businessmen, mechanics, day laborers and professionals. Their devotion to the Union cause was reflected in the case of William P. Powell, a New York Negro physician whose home was sacked in 1863 during the draft riots. Despite the fact that he and his family were forced to take refuge in a police station to save their lives, Dr. Powell, in a published account of the tragedy, wrote:

> As a devoted loyal Unionist, I have done all I could to perpetuate and uphold the integrity of this free government. As evidence of this devotedness, my oldest son is now serving my country as a surgeon in the U.S. army, and myself had just received a commission in the naval service.... I am now an old man, stripped of everything. . . but I thank God that He has spared my life, which I am ready to yield in defense of my country.

Negro abolitionists served as recruiting agents for black troops. Particularly prominent was Dr. Delany, who acted in that capacity, first for the Massachusetts 54th Regiment, then for the Rhode Island Heavy Artillery. In a letter to Secretary of War Stanton, December 15, 1863, he sought to broaden the scope of his recruiting activities by offering to raise troops in the seceded Southern states, provided he was given a War Department order. Dr. Delany came to envision an army of forty thousand Negroes, commanded by colored officers, irresistibly moving through the South to bring the War to a speedy conclusion. It was this vision that brought him an interview with President Lincoln on February 8, 1865. Eloquently, he pleaded his case:

> I propose, sir, an army of blacks commanded entirely by black officers, except such whites as may volunteer to serve, this army to penetrate through the heart of the South, and make conquests with the banner of Emancipation unfurled, proclaiming freedom as they go, sustaining and protecting it by arming the emancipated . . . keeping this banner unfurled until every slave is free, according to the letter of your proclamation.

One week later, Dr. Delany was mustered into service with the rank of major of infantry; in April he was sent to Charleston, South Carolina, where his son, First Lieutenant Toussaint L'Ouverture Delany, was stationed. Before he was able to recruit an "armée d' Afrique," the fighting was over. After the war, he was ordered to duty with the Freedmen's Bureau on Hilton Head Island, South Carolina, where he contributed much to the Reconstruction efforts of the radical Republicans.

The high casualty rate suffered by Negro troops during the War was due in no small measure to the reluctance of the War Department not only to commission available Negro physicians but also to assign a sufficient number of white doctors to Negro regiments. As the big guns roared at Fort Wagner, Port Hudson, Milliken's Bend, Nashville and Petersburg, Negroes died by the thousands. Many who might have been saved died because of lack of medical care. Negro losses during the war amounted to 37,300, the mortality rate of colored troops being 35 per cent greater than among other troops, despite the fact that they were not enrolled until eighteen months after the fighting and dying began.

The War Department's unwillingness to commission Negro practitioners during the Civil War was reflected in the fact that only eight colored physicians were appointed to the Army Medical Corps. Seven of the eight were attached to hospitals in Washington, D.C. The seven were: Drs. Charles B. Purvis, Alpheus Tucker, John Rapier, Wil-

MAJOR ALEXANDER T. AUGUSTA

rank of major. He was placed in charge of the "Freedmen's" Hospital in Washington, then called Camp Barker, the first Negro to head any hospital in the United States. Dr. Augusta was also stationed at Camp Stanton, Maryland, where he encountered racial bias. Two white assistant surgeons at the camp refused to serve under him because he was colored. Their protest resulted in Dr. Augusta being dispatched to Benedict and Baltimore, Maryland, to examine Negro recruits. He was later sent to the Department of the South, where he was stationed until the war ended.

Dr. Augusta was subjected to many indignities while serving his country. On February 1, 1864, he arrived late at a court martial, where he was a key witness, because of his ejection from a street car in Washington, D.C. He had refused to take his place in the section set aside for Negroes. Major Augusta described the incident as follows in a letter to the judge advocate:

> I . . . hailed [a] car at the corner of Fourteenth and I streets. It was stopped for me and when I attempted to enter the conductor pulled me back, and informed me that I must ride on the front with the driver, as it was against the rules for colored persons to ride inside. I told him that I would not ride on the front. . . . He then ejected me from the platform, and at the same time gave orders for the driver to go on. I have therefore been compelled to walk the distance in the mud and the rain, and have also been delayed in my attendance upon the court.

liam Ellis, Anderson R. Abbott, William Powell and Alexander T. Augusta. The eighth, Dr. John V. De Grasse, served with the 35th Regiment. Of this small band of doctors in blue, the most illustrious was Alexander T. Augusta. A free-born Virginia Negro, self-educated, he served his medical apprenticeship in Philadelphia, moved to California and returned East with the intention of deepening his knowledge of medicine. He applied for admission to medical schools in Philadelphia and Chicago but, because of racial bars, was rejected. Finally he matriculated at Trinity Medical College in Toronto, Canada. In 1856, he was graduated with a Bachelor of Medicine degree. Subsequently, he was in charge of the Toronto City Hospital.

In 1863, at the age of thirty-eight, Dr. Augusta joined the Union forces. He was commissioned to serve with the 7th United States Colored Troops as surgeon with the

Because of his color, Dr. Augusta, while in uniform, suffered other affronts. Although a major in the medical corps, he was given no more than the pay of an enlisted Negro soldier, a matter which he brought to the attention of Senator Henry Wilson of Massachusetts. Yet, in spite of these indignities, Dr. Augusta served his government with such distinction and devotion that he was brevetted a lieutenant-colonel in the United States Volunteer Force, to date from March 13, 1865.

DR. JOHN V. DeGRASSE

Dr. John V. De Grasse was another outstanding Negro physician who rendered meritorious and faithful service to his country during the Civil War. As a young man, he was a brilliant student, entering Bowdoin College in 1847 and completing his medical courses there two years later.

He went to Paris to continue his studies and became assistant to the great French surgeon Velpeau. After traveling widely in western Europe, he returned to the United States, where he took up the practice of medicine first in New York City, then in Boston. Here he became so celebrated a practitioner that he was elected a member of the Massachusetts Medical Society, perhaps the first Negro to belong to a medical body. During the Civil War, he served briefly as assistant surgeon with the 35th United States Colored Troops. In appreciation for his services, Governor John A. Andrew presented him with a gold-hilted sword on behalf of the Commonwealth of Massachusetts.

That more Negro physicians did not serve in the Union forces during the dark days of the Civil War was due to the reluctance of the War Department to commission them and to the relatively few trained Negroes available for service. However, the fact remains that those who were allowed to enlist did so and, together with more than two hundred thousand of their colored brothers, fought to preserve the Union and abolish slavery. Victory at Appomattox early in 1865 and the adoption by the states of the Thirteenth Amendment to the Constitution later in the year resulted in the achievement of both these objectives.

CHAPTER FOUR

High Hopes and Expectations

It is a fact worthy of note that this is the only country and the only profession in which such a distinction is now made. Science knows no race, color or condition; and we protest against the Medical Society of the District of Columbia, maintaining such a relic of barbarism. We, for the reasons stated, and in accordance with the spirit of the times, ask Congress to grant a charter to a new Society, which will give all rights, privileges and immunities to all physicians, making only the presentation of a diploma from some college recognized by the American Medical Association, and good standing in the profession, the qualifications necessary for membership.

Memorial of the National Medical Society of the District of Columbia to the Congress of the United States, January, 1870.

THE Civil War was over and so was slavery. The segregation associated with "the peculiar institution" had to be buried if the nation was to be given a new birth of freedom. To many within and outside the medical profession, it seemed only fair that the Negro be assured of his civil rights and an equitable share of the material benefits the country had to offer. There were substantial numbers of white doctors who were ready and willing to improve the professional status of their Negro colleagues. And there were Negro doctors who were eagerly looking forward to successful careers and confidently advancing in private practice. Their hopes and expectations were high.

The revolution which had begun with the Civil War continued during the critical years of radical Reconstruction. Before his death in 1868, Congressman Thaddeus Stevens of Pennsylvania, whose heart was with the Negro and who was hard-set against the Southern gentry, led the drive to set up military Reconstruction governments in the ex-Confederate States, to pass the Fourteenth Amendment to the Constitution and to impeach the man who was dubbed "Jefferson Davis" Johnson. His political counterpart in the Senate, erudite Charles Sumner of Massachusetts, helped to push the revolution one step forward with the adoption of the Fifteenth Amendment granting Negroes the right to vote.

Caught up in the revolutionary ferment, many white doctors joined their Negro colleagues to advance the cause of equal rights and equal opportunities in medicine and health. With indefatigable perseverance, these white practitioners sought to help their Negro associates professionally by establishing schools for their medical education, facilitating their appointment to hospital staffs and supporting their admission into medical societies, including the American Medical Association itself.

HOWARD AND MEHARRY

During the Reconstruction decade, two medical schools, Howard and Meharry, were established for the training of prospective Negro doctors. The medical school of Howard University, earliest of the two, opened its doors in Washington, D.C., on November 9, 1868, to Negro and white students. Present that Monday afternoon at five o'clock in an old frame house on Seventh Street Road, just above Florida Avenue, were five professors and eight students. The building, an abandoned German dance hall, had two floors, the lower of which was occupied by a private family and the upper, by the school. Here, in the front room, lectures were given and dissections made. The school day began at five in the afternoon and ended at nine-thirty in the evening. The semester was slightly less than four months. The student body was an excellent one, eager to learn, punctual in attendance and proficient in study. Of this first class, Dr. Silas L. Loomis, dean of the school, wrote:

> There were eight students who were remarkably punctual in their attendance upon the Lectures, seven were colored and one white, Mr. Bennit of Brooklyn, New York. Every Professor has frequently had occasion to express his surprise that the daily careful examinations of each student has shown an actual advancement in professional education not equalled by any Class heretofore under their instruction. . . . Our first course of Lectures passed with greater satisfaction to the Faculty and Students than in our most sanguine hopes we had anticipated. . . .

During the early years, the student body was, geographically speaking, widely distributed. In 1871–1872, students came from thirteen states (most of them in the North), the District of Columbia, six foreign countries and the West Indies. The school term

DR. SILAS L. LOOMIS

lasted for twenty weeks, with sessions beginning at three-thirty in the afternoon and ending at ten in the evening. The reason for the afternoon starting time was to give needy pupils the opportunity to work for the government, whose official day ended at three. To help financially hard-pressed students, tuition fees were low, ranging from $105 in 1868–1869 to $235 in 1872–1873. During the long depression of 1873, tuition fees were rescinded, not to be reinstated until 1880. Almost from the beginning, the school included women in the student body, and as early as 1872, Mary Dora Speckman was graduated with an M.D. degree. During the next eighteen years, an additional fourteen women were awarded their diplomas. In the meantime, the number of male graduates, including those of the first graduating class of 1871, totaled 238.

The first faculty of Howard Medical School had four white professors: Dr. Silas L. Loomis, dean and professor of chemis-

Medical Department of Howard University.

(Including Medical, Dental and Pharmaceutic Colleges.)

WASHINGTON, D. C.

Incorporated
March 2d, 1867.

863 Graduates.

THIRTY-SEVENTH SESSION (1904-1905) will begin October 1st, 1904, and continue seven (7) months. STUDENTS MATRICULATED FOR DAY INSTRUCTION ONLY. Four years' graded course in Medicine and Dental Surgery. Two years' graded course in Pharmacy.

Instruction is given by didactic lectures, clinics and practical laboratory demonstrations Well-equipped laboratories in all Departments. Unexcelled hospital facilities.

Faculties composed of men in active practice and with years of experience in College and Hospital work. Full corps of Quiz Masters.

Tuition fee in Medical and Dental Colleges, $80. Pharmaceutic College, $70. All students must register before October 12th, 1904.

For further information or catalogue apply to

F. J. SHADD, A. M., M. D.,

901 R Street, N. W.   *Secretary.*

THE HOWARD UNIVERSITY MEDICAL FACULTY, 1869–70

From left to right: Dr. Alexander T. Augusta; Dr. Silas L. Loomis, Dean; Dr. Gideon S. Palmer; Major General O. O. Howard, President; Dr. Robert Reyburn; Dr. Joseph Taber Johnson, Secretary; Dr. Charles B. Purvis; and Dr. Phineas H. Strong.

try and toxicology; Dr. Joseph T. Johnson, secretary and professor of obstetrics; Dr. Robert Reyburn, professor of surgery; Dr. Lafayette C. Loomis, professor of physiology and microscopy; and one Negro, Dr. Alexander T. Augusta, demonstrator of anatomy. Some faculty members also taught in the medical department of Georgetown University, which regarded Howard as "a rival college" bound to surpass it because of "the determination on the part of the 'Niggers' [*sic*] to be educated, and on the part of their friends throughout the North that they would be educated . . .." Georgetown University had already removed Dr. Loomis from his post as full professor in its medical department for his connection with Howard. There was

talk of forcing the resignation of Dr. Reyburn from the medical faculty of Georgetown because of his association with the new school. Those who favored such a move did so because Dr. Reyburn, as surgeon-in-chief of Freedmen's Hospital, one of the largest in Washington, could give Howard "more advantages for clinical instruction than any man in the city . . .." Tremendous pressure was brought to bear upon him, but all to no avail. Dr. Reyburn continued to serve Howard not only as professor of surgery, but also as dean of the school of medicine, 1870–1871 and 1900–1908.

The Howard medical faculty was a strong one because every effort was made to obtain the best men possible. As a result of the sale of lots and money from the Freedmen's Bureau, all of Howard's indebtedness was liquidated by 1870. However, the salaries offered prospective faculty members were lower than those prevailing in the older and better-known schools of the North. For example, in 1871, Howard offered a position on its medical faculty to George F. Barker of New Haven. After carefully considering the proposal, Barker made the following statement:

> Perhaps the most serious matter is whether my family could be comfortably cared for on $3,000 a year in so expensive a city as Washington. . . . Columbia pays $6,000 and my friends who are professors there tell me they can hardly live in New York on that. I am inclined to believe therefore that I could not come to Washington unless on a salary of $5,000 . . ..

Members of the Howard medical faculty were held in high esteem. For a long time they enjoyed the most friendly relations with the American Medical Association and the American Pharmaceutical Society. Similarly, they were cordially received by the Association of American Medical Colleges, although in 1877 that organization, upon objections by the Jefferson Medical College of Philadelphia, refused to seat the Howard delegation, partly because the Howard Medical School permitted men and women to be taught in the same classes.

From 1870 to 1877, several members of the Howard medical faculty were appointed by the President of the United States to serve on the District of Columbia's Board of Health, another reflection of the esteem in which they were held. Included was the distinguished Negro physician Dr. Charles B. Purvis, secretary-treasurer of the Howard University Medical School from 1873 to 1896. Similarly, the British Government thought highly of the Howard medical department. In 1875, the British legation in Washington praised it for its successful work and good standing.

Howard Medical School recognized very early the close relationship between the equal rights movement for Negroes and for women. In 1873, the Medical Alumni Association denounced discrimination against women "as being unmanly and unworthy of the [medical] profession," stating "we accord to all persons the same rights and immunities that we demand for ourselves." In turn, doctors in crinoline, like small and fragile Ann Preston, one of the founders of the medical college for women in Philadelphia, and pretty, persevering Elizabeth Blackwell, first qualified woman M.D. in the country, were outspoken advocates of Negro civil rights as well as unflinching foes of slavery. They and others, like Dr. Harriet K. Hunt and Dr. Marie Zakrzewska, did all they could to encourage Negro women to become doctors. And some did. In 1864, Dr. Rebecca Lee was graduated from the New England Female Medical College. In 1869, Dr. Rebecca Cole completed her course of study at the Woman's Medical College of

GEORGE F. BARKER

DR. MARIE ZAKRZEWSKA

DR. GEORGE W. HUBBARD

Pennsylvania and practiced medicine for half a century in Philadelphia, Columbia, South Carolina, and Washington, D.C.

Unlike the medical school of Howard University, Meharry Medical College was established solely for the education of Negro doctors. Located in Nashville, Tennessee, it was part of the Central Tennessee College, chartered in 1866 and supported by the Freedmen's Aid Society. In 1875, a proposal was made to organize a medical department to provide college-trained physicians to take care of the urgent health needs of the Negro people. The following year, the school opened with less than a dozen students, who eagerly awaited their first lecture in an old frame building at one time used as a barn. Eventually, a four-story brick building was constructed from money furnished by five white men, the Meharry brothers, who in their early years had been befriended by some Negroes.

The moving spirit behind the new school was George W. Hubbard, a thirty-five-year-old New England Yankee with a purpose, ably assisted in his initial endeavors by a white Southerner, Dr. W. J. Snead, a Confederate army surgeon. Hubbard came to Nashville in 1864 to work for the Christian Commission. Later, he joined Sherman's army and marched with it through Georgia. The following year, he taught the 110th United States Colored Troops, first at Gallatin, Tennessee, then at Huntsville, Alabama. After being mustered out of service, he became principal of the Belleview Public School in Nashville. He attended Vanderbilt University and graduated from its medical department in 1879. A man with strong features, a high forehead and a long flowing beard, he had, in the words of the historian of Meharry Medical College, "the vision of a seer, the courage of a warrior and the faith of a saint." For forty-five years, he

Meharry Dental and Pharmaceutical Hall.

Below: Central Tennessee College, Nashville, Tennessee.

The home built for Dr. Hubbard by the alumni and trustees of Meharry Medical College.

The Pharmaceutical Laboratory.

The Dental Laboratory.

administered Meharry, building it until it became the mecca for large numbers of Southern Negroes interested in a medical education. At his side for most of these years was his wife, Pennsylvania-born Sarah Lyon Hubbard.

In the beginning, Dr. Hubbard was assisted only by Dr. Snead, whose medical and surgical knowledge evoked the admiration and respect of the students. The two were soon joined by Dr. N. G. Tucker, who became professor of the theory and practice of medicine. He was an extraordinary teacher, lucid, witty and entertaining. In 1889, Dr. F. A. Stewart, a graduate of the Harvard Medical School, was added to the staff as a lecturer in pathology.

In his *Forty Cords of Wood,* John Edward Perry, class of '95, gives us thumbnail sketches of these faculty members as well as an insight into student life at the Nashville institution. Like many other Meharry students, Perry was a poor boy reared in the South. Born in Texas about 1870, the son of an ex-slave, he picked cotton, fed pigs and milked cows. In order to earn enough to attend school, he sold wood; his father cut it down, while he hauled it to market. The distance was five miles; the price, two dollars a cord. The money he earned from his "forty cords of wood" helped him enter Bishop College, a Baptist school taught by Northerners dedicated to the education of the Negro. After graduation, he became a teacher, hoping in this way to raise enough money to go to Meharry Medical College. There, from 1893 to 1895, he and his fellow students found that "Time was all too short and often we wished the twenty-four hour day might be stretched to thirty-six." His "only recreation aside from fireside jollification was a long walk, usually from 6 to 7 p.m."

Lister's claim concerning the relationship of bacteria to infection was much discussed. Perry and his classmates studied

DR. F. A. STEWART

DR. JOHN EDWARD PERRY

DR. N. G. TUCKER

various germs under the microscope. "We found it very interesting and instructive," he wrote, adding, "I shall always remember the first time I prepared a slide from the sputa of a patient and saw under the microscope the tuberculosis bacilli."

Young Perry also found his teachers exciting and rewarding. In his senior year, he sat in the front row of observers while Dr. Snead operated on a patient, carefully dissecting the tissues and ligating the blood vessels, doing all this "with poise and assurance." He listened to Dr. Tucker lecture on the theory and practice of medicine as related to diseases of the circulatory system. He was particularly impressed by the elderly physician's ability to draw upon his varied clinical experience. He was also charmed by the brilliance and versatility of Dr. Stewart's lectures on pathology.

From 1877 to 1890, Meharry graduated 102 students. For the most part they came from the South and had only the rudiments of a preparatory education. Ex-slaves or the sons of ex-slaves, they were largely without means and, hence, had to work their way through medical school. They took jobs of every kind, including the most menial, all the while devoting themselves to study. That many of them after graduation remained in the South, developing lucrative practices and rising to eminence in their communities, was a testimonial to their perseverance and ability.

FREEDMEN'S HOSPITAL

When on January 1, 1863, President Lincoln took the forward step of declaring all slaves within any state or district in rebellion "forever free," the Civil War was transformed from a defensive struggle for the preservation of the Union into a revolutionary war for the abolition of slavery. Between the Emancipation Proclamation and Appomattox, more than a million Negroes were freed. In 1865, as a result of the

Freedmen's Hospital in 1870.

Because they were unprotected by vaccination, Negro children were very susceptible to epidemics of smallpox.

adoption of the Thirteenth Amendment, another three million were emancipated. With the countryside desolated—farms abandoned, bridges destroyed, river levees broken, railroads ruined—tens of thousands of emancipated slaves wandered about uprooted, "a laboring, landless and homeless class," to use Lincoln's phrase. Free from the old quarter that once gave them shelter and a modicum of health care, they were turned loose, ill-clad, hungry and destitute, waiting and ever hoping for that miracle of miracles, "forty acres and a mule." "Free as the wind," they drifted into "contraband" camps and cities, where unsanitary conditions and abject poverty made them prey to a wide variety of illnesses.

The years immediately following the Civil War were terrible ones for the Negro people. Epidemics of smallpox, yellow fever and cholera swept through the South, resulting in a harvest of death. In 1871, the *Virginia Clinical Record* warned that the largest cities of the South would soon be hit by smallpox and that its ravages would be great, mainly among "the young negro [*sic*] population [which] is entirely unprotected by vaccination." The following year the epidemic struck and spread havoc in Washington and Alexandria, affecting chiefly the colored population. In 1873, Memphis was visited by succeeding waves of epidemics. Thousands died from yellow fever, cholera and smallpox, the latter exacting a particularly heavy toll among Negroes. Similarly, tuberculosis was a great killer. Hardest hit during these years were Negro communities, which, suffering from an appalling lack of food, shelter and clothing, were breeding places for the spread of this dread disease.

The exact number of deaths from disease and starvation among the newly emancipated slaves is not known, but statistics from Charleston, South Carolina, offer some clues. From 1866 to 1871, twice as many of the city's Negroes died as did its whites. Particularly shocking was the mortality rate of colored children under five as compared with that of white youngsters in the same age group. In 1868, almost three times as many Negro children died as did white children, 372 to 136. From these and other figures, it is estimated that in some crowded and unhealthy Southern communities from one-quarter to one-third of the former slaves died during the first years of Reconstruction.

The health gap that existed during slavery between the Negro and white population in the South tended to widen during the post-Civil War era. This is evident from a report made by Dr. F. Tipton of Selma, Alabama, who served the city as registrar of vital statistics for the year 1885. According to the report, the city's death rate among blacks was almost twice as high as among whites. Negro mortality due to various diseases of the pulmonary apparatus was particularly heavy, being four times more numerous among the colored population than among the white. Negroes were also more susceptible to yellow fever, the epidemic of 1878 seriously affecting a large number of them.

They were, likewise, more prone to other epidemics because of the unhygienic conditions under which they lived: houses without windows, chimneys full of smoke, and bedding old and filthy. Dr. Tipton warned Selma's "better classes" that epidemics such as scarlet fever and measles were being carried about town by blacks working for whites in their homes. A white suprem-

GENERAL O. O. HOWARD

acist who looked upon Negroes as "this simple-minded and superstitious race of people," he nevertheless realized that they did the work of the South and, hence, had to be taken care of. In fact, they were irreplaceable as laborers, especially, as he put it, "in our more malarial localities along the sluggish streams of Alabama, Arkansas, Mississippi and Louisiana reeking as they are, like the rice-fields of South Carolina, with the deadliest miasmas . . .."

In the meantime, the group that directed the revolution and Reconstruction from Washington created the Freedmen's Bureau in March, 1865, to help emancipated slaves adjust themselves to their new conditions. Headed by General O. O. Howard, the "Christian Soldier," the bureau turned to the pressing problem of Negro health. During the four and a half years of its existence, the agency gave medical assistance to at least a million Negro patients. It established more than a hundred hospitals and dispensaries.

Among the latter was the celebrated Freedmen's Hospital in Washington, D.C. During the War, thousands of escaped slaves came to the nation's capital. The newcomers took shelter in any building that had four walls and a roof over it, whether it was a broken-down shanty or a deserted barrack. Living quarters were overcrowded, toilet facilities lacking, and destitution, filth and disease rampant. With illness on the increase, the Federal government established new hospitals and enlarged old ones. In the fall of 1863, sick freedmen were treated at Camp Barker, the hospital facilities of which were under the supervision of Major Alexander T. Augusta, then attached to the medical corps. The hospital continued to be directed by the War Department until 1865, when the newly created Freedmen's Bureau was put in charge of the operation. As the health needs of the Negro population grew, there was talk of reorganizing the hospital and running it on a more business-like basis. The urgency of the situation was underlined by the fact that, of the 31,500 Negroes living in Washington and Georgetown in 1866, almost 23,000 suffered from some illness. As a result of heroic efforts, the number of Negro sick subsequently declined. Finally, in 1868, there remained about 350 decrepit and mentally ill patients who were and would continue to be unable to look after themselves during their lifetime.

To care for these helpless people, the Freedmen's Hospital was established on a permanent basis. By order of General O. O. Howard, buildings were erected on the grounds of Howard University. Located at the Corner of Fifth and W Streets, N. W., the group of buildings consisted of a main brick structure, four and a half stories high, for executive offices and lecture halls and four large two-story frame houses for

patients. The entire hospital had a bed capacity of three hundred. Its first surgeon-in-chief was Dr. Robert Reyburn, and its second, Dr. Gideon S. Palmer, both firm believers in racial equality.

In 1881, Dr. Charles B. Purvis was appointed surgeon-in-chief of the Freedmen's Hospital, the first Negro civilian in the United States "to head a hospital under civilian auspices." Born April 14, 1842, in Philadelphia, the son of moderately rich Robert Purvis, the great abolitionist leader, he had every opportunity that wealth and position could offer. From 1860 to 1863, he attended Oberlin College, where he did very well in his studies. Wishing to become a doctor, he transferred to Western Reserve Medical School in Cleveland. After his graduation in 1865, he was offered a commission in the medical corps as acting assistant surgeon with the rank of first lieutenant. He served in the army until 1869, when he became assistant surgeon of Freedmen's Hospital. In that year he was also appointed to the faculty of Howard Medical School, the second Negro to be so honored. As secretary-treasurer, he was

DR. GIDEON S. PALMER

able during the great depression of 1873 to prevent the closing of the school. When President James A. Garfield was felled by an assassin's bullet in 1881, he was one of the doctors called in to attend the stricken Chief Executive, the only Negro physician to have served a president of the United States. Thus, he was already a distinguished member of the medical profession when he was promoted to surgeon-in-chief of the Freedmen's Hospital.

In that capacity Dr. Purvis served with distinction for almost a dozen years. Under him, the hospital grew in size and importance. In 1886, more than five thousand patients were seen; two thousand remained for treatment. Patients and staff respected the commanding presence of Dr. Purvis. A man of resolute determination, he was not one to compromise. To him, medicine was a science, each year bringing new ideas, experiences and achievements. He expected his staff to keep abreast of medical progress. So exacting was he that many of his associates regarded him as overbearing in manner, a very ferocious man who barked rather than spoke. He was a controversial figure, strong, dynamic and imposing. One was either for or against him. Yet all agreed on one fact: his devotion to medicine and the medical profession. For fifty-seven of his eighty-seven years, he was associated with the Howard Medical School, first as faculty member; then as secretary-treasurer, 1873–1896; later as president of the faculty, 1899–1900; and finally as member of the board of trustees, 1908–1926. His years of distinguished service at Freedmen's Hospital did much to assure the appointment of another Negro, Dr. Daniel H. Williams, to the post of surgeon-in-chief.

SHOWDOWN IN THE AMA

During the critical years of the Reconstruction era, Negro doctors, eager to improve themselves professionally, sought ad-

DR. CHARLES B. PURVIS

mission into medical societies. In this endeavor they had the support of a militant band of white physicians who believed in equal opportunities for all. On June 9, 1869, Dr. Alexander T. Augusta and Dr. Charles B. Purvis, two of the seven Negro physicians then practicing in Washington, D.C., were proposed for membership in the Medical Society of the District of Columbia, an affiliate of the American Medical Association (AMA). Both men were Civil War veterans, and Dr. Augusta had been promoted to the high rank of lieutenant-colonel for meritorious services rendered. Both were members of the faculty of the Howard Medical School, Dr. Augusta holding the rank of demonstrator of anatomy and Dr. Purvis, professor *materia medica* and medical jurisprudence. On June 23, Dr. A. W. Tucker, another eminently qualified Negro physician, was similarly proposed for membership in the Medical Society of the District of Columbia. Although all three Negro doctors were reported eligible for admission, their applications were rejected.

This blatantly segregationist action was roundly condemned by Charles Sumner of Massachusetts, who went to the floor of the Senate, December 9, 1869, to introduce a resolution inquiring into the desirability of securing for medical practitioners equal rights and opportunities, without distinction as to color, in the District of Columbia. Speaking on his resolution, this warrior for Negro equality went out of his way to laud the work of Drs. Augusta and Purvis:

> In my opinion, these white oligarchs ought to have notice, and I give them notice now that this outrage shall not be allowed to continue without remedy, if I can obtain it through Congress. The time has passed for any such pretension.

About a month later, the society's leaders, in a published "Appeal to Congress," answered the Massachusetts senator by saying that the question of membership in the medical body was a personal and social matter. Senator Sumner responded by introducing a bill in the Senate on February 8, 1870, to repeal the society's charter. The reason given was plain and pointed: if the organization was to be permitted to change from a professional medical body to merely a social club, and this "in derogation of equal rights of all, it becomes a nuisance and a shame." But the Senate refused to act on the bill.

Senator Sumner's bill was accompanied by a report which showed how the exclusion policies of the District's medical society worked to the disadvantage of Negro physicians. Dr. Augusta was reported to have lost two of his patients to a white physician because he was not a member of the medical body. For the same reason, white practitioners refused to consult with Dr. Purvis on a case involving a patient properly belonging to him.

About a month before Senator Sumner submitted his report, the civil rights group inside the District's medical society tried again to secure the admission of the Negro doctors. On January 3, 1870, Dr. Robert Reyburn, faculty member of Howard Medical School and surgeon-in-chief of the Freedmen's Hospital, introduced a resolution stating, "That no physician (who is otherwise eligible) should be excluded from membership in this Society on account of his race or color." By a vote of twenty-six to ten, the society refused to consider Dr. Reyburn's resolution. At the same meeting, a candidate known to support the admission of the Negro physicians was rejected solely on this ground. Although it was apparent to Dr. Reyburn and his associates that the society was under the control of "gentlemen who served during the war in the Confederate Army," they made one last try. On February 9, 1870, Dr. Joseph Borrows nominated Dr. Augusta, Dr. Purvis and Dr. Tucker for membership, but the nominations were declared out of order because

CHARLES SUMNER

DR. JOSEPH BORROWS

and professional questions, essays and papers were discussed.

> It is a fact worthy of note, that this is the only country and the only profession in which such a distinction is made. Science knows no race, color, or condition; and we protest against the Medical Society of the District of Columbia maintaining such a relic of barbarism.

In conclusion, the memorial urged Congress to charter the new National Medical Society "in accordance with the spirit of the times...."

In the months that followed, the newly established society carefully planned to carry its fight to the American Medical Association. Its annual convention was scheduled to be held in Washington, D.C., in May, 1870. Only twenty-three years old at the time, the AMA was already the recognized center of the organized medical profession of the country. Membership in it gave physicians prestige as well as an opportunity to advance themselves professionally and materially. Negro doctors, wishing to share equally in such benefits, decided to carry their fight for membership directly to the parent body. In this, they had the support of a growing number of white physicians who believed that the time had come to establish racial equality in medicine. The issue was argued at the 1870 convention of the AMA. At stake was whether the national organization would act as a positive force in eliminating segregationist practices in county affiliates or tacitly agree to support such practices by adopting a hands-off policy on the question.

This was the issue on May 3, 1870, as the curtain rose on the opening day of the crucially important 21st annual convention of the association. Two delegations were there to represent the District of Columbia: one, the newly organized National Medical Society, composed of Negro and white physicians; and the other, the regularly constituted and officially recognized all-white body. The point in dispute was

they were not made at a stated meeting as required by the regulations.

This, however, was not the end of the fight. On the contrary, it had just begun. On the evening of January 15, 1870, a meeting was held at the Congregational Church, at the corner of Tenth and G Streets, N.W., to act on the formation of a medical society in the District of Columbia which would extend equal rights and privileges to all regular physicians and surgeons. Out of this meeting, sponsored by the medical faculty of Howard University, emerged the National Medical Society of the District of Columbia, a professional body composed of Negro and white doctors. In a memorial to the Congress of the United States, the new body pointed out that the Medical Society of the District of Columbia was hiding behind the subterfuge that its meetings were merely "social reunions," though parliamentary rules were rigidly enforced immediately joined, and for four long days the question was debated in one form or another.

At exactly eleven o'clock on Tuesday morning, May 3, 1870, President George Mendenhall of Ohio called the convention to order. There was an air of expectancy in Lincoln Hall on that hot and humid day as dignified-looking men, some clean-shaven, others with sideburns, and still others with flowing beards, listened to the majority report of the Committee on Arrangements. A long list of duly accredited representatives was returned, but nowhere on it were the names of the delegates of the National Medical Society. The seating of these representatives, said the majority report, would depend on further investigation of charges.

A hush fell over the hall as militant, outspoken, highly respected Dr. Robert Reyburn presented the minority report. His

DR. N. S. DAVIS

opposition to the regular slate of delegates from the District of Columbia, he stated, was based on the fact that they represented a society which, "in defiance of the ethics of the American Medical Association," issued licenses for the fee of ten dollars to "irregular practitioners" and "persons who [were] not graduates of any respectable college." Accordingly, he urged the seating of a rival slate of delegates, including the Negro doctors Augusta, Purvis and Tucker. There was a stirring in the hall as Dr. N. S. Davis of Illinois proposed that the minority report, together with portions of the majority report, be referred to the Committee on Ethics.

The second day of the convention opened with Dr. Silas L. Loomis of Howard Medical School moving to admit all delegates from the District of Columbia while the question of representation was still pending. The motion was defeated by 142 to 107. Then Dr. Cox moved that none of the delegates from the District of Columbia be seated until the question was resolved by the Committee on Ethics. In the meantime, word began to spread that the committee was planning to delay the submission of its report until the next to the last day of the convention in order to prevent the seating of any delegate belonging to the National Medical Society.

Whether the rumor was true or false, the fact remains that it was not until May 5, the day before the convention adjourned, that the Committee on Ethics submitted its report. The majority (Drs. N. S. Davis of Illinois, H. F. Askew of Delaware and J. M. Keller of Kentucky) recommended that no member of the National Medical Society be admitted as a delegate to the convention. The minority report (by Drs. A. Stille of Pennsylvania and J. J. Woodward of the United States Army) moved that members of the National Medical Society as well as those of Howard Medical School, Freed-

DR. H. F. ASKEW

DR. J. M. KELLER

men's Hospital and Smallpox Hospital be seated as delegates. This would include the Negro physicians, Augusta, Purvis and Tucker, as well as such white practitioners as Reyburn and Loomis.

Then the parliamentary maneuvering began in earnest. After motions were made to accept the majority and minority reports, Dr. E. L. Howard of Maryland moved to table the minority report. Vice-President Sayre of New York, in the chair at the time for President Mendenhall of Ohio, ruled that, on the motion to table, all those from the District of Columbia who had been favorably reported upon by the Committee on Ethics were entitled to vote. An angry roar rose in the hall as the temporary chairman's ruling was announced, for this was what was actually at issue before the convention. As the uproar subsided, the vote on the motion to table was begun. With the Southern states and the District of

Columbia voting practically as a solid block, the minority report was laid aside by a vote of 112 to 80. According to an authority on the subject, if the representatives from the District of Columbia had not been allowed to vote on their own seating, the vote to table would have been defeated seventy-seven to seventy-six.

Steamroller tactics notwithstanding, the desegregationists returned on the following and final day of the convention to continue the fight for equal rights. Dr. G. S. Palmer of Maine moved that the majority of the Committee on Ethics inform the convention on what principle the delegation from Howard Medical School had been excluded from membership in the American Medical Association. Dr. N. S. Davis of Illinois promised to present the majority's position in writing. As the closing minutes of the session approached with still no report from Dr. Davis, Dr. J. L. Sullivan of

Massachusetts rose to offer the following resolution: "That no distinction of race or color shall exclude from the Association persons claiming admission and duly accredited thereto."

At this point, Vice-President Sayre moved that the vote on Dr. Sullivan's resolution be temporarily suspended so that Dr. N. S. Davis of Illinois could be given time to explain the majority report of the Committee on Ethics. He explained that only delegates from the National Medical Society and not from Howard Medical School or "any other medical institution in the District of Columbia" were excluded. Then the Sullivan resolution on equal rights for Negro doctors was tabled. As if to whitewash the whole matter, another resolution was entertained to the effect that considerations of race and color had nothing whatsoever to do with the decision on the question of the admission of the Washington delegates and that, therefore, the majority report of the Committee on Ethics be declared, "as to all intents and purposes, unanimously adopted by the Association." The resolution was passed, and the convention was adjourned.

The action taken by the American Medical Association at its 21st annual meeting did not stop the civil rights forces, black and white, from continuing their fight for integration in medicine. A report of the dean of the medical department of Howard University in 1870 condemned the AMA "as degrading itself on a pretense of violation of the Code of Ethics, whilst—as was notorious and patent to all that were present—the real reason was that one of the delegates was not of the Caucasian race." The battle for AMA membership was renewed in 1872, when the National Medical Society, by then called the Academy of Medicine, requested the Philadelphia convention to seat its delegates. As in 1870, so in 1872, the association turned down the request. Two years later, a similar petition

was rejected, the AMA ruling that since the Medical Association of the District of Columbia was a duly constituted body, its wishes regarding the exclusion of Negro doctors from membership had to be respected.

As a result of the continued refusal of the Washington society to admit Negro doctors to membership, a group of white physicians organized in 1884 the Medico-Chirurgical Society of the District of Columbia, a biracial body. The original group included Dr. Robert Reyburn and, in all probability, Dr. Silas L. Loomis. Two other veterans of the integrationist battles of the late sixties and early seventies, Drs. Augusta and Purvis, though sympathetic with the aims of the new organization, remained outside of it, preferring to fight Jim Crow in their own way. Apparently, there were many others like them, for the new body made

DR. J. R. FRANCIS

little progress. In 1891, Dr. J. F. Shadd and in 1894, Dr. J. R. Francis applied to join the all-white Medical Society of the District of Columbia. Although they obtained a majority of the votes cast, they failed to receive the two-thirds necessary for admission. Following these defeats, the Medico-Chirurgical Society was revived in 1895 and subsequently became all-Negro since its white members died and were not replaced by others.

Similarly, the exclusionist policies of other affiliated AMA bodies forced Negro doctors to organize into separate professional societies. In 1886, a group of Negro physicians established the Lone Star State Medical Association of Texas. The guiding spirit behind the new organization was Dr. Monroe A. Majors, a Meharry graduate, who shortly thereafter had to leave Texas for the West Coast to escape hanging by segregationist elements. In 1887, another all-colored medical body, the Old North State Medical Society of North Carolina, was formed. It was destined to enjoy a long and distinguished history.

The organization of separate Negro medical societies in the 1880's was the natural concomitant of the local autonomy or "home rule" policy adopted by the American Medical Association in the 1870's. In turn, the policy was part of a much larger political movement which was then coming to the fore. With the flood tides of radical Reconstruction receding from 1872 onward, the Negro people in the South were increasingly left to the none-too-tender mercies of their former masters. "Black Codes" were revived, the Ku Klux Klan rode again, and a new form of economic bondage, sharecropping, emerged. These roadblocks to freedom made increasingly

DR. MONROE A. MAJORS

difficult the fight of the Negro masses for the franchise, land reform and civil rights. The *coup de grâce* was administered in 1877, when the Hayes-Tilden contest over the presidency led to a formal agreement in which the Republicans contracted to permit Southern Democrats to deal with the Negro people as they wished. As a result of this compromise of 1877, the Republican Hayes became President by a single electoral vote, and Federal troops were recalled from the South. With this stab in the back, the Negro-white coalition for racial equality was dealt a heavy blow. The achievement of equal rights for the Negro people remained, and still remains, one of the unfinished tasks of what has been aptly described as "The Second American Revolution."

CHAPTER FIVE

Grim Realities

Conceived in no spirit of racial exclusiveness, fostering no ethnic antagonisms, but born of the exigencies of the American environment, the National Medical Association has for its object the banding together for mutual co-operation and helpfulness, the men and women of African descent who are legally and honorably engaged in the practice of the cognate professions of Medicine, Surgery, Pharmacy and Dentistry.

Dr. Charles V. Roman, in response to an address of welcome by the Borough President of Manhattan to the National Medical Association at its convention in New York City, 1908.

The Negro death rate is . . . undoubtedly considerably higher than the white. . . . The excess is due principally to mortality from consumption, pneumonia, heart disease and dropsy, diseases of the nervous system, malaria and diarrheal diseases.

Dr. W. E. B. Du Bois, ed., *The Health and Physique of the Negro American,* 1906.

BY 1890, the majority of the former Confederate states had succeeded in repealing the civil rights laws enacted during Reconstruction; and the modern system of legal segregation and discrimination began in the South. It continued thereafter with unabated intensity until the adoption of the Oklahoma constitution in 1910. In the meantime, influential circles in the North accepted the Southern system with "understanding." Said President Charles W. Eliot of Harvard in 1907: "Perhaps if there were as many Negroes here as there, we might think it better for them to be in separate schools. . . . If they were equal in numbers or in a majority, we might deem a separation necessary." It was no accident that during these two decades the United States assumed "the white man's burden" in colonial possessions as far apart as the Caribbean, Hawaii and the Philippines.

These were the grim realities that shattered the hopes of Negro doctors for racial equality in the late nineteenth and early twentieth centuries. From 1890 to World War I, Negroes in medicine were faced by a new system of racial segregation and discrimination popularly known as Jim Crow—"overt and legal" in the South and "covert and extra-legal" in the North. To meet the new situation, Negro doctors as well as nurses were forced to establish their own medical schools and professional organizations.

In the South, and to a lesser degree in the North, medical schools were closed to Negro students. In the border states and the old Confederacy, where the bulk of the colored population lived, it was impossible for Negroes to enter white medical colleges. Typical of the section's attitude was the position taken by the dean of a St. Louis

The University of Pennsylvania Medical School.

medical college who, in response to a circular asking if any Negro students were in attendance, exploded: "If you are looking for niggers [*sic*] go to Boston or other 'nigger' loving communities. *None,* thank God !! *None,* by God, sir! And what's more, there never will be any *here.*" Although the over-agitated dean had a somewhat exaggerated idea of what was happening in the North, it was nevertheless true that, here and there, highly qualified Negro students were given the opportunity of entering some of the older medical schools of the East, such as Harvard, Yale and Pennsylvania, and the newer ones of the Midwest, such as Indiana, Northwestern and Michigan. However, the number of Negro doctors graduating from these and other white Northern schools was miniscule in comparison to the number taking their M.D. degrees at Negro schools. In 1895, of 385 Negro physicians tabulated, only 27, or 7 per cent, came from white medical schools. In 1905, 213, or 14.5 per cent of a tabulated 1,465 Negro doctors, were graduates of white institutions. From 1890 to the end of World War I, almost 2,400 physicians were graduated from Howard and Meharry.

SCHOOLS AND ORGANIZATIONS OF THEIR OWN

Beginning in 1882, but especially from 1888 on, a half-dozen Negro medical schools were founded to supplement the work of Howard and Meharry. All six disappeared during the early twentieth century, but not until a thousand students had been graduated from them, nearly half of whom passed their state board examinations.

Of the six institutions, the most successful was the Leonard Medical School of Shaw University in Raleigh, North Carolina. It was established in 1882 and was supported by the Baptist Mission Society for Negroes. The North Carolina state legislature contributed the site for a medical building as well as a hospital, dispensary and dormitory. There were six students in

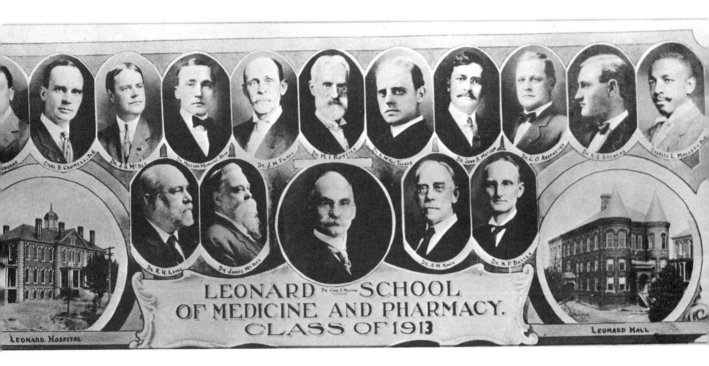

The Hospital and Medical Building of the Leonard Medical School.

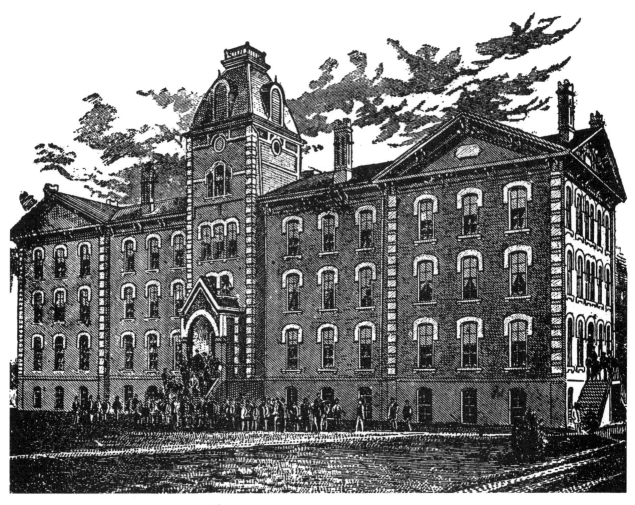

Shaw University in Raleigh, North Carolina.

the school's first graduating class. There-after, the number steadily increased; by 1915, over five hundred students had been graduated.

Students came to the school from every section of the country, as well as from Liberia, Trinidad and Jamaica. Among the school's graduates were such outstanding physicians as Dr. L. L. Burwell, a poor farm boy who became a successful Selma, Alabama, practitioner; Dr. J. W. Jones, who was so busy a physician in Winston-Salem, North Carolina, that he made as many as forty-five calls a day; Dr. J. A. Kenney, family physician of Booker T. Washington and one-time secretary of the National Medical Association; and Dr. L. Martin,

a Philadelphia radiologist who became a certified specialist. Leonard's faculty was composed of leading white physicians of Raleigh. By 1912, its medical building was equipped with lecture halls, a dissecting room and a laboratory, while its hospital was capable of housing eighty patients. But despite all this, the school was closed in 1915 because it was unable to meet the rising medical standards set forth in the Flexner Report on Medical Education, published in 1910.

Second only to the Leonard Medical School in the number of graduates was the Medical Department of the University of West Tennessee. During the twenty-three years of its existence (1900–1923), it grad-

The residence of Dr. J. W. Jones of Winston-Salem, North Carolina.

DR. L. L. BURWELL

The well-equipped drugstore of Dr. Burwell.

uated 266 students. Its founder was Dr. Miles V. Lynk, a prominent Negro physician and medical educator. Born in 1871 on a farm near Brownsville, Tennessee, he spent his early years farming, cutting wood and studying in a country school. In his autobiography, *Sixty Years of Medicine,* he wrote of his boyhood as follows:

> At an early age I had an ardent desire to become a doctor. With this end in view I cultivated home study, literally attended 'PINE KNOT COLLEGE.' I soon became interested in history, biography and current events. As a supplement to my limited school facilities, my home-study enabled me at the age of 13 years, to pass the teacher's examination in my county and thus obtain a teacher's certificate, which because of my youth I could not use.

After a brief apprenticeship to a physician, young Lynk entered Meharry and, at the age of nineteen, was graduated with his M.D. degree, second in a class of thirteen. In December, 1892, when he was but one year out of medical school, he published *The Medical and Surgical Observer,* the first Negro medical journal in the country. At the turn of the century, Dr. Lynk and his wife mortgaged their home to provide initial funds for the establishment of the medical college of the University of West Tennessee. Its financial resources were so limited that in 1909 the school was found to have little equipment, a small hospital for clinical training and a dispensary without records. The Memphis institution finally closed in 1923, but not before it had graduated such eminent Negro physicians as Dr. Willard M. Lane, assistant professor of surgery at Howard, and Dr. John S. Perry, president of the Medico-Chirurgical Society of the District of Columbia.

Like Dr. Miles V. Lynk, Dr. Henry Fitzbutler, founder and dean of the Louisville National Medical College, was devoted to the cause of Negro medical education. Born in 1842, in Ontario, Canada, he completed district school and financed his further education by working as a farm hand, school teacher, lumberman and surveyor. At the age of thirty, he was graduated from the medical school of the University of Michigan. Thereupon, he moved to Louisville, Kentucky, the first Negro to enter the medical profession in that state. From the beginning, he felt the full force of

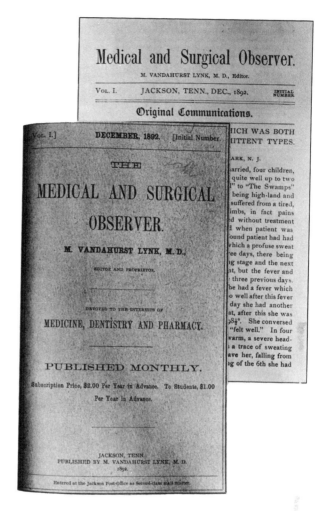

DR. MILES V. LYNK

racial discrimination. One day he answered an emergency call to treat a girl who had been severely burned while cooking. Also summoned were seven other doctors, all white. Dr. Fitzbutler, who had his emergency kit with him, asked the white physicians present to assist him. They replied, "We won't work with a Negro." Accordingly, he worked alone and saved the girl, despite the fact that about five-eighths of the surface of her body had been burned. A similar anti-Negro bias pursued him when he tried to practice in Louisville hospitals and to attend medical lectures.

As the years passed, Dr. Fitzbutler thought of establishing a medical college open to all, regardless of color. In 1888, the Kentucky state legislature granted him and his associates permission to establish

DR. HENRY FITZBUTLER

DR. SARAH H. FITZBUTLER

a school of medicine in Louisville. In a rented hall, the Louisville National Medical College opened its doors to six students. The following year, the school had its own building at 114 West Green Street, and it later acquired a hospital of its own, maintained chiefly by Dr. Fitzbutler's own funds. After his death in 1901, the work of the school was carried on by Dr. W. A. Burney, a close associate of his in the fight for equal educational opportunities. Dr. Burney was ably assisted by Dr. Fitzbutler's wife, herself a graduate of the school. An amiable, compassionate woman, Dr. Sarah H. Fitzbutler served as superintendent of the Auxiliary Hospital, which the Flexner Report described as small but scrupulously clean. In 1909, the school had twenty-three faculty members and forty students. Two years later it closed its doors because of its inability to meet the new standards established for accreditation.

A similar fate befell the three remaining medical schools that were founded for the education of Negro doctors. Flint Medical College of New Orleans, established in 1889, graduated in its span of twenty-two years 120 medical students. Among them was Dr. J. H. Lowery of Louisiana, who headed a successful civil rights fight to secure equal accommodations for Negroes on the state's railroads. Knoxville (Tennessee) Medical College, founded in 1895, was in existence for at least a half-dozen years and had over forty-five graduates. Concerning the last of these Negro medical schools, the Chattanooga (Tennessee) National Medical College, very little is known beyond the fact that it was listed as having nine students in its 1903–1904 session and one graduate in 1904.

The color line forced Negro doctors to establish separate professional bodies as well as separate medical schools. Racial exclusion and "token" membership policies kept most Negro physicians out of regularly recognized AMA county and state medical societies. In the latter half of the 1880's, Negro doctors organized two professional bodies of their own, one in Texas, the other in North Carolina. As early as December, 1892, Dr. Miles V. Lynk, in his *Medical and Surgical Observer,* advocated "an Association of medical men of color, national in character." To establish such a national organization, Dr. Lynk conferred with a number of leading Negro physicians. He particularly singled out Dr. Robert F. Boyd, whom he considered the foremost Negro practitioner of the day. "He was always affable, farsighted, a friend of young men and bristling with energy," Dr. Lynk wrote, adding, "I was glad to class him as one of my friends."

Like most of his colleagues, Dr. Robert F. Boyd was a poor boy who worked his

DR. ROBERT F. BOYD

Dr. Boyd's residence in Nashville, Tennessee.

way through college and medical school to become a doctor. Born July 8, 1858, in Pulaski, Tennessee, of slave parents, he spent most of his boyhood working on a farm except for a brief period learning the trade of brickmasonry. He attended school in Pulaski, where he studied the three R's. Forced to work during the day, he went to school at night, eventually graduating from Central Tennessee College and Fisk University. He then entered Meharry, graduating with honors in 1882. Five years later, he was awarded a D.D.S. degree, whereupon he began the practice of medicine and dentistry. Not satisfied with a minimal professional education, he did postgraduate work in surgery at Ann Arbor and in diseases of women and children at the Postgraduate Medical School and Hospital in Chicago. He returned to Nashville, where he built up a large practice, taught at Meharry, and ran for mayor in 1893, when both major parties spurned the Negro vote. He died suddenly in 1912 at the age of 54, one of the most outstanding and wealthiest Negro physicians in the country.

In 1895, Dr. Boyd and Dr. Lynk were both in Atlanta, Georgia, attending the Cotton States and International Exposition. The two men agreed that the time had come to launch a national medical association for Negroes. They obtained permission to use the First Congregational Church for a meeting. On a Wednesday afternoon in October, 1895, with Professor I. Garland Penn, commissioner of the Negro division of the exposition, in the chair, the meeting was called to order. After stating that the purpose of the meeting was to organize a national association of colored physicians, dentists and pharmacists, Professor Penn asked for reactions to the proposal. Each of the twelve doctors present agreed that such an organization was needed, and the group proceeded to elect Dr. R. F. Boyd of Nashville, president; Dr.

I. GARLAND PENN

D. H. Williams of Chicago, vice-president; Dr. D. L. Martin of Nashville, secretary; Dr. D. N. C. Scott of Montgomery, treasurer; and Dr. H. R. Butler of Atlanta, chairman of the executive board.

The spirit behind the National Medical Association was graphically expressed in 1908 by Dr. Charles V. Roman, who, in response to an address of welcome to the Association by a New York City official, stated:

> Conceived in no spirit of racial exclusiveness, fostering no ethnic antagonisms, but born of the exigencies of the American environment, the National Medical Association has for its object the banding together for mutual co-operation and helpfulness, the men and women of African descent who are legally and honorably engaged in the practice of the cognate professions of Medicine, Surgery, Pharmacy and Dentistry.

During the first eight years of its existence, the association made little progress; in 1904 it had less than fifty members, but, by 1912, it had over five hundred members, with affiliated bodies in a number of Northern and Southern states.

Typical of the association's early annual conventions was the one held in New York City in 1908 and described in the New York *Evening Post* of August 27 as "Negro Doctors' 'Clinic Day.'" According to the dispatch, the day before at nine in the morning, the delegates gathered at Lincoln Hospital in New York City to watch extremely delicate and masterful operations by Drs. Austin M. Curtis of Washington, D.C., Daniel H. Williams of Chicago, and John E. Hunter of Lexington, Kentucky. In the afternoon, the delegates convened at the Plaza's assembly rooms to hear a number of solid scientific papers. In the evening, Dr. Williams lectured to a capacity crowd on "Crushing Injuries of the Extremities," illustrating his subject by forty stereopticon views taken from his own practice.

In 1908, to help Negro doctors raise their professional standards, the association's executive board recommended the publication of a magazine. The first issue of the *Journal of the National Medical Association* appeared in March, 1909, under the editorship of Dr. Charles V. Roman, a past president. A forceful personality and a man of great intellectual capacity, Dr. Roman was high in the councils of the association and was the leader of the Southern wing of the Negro doctors in the organization. Although born in Pennsylvania and raised in Canada, he spent virtually his entire medical life in the South. He was graduated from Meharry in 1890, practiced medicine for twelve years in Dallas, Texas, and accepted President Hubbard's offer in 1904 to head the new department of ophthalmology and oto-laryngology at Meharry. Of his decision to teach at the Nashville institution— he had intended to stay for four or five years but instead remained a lifetime—he wrote, "I was drawn into the altruism that controlled his [Hubbard's] life, I gave up *my*

JOURNAL
NATIONAL MEDICAL ASSOCIATION
A QUARTERLY PUBLICATION DEVOTED TO THE INTEREST OF THE NATIONAL MEDICAL ASSOCIATION AND ALLIED PROFESSIONS OF MEDICINE, SURGERY, DENTISTRY AND PHARMACY . . . . .

Vol. 1   January - March, 1909   No. 1

"Conceived in no spirit of racial exclusiveness, fostering no ethic antagonism, but born of the exigencies of American environment, the National Medical Association has for its object the banding together for mutual co-operation and helpfulness, the men and women of African descent who are legally and honorably engaged in the practice of the cognate professions of Medicine, Surgery, Pharmacy and Dentistry" . . . . .

NMA

PUBLISHED AT TUSKEGEE INSTITUTE, ALA.

DR. CHARLES V. ROMAN

Dr. C. V. Roman (seated in center) with the 1914 editorial staff of the Journal of the National Medical Association. From left to right: Dr. J. A. Kenney, Sr.; Dr. W. A. Alexander; Dr. R. C. Brown and Dr. U. G. Dailey.

plans for *his.*" For ten years, Dr. Roman edited the *Journal of the National Medical Association.* From the beginning, the quarterly showed a high degree of scholarly competence. This was due in no small measure to the work of managing editor Dr. John A. Kenney, whose original recommendations led to the establishment of the journal.

From 1890 to 1914, Negro doctors were concerned not only with their own professional progress, but also with that of Negro nurses. Fully cognizant of the importance of nursing, they did everything possible to establish training schools for Negro girls eager to devote themselves to the profession. The following story illustrates the point. About 1890, Emma Reynolds came to Chicago from Kansas City to study nursing. Because of her color, every training school in the city turned her down. Her brother, the Reverend Louis H. Reynolds of St. Stephen's African Methodist Church, thought that Dr. Williams, Chicago's leading Negro physician, could help her. When Dr. Williams was asked if he could arrange for the young lady's admission to a nursing school, he said: "No, I don't think I'll try to get Miss Reynolds into a training course. We'll do something better. We'll start a hospital of our own and we'll train dozens and dozens of nurses!" Dr. Williams kept his word, for in the early part of 1891, the Provident Hospital opened its doors with an eighteen-month training course for nurses. Among the seven students who enrolled was Emma Reynolds.

Miss Reynolds' experience was common to most Negro women seeking admission to the country's nursing schools. In the South, none were open to them; in the North, only a few accepted them. One of these was the New England Hospital for Women and Children in Boston, the first American institution to introduce a regular course for training nurses. Headed by Dr. Marie Zakrzewska, a militant exponent of equal rights for women and Negroes, the hospital graduated by 1899 a half-dozen Negro nurses. Among them was Mary Eliza Mahoney, the first colored graduate nurse in the country. She was thirty-three years old in 1878 when she entered the New England Hospital for Women and Children to begin a sixteen-month course. A bundle of energy, weighing scarcely ninety pounds, she worked sixteen hours a day, seven days a week, washing, ironing, cleaning and scrubbing, for that was the lot of student nurses at the time. Of the forty applicants in her class, only three remained to receive their diplomas on August 1, 1879, two white girls and Mary Mahoney.

Before the turn of the century, a few other hospital training schools in the North joined

MARY ELIZA MAHONEY

the New England Hospital for Women and Children in graduating Negro nurses. Among them were Woman's Hospital in Philadelphia, old Blockley in the same city, Jefferson Park Polyclinic in Chicago, and the Woman's Infirmary in New York. In light of the rigidly developing patterns of segregation and discrimination, Negroes were forced to organize schools of their own for the training of nurses. As early as 1881, they established such a school at Spelman College, Atlanta, Georgia. This school, the first of its kind, remained open until 1921.

In the 1890's and early 1900's, a number of other institutions followed: America's oldest continuing school for Negro nurses established at Provident Hospital, Chicago, by Dr. Williams, in 1891; Dixie Hospital Training School, in 1891, with the help of Hampton Institute; the Tuskegee Institute Hospital and Nurses' Training School in Alabama, in 1892; the Freedmen's Hospital Nursing School, organized by Dr. Williams in Washington, D.C., in 1894; the St. Agnes School in Raleigh, North Carolina, in 1895; the Frederick Douglass Hospital School, founded by Dr. Mossell in Philadelphia, in 1895; the McDonough Memorial Hospital Nursing School in New York City, in 1898; the Mercy Hospital School in Philadelphia, in 1907; and the Perry Sanitarium and Nurses' Training School in Kansas City, Missouri, in 1910.

As a result of the founding of all-colored training schools, the number of Negro graduate nurses steadily rose. In comparison with white nurses, employment opportunities for colored ones were distinctly limited. Negro nurses, even graduate ones, did not find it easy to obtain work. Jessie Sleet Scales, a graduate of Chicago's Provident Hospital, class of 1895, grew footsore and weary as she pounded the sidewalks of New York looking for work. That she was a graduate nurse when such nurses were a rarity meant nothing. That her skin was colored meant everything. An organization finally agreed to employ her on an experimental basis. So competent was this Negro nurse that the experiment lasted for nine years, until she married. Few Negro nurses succeeded in finding employment in health agencies or nursing organizations, and those who did were generally assigned to Negro patients.

Little or nothing was done by the Nurses' Associated Alumnae of the United States and Canada (later known as the American Nurses' Association) to help Negro graduate nurses overcome the special problems facing them. Relatively few were members of the national organization, since membership was open only through nursing school alumnae bodies. The latter were virtually non-existent in most of the schools where colored nurses were admitted for training.

The Mercy Hospital School for Nurses, in Philadelphia.

The first hospital of Tuskegee Institute.

The first nursing class at Tuskegee Institute.

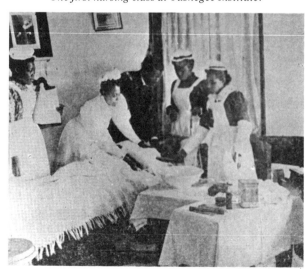

By 1908, a growing number of Negro nurses felt that the only way they could improve their conditions was to establish a professional body of their own. The initiative was taken by Martha Franklin of New Haven, who issued a call to organize a national association of colored nurses. Miss Franklin's call had the backing of Adah B. Thoms, president of the alumnae association of the Lincoln Hospital Training School for Nurses. Under the sponsorship of this organization as well as of the Lincoln Hospital, a meeting was held on August 25, 1908, at St. Mark's Methodist Church in New York City, with fifty-two nurses present. After three days of deliberation, the National Association of Colored Graduate Nurses was launched. Many of its twenty-six charter members were also members of the Nurses' Associated Alumnae of the United States and Canada.

The new organization was warmly backed by the National Medical Association, which was meeting at the time in New York City. Several NMA members came to address

THE FIRST ANNUAL CONVENTION
of
COLORED GRADUATE NURSES
will be held in
ST. MARK'S CHURCH,
W. 53rd Street, New York City, N. Y.,
AUGUST 25, 26, 27, 1908.
...ing Session, 10 o'Clock.   Afternoon Session, 2 o'C...
You are earnestly requested to be present.

the assembled nurses. Dr. E. P. Roberts, one of the first Negroes to serve in the clinics of the New York City Health Department, spoke on the opportunities for colored nurses in that field. Dr. John B. Hall of Boston, a friend of graduate nurse Mary Mahoney, urged delegates to come to Boston for their next meeting. Dr. Daniel H. Williams offered the nurses his whole-hearted support.

The next annual convention of the National Association of Colored Graduate Nurses was held in Boston in 1909. Membership had doubled within the year, and locals had been organized in as many as ten states. At its meeting, the convention decided to work for state registration acts to raise professional nursing standards, but to insist that such laws should exclude any double standard based on race. In Georgia, Negro nurse Ludie Andrews of Atlanta instituted legal proceedings which forced the Georgia State Board of Nurse Examiners to eliminate certain discriminatory practices.

During these early years, Adah B. Thoms was indispensable to the organization. A native of Virginia, she completed her nursing courses at the Woman's Infirmary of New York City in 1900. Associated with

DR. E. P. ROBERTS

the newly established Lincoln Hospital Training School, she served first as an assistant and then as acting superintendent of nurses. For seven years she headed the National Association of Colored Graduate Nurses, throwing the organization's full weight behind the drive for equal opportunity for Negroes in nursing. During World War I, she led a courageous fight for acceptance of Negro nurses in the American Red Cross and in the Army Nurse Corps.

FOUR OUTSTANDING DOCTORS

At the turn of the century, Negroes had their "big four" in medicine: Dr. Daniel Hale Williams, Dr. George Cleveland Hall, Dr. Austin Maurice Curtis and Dr. Nathan Francis Mossell. All four of these distinguished physicians had one interest in common: hospitals for the care of colored patients and the professional improvement of colored doctors and nurses.

July 9, 1893, was a desperately hot and oppressively humid day. Tempers in Chicago escalated as the temperature rose. A brawl broke out in a bar not far from the Provident Hospital. A Negro expressman, James Cornish, was stabbed in the region of the heart and was rushed to the hospital. He was examined by a slim, erect, faultlessly groomed physician, Dr. Daniel H. Williams, founder of the Provident Hospital. Although the wound seemed superficial, the patient began to complain of pain around the heart. The face on the pillow darkened as a coughing spell set in. What should he do—the doctor asked himself. The best medical opinion suggested that heart wounds be left alone. But, if he did nothing, the man would probably die. As he debated with himself what course to follow, the patient's pulse became fainter. At this point Dr. Williams hesitated no longer and, turning to intern Elmer Barr, quietly said, "I'll operate."

DR. DANIEL HALE WILLIAMS

Six doctors, four white and two colored, were invited to attend the operation. Dr. Dan, as he was affectionately called, set to work with no X-ray pictures to direct him, no trained anesthetist to assist him, no blood transfusions to keep the patient alive, no chemotherapeutic drugs to correct an infection, no artificial airway to keep the windpipe open, and no previous surgical experience to guide him. Working swiftly and deftly, Dr. Dan entered the thoracic cavity and proceeded to perform a surgical exploration of the heart. He decided that the heart muscle itself needed no suture, but that the pericardial sac did. After performing the necessary suture, he applied a dry dressing. The operation was over. Not only did the patient survive, but he lived for at least another twenty years.

Shortly after the operation, a reporter from the publication *Inter Ocean* interviewed Dr. Williams. In due time the readers of the journal were informed of what had happened in an article headed "Sewed Up Heart!" Subheadings announced the rest of the story: "Remarkable Surgical Operation" and "Dr. Williams Performs Astonishing Feat." Although the article was technically misleading (Dr. Williams "sewed up" the pericardium and not the heart), nevertheless, it was correct in describing the operation as "astonishing." It was one of the first of its kind to be performed. On September 6, 1891, almost two years before Dr. Williams' surgical feat, Dr. H. C. Dalton performed a successful pericardial operation in St. Louis. It should be noted, however, that Dr. Williams knew nothing of this operation when he performed his own on James Cornish.

Dr. Williams was only thirty-seven and ten years out of medical school when his history-making operation took place. Born in Pennsylvania, he grew up in Wisconsin, working part time as a barber in Harry Anderson's Tonsorial Parlor and Bathing Rooms and spending the rest of his time attending school, reading books, and listening to lectures. After graduating from the Classical Academy in Janesville, he decided to become a doctor. He was fortunate to serve a two-year apprenticeship under Dr. Henry Palmer, a busy and capable physician, active in AMA affairs and one-time vice-president of the organization. Dr. Palmer liked the bright, eager, serious-minded young man who was so quick to learn. By 1880, young Williams was ready to go to medical school. With credentials from Dr. Palmer, he set out for Chicago, where he was admitted to Chicago Medical College, then affiliated with Northwestern University. He worked and studied hard to keep abreast of the leaders in his class. After three terms of six months each, the one-time barber, who was nimble with scissors and blade, achieved his goal. In the last week of March, 1883, he stepped to the platform of the Grand Opera House to receive the coveted M.D. degree. He opened an office at Thirty-first and Michigan Avenues, the fourth Negro doctor in Chicago. His practice was successful, and he became quite prosperous.

Dr. Williams was a man on the move. One idea obsessed him: the establishment of a biracial hospital where Negro physicians and nurses could be trained and Negro patients cared for. In 1890, he swung into action and one year later opened Provident Hospital with a biracial staff of doctors and a training school for nurses. At last Chicago's Negro population of ten thousand could go to a hospital without fear of racial discrimination. From the very beginning, Dr. Williams put Provident on a solid basis. As the hospital's reputation grew, so did that of its founder. In 1893, President Grover Cleveland appointed Dr. Williams surgeon-in-chief of the Freedmen's Hospital in Washington, D.C., to succeed Dr. Charles B. Purvis. As head of the largest Negro hospital in the country, Dr. Williams proceeded to make innovations and expand operations. He reorganized the surgical services and established a nursing school. The horse-drawn ambulances of the Freedmen's Hospital clattered about the nation's capital picking up Negro patients, some of whom had been turned away from white hospitals. The scope of the outpatient clinic was enlarged to take care of the increasing health needs of Washington's Negro population. In 1898, Dr. Williams was succeeded as surgeon-in-chief by Dr. Curtis, who had interned under him at Provident.

Dr. Williams returned to Chicago. He took up where he had left off at Provident Hospital, but things had changed. While he had been away, Dr. George C. Hall had managed to become a leader of the Provident staff. A running battle ensued between the two, and Dr. Hall emerged as the victor. After almost two decades of service, Dr.

PROVIDENT HOSPITAL, 36th and Dearborn Streets

Provident Hospital founded in 1891 by Daniel Williams, one of Chicago's foremost physicians, for almost thirty-five years, has paved the way for the training of nurses and internes in Chicago. It has gained a nation-wide recognition for the advancement of medical and health measures, especially among the members of the race. In addition to its educational influence, it is an institution that alone answers an imperative demand today in Chicago, and it deserves the support of all citizens, if the inevitable increase in sickness and mortality is to be checked.

Beginning in 1891 with practically no resources, the Hospital has trained and graduated over two hundred nurses, who are making an enviable reputation in their profession. Numbered among the physicians who have taken internship at Provident are some of the race's most prominent professional men.

Some statistics will show the progress the institution has enjoyed in its history:

Number of pay patients treated 1891-1926	30,446	Expense Budget, First Year	$ 5,429
Number of free patients treated 1891-1926	102,866	Expense Budget 1926	$78,719
Capacity for service (number beds)	65	Attending Staff over	50
Average Daily Occupancy, 1926	51	Visiting Staff	75
		Number of paid employees	28

The Hospital has on its staff some of the leading colored and white physicians and surgeons in the country, thus giving to the patients the best possible treatment and care known to the medical profession.

The payroll in 1892 was $1,795.00; 1902, $4,214.00; 1912, $7,268.00; 1922, $17,160.00; 1925, $20,378.88 Fixed assets in 1923 were $112,402.87. Fund Investments, $117,639.16. Less Accounts payable, $170,521.55. Net Worth, $170,588.12, Less Deficit, Hospital Account, $66.57.

The $1,000,000 drive for a greater Provident and bigger nursing quarters will add fifty more rooms for Nurses, 150 beds and a Modern General Hospital. Representatives of twenty-one different nationalities have been treated here.

The Nurse's Training School is one of the best in the country with an enrollment of 29 in 1923, 32 in 1924, 36 in 1925 and the graduating classes in the same years respectfully, 11, 4 and 7.   Lillian Haywood and Emma A. Reynolds were the first two nurses to graduate, the first from Honolulu and the other became a physician in New Orleans. Almost half of the 206 who have completed the course were from Chicago, the others from some 37 states and four from foreign countries.

The Children's Department was organized April, 1906, which established a Diet Kitchen for babies.

Williams severed his connections with Provident. Thereafter, as a member of the attending staff of St. Luke's, he ran one of the largest gynecological services in Chicago.

Dr. Williams was one of the best-known physicians of his day. One of the founders of the National Medical Association and its first vice-president, he was also a member of the city and state medical societies and of the AMA. In 1913, he became a charter member of the American College of Surgeons, the first, and for many years the only, Negro belonging to that body. An article in *The Crisis* of September, 1915, referred to him as "the most noted colored physician in the United States." Years later, the authoritative *Dictionary of American Biography* spoke of him as "undoubtedly the most gifted surgeon and most notable medical man the colored race [has] produced."

Despite his eminence in the surgical world, Dr. Williams, who had created a

DR. GEORGE CLEVELAND HALL

method by which the living heart could be sutured, had his own heart broken by racial prejudices. Worn out by his efforts to overcome the great odds against him, Dr. Williams retired into self-exile for almost a decade and a half before his death in 1931. A scholar and scientist, reserved and sensitive, he withdrew from active participation in medical and scientific affairs before the full flowering of his genius. In the words of a close friend, Dr. Carl G. Roberts, himself a leading Negro physician, Dr. Williams went into self-retirement in the face of the "big white fog."

The second of the "big four" was Dr. George Cleveland Hall, a leading Chicago surgeon and diagnostician. A suave politician, which his contemporary Dr. Williams was not, he spent almost all of his medical career at Provident Hospital. Born in Ypsilanti, Michigan, February 22, 1864, he was educated in its public schools, was graduated from Lincoln University with the highest honors and received his M.D. degree in 1888 from Bennett Medical College in Chicago.

DR. CARL G. ROBERTS

Provident Hospital was Dr. Hall's life. Six years after his graduation from medical school, he began an association with Provident that was to continue to the time of his death thirty-six years later. From 1894 to 1930, he served the Chicago hospital in one capacity or another: as assistant in gynecology, surgeon, chief of staff, member of the board of trustees and chairman of the medical advisory board. His pre-eminent position at Provident came only after a long and bitter fight with Dr. Williams. The feud between the two men began when Dr. Williams returned from Freedmen's Hospital to find Dr. Hall entrenched in a position of leadership. Dr. Williams looked upon Dr. Hall as a Machiavellian upstart and, surgically speaking, a "butcher." He sought to embarrass his rival, berating him before patients and members of the hospital board. Dr. Hall replied in kind. The feud between the two spilled over even into the National Medical Association. The vendetta reached a pinnacle about 1910 with the

resignation of Dr. Williams from the hospital he had founded. From then on, Dr. Hall became the undisputed leader of Provident, which he molded in his image. He held the staff together and organized the hospital's first postgraduate course. He dreamed of a greater Provident Hospital and, with the help of Julius Rosenwald and Dr. Frank Billings, raised three million dollars for a new, up-to-date building, which was opened in 1933, shortly after his death.

Dr. Hall was not only a good mixer and raconteur but also a highly qualified surgeon and therapist. Regarded as one of Chicago's chief Negro physicians, he conducted surgical clinics before Negro medical associations in Alabama, Tennessee, Kentucky, Virginia, Georgia and Missouri. In addition, he helped establish infirmaries throughout the larger cities of the South.

Dr. Hall was a spirited fighter for Negro rights. He was responsible for bringing the National Urban League to Chicago. He was active in the National Association for the Advancement of Colored People and was among the founders of the Association for the Study of Negro Life and History. His activities for Negro betterment also made him a director and treasurer of the Frederick Douglass Center. A public library in Chicago bears his name.

The third of the "big four" was Dr. Austin Maurice Curtis, a protégé of Dr. Williams and one of the Provident group of Chicago surgeons at the turn of the century. He was born in Raleigh, North Carolina, in 1868, attended the city's public schools, was graduated from Lincoln University, and at the age of twenty-three obtained his M.D. degree from Northwestern. In 1891, he attracted the favorable attention of Dr. Williams, who offered him an internship at newly founded Provident Hospital. The following year, he was appointed a surgeon on the hospital's visiting staff and opened

DR. FRANK BILLINGS

DR. AUSTIN MAURICE CURTIS

an office. His practice and his reputation grew steadily. In 1895, there was an opening on the surgical staff of Cook County Hospital. The Negro leaders of Chicago were determined to ensure the appointment of a Negro to the post. On December 28, more than a dozen Negro doctors met in the office of Theodore W. Jones, recently elected to the office of county commissioner. After advising those present of the opening, Jones suggested that they select a qualified candidate to fill the vacancy. Two candidates were proposed, Dr. Curtis and Dr. J. N. Croker. After six close ballots, Dr. Curtis was the unanimous choice. On January 6, 1896, he was invited to serve on the surgical staff of the Cook County Hospital, the first such Negro appointment to a non-segregated hospital.

In 1898, Dr. Curtis was named surgeon-in-chief at Freedmen's Hospital, Washington, D.C., to succeed his old friend and mentor, Dr. Williams. For three years Dr. Curtis headed the hospital, which was still lodged in its original old brick building on grounds belonging to Howard University. A daring but not reckless surgeon, he soon established a national reputation. He emphasized the need for correct diagnosis, impressing this fact upon his staff as he walked in short, quick strides through the wards, his deep booming voice loud enough for all to hear. He was a man of tremendous energy, admired and respected by his associates. Among the latter was Dr. William Alonza Warfield, Howard Medical School, class of '94, first assistant surgeon who succeeded his chief on October 1, 1901. Dr. Curtis ended his illustrious career as professor of surgery at Howard (1928–1938).

Dr. Nathan Francis Mossell was the only member of the "big four" who did not come from Chicago. Just as Dr. Williams' name is associated with Chicago's Provident Hospital, so Dr. Mossell's is coupled with Philadelphia's Frederick Douglass Memorial Hospital. Born in Hamilton, Ontario,

DR. WILLIAM ALONZA WARFIELD

Canada, July 27, 1856, he was the son of free Negro parents who had left Baltimore to raise a family in an atmosphere of freedom. When the Civil War was over, his parents felt that the time was ripe to return to the United States. The family moved to Lockport in western New York State. The town had a separate school for Negroes, and the elder Mossell led the successful fight to have it closed. In this way, the boy was able to attend an integrated school from the beginning. As a young man, he worked his way through Lincoln University and decided upon his graduation in 1879 to become a doctor.

Young Mossell applied for admission to the oldest medical school in the country, the University of Pennsylvania. He was undaunted by the fact that no Negro had ever been admitted before. By nature no "Uncle Tom," he decided to take the direct approach. He personally went to see Dr. James Tyson, dean of the school, who, when the interview was over, said: "We have a greater medical school than Harvard or Yale and since they have admitted Negroes, we will." On the opening day of school, Mossell was told to sit behind a screen. He refused. When he sat down on a bench, no student sat next to him. For months this went on, but eventually a few friendly students took seats alongside him. In the end, all did the same. At commencement exercises in 1882, when he stepped to the platform to receive his diploma, he was greeted by such applause that the provost had to request the audience to stop so the proceedings could continue in an orderly fashion.

Next, Dr. Mossell tackled the Philadelphia Medical Society. His sponsor for admission was a Southerner, Dr. J. Britton Massey. When the opposition formed, Dean James Tyson, who had endorsed the application, said, "Dr. Mossell was graduated with an average higher than three-

DR. NATHAN FRANCIS MOSSELL

fourths of his class." The opposition evaporated. Dr. Mossell was admitted, and a second hurdle was overcome.

After studying at Guy's and St. Thomas' Hospitals in London, Dr. Mossell was ready for the third hurdle: the founding of a hospital in Philadelphia where Negro patients could be cared for and Negro physicians and nurses trained. On October 31, 1895, the Frederick Douglass Memorial Hospital and Training School for Nurses opened its doors to people of all races and creeds. During its first year, most of the patients were Negroes, and 86 per cent of the contributions to support the institution came from Negroes. In 1898, it treated returning Spanish-American War veterans for typhoid fever. The hospital continued to grow, and two more properties were acquired in subsequent years.

In 1905 the Frederick Douglass Memorial Hospital was faced by a serious crisis. A group of young physicians led by Dr. Edward C. Howard wanted greater opportunities, especially in performing operations.

Dr. Mossell, emphasizing the need for excellence, refused to accede to the demands of the dissidents. In the ensuing struggle, Dr. Mossell was castigated as a "dictator" and "tyrant." He answered charges with countercharges. In the end, the dissidents broke away and in 1907 established Mercy Hospital on the northwest corner of Seventeenth and Fitzwater Streets. It was not until 1948 that the schism was healed and a new institution, the Mercy-Douglass Hospital, emerged.

In the meantime, the Frederick Douglass Memorial Hospital continued to grow. In 1908, a new building, costing $118,000, was constructed. The enlarged hospital had seventy-five beds and a potential capacity of one hundred. The state of Pennsylvania contributed part of the cost of construction. By 1912, the hospital had about 3,500 in-patients and 40,000 out-patients. Had Dr. Mossell been willing to guarantee internships to Negro graduates of medical schools in the Philadelphia area, whether qualified or not, the state government willingly would have granted the hospital financial support. But this Dr. Mossell would not do. He refused to accept anything but the highest standards in medical and hospital care.

Dr. Mossell was active in the fight for

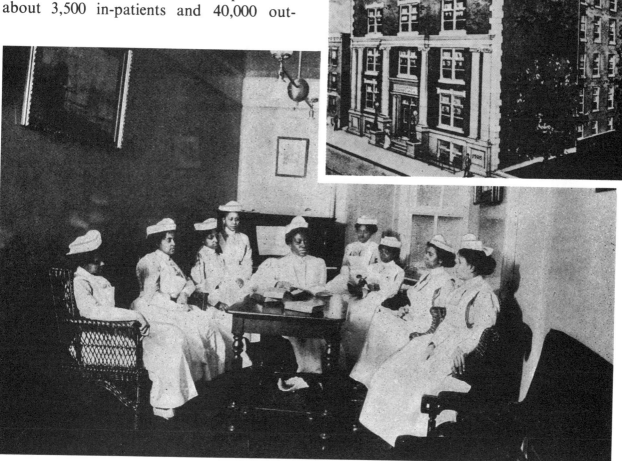

A class of nurses studying at the Frederick Douglass Memorial Hospital.

racial equality. He joined others in driving out of Philadelphia the anti-Negro play *The Clansman* and in protesting against the showing of *The Birth of a Nation*. He organized a Thaddeus Stevens Memorial Association which annually paid homage to the celebrated abolitionist leader. As Dr. Mossell grew older—he lived to the age of ninety—he took great delight in looking through his scrapbooks, which included abundant clippings dealing with his famous nephew Paul Robeson, one of America's most celebrated actors and a militant champion of Negro rights.

HOSPITAL CONSTRUCTION AND HEALTH EDUCATION

During the period of emerging Jim Crow, Negro physicians and civic leaders turned to the establishment of hospitals and the promotion of health education to ease the burden of the ill and to prevent sickness from attacking the healthy. Hospital building was undertaken to offset the ever-increasing inequities with respect to health care facilities and practices. In the South,

where the vast majority of the Negro people lived, there were either no hospital accommodations for blacks or poorly equipped and badly neglected colored wards, from which Negro physicians were virtually excluded. In the North, conditions were a little better, but far from satisfactory. According to a survey which was reported in 1912, nineteen of twenty-nine hospitals in New York City indicated they would not discriminate against Negro patients. The same survey showed that, of nineteen hospitals, sixteen would deny Negro doctors the right to attend patients or perform operations. To overcome discriminatory practices in hospital facilities, Negro doctors took the lead in building hospitals for the care of Negro patients and the training of professional personnel. They had the backing of Negro schools, churches and private individuals. Only Freedmen's Hospital in Washington, D.C., had Federal government support.

Hospitals under Negro auspices were established in practically every Southern state. Probably the most famous was the Tuskegee Institute Hospital and Nurses' Training School in Alabama.   Founded

Freedmen's Hospital in Washington, D.C.

Dedication of the John A. Andrew Memorial Hospital in 1912.

in 1892, it grew from an institution primarily for the care of sick Tuskegee students and teachers to one serving the health needs of the townspeople, neighboring communities and even out-of-state patients. In 1902, Dr. John A. Kenney was chosen to head the institution; within a decade, it had a two-story building with up-to-date wards, classrooms and operating rooms equipped in the most modern fashion. The building was named the John A. Andrew Memorial Hospital after the Civil War governor of Massachusetts. At Tuskegee, colored doctors received invaluable training at the famous John A. Andrew's clinics; colored nurses were graduated and sent out to practice in the North, East, West and particularly the South; and colored patients by the thousands were cared for.

In addition to Tuskegee, other Southern cities had hospitals established and controlled by Negroes. In Atlanta, Georgia, there was the Fair Haven Infirmary, organized by Dr. Henry R. Butler, one of the first Negro physicians to establish a permanent practice in the city and a founding father of the National Medical Association. Montgomery, Alabama, "the cradle of the Confederacy," had its Hale Infirmary,

founded by Dr. Cornelius N. Dorsette, one-time teacher of Booker T. Washington and the state's first licensed Negro practitioner. Some years after Dr. Dorsette's death in 1897, the hospital was reorganized and enlarged. In Durham, North Carolina, Lincoln Hospital was founded with Dr. A. M. Moore as its guiding spirit. It was he who convinced Washington Duke to build the hospital instead of a monument to the Negro people on the campus of Trinity College. Clarksville, Tennessee, and Selma, Alabama, had two privately owned hospitals. The Home Infirmary in Clarksville was established by Dr. Robert T. Burt and for years was the only hospital of its kind in the city. The infirmary in Selma was founded by Dr. Lincoln L. Burwell with the idea of giving the Negro the same chance for health and recovery as others had. In 1899, Dr. W. T. Merchant and Dr. Ellis Whedbee opened the Red Cross Hospital in Lexington, Kentucky, to provide the city's Negro physicians with hospital facilities for their patients.

In the North, too, hospitals were established under Negro direction. In addition to Provident Hospital in Chicago and Fredrick Douglass Memorial Hospital and

DR. HENRY R. BUTLER

DR. CORNELIUS N. DORSETTE

Mercy Hospital in Philadelphia, facilities were founded by Negro doctors in other Northern cities. In New York City, there was the short-lived McDonough Memorial Hospital, named after slave-born practitioner David K. McDonough. Opened in 1898 at 439 West 42nd Street, "in the very center of Little Africa," the institution was the first voluntary hospital to open its doors to doctors, nurses and patients without regard to race, creed or nationality. Dr. Peter A. Johnson, one of the founders of the National Urban League and a president of the National Medical Association, served as surgeon-in-chief of the institution. In Boston, Dr. C. N. Garland, who received his M.D. degree from the Leonard Medical School of Shaw University and took his postgraduate work in England, established the Plymouth Hospital in 1908. In Washington, D.C., Dr. John R. Francis, a member of one of the oldest colored families in the city, a graduate of the medical

school of the University of Michigan and a member of the board of trustees of Howard University, was the first Negro to establish a sanitorium for Negro patients in the nation's capital.

Negro hospitals were established also west of the Mississippi. The first was the Douglass Hospital in Kansas City, Kansas, founded in 1899 by two able physicians, Dr. Solomon H. Thompson and Dr. Thomas C. Unthank. Support for the venture came from the packing-house workers. With the help of private and public funds, the new hospital grew steadily. It served all ethnic groups, helped give Negro doctors additional clinical experience and prepared Negro women for nursing careers. Across the state border in Kansas City, Missouri, Dr. John E. Perry founded the Perry Sanitarium in 1910, with twenty beds and six nurses. Patients came from Kansas and Oklahoma as well as Missouri. Four years before the institution's founding, Dr. Perry and Dr. Unthank suggested that Kansas City's municipal hospital should open a ward where Negro doctors could treat patients. The newspapers immediately ridiculed the suggestion. Undaunted, Dr. Perry and Dr. Unthank stuck to their guns.

In 1910, when a new city hospital was built for indigent white patients, the older building was given, in characteristic racist fashion, to Negroes and Mexicans. Four Negro physicians were selected as members of the staff of what became known as City General Hospital No. 2. This limited opening of public hospital facilities came immediately after Dr. Perry established his own sanitarium.

Despite these and other efforts, Negro doctors and their supporters were unable to establish enough hospitals to take care of even the minimum health needs of the colored people. During the last decade of the nineteenth century and the first decade of the twentieth, the Negro population of the country increased by one-third—from

approximately 7.5 million in 1890 to 10 million in 1910. The number of hospitals established during this period under Negro auspices was entirely inadequate to meet growing Negro health needs. Dr. Du Bois listed forty-one private hospitals admitting colored patients in 1900; 78 per cent of them were below the Mason-Dixon line. In 1912, there were sixty-five; 83 per cent were in the South. If public hospitals had been added to these figures, there still would not have been enough hospital facilities in the country to cope with the health requirements of Negro Americans.

The shortage of professional personnel added to the health woes of the Negro people. This deficiency was the by-product of such Jim Crow obstacles as inadequate schooling, low family incomes and bleak professional futures—enough to discourage all but the most dedicated to pursue medical careers. The result was an acute shortage of Negro doctors. In 1910, there were 3,409 Negro physicians in the country as

Lincoln Hospital in Durham, North Carolina.

compared to 909 in 1890. Despite this almost fourfold increase, Negro doctors in 1910 constituted only 2.5 per cent of all physicians. In that year there were 135,000 practitioners in the country, a ratio of approximately one physician to 684 people for the United States as a whole and only one Negro doctor to each 2,883 Negroes. In 1910, the total population of the United States was 92,400,000, of whom 9,828,000 were Negroes.

Increased health deficiencies among Negro Americans accompanied the shortage of medical personnel and hospital accommodations. These health deficiences were strikingly disclosed in a monograph, *The Health and Physique of the Negro American,* edited by the well-known Negro sociologist Dr. W. E. B. Du Bois and published in 1906. In this Atlanta University publication, Dr. Du Bois marshalled statistical data to indicate how deprived the Negro people were of health care. In 1890, the death rate per 1,000 living was 27.4 for the Negro and 19.5 for the white; in 1900, the figures were 25.3 and 17.3 respectively. Mortality among Negro infants was particularly high; for every 1,000 living colored children under one year of age, there were 458 who died in 1890 and 344 in 1900. The disease that killed more Negroes than any other in 1890 and 1900 was consumption, with pneumonia and nervous system disorders close behind. In summing up the situation, based on statistical data as of 1900, the study observed:

> The Negro death rate is . . . undoubtedly considerably higher than the white. . . . The excess is due principally to mortality from consumption, pneumonia, heart disease and dropsy, diseases of the nervous system, malaria and diarrheal diseases.

The comparatively poor health of the Negro people was essentially the result of indigence and discrimination. For the most part, Negroes were sharecroppers on South-

The

Health and Physique

of the

Negro American

Report of a Social Study made under the direction of Atlanta University; together with the Proceedings of the Eleventh Conference for the Study of the Negro Problems, held at Atlanta University, on May the 29th, 1906

Edited by
W. E. Burghardt Du Bois
Corresponding Secretary of the Conference

The Atlanta University Press
Atlanta, Georgia
1906

ern plantations or workers employed in the least rewarding and least desirable jobs in mills, railroads and households. Housing conditions were miserable in both the rural slums of the South and the blighted urban areas of the North. The relationship between ill health and sociological conditions was not lost on some Negro physicians of the time. In 1909, Dr. S. P. Lloyd of Savannah gave the reasons for the high death rate among Negroes as the lack of education, bad landlords and poor housing conditions.

To offset the health deficiencies of the colored people, Negroes launched a campaign of health education. In 1915, Negro

DR. JOHN A. KENNEY

DR. A. M. TOWNSEND

National Health Week was initiated by Booker T. Washington at Tuskegee. Co-sponsoring the movement, which was designed to focus attention on the health needs of the Negro, were Howard University, the National Medical Association and the National Insurance Association.

The National Medical Association played a particularly important role in the drive to improve the health of the Negro people. Special commissions were appointed by the association to study and report on a number of diseases as they related to Negroes. In 1910, three such commissions were named: the tuberculosis commission, headed by Dr. Marcus F. Wheatland of Newport, Rhode Island; the hookworm commission, presided over by Dr. John A. Kenney of Tuskegee, Alabama; and the pellagra commission, chaired by Dr. A. M. Townsend of Nashville, Tennessee. All three physicians were authorities in their special field, Dr. Townsend having been credited with recognizing the first case of pellagra in Nashville.

Particular attention was focused on the subject of tuberculosis, an especially virulent killer. Special tuberculosis sanatoria were established for Negroes, and anti-tuberculosis leagues were organized from 1907 to 1909 by Negro medical societies in Louisiana, Alabama, Virginia and the District of Columbia. In Norfolk, Virginia, the Anti-Tuberculosis League opened a free clinic for colored patients suffering from pulmonary tuberculosis. In one year, sixty-four Negroes were seen and 1,685 follow-up visits made. The clinic had a nurse in charge and seven doctors on the staff. In New York City, Dr. Peter A. Johnson served in the tuberculosis department of the Board of Health. Dr. A. Wilberforce Williams of Chicago, one of the first Negro physicians to contribute articles on health to Negro newspapers, helped create an early interest in tuberculosis. At the organizing meeting of the National Association of

Colored Graduate Nurses in 1908, the high number of deaths from tuberculosis among the Negro people, in the North and the South, was discussed.

Other Negroes in medicine also were educating colored Americans on ways and means of improving health. In 1908, the Bay State Medical Society of Boston held a series of lectures attended by people in all walks of life on such subjects as personal and practical hygiene, water contamination, medical uses of water, infant feeding, milk contamination and the origin and control of tuberculosis. Similar discussions were held by the North Jersey Medical Society, which set aside four meetings for this purpose. Tuskegee Institute published health bulletins under the direction of its resident physician. Topics included "Tuberculosis," "Typhoid Fever" and "The Danger of Flies." Lectures on tuberculosis and hookworm were given to farmers, churchgoers, teachers and students. In Nashville, Tennessee, Dr. Robert F. Boyd, head of the Anti-Tuberculosis League, held meetings in churches to instruct people in the cause, prevention and cure of "the Great White Plague." Better food, sanitary conditions and personal hygiene were emphasized.

Thus, in the quarter of a century prior to World War I, Negroes, working largely on their own, made some notable progress in medicine and health. They established medical and nursing schools, organized professional bodies, built hospitals, and carried on a campaign of health education. These were no mean achievements for a people living under the corrosive humiliation of daily Jim Crow intimidation and deprivation. It took courage and dignity to move forward. But, even as this was being done, profound technical advances were taking place in medicine which rendered obsolete many of these gains.

CHAPTER SIX

Against Great Odds

We are all your good friends and it is a most unpleasant thing to have to tell you that just because you are colored, we can't arrange to take you comfortably into the hospital. I am quite sure that most of the internes [sic] who come to us next year will not give us as good work as you are capable of doing . . ..

Letter to Dr. Lillian Atkins Moore, dated March 2, 1923.

In answer to yours of June 11th asking for admission to our school for Nurses, please note that it is impossible for me to consider your application. . . . Trusting that you may realize that you cannot enter our school and with best wishes,

I am, Yours very truly

Letter to a Negro applicant from the Superintendent of Nurses of a California county hospital, reproduced in *The Crisis*, April 1930.

In the field of medicine I know I could have done much more had racism never been encountered.

Dr. Thomas R. Peyton, *Quest for Dignity: An Autobiography of a Negro Doctor*, 1950.

FROM World War I to the end of World War II, Negro physicians and nurses continued to fight against great odds. There were new hurdles to overcome as a veritable revolution took place in the field of medicine. Great medical centers and research institutes sprang up. Large outlays of capital went into new buildings and equipment. Diagnostic innovations and therapeutic discoveries followed each other with bewildering rapidity. The medical literature became so voluminous that few were able to keep abreast of it. So all-pervading was the revolution in medicine that serious problems of readjustment arose. These problems confronted all, but most formidably the Negro physicians and nurses.

NEW HURDLES TO OVERCOME

New techniques rendered obsolete the half-dozen medical colleges which Negro doctors had worked so hard to establish prior to the outbreak of World War I. Organized in the horse-and-buggy days of the late nineteenth century, these educational institutions were unable to meet the demands of the automobile age of the early twentieth century. The Flexner Report on Medical Education, with its high professional requirements, sounded their death-knell. By 1914, four of the six schools had disappeared. Then, in 1915, the largest one, Leonard Medical College, gave up the unequal battle; it was followed eight years later by the second largest, the Medical Department of the University of West Tennessee.

Even Howard and Meharry encountered great difficulties. It was obvious after World War I that, unless these two schools took vigorous steps to acquire new plants and better-trained teachers, their accreditation might be lost. In fact, Meharry was placed on temporary probation; and although Howard was able to retain its Grade A rating, it was in danger of losing it. To continue operating, both schools required the kind of grants that were being made by various foundations to meet the needs of the new revolution in medicine. The Rosenwald, Rockefeller and National Research Foundations responded by granting the necessary funds.

DR. NUMA P. G. ADAMS

Two men joined to build a stronger Howard Medical School. One was a farsighted and effective administrator, Dr. Mordecai Johnson, President of Howard University; the other was a quiet, determined man, Dr. Numa P. G. Adams, first Negro dean of the medical college. During the booming twenties, the Rockefeller group agreed to give Howard $250,000 for a new medical building provided the university raised a similar amount. When Dr. Mordecai Johnson assumed the presidency in 1927, his first task was to raise the required sum. With great resourcefulness, he succeeded in obtaining the funds by contributions from the school's alumni and friends. Consequently, a modern and well-equipped building was added to the medical college.

Now that the bricks were there, the school needed a strong faculty and qualified students. It fell to the lot of Dean Adams to procure both for Howard. Born in Virginia, February 26, 1885, Numa Adams early in

DR. MORDECAI JOHNSON

life learned the habit of painstaking scholarship. As a boy, he helped his grandmother collect and dispense medicinal herbs. Under her guidance, he learned to recognize the prime importance of careful investigation and accurate information. Serious beyond his years, he developed into a fine student. He was graduated from high school with honors and, after a short period of teaching in public schools, attended Howard University, receiving his B.A. degree, *magna cum laude,* in 1911. The following year Columbia University awarded him a master's degree in chemistry. Because of his academic achievements, Howard appointed him to an instructorship in chemistry.

Promotion followed promotion, and by 1918, he was made head of the department. A year later, he resigned from his post to enter Rush Medical College, where he worked his way through school by playing the saxophone. Upon his graduation in 1924, he took up the practice of medicine and, on June 4, 1929, was appointed dean of the Howard Medical School as a result of President Johnson's decision to break with the past by appointing a Negro to the position.

During his eleven-year tenure as dean, Dr. Adams strove to make Howard a medical school of the highest excellence. To achieve his objective, he was resolved to build a strong faculty, bringing in as many new men as possible. Ever on the alert for prospective instructors, he searched the country for talented and promising Negroes. Firmly convinced that a well-trained Negro could do as well as any well-trained white man, he obtained foundation fellowships to train colored physicians for faculty

Rush Medical College, Chicago, Illinois.

posts. He encouraged young men doing advanced work to acquire a Ph.D. degree or its equivalent, in addition to their M.D. degree. He tried to raise faculty salaries to keep the best men at Howard and at the same time to attract younger men. He proposed initial yearly salaries of $3,500 for fellows, with annual increases of $500 to a maximum of $6,000 a year. The Great Depression intervened to make difficult the realization of his proposals.

Dr. Adams sought to improve the caliber not only of the Howard medical faculty but also of its student body. He advocated the raising of entrance requirements to reduce the size of the freshman class. With smaller entering classes, more time could be given to the individual student. Although his policy of restricting student enrollment was severely criticized, Dean Adams refused to discontinue it. The result was a scholastically improved student body. The last four classes admitted while he was dean had a perfect record in passing state board licensing examinations.

Toward the close of his tenure, Dean Adams found himself virtually isolated because of the uncompromising stand he had taken on issues of policy. Even those whom he had befriended turned against him. On one occasion, he confided: "I have learned from other experience that people for whom one has done the most, can be the most unappreciative. And I know that at this time I haven't got a 'friend' in the Medical School." Ill in health, tired and alone, he died "a martyr to his job" in Billings Hospital, Chicago, on August 29, 1940, but not before the future of Howard as a first-class medical school was ensured.

While Howard was maintaining its Grade A rating, Meharry was moving toward it. At the college's commencement in 1923, President John J. Mullowney announced that Meharry, for the first time in its history, was recognized by the American Medical As-

JOHN J. MULLOWNEY

sociation as a Grade A institution. To obtain such recognition, the college had raised an endowment fund of over half a million dollars, had renovated the hospital associated with it and had established a department of pathology headed by Dr. William S. Quinland, a Rosenwald Fellow at Harvard. Dr. Quinland, a native of the British West Indies, was an unusual student. In his four years at Meharry, his general average was 98 per cent. In 1919, upon completion of his course of studies, he was awarded the first of the new Rosenwald medical scholarships for graduate work in bacteriology and pathology at Harvard Medical School. In 1922, he returned to Meharry, where he remained for a quarter of a century as professor of pathology.

Similarly, Dr. Michael J. Bent was sent under a Rockefeller grant to Columbia and Harvard to do graduate work in bacteriology. On his return to Meharry, he was appointed professor of bacteriology and, in 1941, dean of the school. From 1919 to 1948, thirty Meharry graduates were given fellowships at leading Eastern and Midwestern universities for advanced study preparatory to teaching anatomy, psychology, radiology, pediatrics, pathology, medicine, bacteriology, surgery, urology, psychiatry and neurology.

In the meantime, foundation funds were obtained to provide Meharry with the latest physical facilities. By 1933, medical, dental and hospital buildings were completed at a cost of more than $2,000,000. The General Education Board gave $1,500,000; the Rosenwald Fund, $250,000; Mrs. George Eastman, $200,000; Edward Harkness, $50,000; and others, lesser amounts.

The major figure in the Meharry faculty during these years was Dr. John H. Hale, who was most closely identified with the teaching of surgery. In the early 1920's, he became director of the division of surgery of the postgraduate department, chief of staff of the department of surgery of the George W. Hubbard Hospital, and clinical professor of surgery on the Meharry faculty. In 1938, he was appointed chairman of the department of surgery and head of the hospital committee; he served in these posts until his death six years later. He was an able surgeon, performing during his lifetime about thirty thousand operations. In recognition of his eminent career, he was elected thirty-sixth president of the National Medical Association and after his death was honored by having a low-rent housing project in Nashville named after him.

With Grade A accreditations, Howard and Meharry continued to provide the country with the bulk of its Negro physicians. From 1910 through 1947, these

The Meharry Medical College.

two schools graduated 3,439 students, 101 of whom were women. Relatively few Negro doctors received their medical education at other schools. As late as World War II and the years immediately following it, the number of Negro physicians graduating annually from schools other than Howard and Meharry was less than 10 per cent, or ten to fifteen students a year.

The same situation was true of medical school enrollment. In 1947, fall registration indicated a total of 82 Negro students at twenty Northern and Western schools, as against 590 at Howard and Meharry. In that year, there were approximately 25,000 medical students in the country. If Negroes had been enrolled in proportion to population, there would have been approximately 2,500 of them in medical schools. But because of the Jim Crow character of medical education—complete exclusion of Negro students in the South and "token" admission in the North—there was a deficit of about 1,900. Lest one think that Negro students were not anxious to enter medical schools, it should be noted that in 1947 Howard admitted only 74 of its 1,351 applicants, and Meharry, only 55 of its 800.

In the age of modern medicine, education did not stop with graduation from medical school. Doctors went on to do postgraduate work in the form of the one-year internship and in some cases continued through residency training. Both the internship and the residency had to be done in accredited hospitals.

The internship was particularly important as it gradually became a prerequisite for a license to practice. This presented Negro physicians with an acute problem because of the small number of accredited hospitals that would accept colored trainees. No matter how well qualified Negro applicants for internships were, there was always the likelihood of their being rejected because of their race. Dr. Lillian Atkins

Dr. JOHN H. HALE

Moore, an outstanding Negro student at Woman's Medical College, Philadelphia, received the following communication, dated March 2, 1923, from the medical director of a hospital:

> I was a little surprised to get your letter in regard to an internship. . . . I was told we could not possibly undertake to give you a service here. We are all your good friends and it is a most unpleasant thing to have to tell you that just because you are colored, we can't arrange to take you comfortably into the hospital. I am quite sure that most of the internes [sic] who come to us next year will not give us as good work as you are capable of doing . . ..

In the late 1920's, of the non-Negro hospitals of the country, only three large ones, Cook County in Chicago, and Harlem and Bellevue in New York, accepted colored interns. Of the Negro hospitals, only twelve were at that time approved for 68 internships; and Freedmen's Hospital in Washington, D.C., had as many as 24. Since there were more than a hundred Negro graduates each year, this meant a deficit of 30 or more internships annually. The situation gradually improved during the 1930's as the available supply of Negro internships jumped from 68 to 168.

Some progress was made also during these years in regard to residencies for Negro physicians. Whereas in the 1920's there were no such posts available, in the 1930's they began to appear increasingly at accredited Negro hospitals. By 1939, seven of them reported a total of 31 residencies for Negro physicians in eight specialties. Five years later, 25 additional residencies were approved, excluding those established at Harlem Hospital.

The residency was a reflection of the growing trend toward specialization. In his autobiography, *Quest for Dignity,* published in 1950, Dr. Thomas R. Peyton vividly describes the difficulties Negro physicians faced during this period in their efforts to specialize in medicine. Born in Brooklyn, New York, Dr. Peyton was graduated from the Long Island College of Medicine in the early 1920's—the only Negro in a class of one hundred. He interned at Mercy Hospital in Philadelphia, a Negro institution, and began to practice medicine in the Negro section of Jamaica, Long Island. He did well, and with the end of the boom years, he decided to specialize in proctology. When he applied for training at a large New York hospital with a clinic that was outstanding, the superintendent informed him that he could do nothing for him because of the

The George W. Hubbard Hospital, Nashville, Tennessee.

Freedmen's Hospital, Washington, D.C.

administration's fear that patients would object to being treated by a Negro.

> Tongue-tied with astonishment, I recovered sufficiently to state that I was a licensed physician in general practice and interested solely in scientific medicine. As a member of the city and county medical groups, I was called upon to treat people of all races and had been doing so for several years.

The superintendent, however, could not be moved; he was merely following instructions and was sorry.

Young Dr. Peyton, eager to pursue the study of proctology, refused to accept a negative answer. If he could not do this in his own country because of anti-Negro bias, he determined to go abroad. He studied in Paris and London under internationally recognized rectal surgeons. As one of his preceptors put it, he could see "no reason why postgraduate courses should not be open to . . . anyone sincerely desiring to progress in proctology."

Dr. Peyton returned to America to work among his people as a proctologist. In addition, he began to publish original articles in the field of his specialty. But he still found that the color of his skin was enough to bar him from staff privileges in white hospitals, participation in specialists' meetings and membership in the national proctologic society. On one occasion, a prominent rectal specialist requested that an invitation be sent to Dr. Peyton to attend a national conference of proctologists to be held in Norfolk, Virginia, "but received an instant flat refusal to admit me or any Negro M.D. to the meeting." Commenting on this, Dr. Peyton writes, "I wanted to hear those talks as freely as I had done in Europe, for America was my home." His membership in the American Proctologic

Society was turned down because he was not white, "a requirement" which, as he put it, "God had made it impossible for me to meet." Given these experiences, he concluded: "In the field of medicine I know I could have done much more had racism never been encountered."

The difficulties facing Dr. Peyton during these years were shared by other Negro physicians who wanted to devote themselves to the specialties of their choice. Very few hospitals were open to them for such training. In addition, they were by and large systematically excluded from election to specialty boards. The American College of Surgeons, founded in 1913, with the celebrated Negro practitioner Dr. Daniel H. Williams as a charter member, refused to accept another Negro for at least two decades. Finally, in 1934, Dr. Louis T. Wright, one of the country's foremost surgeons, was elected to a fellowship. Although it was expected at the time that other prominent Negroes would be admitted to the college, this was not done until many years later and then only after a prolonged struggle. Under such adverse conditions, there were few Negro specialists in the country. In fact, as late as 1947, only ninety-three Negroes in the entire United States were certified specialists.

Thus, during the period from World War I to the end of World War II, Negro physicians had to surmount new obstacles. In addition to continuing patterns of racial segregation and discrimination, they were faced with continually rising standards at every professional level—medical school, internship, residency and postgraduate specialization. Gone were the days when the training of a doctor consisted of a brief period of apprenticeship under a preceptor or a one-year or two-year stint of medical lectures. Now seven to ten years' training was required before a doctor could even begin to practice.

Large funds were needed to finance prospective doctors. Relegated to an inferior economic position, the vast majority of Negroes—unskilled laborers, sharecroppers and domestic servants—were financially unable to see their children through high school, premedical school, medical college and the period of internship. Even Negroes in the middle-income bracket—businessmen, professionals and tradesmen—had to think twice before assuming the burden of keeping their sons and daughters in school for so many years. Undergraduate medical scholarships were few in number.

In addition to financial difficulties, Negroes who looked forward to a career in medicine were confronted by an educational system which gave them an inadequate scholastic preparation from the beginning. In the South, the "separate-but-equal" schools which Negro children attended were poorly financed and inadequately staffed. Those who managed to graduate were ill-prepared to continue their studies. In the North, the situation was somewhat better, but still not good enough. In the larger cities and towns where segregation by neighborhood prevailed, schools in the Negro ghettos, though better equipped and staffed than in the South, were run-down, overcrowded and much inferior to those in most white areas. Drop-outs were a serious problem as relatively few Negroes attended high school and still fewer, college. Only the cream of the crop was able to matriculate into medical school, graduate, take an internship and pass stiffer and stiffer state board licensing examinations.

And for those who achieved this, then what? If they lived in the South, they had to practice in segregated areas. In addition, because of color, they were barred from membership in county and state medical societies and thus were denied the benefits of participation in professional conferences designed to bring to the attention of physicians the latest in medical developments. Similarly, they were excluded from hospital staff appointments, except the few that were open to them in Negro institutions. Even in these colored hospitals, they were often forced to share staff privileges with white physicians. In North Carolina, for example, the medical staffs of three Negro hospitals, the L. Richardson Memorial in Greensboro, the St. Agnes in Raleigh, and the Good Samaritan in Charlotte, included not only colored, but also white doctors. It was only after a bitter fight that a Negro staff supplanted a white one at the government-supported Tuskegee Hospital for Disabled Negro Veterans. Deprived of clinical facilities in hospitals and kept out of county and

state medical societies, Negro physicians in the South were virtually isolated from the main currents of modern medicine, and as a result, some tended to retrogress. It was, therefore, not too difficult to make Negro patients believe that, no matter how bad a white physician might be, he still was better than a colored one.

In the North, too, Negro physicians were faced by racial restrictions, albeit in a less blatant form. Although theoretically free to practice anywhere they wished, colored doctors in Northern cities ran into all kinds of practical difficulties when they attempted to establish offices outside the Negro community. Dr. Peyton, in his *Quest for Dignity*, tells of his experience when he moved to Los

The Tuskegee Veterans Administration Hospital, Tuskegee, Alabama.

Angeles in 1944 to practice medicine there. Upon his arrival, he tried to lease an office in a building where there was a large number of doctors and dentists. He was told on the telephone that one was available. When he hurried over to see it, he was met by an agent who was so taken aback that he could only manage to stutter, "Why—uh—uh—I didn't know you were a Negro!" Unable to rent an office in a professional building, Dr. Peyton did the next best thing. He bought a house and began practicing medicine there. Soon an attempt was made to evict not only him but also other Negroes who had attractive homes in the area. Only a court decision prevented the evictions from taking place.

De facto segregation in housing forced the vast majority of Negro doctors in the North to practice within, or on the edge of, colored neighborhoods. As a result, practically all their patients were Negroes. The bulk of their clientele was drawn from the lower- and middle-income groups. Wealthy Negro patients, as Dr. Peyton put it, "invariably went to white doctors. They didn't believe a Negro specialist could possibly know anything. Also, there was that odd attitude assumed by wealthy Negroes who think their selection of white doctors lends to the selector a certain superiority."

Negro doctors also lost a substantial number of better-paying patients because of lack of staff privileges in white voluntary hospitals. Even in the North, where the legal rights of Negroes were recognized, such hospitals might or might not take colored patients. Those that did would admit them only upon the recommendation of physicians having staff privileges. Since very few Negro doctors served on the staffs of these private hospitals, colored patients could gain admission only through referral of white physicians with such connections. For most Negro doctors this meant handing over their seriously ill patients to white physicians, a procedure which might well result in losing them.

Other subtle racial restrictions worked to the disadvantage of Negro physicians in the North. Although membership in county and state medical societies was open to all, regardless of race, few, if any, Negroes held positions of influence in them. The planning of conferences and selection of speakers were not in their hands. But at least they were better off than their colored colleagues in the South, for as members they had the opportunity of listening to and discussing the medical papers presented and occasionally of being invited to read one of their own. Moreover, they had a greater opportunity than in the South to serve on hospital staffs and thus gain valuable clinical experience. But, even in this area, the color line in white hospitals was so strong that only a small number of Negro doctors was able to secure appointments to them. It was only after a long and bitter fight that Negroes were admitted to the staffs of some Northern tax-supported institutions. And it was only in isolated instances that they served on the staffs of white voluntary hospitals.

A composite picture of the average Negro physician practicing in 1945 was given in a study begun in that year by Dr. Paul B. Cornely. It was published in the *Journal of the National Medical Association,* in March, 1951, under the title "The Economics of Medical Practice and the Negro Physician." On the basis of data furnished by 417 colored practitioners, Dr. Cornely found that the Negro doctor who was practicing at the close of World War II was in most instances a private physician without any other source of income; that generally he had an office alone, with equipment costing under $5,000, and an office staff consisting usually of one person; that he lived in a home for which he paid from $5,000 to

$10,000; and that he carried life insurance below $25,000. His annual gross income was $10,267, of which he collected 80 per cent and spent less than 40 per cent to maintain his practice. He saw 155 patients a week and spent about seven hours a day in his office and additional hours for hospital and home calls. Dr. Cornely concluded his study by observing that the average income of the Negro physician was likely to be 25 to 30 per cent lower than that of the white practitioner and that his patient load might be larger than that of his white colleague.

Thus, for the Negro doctor there was at the end of the rainbow a Jim Crow medical economic status, just as at the beginning there was a Jim Crow medical education. It was therefore not surprising that the number of Negro physicians remained almost stationary in the period between the two world wars. In 1920, there were 3,855 Negro doctors in the country; in 1930, 3,770; and in 1942, 3,810. In the latter year, colored practitioners comprised 2.1 per cent of the 180,496 physicians in the country, despite the fact that the Negro population was slightly more than 10 per cent of the total population. Whereas in 1942 there was one doctor for every 742 persons in the United States as a whole, there was one colored physician for every 3,377 Negroes.

Like Negro doctors, Negro nurses found the odds heavily stacked against them. Professional training and advancement were generally closed to them. It will never be known how many Negro women were the recipients of cryptic notes like the following, sent to a colored applicant in the early 1920's by the superintendent of nurses of a California county hospital:

> In answer to yours of June 11th asking for admission to our school for Nurses, please note that it is impossible for me to consider your application. This matter was taken up some time ago and definitely settled. Trusting that you may realize that you cannot enter our school and with best wishes, I am, Yours very truly.

DR. PAUL B. CORNELY

This letter was reproduced in *The Crisis*, April, 1930, under the heading, "'Jim-Crowing' Nurses," and was part of a communication sent by Osolee M. Ruffin, a social worker of Oakland, California. In her communication, Mrs. Ruffin told of the fight carried on by the Alameda County League of Colored Women Voters to open the county hospital to Negro student nurses. Despite the fact that the hospital was tax-supported and the state laws of California prohibited racial discrimination, the medical director and superintendent of nurses used "any silly thing for an excuse" to exclude Negro student nurses from the hospital's training program. Finally, in 1927, both officials resigned, and in the following year two Negro students were admitted for training. But so deeply embedded were racial prejudices that the two were given an unheated and segregated room located in the basement of the annex building, with steam and sewer pipes overhead. The correspondent finished her letter on the following militant note:

> Kind sir, may the world know that what I failed to do was to sanction segregation in an institution in a county where the laws of the state give equal rights to every taxpayer, just for the sake of saying, "We got colored nurses in training."

The same kind of fight occurred in other parts of the country. But progress in opening white nursing schools to the training of Negroes was slow. As late as 1941, there were only fourteen such schools in the country. In that year most Negro student nurses were enrolled in twenty-nine all-colored schools.

Similar difficulties were encountered by trained Negro nurses when they tried to improve themselves professionally by taking advanced courses. In 1928, the list of nursing schools accredited by state boards showed only one Negro school offering such work. Some white schools in the North, such as Columbia University, Western Reserve, City College of Detroit, the Pennsylvania School of Social and Health Work and the University of Chicago, admitted only a limited number of Negroes to advanced courses. In 1935, colored nurses at Freedmen's Hospital in Washington, D.C., aspiring to positions above staff level were denied admission to Catholic University. Unable to budge the school's administration, Mrs. Marion Brown Seymour, assistant superintendent of nurses at Freedmen's Hospital, turned for help to the National Association of Colored Graduate Nurses. The organization brought the matter to the attention of a prominent Catholic clergyman. The university soon reversed its position, and the first Negro student nurse was admitted early in 1936.

Despite the obstacles facing them, Negro women entered the nursing profession in increasing numbers. In 1910, there were 2,433 of them; in 1920, 3,331; in 1930,

5,589; and in 1945, an estimated 9,000. A survey made in the early 1930's showed that all Negro nurses were high school graduates. As many as 45.4 per cent went on to college, and 3.6 per cent of them received their degrees. A considerably higher percentage attended college after 1915 than prior to that date, one indication that professional standards in nursing were on the rise. Another indication was that, after graduation from training school, 18.1 per cent served internships and 4.5 per cent took postgraduate work.

In addition, the survey revealed that Negro nurses were largely concentrated in the deep South and in the big cities of the North. However, in six Southern states where the Negro population was sizeable (Texas, Oklahoma, Louisiana, Arkansas, Mississippi and Kentucky), there were relatively few trained Negro nurses. Even the number in the remaining nine Southern states and the District of Columbia, compared to the total in Illinois, Michigan, Pennsylvania, New Jersey and New York, was not very impressive. In the North and South alike, Negro nurses were mainly concentrated in the urban centers. In this connection it is significant to note that a substantial part of the Negro population of the South, unlike that of the North, lived in rural communities.

Negro nurses faced discriminatory treatment on the job as well as in hiring practices. In the South, they were regarded as a species of domestic servant and treated as such. In white hospitals with Negro wings, they were assigned the task of handling rather than of treating patients. Although conditions were somewhat better in the North, there, too, they felt the heavy hand of discrimination. Prior to 1929, except for Harlem Hospital, no Negro nurses were employed in New York City's municipal hospitals. In that year, however, a Negro was admitted to the nursing staff of the Sea View Hospital on Staten Island, and in 1934, three colored nurses were added to the Queens General Hospital. The first breakthrough in the city's voluntary hospitals came in 1935, when Lebanon and Montefiore accepted colored nurses on their staffs.

The Great Depression of the 1930's hit Negro nurses hard. So bad were conditions that, during one year, it was necessary to use money from the Rosenwald Fund to finance in part the salaries of colored nurses in eleven Southern states. In 1940, the same fund granted money for a study covering employment opportunities for Negro nurses. Letters and questionnaires were sent to organizations selected from a list furnished by the National Organization for Public Health Nursing. According to the survey, opportunities for Negroes in this field did not markedly improve during the decade of the thirties. Whereas in 1930 twenty organizations reported the employ-

ment of 91 full-time Negro nurses, in 1939 there were twenty-two reporting 103 full-time jobs.

During the Depression years, the Rosenwald Fund was used also to advance the work of the National Association of Colored Graduate Nurses. With the fund's help, the association was given a new lease on life in 1934, when it established a national office at the Rockefeller Center in New York City. With Mabel K. Staupers, a registered nurse, as executive secretary, an all-out campaign was launched for the admission of more Negro students to nursing schools, the establishment of scholarships, especially for Negro graduate nurses, and more job opportunities for Negro personnel. To achieve the latter, a working relationship was established with three major nursing organizations in the field.

An intensive membership campaign was also launched and the *National News Bulletin,* official organ of the association, authorized. In 1938, with the aid of Dr. M. O. Bousfield, a representative of the Rosenwald Fund, the National Advisory Council was organized to back the program of the National Association of Colored Graduate Nurses. High on the list for action was the promotion of progressive health legislation. Both the association and its National Advisory Council worked actively for passage of the National Health Act of 1939.

MEDICAL CONTRIBUTIONS

During the first half of the twentieth century, a number of talented Negroes made striking contributions to the progress of American medicine. Their achievements might well have been greater had there been no built-in color prejudice. That they were able to accomplish what they did was largely the result of their own extraordinary talents, courage and unswerving dedication to science. Through their productive and

MABEL K. STAUPERS

DR. WILLIAM A. HINTON

creative research, they did much to help improve the health and prolong the lives of countless Americans, black and white alike.

Consider the work of Dr. William Augustus Hinton, who devoted his life to fighting venereal diseases. When the Wassermann, Kahn and Hinton tests for syphilis are mentioned, few know that Hinton was a Negro. Concerning him, a writer in the *Boston Daily Globe* of September 15, 1952, remarked:

> It is 40 years since Dr. William Hinton was graduated from Harvard Medical School and began a career which brought him renown in the field of social diseases throughout the world. . . . Retired on June 30 at 68 years of age from the position he has held for 38 years as chief of the Department of Clinical Laboratories at the Boston Dispensary, Dr. Hinton will continue as consultant and as director of the Massachusetts Department of Public Health Institute of Laboratories. He still teaches at Harvard Medical School, too, though salaries there cease at the retirement age of 65.

Born in Chicago in 1883, William A. Hinton was graduated with a B.S. degree from Harvard in 1905 and with an M.D. degree, with honors, in 1912. Interested in scientific research, he decided to restrict his practice and went to work in the laboratory of the Massachusetts General Hospital, where he studied the effects of syphilis from the postmortems of children afflicted with the disease. He showed so much promise that, in 1915, he was appointed director of the Wassermann Laboratory of the Massachusetts Department of Public Health. In the same year, he became chief of the laboratory department of the Boston Dispensary, where his interest in venereal diseases was greatly stimulated by Drs. Abner Post and Morton Smith. Meanwhile, he was appointed instructor in bacteriology at Harvard.

There were not enough hours in the day for Dr. Hinton as he worked with microscope, test tube and slides. To be close to his work, he searched for a home within a twenty-mile radius of his beloved laboratories in Boston. In 1916, he and his young bride, a native of Macon, Georgia, settled in Canton. "We had no money," the couple recalled many years later, "but we bought something which we could swing. We'd do so much each year, then our money would give out and we'd wait another year to do something else." Dr. Hinton loved to work with his hands; he was a skilled carpenter and an accomplished gardener. In his spare time—the precious little there was of it—he added a porch, garage and extra rooms to his house and beautified the grounds around it by planting trees and putting in flowers. The Hintons' home in Canton was a place of unusual beauty.

In the meantime, Dr. Hinton achieved a worldwide reputation. He discovered a flocculation method for the determination of syphilis. One of the most sensitive tests devised, it was known by his name. He was also co-originator of the Davies-Hinton tests of blood and spinal fluids. His book *Syphilis and Its Treatment*, published in 1936, was hailed on both sides of the Atlantic. In England, it was acclaimed by the highly esteemed British medical journal, *Lancet*, and in the United States, it was greeted as a unique contribution to the field. Embodying over twenty years of research in laboratory and clinic, the book became a standard reference work. Its approach to the problem was fresh and stimulating. To Dr. Hinton, contracting syphilis was not due to race, but to the socio-economic condition of the patient. A disease of the underprivileged, it was the by-product of poverty and ignorance.

Dr. Hinton was as devoted to teaching as he was to research. He established a school for technicians at the Boston Dispensary. Evolving from classes for volunteers, the school in a twenty-year period graduated 432 students, all of whom were immediately employed by hospitals and laboratories throughout the country. At the same time, he taught a generation of students at Harvard Medical School, where he served as clinical professor and professor emeritus.

Dr. Hinton was a man of great charm and talent. He was a hard worker, enthusiastic and unusually capable. Adversity did not stop him. Even the loss of a leg in an automobile accident in 1940 did not keep him from going on and doing things. Despite his many achievements, he was a modest man. When the National Association for the Advancement of Colored People awarded him the Spingarn Medal for his important contributions to American life, he declined the honor on the ground that he wanted to wait until he had achieved a great deal more.

Similarly, Dr. Solomon C. Fuller of Boston broadened the horizons of medical knowledge by his major contributions in neuropathology and psychiatry. The son of

DR. SOLOMON C. FULLER

a coffee planter and government official in Liberia, he came to the United States in 1889, when he was seventeen years old. Four years later, he received his baccalaureate degree from Livingstone College, Salisbury, North Carolina. Intent on becoming a doctor, he entered the Long Island College Hospital in Brooklyn but transferred to Boston University, where he received his M.D. degree in 1897. Two years later, at the age of twenty-seven, he was appointed to the faculty of the Boston University Medical School, where he taught pathology, neurology and psychiatry for more than thirty years.

Upon his graduation from medical school, Dr. Fuller received an internship at Westborough State Hospital in Massachusetts and two years later was appointed pathologist. Following this, he studied under Professor Dunham at the Carnegie Laboratory in New York, Professors Kraepelin and Alzheimer at the Psychiatric Clinic of the University of Munich, and

MEDICAL CONTRIBUTIONS 105

DR. WILLIAM H. BARNES

Professors Bollinger and Schmaus at the pathological institute of the same university. By 1913, he was chosen editor of the *West-borough State Hospital Papers,* a scientific publication devoted to various aspects of mental disease.

Dr. Fuller wrote widely on pathologic, neurologic and psychiatric subjects. His contributions appeared in medical books and journals. He was best known for his work on dementias and for several papers on Alzheimer's disease. His suggestion that this mental disorder was caused by something other than arteriosclerosis was upheld in 1953, the year he died. He was a member of the American Psychiatric Association, the Boston Society for Psychiatry and Neurology, the New York Psychiatric Association, and also the Massachusetts Medical Society, the New England Medical Society and the American Medical Association.

Dr. Fuller practiced medicine in both Boston and Framingham, where he had an

office in his home at 31 Warren Road. He loved gardening, was a skillful bookbinder and enjoyed music. A diligent and meticulous worker, he became totally blind toward the close of his life. Shortly before his death, he was visited by a friend who wrote: "I saw and talked with him: though blind, his memory was excellent, his speech flawless, his interests alive. He knew he had not long to live, but accepted the fact in his usual philosophical manner, like the perfect gentleman he was."

Another renowned Negro contributor to medicine was the otolaryngologist Dr. William H. Barnes of Philadelphia. Born of poor parents, April 4, 1887, he was able to pursue a higher education only because of his unusual brilliance as a student. In 1908, he ranked so high on a competitive examination that he was awarded a scholarship to the medical school of the University of Pennsylvania. Four years later he was awarded his M.D. degree, and after a period of internship, he was appointed assistant otolaryngologist at Frederick Douglass Hospital in Philadelphia. In 1921, after seven years of private practice, he decided to do postgraduate work in the disorders of the ear, nose and throat. He studied first at the University of Pennsylvania and then attended the University of Paris and the University of Bordeaux.

Hard work and study in his specialty bore fruit. Dr. Barnes was made chief otolaryngologist at the Frederick Douglass Hospital and clinical assistant otolaryngologist at Jefferson Medical College Hospital. In 1927, he was elected a diplomate of the American Board of Otolaryngology. During the early thirties, he established and presided over the department of bronchoscopy at Mercy Hospital and was appointed lecturer and consultant in bronchoscopy at the Howard Medical School.

Dr. Barnes was famous for his bloodless operative techniques. A friend and student of Dr. Chevalier Jackson, he followed the methods of this noted Philadelphia bronchoscopist and, in the course of time, made innovations of his own. In 1926, he demonstrated at a meeting of the Philadelphia Laryngological Society an instrument he had invented to make easier an approach to the pituitary gland in operative work. He devised other surgical instruments and made useful additions to older ones.

Up to the time of his death in 1945, Dr. Barnes played a prominent role in the political as well as medical life of Philadelphia. A firm believer in integration, he tried to bring racial equality and human dignity to his native city. As a doctor, he knew the importance to health of good living quarters and so carried on for years an active fight for better housing for Negroes.

Like Dr. Barnes, Dr. Louis T. Wright was not only a distinguished medical scientist, but also a militant advocate of Negro rights. A prominent member of the National Association for the Advancement of Colored People, he served as chairman of the board and was responsible for the establishment of a board committee on health. In 1940, he was awarded the association's Spingarn Medal for his work as one of the country's foremost surgeons and champion of equal rights. He was active in the New Deal fight for a fair employment practice code and in pushing Negro demands for job equality in the labor movement. His battle for the elimination of the color line at Harlem Hospital and his fight against racial discrimination in the American College of Surgeons will be discussed later.

Born in La Grange, Georgia, Louis Wright came north to study medicine and graduated from Harvard Medical School in 1915, at the age of twenty-four. While a student in obstetrics at Harvard, he was told that he could not deliver babies at the Boston Lying-In Hospital. His response to this was that, since he had paid his tuition like the other students, he intended to receive the same kind of treatment. He won his point, and as a result, the practice of having Negro students deliver babies under the supervision of a Negro physician, separate from the rest of the class, was discontinued. A student of marked ability—he was graduated from Harvard Medical School with honors—he did not hesitate to take time from his studies to picket and protest against racial injustice. For three weeks he walked in front of a Boston theater demanding that D. W. Griffith's anti-Negro motion picture, *The Birth of A Nation*, be withdrawn.

After graduating from Harvard Medical School in 1915, Dr. Wright returned to Atlanta, Georgia, to practice medicine. When the First World War broke out, he joined the army's medical corps, was shipped to France as a lieutenant and stationed in the Vosges sector, where he was ordered to make a medical survey of the area prior to the launching of an offensive.

DR. LOUIS T. WRIGHT

The main building of the Harlem Hospital Center in New York City.

In France, he was gassed and hospitalized. Before returning home, he was promoted to the rank of captain.

In 1919, Dr. Wright became the first Negro to be appointed to a New York City municipal hospital. For more than thirty years, he served Harlem Hospital with distinction. As a member of the attending staff, director of the department of surgery and president of the medical board, he did much to impress upon the institution his twofold idea of excellence and equality in medicine. Regarded as one of the nation's great surgeons, he made significant contributions to the development of his specialty. His section on skull fractures in *The Treatment of Fractures,* edited by Dr. Scudder, successfully challenged traditional theories on the treatment of such cases. He devised a blade plate for the operative treatment of fractures about the knee joint and a brace

for cervical vertebrae fractures. He invented an intradermal vaccination against small-pox; and, under his supervision, the first tests on aureomycin were made on human beings. He also engaged in cancer research under a grant from the Damon Runyon Fund. For his noted work in surgery, he was admitted in 1934 to fellowship in the American College of Surgeons.

Another illustrious Negro surgeon was Dr. Charles R. Drew, whose pioneer work in blood research was responsible for saving innumerable lives during World War II. The story of his career points up the tragic loss of the human potential in a racist-oriented society.

Dr. Drew was born in Washington, D.C., in 1904. His father was a worker, and his mother, a graduate of a training school for teachers. As young Drew grew to manhood, it was evident that he was not only a good

DR. CHARLES R. DREW

student but a fine athlete. At Amherst, he was voted the most valuable baseball player, was elected captain of the track team and starred as a halfback. When he was graduated in 1926, he was awarded the Howard Hill Mossman Trophy as the man who contributed the most to Amherst athletics during his four years in college.

While coaching basketball and football at Morgan College, Drew decided to become a doctor. Aware that he needed additional funds for his education, he supplemented his income by working as a referee. Within a few years, he had saved enough to enter McGill Medical College. There he achieved an enviable scholastic record. At the end of his junior year he was elected to Alpha Omega Alpha, the medical honorary fraternity, and at the close of his senior year he was awarded the Williams Prize, given annually to the top five men in the class. In 1933, at the age of twenty-nine, he received his M.D. degree from McGill.

Two years later, Dr. Drew joined the faculty of Howard Medical School. Regarded by Dean Adams as one of his brightest young men, he was awarded a General Education Board fellowship to Columbia University Medical School. There he worked with Dr. Scudder and his group in blood research. His specific project was to discover how blood could be preserved and used for transfusion purposes. Working as many as eighteen hours a day, he gathered together a mass of scientific data which was published in 1940 in a pioneer and definitive treatise, *Banked Blood: A Study in Blood Preservation.* Recognizing his contribution, Columbia University awarded him the degree of Doctor of Science (medicine).

At the outbreak of the Second World War, Dr. Drew received an urgent cablegram from Dr. John Beattie, director of the research laboratories of the Royal College of Surgeons. The cablegram read as follows: "Could you secure five thousand ampules of dried plasma for transfusion. Work immediately and follow this by equal quantity in three to four weeks. Contents should represent about one pint of whole plasma." Dr. Drew was stunned by the request of his former professor of anatomy at McGill. He knew there was no such amount of dried blood in the entire world. But this did not stop him. He set to work, and by September, 1940, at the height of Nazi Germany's blitzkreig of England, he headed the "Blood for Britain" project. The following year, he was selected as the director of the American Red Cross Blood Bank and as assistant director of blood procurement for the National Research Council.

Modest, alert and hard-working, Dr. Drew proceeded to set up the blood bank project and to train the necessary staff. He refused to suffer in silence the humiliating practice of segregating the blood of Negro and white donors, for like all other competent medical scientists, he maintained that all human blood was the same and had no relation to race. At a time when it was customary to incorporate leading medical authorities into the armed forces, he was "let go" and "permitted" to return to a professorship in surgery at Howard Medical School. Rumor had it that the position he held in the blood bank was too high a post for a Negro. He returned to Howard, where he refused to discuss the subject of his "resignation." Not one to dwell on the past, Dr. Drew threw himself into teaching. He was particularly happy in the presence of students. They inspired him, and he inspired them. He was ever on the alert to obtain residencies for his "boys" and to see them later certified by the American Board of Surgery.

His unique research in blood plasma brought him many honors. Dr. Drew was elected a fellow of the International College of Surgeons, received the Spingarn Medal of the National Association for the Advancement of Colored People, was made a vice-president of the American-Soviet Medical Society, and obtained the honorary degree of D.Sc. from both Virginia State College and Amherst. Honest, genial, forthright, he was one who modestly bore these honors without losing the common touch. Just before his untimely death in an automobile accident in 1950, he was planning a series of new research projects.

Negro medical scientists also made contributions to the development of modern dermatology. Particularly important was the work of Dr. Theodore K. Lawless of Chicago. Born in Louisiana in 1894, he studied medicine at Kansas and Northwestern, and dermatology in France, Austria and Switzerland. Practicing in the heart of Chicago's Negro community, he established one of the largest skin practices in the city. His contributions to the medical literature on dermatology and syphilis were significant; and his research on the cure

Dr. Drew, assisted by a nurse, serving as a civil defense worker during the Second World War.

DR. THEODORE K. LAWLESS

of leprosy, outstanding. In recognition of his work, he was appointed lecturer and demonstrator in the department of dermatology at Northwestern, associate examiner in dermatology for the National Board of Medical Examiners and special lecturer in dermatology for Cook County Hospital.

Though not a physician, Dr. Ernest E. Just, one of America's most eminent biologists, deserves to be mentioned in any discussion of contributions made by Negroes to modern medicine. For many years, he was closely associated with the medical profession as professor of physiology at Howard Medical School. It was largely through his efforts that the National Research Council in the early 1920's awarded three fellowships to Howard medical graduates for careers in teaching and research.

Born in Charleston, South Carolina, in 1883, he studied at Dartmouth and earned his doctorate at the University of Chicago. He contributed many papers to scientific

journals and was associate editor of the *Biological Bulletin,* the *Journal of Morphology,* and *Physiological Zoology.* His book, *The Biology of the Cell Surface,* published in 1939, two years before his death, represented a lifetime of research. In it, he rejected the traditional theory that the germ cells were absolutely independent of the rest of the body. Stressing the importance of environment, he called for a dialectical approach to the life process.

Dr. Just became a vice-president of the American Society of Zoologists and was the first recipient of the Spingarn Medal of the National Association for the Advancement of Colored People. Like other Negro scientists, he felt the full impact of Jim Crow. To escape color prejudice in America, he spent many years abroad in study and research. Deep inside him, he felt the hurt of racism; in the words of Dr. Samuel M. Nabrit, he was "frustrated and embittered."

DR. ERNEST E. JUST

CHAPTER SEVEN

Fighting Back

Our hats are in the air to Tuskegee and Moton. . . . He and the Negro world demanded that the Government Hospital at Tuskegee be under Negro control. Today, at last, it is.
The Crisis, September 1924.

. . . Ousts Board in Harlem Hospital: Negroes Are Added.
Headline in *The New York Times,* February 14, 1930.

Our death rate is without the slightest doubt a death rate due to poverty and discrimination.
Dr. W. E. B. Du Bois, "Postscript: Our Health," *The Crisis,* February 1933.

DURING the interim between World War I and World War II, Negroes in medicine, aided by Negroes in civil rights activity outside medicine, fought against racial discrimination in its blatant Southern form and in its more subtle Northern one. Their struggle centered on two hospitals, Veterans Hospital No. 91, at Tuskegee, Alabama, and Harlem Hospital, in the heart of New York City's Negro ghetto.

Although Negroes constituted slightly more than one-tenth of the total population, they made up nearly one-seventh (380,000) of those serving in the armed forces of the United States during the First World War. So entrenched were Jim Crow practices that, of the two hundred thousand Negroes in France, about three-fourths were assigned to labor battalions. The remaining one-fourth managed to see front-

line action, fighting gallantly at Champagne, Metz and the Argonne Forest.

During the war, a total of 356 Negroes were commissioned as medical officers; many of them saw action overseas with Negro units, chiefly, though not entirely, with the 92nd Division. Among those serving in France were Dr. Louis T. Wright, future director of the department of surgery at Harlem Hospital, Dr. Joseph H. Ward, later to become chief medical officer of the Tuskegee Veterans Hospital, and Dr. Charles H. Garvin, the first Negro to be appointed to a Cleveland hospital. Dr. Garvin was also the first Negro during World War I to be commissioned in the medical corps and the first to attend the army medical school in Washington.

Concerning the excellent work of the Medical Department of the 92nd Division,

DR. CHARLES H. GARVIN

Colonel C. R. Reynolds, chief surgeon of the A.E.F.'s Second Army, had this to say: "I desire to express my admiration and appreciation of the splendid hospital organized and administered by the Medical Department of the 92nd Division at Millery." Negro nurses were not accepted by the army until after the war had ended and then only to meet the emergency created by the influenza epidemic of 1918. Eighteen Negro nurses were mobilized and sent by the surgeon general to Camp Sherman, Ohio, and Camp Grant, Illinois. In characteristic Jim Crow fashion, they were assigned to separate living quarters. Once the emergency was over, they were discharged.

BREAKTHROUGH AT TUSKEGEE AND HARLEM

Following the end of the war, the United States Veterans Bureau began building hospitals for disabled soldiers throughout the country. With the exception of some isolated wards, little was available to meet the needs of colored veterans. Negro soldiers who had risked their lives in a war allegedly fought for democracy were outraged by this latest disregard of the basic democratic right of equality for all. Where was the new and better world that they had been promised and that they had gone off to fight for?

In June, 1918, a leading Negro journal had expressed Negro aspirations as follows: "Out of this war will rise, too, an American Negro, with the right to vote and the right to work and the right to live without insult." So far as the Negro veterans of World War I were concerned, "the right to live without insult" meant an equal opportunity to enjoy the benefits of first-class hospitalization when they needed it. In this, they had the support of an aroused Negro public opinion, which in the end succeeded not only in establishing a hospital for Negro veterans but also in staffing it with Negro personnel.

The Harding administration, faced by mounting pressure to do something for disabled colored soldiers, approached Tuskegee Institute for advice on how to meet the problem. From the administration's viewpoint, this was a logical move, for Tuskegee was long associated with the activities of Booker T. Washington, whose ideological thought stemmed from the compromise of 1877. It was he who had urged the Negro people to turn from political action and the struggle for civil rights to industrial training and individual responsibility. By hammering away at the idea of self-improvement and accommodation, he had all but emasculated the Negro movement precisely when the Southern leaders were aggressively erecting the legal system of segregation. Because the Harding administration believed that the spirit of Booker T. Washington was still alive at Tuskegee (barely a half-dozen years

BOOKER T. WASHINGTON

had elapsed since his death in 1915), it anticipated no undue trouble in dealing with this Southern center of "safe and sound" Negro leadership.

But times had changed, and the Tuskegee of 1921 was not that of 1895 or 1905, when Booker T. Washington was at the height of his popularity. More than a quarter of a century of unabashed Jim Crow and a war to make the world safe for democracy had brought into being a more militant Negro movement. The National Association for the Advancement of Colored People, organized in 1910 by a group of prominent liberals and socialists, reflected the new trend. Under the leadership of the renowned Negro author and scholar Dr. W. E. B. Du Bois, it developed a more aggressive and comprehensive approach to the question of the Negro's place in American life than that expounded by Booker T. Washington. To Dr. Du Bois and his associates, Washington's idea of adjustment and submission was dangerous in a period of rising Jim Crow because it served only to undermine Negro self-respect and confidence. Dr. Du Bois and his colleagues, basing their actions on the militant strategy of self-assertion, urged Negroes to use every method available to fight for the rights and dignity due all men. As a result, the NAACP stepped up the battle to eliminate discriminatory practices in American life, including those in medicine and health.

By the early 1920's, even Tuskegee, the stronghold of the Booker T. Washington forces, was caught up in the movement of greater Negro militancy. With the help of the National Association for the Advancement of Colored People and the National Medical Association, Tuskegee rose to the occasion and fought to a successful conclusion the main issue in dispute: the appointment of an all-Negro staff to a publicly supported, all-Negro veterans hospital.

In 1921, the Veterans Bureau and Tuskegee Institute agreed to the construction of a hospital on three hundred acres of land owned by the institute. At a cost of $2,500,000, a hospital, consisting of six hundred beds in twenty-seven permanent buildings, to treat primarily neuropsychiatric patients, was completed and dedicated on Lincoln's birthday, February 12, 1923. In the meantime, the Veterans Bureau appointed a white physician, Colonel Robert C. Stanley, as superintendent of the hospital, despite a promise made to Dr. Robert R. Moton, President of Tuskegee Institute, that he would be consulted prior to any such appointment.

Under Superintendent Stanley's direction, plans were made to open the hospital "with a full staff of white doctors and white nurses with colored nursemaids for each white nurse, in order to save them from contact with colored patients!" To forestall

DR. ROBERT R. MOTON

DR. CHARLES M. GRIFFITH

the execution of these plans, Dr. Moton wrote to President Harding on February 14, 1923, requesting him to give Negro physicians and nurses an opportunity to qualify for service in the hospital through special civil service examinations. After conferring with Dr. Moton, President Harding granted the request. General Frank T. Hines, director of the Veterans Bureau, was sent to Tuskegee to initiate a gradual change in the medical staff from white to black. Meanwhile, Superintendent Stanley, who had declared there could be no mixture of the races on the hospital staff, was replaced by Dr. Charles M. Griffith, who was directed by General Hines on his visit to Tuskegee to make preparations for a changeover in staff from white to Negro.

Pressure on the part of the National Association for the Advancement of Colored People helped bring about the removal of Dr. Stanley. Especially impor-

tant were the behind-the-scene activities of Walter F. White, assistant secretary of the NAACP, James Weldon Johnson, secretary, and James A. Cobb, attorney. Through their efforts, government officials in the highest echelons were made aware of the importance of staffing the hospital with Negro personnel and of protecting them against intimidation on the part of prominent Tuskegee citizens, many of whom were members of the resurgent Ku Klux Klan.

In fact, local Klansmen were so incensed at having Negro doctors and nurses at a hospital housing neuropsychiatric and tubercular Negro veterans that they paraded at the Tuskegee Institute and burned a cross on the front lawn of Dr. John A. Kenney's home. When Dr. Kenney, a close friend of the late Booker T. Washington and editor-in-chief of the *Journal of the National Medical Association,* refused to repudiate his stand for a Negro staff, he became a "marked man." Anonymous threats were made against him. Dr. Kenney sent his family North, and when a few days later he was told by a white patient that the Klan was plotting to kill him, he also went North.

Dr. Kenney went to the home of Dr. George Cannon, Sr., then chairman of the executive board of the National Medical Association. A committee was promptly organized to bring the matter of Dr. Kenney's flight from Tuskegee and the question of a Negro staff at the hospital to the government's attention. Several conferences were held with President Harding and General Hines, which resulted in agreement on the staffing of the veterans hospital at Tuskegee with Negro personnel. Meanwhile, the National Medical Association alerted its members to the basic issues involved in the fight. In his presidential address in 1923, Dr. J. Edward Perry spoke of his having travelled 5,280 miles, addressing one thousand physicians, surgeons, dentists and pharmacists; of his organization having printed and mailed eight thousand pieces of literature; and of his having "used [his] office to its fullest extent in influencing the Veterans Bureau director as to the personnel of the Veterans Hospital at Tuskegee . . . ."

After a two-month stay in the North, Dr. Kenney returned to Tuskegee to continue the fight. He remained until September 1, 1924, when he resigned his post as medical director of the John A. Andrew Hospital and left for Newark, New Jersey, to enter private practice. But, before his departure, he had the satisfaction of knowing that he and others, with their backs to the wall, had stood fast, fought back—and won. "Our hats are in the air to Tuskegee and Moton," wrote Dr. Du Bois in *The Crisis,* September, 1924. "He and the Negro world demanded that the Government Hospital at Tuskegee be under Negro control. Today, at last, it is."

Signaling the new order was the replacement in July, 1924, of Dr. Charles M. Griffith by Dr. Joseph H. Ward, a Negro physician from Indianapolis, as medical officer-in-chief of the Tuskegee Veterans Hospital. Dr. Ward was a World War I veteran who served overseas, was promoted from second lieutenant to major in the medical corps, and at the time of his appointment, held the rank of lieutenant-colonel. During his twelve years as head of the Tuskegee institution, he made an enviable record for himself as an administrator. In 1936, Dr. Ward was succeeded by Dr. Eugene H. Dibble, Jr., a former member of the hospital's staff, who was then medical director of the John A. Andrew Hospital in Tuskegee.

In the meantime, the National Medical Association was recruiting competent Negro physicians and other professional staff members. On June 2, 1923, Dr. L. B. Rogers, medical director of the Veterans

DR. JOSEPH H. WARD

DR. TOUSSAINT T. TILDON

Bureau, sent a letter to the association, recognizing it as the "official organ of the medical profession of the Negro race" and requesting it "to submit a list of experienced physicians qualified in this important service." Playing a conspicuous role in the recruitment program was Dr. Michael O. Dumas, high in the association's councils. Working closely with the Veterans Bureau, Dr. Dumas, assisted by Dr. Kenney, arranged with Dr. Solomon C. Fuller, Boston University's celebrated Negro neurologist and psychiatrist, to train a small group of recent Negro graduates from the medical schools of that area. On November 21, 1923, four Negro physicians, three recent graduates of the Boston University Medical School and the fourth from the Harvard Medical School, were recruited from the training program and reported for duty in the neuropsychiatric service. One of the group, Harvard-educated Dr. Toussaint T. Tildon, later became clinical director and still later, hospital director.

By the close of the 1920's, so excellent was the National Medical Association's recruitment program that the Tuskegee Veterans Hospital was staffed completely by Negro doctors of the highest caliber. Wrote Dr. Louis T. Wright in *The Crisis* of September, 1929: "I am told that this hospital has been rated since it was first established as one of the best managed Veterans Hospitals in the country, both as to administration and in the character of scientific work done."

It was at this time that Dr. Wright and other Negroes were leading the fight at Harlem Hospital to improve the lot of Negro patients and to gain greater Negro representation on the staff. Located on Lenox Avenue in New York City's borough of Manhattan, Harlem Hospital was overcrowded almost from the day it opened, April 13, 1907, with a bed capacity of 150. As early as 1911, plans were made to expand the physical plant as the average daily census of the hospital reached 184 and total yearly visits to its out-patient department were 108,502. Four years later, a new wing was added to increase the bed capacity to 390. Yet, in spite of this increase, facilities continued to prove inadequate during and immediately following World War I as Harlem received its first great wave of Negro migration from the South. So rapidly did the colored community grow that Harlem Hospital, unable to adjust itself to the situation, became the center of bitter controversy. By the early 1920's, its administration was being charged with gross inefficiency and racial prejudice.

Alderman George W. Harris, editor of a New York City newspaper, laid down the opening barrage by demanding that Harlem Hospital admit Negro doctors and nurses to its staff. The only Negro on the staff at the time was Dr. Louis T. Wright, who was appointed in 1919 as clinical assistant in the out-patient department, the lowest possible staff appointment. Dr. Casmo D. O'Neil, who was directly responsible for Dr. Wright's appointment, was roundly denounced and promptly demoted. When Dr. O'Neil's demotion was brought to Mayor Hylan's attention, the mayor quickly selected him to head Fordham Hospital.

Another result of Dr. Wright's appointment to the staff was the resignation of four physicians who refused to serve with a Negro. In 1923, when Harlem Hospital established a training school for Negro nurses, some staff physicians expressed their unwillingness to work with colored nursing personnel. One surgeon was reported to have remarked "that he would not operate in the presence of a 'nigger [*sic*] woman,' " after which he "pulled his gloves off and walked out of the Operating Room." The same anti-Negro bias was said to exist in the treatment of colored patients. The North Harlem Medical, Dental and Pharmaceutical Society engaged William Nelson Colson to investigate the matter. The investigation revealed shocking abuses in the way Negro patients were being treated.

As a result of newspaper publicity, political pressure began building up for a sweeping investigation of discriminatory practices at Harlem Hospital. Unlike Negroes in the South, those in the North had suffrage. Since Tammany Hall was fully aware of the vital importance of the Negro vote in Harlem, it agreed to concede to the mounting pressure being exerted by the NAACP, the Negro press and organized Negro medicine for an inquiry into the affairs of the hospital.

Mayor Hylan then appointed David A. Hirshfield, Commissioner of Accounts, to

The original Harlem Hospital, shown above, became inadequate by 1906, and its facilities were transferred to a new building at its present location on 136th Street and Lenox Avenue.

DR. JOHN W. BRANNAN

conduct the investigation. The North Harlem Medical, Dental and Pharmaceutical Society engaged Attorney Aiken A. Pope to represent it at the public hearings. During the investigation, Alderman Harris effectively presented instance after instance of discriminatory practices at the hospital. After several weeks of public hearings, a report which was sympathetic to Negro demands was made to the Mayor. Agitation, however, continued; and as a result, the situation at Harlem Hospital became an issue in the mayoralty campaign of 1925.

Meanwhile, the city government attempted to placate the Negro community. On February 1, 1923, Mayor Hylan appointed Dr. John J. McGrath a member of the Board of Trustees of Bellevue and allied hospitals for a term of seven years to replace Dr. John W. Brannan, who had been president of the board for more than fifteen years. Dr. Brannan, concerned about the employment of Negro physicians,

once asked the superintendent of the outpatient clinic whether the white patients objected to being treated by Negro doctors. The administrator answered the question by observing that the white patients "liked the colored physicians better because they received better treatment from them." Some months after the replacement of Dr. Brannan, Harlem Hospital established a training school for Negro nurses. The racial imbalance in nursing personnel was gradually rectified as colored nurses were appointed and white nurses transferred to other hospitals.

Following the mayoralty campaign of 1925, further concessions were made to appease the Negro community. In 1926, three Negro doctors were added to Harlem Hospital's visiting staff. At the same time, Dr. Wright was promoted to the rank of assistant visiting physician. By 1929, there were seven Negro doctors on the in-service staff of sixty-four. By then, too, the newly created Department of Hospitals announced its intention of expanding Harlem's physical facilities in order to cope with the increased patient load.

However, the situation at Harlem Hospital was rapidly deteriorating. Morale was low, patients were being neglected, and factionalism on the staff was rife. To prevent chaos, Commissioner of Hospitals William Schroeder, Jr., late in the summer of 1929, appointed a committee to conduct a survey of the hospital's staff. The result was a drastic and sweeping reorganization of the municipal institution.

On February 14, 1930, *The New York Times* ran a front-page story which told of the ousting of the medical board of Harlem Hospital and of the addition of Negro doctors to the staff. According to the report, orders were issued the day before by the Commissioner of Hospitals to reorganize Harlem Hospital. Dr. Thomas A. Martin replaced Dr. Arthur M. Shadry as director of medicine. Twenty-three white and two Negro physicians were dismissed from the staff, while twelve colored doctors were added. As a result of these changes, the hospital's surgical division had seven Negroes and seven whites; the medical staff, four Negroes and four whites; the obstetrical staff, two Negroes and two whites; the division of pediatrics, one Negro and one white; the ophthalmology staff, two Negroes and one white; and the division of hematology, one Negro and three whites.

The next day, the forty-six-man medical board (nineteen of whom were Negroes) met to elect officers. Dr. John F. Connors, surgical director, was chosen president to replace Dr. Arthur M. Shadry, who had been medical director before the shake-up. Dr. Connors, a pivotal figure in the controversy, was the acknowledged leader of the white physicians at the hospital who favored greater Negro representation on the medical staff. Dr. Thomas A. Martin was elected vice-president and Dr. Louis T. Wright, the Negro champion of equal rights, secretary. After announcing the results of the election, the Commissioner of Hospitals told reporters: "The reorganization is in the interest of the patient rather than of the men having aspirations for medical appointments."

Reorganization having been accomplished, Negro physicians on the staff, like Dr. Louis T. Wright and Dr. Peter M. Murray, were determined to make Harlem Hospital a first-rate institution. Dr. Wright was an uncompromising foe of professional incompetency, white or black. A firm believer in medicine of the highest quality, he favored the appointment of only those who showed proficiency and promise in their work. Because of his high standards, he fought to remove unqualified white physicians from the staff and to block the appointment of unqualified Negro doctors. Consequently, he was bitterly opposed by

both sides; he was even forced to face, in the words of his friend Dr. Du Bois, an " 'investigation' on demand of colored physicians before that very hospital head who opposed any Negro appointee to any position in Harlem Hospital." Yet, like Dr. Mossell before him, he refused to compromise his principles. Nothing could deter him in his determination to provide Harlem Hospital patients with the best medical and surgical care available.

Dr. Peter M. Murray shared Dr. Wright's desire for the very best in medical service. Born in Houma, Louisiana, Dr. Murray received his M.D. degree from Howard Medical School in 1914. After doing graduate work in surgery and gynecology and serving as medical inspector in the public schools of the District of Columbia, he came to New York to engage in private practice. During the 1920's, he became generally known in Harlem as an able

DR. PETER M. MURRAY

surgeon and gynecologist. In 1929, he was appointed to Harlem Hospital as a provisional assistant adjunct visiting in gynecology. The following year, as a result of the hospital commissioner's reorganization order, he became a member of the hospital's surgical division.

Although Dr. Murray believed that the Harlem Hospital shake-up was a step forward, he was of the opinion that the reorganization plan had to be supplemented if high-quality medicine was to be achieved. On March 22, 1930, *The New York Times* quoted him as saying:

> The reorganization by Dr. Greeff [Commissioner of Hospitals] accomplished some good, but did not go far enough. The hospital now needs competent and experienced white physicians and surgeons to instruct the younger staff members. We believe that proper professional training should come through physicians of all races working together. The medical board and the surgical director [Dr. John F. Connors] should have brought more competent physicians into the institution.

He went on to point out that if steps in this direction were not taken, there would be an inevitable breakdown of hospital services, with the distinct possibility that Negro physicians would be blamed for this. So serious did he consider the situation to be that he and Dr. James T. W. Granaday of the medical staff resigned in protest against the manner in which the institution was being run. Later, they agreed to remain only because of the hospital's lack of sufficient medical personnel. Similar misgivings concerning the operation of the hospital were expressed by the North Harlem Medical Society, which elected a committee of seven to present its grievances to the hospital commissioner.

The fight to integrate and improve Harlem Hospital continued throughout the 1930's and well into the 1940's. By the beginning of 1932, the in-service Negro staff numbered thirty-eight; five were dentists.

Twenty-seven Negroes were on the out-patient staff, including five dentists and fourteen interns. Thereafter, the number of Negro physicians and surgeons on all staffs increased. By the middle of the 1940's, the house and visiting staff leveled off at about one-half Negro and one-half white.

Steady progress was also made in giving Negro doctors positions of greater responsibility. Dr. Wright was made surgical director. However, in announcing this appointment, the Commissioner of Hospitals, Dr. Goldwater, made it clear that it would be for one year only, despite the practice of continuing such appointments indefinitely. Although Dr. Wright made an enviable record during the year (the death rate from traumatic injuries was reduced by 20 per cent), he was dropped; and a white physician was appointed in his place. This prompted *The Crisis* of March, 1939, to inquire editorially "whether Commissioner Goldwater is interested in the health of the people of Harlem or in the color of his appointees to hospital posts?" Four years later, Dr. Wright became director of the department of surgery, a position he held until his death in 1952. Meanwhile, other well-qualified Negro physicians were promoted to positions of responsibility. In the years immediately following the Second World War, seven Negroes held the rank of chief of service: Louis T. Wright and Ralph Young in surgery, Peter M. Murray in gynecology, Paul Collins in ophthalmology, Neville Whiteman in medicine, Harold Ellis in neurology and psychiatry and E. R. Alexander in dermatology.

Agitation for staff integration at Harlem Hospital was accompanied by a corresponding drive to obtain better facilities and services for patients. In 1932, the hospital had a patient load of 11,510, with Negroes constituting 83 per cent of the total. The greatest number of patients in the institution at one time was 441. The official bed accommodation was 325, of which 52 were bassinets. So overcrowded were the in-service facilities that double rows of beds were placed in the middle of the wards and, at times, even in the corridors. Equally overtaxed were the facilities of the out-patient department, whose daily attendance at times exceeded 1,000, practically all of whom were Negroes.

The continuing urgent demand for expansion of the physical plant became so great that, during the early 1930's, construction proceeded on a new Women's Pavilion, which was dedicated January 4, 1935. It was an eight-story, brick building with a bed capacity of 282, in addition to 114 bassinets. By 1937, the hospital's total number of beds was 665. Yet, despite an almost two-fold increase in bed capacity since 1915, the institution was unable to cope with the increasing hospital needs of Harlem's Negro population. The shortage became even more acute in the early 1940's as Negroes left the South for wartime jobs in New York and other cities in the North and West.

During World War II, the need for additional hospital facilities in Harlem was so great that fifty-year-old Sydenham Hospital was reorganized along interracial lines. In 1943, six Negroes and six whites were added to Sydenham's Board of Trustees with the purpose of integrating Negro doctors, nurses, technicians and administrative personnel. A year after its first meeting on December 20, 1943, the reorganized board of trustees issued an annual report which showed significant progress in the attainment of its goals. For the first time in the history of any Grade-A voluntary hospital, the report stated, a Negro physician was appointed to the executive committee of the medical board. He was Dr. Peter M. Murray, attending physician in obstetrics and gynecology and veteran leader in the Harlem Hospital fight for integration. In addition to Dr. Murray, twenty-two other Negro physicians were made members of the medical staff.

According to the report of the trustees, the public and private response to the hospital's interracial program was excellent. With more financial aid given to Sydenham than in the past, half of its $350,000 building fund had already been raised. The campaign for funds was continuing, and upon its success depended the achievement of a project designed "to provide a congested community with adequate hospital facilities" and to inspire other private and public hospitals to adopt "interracial cooperation in hospital care" as part of "good Americanism and sound practice." Following Sydenham's example, three other voluntary hospitals in greater New York were reported to have added Negro doctors to their staffs, and six hospitals had added Negro nurses.

Negro physicians hailed Sydenham's efforts as a significant contribution to the establishment of a new type of hospital. In a signed editorial, "Post-War Planning for 'Negro' Hospitals," in the January, 1945, issue of the *Journal of the National Medical Association,* Dr. Charles H. Garvin observed:

> With this voluntary cooperative interracial plan we have medical democracy in action. It is my opinion that hospitals of this type will be a blow against "Jim Crow." Well equipped hospitals with no discrimination in their directorial and medical boards, with full facilities open to all patients regardless of race, answers our question.

Toward the close of the editorial, Dr. Garvin sounded a note of caution. He warned against the possibility that such an interracial type of hospital might become, like Provident in Chicago, an all-colored facility. However, he was of the opinion that, with constant vigilance and complete honesty, this eventuality could be averted.

THE WILL TO SURVIVE

During the quarter of a century following the First World War, Negro Americans were engaged in another fight, the day-by-day struggle to survive. For the most part working people—sharecroppers, unskilled laborers and household servants—they lived on the ragged edge of poverty with all its attendant health hazards. Slum conditions, family disorganization, inadequate nutrition and lack of knowledge of hygiene exposed them to the dangers of pulmonary tuberculosis, communicable childhood diseases, syphilis, gonorrhea, parasitic disorders and prenatal and maternal complications.

Since their incomes were insufficient to meet even the minimum of medical costs, Negroes depended on charity for health services. If such were available, they were forced to suffer the indignity of second-class treatment, not only because they were poor, but also because they were colored. Even the relatively few Negro Americans who were able to pay found health facilities closed to them because of Jim Crow practices. As a result of distinctions of social class and poverty, on the one hand, and racial discrimination, on the other, the health status of Negroes, as compared to whites, continued to remain unfavorable during this twenty-five-year period. However, these years saw some narrowing of the health gap between the two races, unmistakable proof of the steady advance of modern medicine and the indomitable will of the Negro people to survive.

The advent of medical research on a scale hitherto unknown made for notable progress in the improvement of health and the prolongation of life. Despite the fact that the Negro people shared some of the benefits of this medical breakthrough, statistical data still showed striking racial differences in the incidence of disease and death rates.

During the period between the two world wars, vital statistics revealed a lower life expectancy and a higher mortality and morbidity rate among blacks than among whites. In 1940, the expected life span of nonwhites was 51.5 years for males and 54.9 for females, while that of whites was 62.1 for males and 66.6 for females, a discrepancy of roughly eleven years in males and twelve in females. The difference was even greater in 1930, with the life expectancy of both races and sexes lower that year. In 1940, the death rate for nonwhites was 33 per cent higher than for whites, 13.8 per 1,000 as against 10.4. Ten years before, 17 nonwhites out of every 1,000 died, as compared to 11 whites.

In 1927, five diseases (tuberculosis, cancer, heart disease, cerebral hemorrhage and pneumonia), along with fatal accidents, accounted for two-thirds of the Negro death rate. Compared to white mortality rates, Negro death rates from tuberculosis were particularly high. In New York City in 1931, five times as many Negroes died from this disease as whites; while in Pittsburgh in 1933, tuberculosis was responsible for 17.7 per cent of all Negro deaths, as against 4.4 per cent of all white deaths. Similarly, the Negro mortality rate from pneumonia far exceeded the white rate. According to a study made in Pittsburgh in 1933, pneumonia accounted for 17.5 per cent of the total number of Negro deaths, compared to 9.0 per cent of white deaths. Negro infant mortality rates were disproportionately high. In 1929–1931, in New York City's borough of Manhattan, where Harlem is located, the death rate per 1,000 live births was 98 for Negroes and 67 for whites. In 1940, a United States Government report, based on official statistics for 1936–1938, came to the conclusion that mortality rates for Negro mothers as well as for Negro babies were "far higher than those for the United States as a whole."

These disturbing figures, however, do not

DR. W. E. B. DU BOIS

tell the whole story since the racial groups compared were not at all similar. As Dr. Du Bois so aptly pointed out in *The Crisis* of October, 1927, there was, on the one hand, "a great mass of white people, aided by large immigration in the past and considerable in the present, with the advantage of hospital service, trained physicians, sanitary homes and selected areas for the richer classes" and, on the other hand, a Negro population, only a few generations removed from slavery, under severe economic pressure and great mental and physical stress due to prejudice and migration. In view of the differences in the economic and social level of the racial groups involved, Dr. Du Bois suggested that it would be better to compare each group with its own health status in the past to obtain a truer picture of the situation. Such a comparison, he wrote, "shows that the Negro death rate has been reduced 50 per cent in the last forty years."

The observations of Dr. Du Bois were in agreement with those expressed by Dr. Louis Dublin, statistician of the Metropolitan Life Insurance Company. Concerning the improvement in the health status of the Negro people, Dr. Dublin wrote:

> The pessimism which prevailed thirty and more years ago with regard to his [the Negro's] future is now no longer even remotely justified. The doleful prophecies of those who saw the race problem solved through his extinction have been absolutely discredited by recent events. A race which lives in many areas under what are still primitive conditions of sanitation is today enjoying an expectation of life of about forty-six years which is equal to that of white Americans only thirty years ago. In comparison with a death rate of 35 to 40 per 1,000 in Reconstruction days, the Negro mortality is now only 17 per 1,000—a death rate about the same as the rate for a number of European countries before the World War.

Yet, despite the progress made, Negro mortality and morbidity rates continued to be high. In 1915, Booker T. Washington, in inaugurating Negro Health Week, estimated that 45 per cent of Negro deaths could be prevented and that 450,000 Negroes were seriously ill at all times. He put the cost of this illness at $75,000,000 a year and the cost of illness and death at $100,000,000 annually. Identical figures as to costs were given about a decade and a half later in a report prepared by the Interracial Committee of Montclair, New Jersey. The report, the result of a survey under the direction of Dr. John A. Kenney, presented additional information to the effect that Negroes spent a billion dollars annually on medicines, mostly patent drugs.

Socio-economic patterns played a significant role in undermining Negro American health. "Our death rate," wrote Dr. Du Bois in *The Crisis* of February, 1933, "is without the slightest doubt a death rate due to poverty and discrimination." Continuing, he observed: "As a problem of poverty, our death rate can ultimately be brought down to normal size only as our income is increased." But even with an increased income, the problem of Negro health, he pointed out, would not be settled, for there still remained "race discrimination." On this point, he noted:

> Even for those of us who are able to pay, hospital doors are today half-closed in our faces; parks, swimming pools and recreation centers often will not admit us; projects for improved housing seldom include us; and available food supply, particularly in cities, is vitiated by the custom of dumping the worst food at the highest prices in Negro districts . . . .

The great mass of Negro Americans, however, did not fall into the category of those who were able to pay. On the contrary, as sharecroppers, unskilled laborers and domestic servants, they received incomes so low that they were barely able to subsist. Like their impoverished white counterparts, they lived in poverty throughout the golden twenties as well as during the depression of the thirties. Their poverty, however, was unique in the world of American poverty, for, in addition to economic oppression, they suffered the burden of racial discrimination.

In the America of the period between the two world wars, Negro poverty was as appalling as it was all-pervading. In the rural areas of the economically backward South, it was rooted in a tenant-cropper system which emerged during and after Reconstruction as a substitute for the old order of slave labor. Semi-feudal in character, the tenant-cropper system provided for the payment of a fixed share of the crop to the plantation owner for the use of the land and additional charges for food, seed, fertilizer and "supervisory" services. Negro share-tenants and sharecroppers were fortunate if, after a year's labor, they were able to break even. More often than not, they found themselves in never-ending debt. Submarginal producers, they barely managed to keep alive, despite the fact

that their black backs and black hands produced a sizeable share of the wealth of the South.

Similarly, in the urban areas located in the old Confederacy, the economic plight of the Negro worker was tragic and desperate. With the exception of a small number of middle-class businessmen and professionals, the vast majority of Negro city dwellers were unskilled workers and household servants. Poorly paid and frequently unemployed, they had much less than what was needed to provide themselves and their families with the bare necessities of life.

To escape from chronic deprivation and constant intimidation, many of the more venturesome Negroes migrated to the North. During World War I, Northern industry boomed as first the Allies, and then the United States, demanded food, steel, copper and war materiel. With labor scarce, businessmen sent agents to the South to recruit Negroes as they had recruited Irish, Italians, Poles and Czechs in the nineteenth century. Jobs were promised and railroad tickets offered. Almost a half-million Negroes, responding to the siren call of economic security and freedom, left the eleven states of the old Confederacy from 1910 to 1920. Nearly 800,000 more moved away during the twenties and were followed by almost another 400,000 during the thirties.

Thus, in the early twentieth century, the North served the South in much the same way as the West had served the East in the nineteenth, namely, as a "safety valve" for discontent. The influx of nearly 1,700,000 Negroes from 1910 to 1940 served to double the Negro population of the North, increasing it from 1,900,000 in 1910 to under 4,000,000 in 1940. By contrast, the colored population within the old Confederacy rose 12 per cent, reaching more than 8,000,000 in 1940.

Negro workers, who constituted the bulk of the colored population in the North, found themselves living in poverty or very close to it. Northern industry either used them as strikebreakers or gave them jobs so exhausting and poorly paid that even the foreign-born would not take them. It was only through great perseverance and endurance that Negroes were able to make their way into and remain part of Northern industry. Despite discriminatory practices by management groups and many old-line craft unions, they were moving forward and by 1930 constituted 7.3 per cent of all workers in manufacturing and mechanical industry. Paid approximately half as much as white workers, they were also the first to lose their jobs. They were especially hard hit during the depression years. Even in 1940, when relatively good times returned, largely as a result of the outbreak of another war in Europe, there were still more than one million Negroes unemployed.

Impoverishment and deprivation were formidable barriers to good health. In the rural areas of the South, Negro share-tenants and croppers were housed in overcrowded, unventilated and unsanitary shacks. Poorly fed and medically neglected, they were susceptible to every kind of illness.

The same situation existed also in the black communities of Southern cities, where expendable Negro laborers and menials lived in ghettos with unpaved, sand-rutted streets and in homes without proper ventilation or sanitation. In an article in *The Crisis* of January, 1942, on "Negro Health in Jacksonville [Florida]," Dr. C. E. Frederick Duncan, medical director of Brewster Hospital, asked whether in such Gehennas it was "to be wondered at that Negroes [were] more exposed to contagious and infectious diseases than non-Negro groups."

In the North, too, where neighborhood segregation prevailed, the Negro poor were consigned to dilapidated tenements, decrepit houses, basements, cellars and even converted stables. Fleeced by slum landlords and get-rich-quick real estate operators, they lived in quarters where light and ventilation were non-existent and toilet facilities lacking, with overcrowding a serious problem. Regarding tuberculosis, a common disease in the Negro ghetto because of bad housing conditions and inadequate nutrition, a writer observed in *The Crisis* of April, 1939:

> It is shocking to note that a race which has a much higher percentage of the disease is held to an economic level favoring its incidence, and that this people is largely denied the benefit of all modern methods that science has given humanity with which to fight it.

Concentrated in the worst slums and faced by festering poverty, low-income Negroes who needed the most medical care received the least. In many rural and urban areas of the South, it was common for poverty-stricken Negroes to die without any kind of medical care. According to an article by Dr. Midian O. Bousfield in the *Bulletin of the History of Medicine,* January, 1945, there were "southern states where at least twenty per cent of the Negro population die without a doctor during their last illness." In the deep South, where the poll tax prevailed and the disenfranchisement of the Negro was an accomplished fact, the amount of money spent for the medical care of indigents, particularly of blacks, was negligible. There were few state and city clinics where the Negro poor could go for medical help. Only in the most extreme cases were Negroes admitted to "white" hospitals and then only to the colored wards, from which they were discharged as speedily as possible.

In the Northern cities, where Negroes had the right to vote, politicians were more circumspect than in the South, and as a result, health facilities were more available to colored indigents. But so great was the demand for such facilities that they proved totally inadequate to meet even minimum health needs. A case in point was Harlem Hospital in the heart of New York City's Black Belt. Although Harlem Hospital theoretically served only its own neighborhood, it actually admitted patients from other parts of the city. Consequently, it was constantly overcrowded and, because of an austere city budget, woefully understaffed.

The demands made on Harlem's outpatient clinic were staggering. From 1920 to 1932, dispensary visits increased by more than 300 per cent, from roughly 80,000 to 250,000. The number of visits in 1932 nearly doubled in comparison to 1927. So overcrowded were its facilities that the syphilis clinic was forced to exclude new patients and limit old ones to no more than 300 per session. Similarly, the bed capacity of Harlem Hospital was inadequate to meet even the barest needs of the neighborhood. In 1937, Harlem had a Negro population of slightly more than two hundred thousand. Despite increases in bed capacity, Harlem Hospital had only 665 beds. An editorial in *The Crisis* of April, 1937, underscored the inadequacy of the hospital's facilities by citing the fact that St. Louis, with a colored population of ninety thousand, had a new municipal hospital for Negroes with a bed capacity of 685.

Similarly, public health services in impoverished Negro communities were far from adequate. Under the impact of the progressive movement of the early twentieth century and the New Deal of the 1930's, the first hesitant steps were taken by city, state and Federal governments to launch a public health program based on the recognition that poverty and slum conditions brought with them a high sickness and death rate. To lower the incidence of tuberculosis, syphilis, childhood diseases and complications of childbirth, public health doctors

and nurses were sent into the slum areas of Southern states and Northern cities. Included in the task force was a small band of Negro professional personnel. Their number increased slowly but steadily, particularly after 1930, when city health departments in New York, Louisville, Detroit, Baltimore, Boston, Philadelphia, Chicago and Birmingham began to make a token show of racial equality by appointing some Negro physicians to their staffs. Similarly, public health centers were established in colored communities and staffed with Negro doctors and directors.

New York, Baltimore, Louisville, Birmingham and Philadelphia got money for this from the Rosenwald Fund; its fifteen-year program in Negro health was brought to a close in 1942 after the expenditure of more than $1,600,000. In addition to enabling the establishment of health centers, the money was used for the development of Negro hospitals and for the control of syphilis, tuberculosis and maternal and infant mortality.

The Public Health Nursing Service was particularly important in providing the Negro poor with medical care not otherwise available. In 1930, there were an estimated 4,986 public health nurses in the country. Of these, 471 were colored. Despite the agency's expansion during the New Deal, it found itself too limited in personnel and money to meet the staggering health needs of low-income groups. Nevertheless, its mere presence showed what valuable work could be done in reducing the high incidence of death and illness among underprivileged Negroes.

Public health nurses, working both in the backward rural areas of the South and in the urban slums of the North, instructed expectant mothers in prenatal care, immunized children against contagious diseases and paid special attention to undernourished youngsters. They conducted clinics for diseased children, tubercular patients, sufferers from venereal diseases and patients complaining of eye, ear, nose and throat disorders. They also performed corrective work of an orthopedic nature. During the early 1940's, they were aided in at least one aspect of their work by the nurse-midwife. The impossibility of reaching Negro mothers in the South brought about the official recognition of this new cog in the public health machinery. By the close of World War II, there were three schools for Negro nurse-midwives—in New York, Kentucky and Alabama.

Racially discriminatory treatment also tended to lower the health standard of Negro Americans between the close of World War I and World War II. By restricting the availability of medical manpower and hospital facilities, Jim Crow practices made it more difficult for Negroes to achieve better health. In the overtly segregated areas of the South and the more subtly segregated areas of the North, there were few physicians in relation to the number of Negroes needing medical care. Almost exclusively, these physicians were Negroes.

Since racial discrimination in medicine tended to reduce their number and limit their professional development, the shortage of well-trained physicians in most colored communities was critical. For example, in 1942, there were 3,810 Negro physicians in America—one to every 3,377 Negroes. By states, the ratio ranged from one to 1,002 in Missouri to one to 18,527 in Mississippi. With 55 per cent of the total number of Negro doctors practicing in the South and 45 per cent in the North, there was one colored physician to 4,150 Southern Negroes and one to every 2,500 Northern blacks. Minimal health standards, it was believed, required the ratio to be one physician to every 1,500 persons. The national average in 1942 was one to every 750 persons.

Similarly, the color line in medicine re-stricted the availability of hospital facilities. With the exception of some tax-supported hospitals and a few biracial, voluntary institutions, Negro patients, even those able to pay, were forced to look to their own hospitals for treatment. According to a 1930 survey, there were relatively few hospitals for Negroes in the country. In that year, they numbered 225 out of a total of 7,259. All of them combined furnished one bed for every 1,914 colored Americans. Fourteen years later, general statistical data indicated a decrease in the number of hospitals for Negroes but a relative increase in the ratio of beds available to the colored population.

In 1944, according to a commission that studied hospital care, there were 124 hospitals in the country which served Negro patients exclusively. In twenty-three states and the District of Columbia, they had twenty thousand beds. With roughly 13,700,000 Negroes in the U.S., this meant one bed to each 685 of the colored population. Of the 124 hospitals for Negroes, 112 were operated by non-governmental bodies and the remaining 12, by Federal, state or municipal governments. Only 23 of the hospitals for Negroes were fully approved by the American College of Surgeons, and 3 others were officially sanctioned on a provisional basis. Only 9 were approved for the training of interns by the AMA Council on Medical Education and Hospitals.

The same commission on hospital care, in its published report of 1947, summarized the effects of racial discrimination on medical attention in the following manner:

> In general, there is not now available to them [Negroes] the same quality or quantity of medical and hospital care as there is for the white population. This is due, in part, to inadequate facilities, to the inferior quality of those which are available, and to the inadequate number and quality of Negro physicians and nurses.

This was true despite the fact that, in the

committee's words, "[Negro] health needs are greater than those of the white population."

WORLD WAR II

Everywhere the Negro turned, he faced Jim Crow. Even when he wanted to enlist in the service of his country, he had to "fight for the right to fight." During the Second World War, the National Medical Association and the National Association of Colored Graduate Nurses did everything in their power to make the government aware of the desirability of fully mobilizing Negro doctors and nurses in the struggle against the Axis powers.

When the United States declared war on Germany, Italy and Japan in December, 1941, the National Medical Association set up a committee to collect data on available Negro medical personnel. Acting also as a liaison group, the committee held several meetings with the Secretaries of the Army and the Navy and the Surgeon General of the Army. Officially recognized as the spokesman for the Negro medical profession, the committee was finally made a subcommittee of the Procurement and Assignment Service. On February 17, 1943, it was agreed that five hundred Negro physicians should be incorporated into the armed forces. Before the end of the war, about six hundred Negro doctors were serving. This constituted approximately 16 per cent of the total number of Negro practitioners in the country.

The National Association of Colored Graduate Nurses also worked and fought for the incorporation of Negro nursing personnel into the armed forces. Remembering that only eighteen colored nurses had been permitted to enlist in World War I, and this only after the signing of the armistice, the association immediately launched a drive for the recruitment of nurses regard-less of race. So successful was the campaign that, shortly after the entrance of the United States into the war, the Army agreed to grant commissions to a group of Negro nurses trained in the public health service and in small and large hospitals. About a year after Pearl Harbor, there were nearly two hundred colored nurses in the Army; by the close of the war, there were approximately five hundred. The Navy permitted the enlistment of only four Negro nurses during the war. That more of the country's nine thousand colored nursing personnel would have joined the Army and Navy had they been given the opportunity was the gist of an editorial in *The Crisis* of February, 1945, entitled "No Negro Nurses Wanted."

Many colored nurses enlisted during the war with the idea of being assigned to overseas duty. As Lieutenant Chrystalee Maxwell, staff nurse at the Los Angeles General Hospital, put it: "When I signed up in Los Angeles, I asked for overseas duty. I think that if our boys can go to the ends of the earth to fight, we should go along and do what we can to make it easier for them. The sooner they send me the better I will feel." The National Association of Colored Graduate Nurses backed the right of Lieutenant Maxwell and others for overseas service. In response to the association's insistent demand that Negro nurses be assigned to duty wherever needed, Colonel Florence A. Blanchfield, superintendent of the Army Nurse Corps, wrote on January 3, 1944: "Colored nurses have a definite contribution to make to the nursing services of the Army, and careful consideration is now being given to determine how their services may be fully realized."

Despite reassuring statements, the armed forces adopted an overall Jim Crow policy in respect to medical personnel. There was considerable controversy in Negro medical circles when army plans called for

Despite enlistment difficulties, many Negro nurses served their country during the Second World War.

activation of the 93rd all-colored Division at Fort Huachuca in southern Arizona and the establishment there of a hospital. Many Negro physicians expressed misgivings concerning the Jim Crow orientation of these plans. However, feelings were sublimated in view of the urgency of the situation. Working overtime, Negro medical officers soon organized a large and well-equipped hospital in the Arizona desert, which eventually had one thousand beds.

Its commander, Lieutenant-Colonel Midian O. Bousfield, a Negro physician from Chicago, was assisted by a hospital staff of ten majors, ten captains and fifteen to twenty lieutenants. Early in July, 1942, ten Negro nurses joined another nurse who was already there to form the nucleus of a nursing staff which within six months grew to approximately one hundred. Directed by Lieutenant Susan E. Freeman, previously head nurse at Freedmen's Hospital, Washington, D.C., the Negro nurses soon helped make the hospital as

LT. COLONEL MIDIAN O. BOUSFIELD

fine a one "as Uncle Sam has in his entire Army." Associated with it was a medical officers replacement pool and also two physiotherapy training schools, one for WAC's and one for civilians. Two hospitals of 150 beds each were organized for overseas duty. During the war, Negro physicians and nurses were also assigned to mixed hospital staffs, such as those at Fort Bragg, North Carolina, and Camp Livingston, Louisiana.

Under the impact of the intense global struggle of war, the question of the integration of the Negro in medicine commanded greater attention. In 1944, a special committee of the Medical Society of the County of New York was appointed with Dr. Peter M. Murray as chairman. The committee recommended that the society go on record in favor of the admission of more Negro medical students to schools in New York County; the integration of qualified Negro physicians as interns, residents and members of hospital staffs in the city; and the elimination of racial considerations for election into the American College of Surgeons. Supported by members of the Physicians' Forum, a nationwide white professional organization, the recommendations were approved at a meeting of the society in April, 1944.

On December 8 and 9, 1944, the Physicians' Forum sponsored a national conference in Washington, D.C., on problems of medical care. Among the subjects discussed were medical treatment for war veterans of minority groups and the integration of Negro physicians in schools and hospitals. A panel session devoted exclusively to problems confronting veterans urged that medical care be made accessible to all members of minority groups on an equal basis. At a luncheon meeting presided over by Dr. Ernst P. Boas, chairman of the Physicians' Forum, Dr. Paul B. Cornely, head of Howard University's department of bacteriology, preventive medicine and public health, pointed out the need for utilizing Negro physicians in the Veterans Administration and integrating them with other doctors. At the same session, Professor Marion Hathway, of the public health department of the University of Pittsburgh, emphasized the importance of a wide base for the selection of medical personnel, saying:

> There must be some provision for the medical education of promising young people particularly of the large Negro minority as well as youth in lower income brackets that cannot afford this education.

Encouraged by the growing support of progressive-minded white physicians, Negroes in medicine and health hopefully looked to the future as World War II came to an end.

CHAPTER EIGHT

Moving Forward

We aver that this part of the Constitution of the American Medical Association under which the members of a county society in the South can, through color prejudice, prevent the membership of Negroes (regardless of their qualifications) in the American Medical Association, should be changed as being unworthy of that great organization.

"An Appeal to the A. M. A. in Behalf of Negro Physicians in the South," Editorial, *Journal of the National Medical Association*, September 1947.

Steadily and purposefully the national nursing organizations have faced the fact that health knows no man-made barriers, does not recognize racial, religious or ethnic origins . . .. The A.N.A. congratulates the N.A.C.G.N. on its outstanding achievements in behalf of Negro nurses in this country.

Tribute to the National Association of Colored Graduate Nurses by the American Nurses Association, January 1951.

The lack of adequate hospital facilities is perhaps the greatest single deterrent to the acquisition of adequate medical care by the Negro. . . . It operates in devious ways to rob the patient of adequate diagnosis and treatment and to stifle the ambition and scientific advance of the physician.

Dr. John E. Moseley, May 1949.

THE participation of 1,174,000 Negro Americans in World War II, the defeat of the Axis powers, the rise of the submerged colored peoples of Asia and Africa, social revolutions from Prague to Peking, the advent of the Fair Deal—all combined to create a climate of opinion conducive to the emergence of a strong civil rights movement. Beginning during the years immediately following the Second World War, the civil rights movement had the support of an ever growing number of Negroes and whites, drawn from every walk of life, who optimistically anticipated the dawn of a new era of peace, prosperity and brotherhood. The fight for racial equality gained momentum when the dominant Democratic Party, under the leadership of President Truman, seeking the Negro vote particularly in the big cities of the North, was forced by the pressure of progressive forces to incorporate the principle of non-discrimination into major pieces of legislation. The initial phase of the battle culminated in the landmark decision of the Supreme Court on school desegregation in May, 1954.

The second phase of the civil rights movement was ushered in when a colored woman, Rosa Parks, in December, 1955, refused to give up her seat on a bus to a white man in Montgomery, Alabama. A Negro boycott of the city buses followed, bringing in its wake the desegregation of the municipal transportation system. This demonstration of Negro militancy and solidarity was matched by the successful struggle of the Negroes of Little Rock, Arkansas, to desegregate the city's public schools in accordance with the Supreme Court's decision. As a result of the increasing Negro agitation, new civil rights organizations emerged. Adopting the tactic of non-violent civil disobedience, they dramatized the plight of the Negro people in such a way as to arrest national attention. The battle for racial equality found added impetus in international events of major significance. The Dark Continent moved into the mainstream of history as one African country after another threw off the yoke of colonialism, became independent and gained membership in the United Nations. There, colored men spoke out very sharply against apartheid in South Africa and Jim Crow in the United States. Negro Americans were inspired with a new sense of pride and purpose. The struggle for racial equality and human dignity was quickened as a new generation of militants appeared in the early sixties to demand "Freedom Now!"

The civil rights movement of the decade and a half prior to 1960 was accompanied by tactical victories in almost every aspect of American Negro life. Slowly but steadily, the walls of fortress discrimination were breached, and the stage was set for "Operation Clean-Up." Throughout the post-World War II years, Negro doctors, nurses and patients, aided by progressive white elements, inched ahead as the opposition was forced to give way in professional bodies, training schools and hospitals.

PROFESSIONAL ASSOCIATIONS

In 1945, when the Second World War ended, the American Medical Association was almost a century old. In its organizational structure, the AMA was a federation of county and state medical societies. Membership in the parent body as well as in state units was open only to members of local affiliates. For almost seventy-five years, representations had been made to the national organization concerning the exclusion of Negro physicians from county and state societies in the South and, hence, from the AMA itself. However, all such representations had been brushed aside by the parent association on the ground that its constitution and organization prohibited it from intervening.

In the aftermath of World War II and with the rise of a broader, more militant civil rights movement, Negro and white physicians returned to the attack and forced the national organization to face the issue. In an editorial entitled "An Appeal to the A.M.A. in Behalf of Negro Physicians in the South," the *Journal of the National Medical Association* in September, 1947, put the issue as follows:

> We aver that this part of the Constitution of the American Medical Association under which the members of a county society in the South can, through color prejudice, prevent the membership of Negroes (regardless of their qualifications) in the American Medical Association, should be changed as being unworthy of that great organization. We herewith appeal to that honorable body to take such action. Truth, right, reason and fair play demand that it *shall* be done.

The journal appealed to its readers to make this the paramount issue of the day. It also supported the position taken by Dr. Charles R. Drew, world-famous Negro medical scientist who, in an exchange of letters with the editor of the AMA *Journal,* urged that body to start the second century of its life by ridding itself of racial prejudice.

White doctors, too, took up the fight for the admission of Negro physicians to the AMA. On January 26, 1948, the New York County Medical Society adopted a resolution backed by the Physicians' Forum requesting the national organization to change its constitution in such a way as to prohibit a constituent body from excluding any qualified physician because of race. Because it was believed that the resolution had little chance of being adopted by the AMA in national convention, a committee was appointed to confer with Negro doctors on the matter. When Dr. Peter M. Murray informed the committee that Negro physicians favored the resolution and would much rather sacrifice any advantages that might accrue from membership in the association than give up principle, the resolution was adopted by the county body and later by the New York State Medical Society.

The New York County Medical Society's resolution was duly submitted to the 1948 AMA convention in Chicago. It provided for the following constitutional amendment: "No constituent association [should] exclude from membership any physician for other than professional or ethical reasons." The amendment was accompanied by a resolution which stated that the "exclusion of physicians on the basis of race constitutes an affront to our colleagues, a degradation of the honored traditions of our profession and a violation of our American democratic ideal."

To defeat the proposed resolution, the segregationist forces employed the same parliamentary tactics in Chicago as their predecessors had at the Washington convention almost eighty years earlier. Floor debate on the New York resolution was avoided by referring the matter to a committee which submitted the following counterproposal: ". . . that the county medical society is the sole judge of whom it shall elect to membership, provided the applicant meets the medical requirements for membership and is so recommended." A repetition of the "home rule" stand of 1870, the Southern-inspired resolution was adopted as a substitute for the one from New York. To doctors of both races who were working for better understanding in medicine, the resolution represented a slap in the face. In an editorial entitled "Racism Rules A.M.A. Policies," the *Journal of the National Medical Association,* January, 1949, made the following comment:

> The reactionary forces within the American Medical Association have won a temporary victory. . . . Progress cannot be forever stayed and some day right will prevail. . . . Our unremitting efforts will be joined with those of other fair-minded people until the American Medical Association redeems itself in the eyes of a critical world.

The fight for racial equality continued as fair-minded white physicians in increasing numbers sided with their Negro colleagues. Liberal sentiment became evident even in some of the association's constituent bodies in the South. In December, 1948, the Baltimore County Medical Society voted unanimously to accept Negroes into membership. In 1949, a Negro physician was admitted to the county and state medical associations in Oklahoma. In the same year, the Missouri State Medical Association agreed to delete the word "white" from its membership section, and soon after the St. Louis Medical Society voted to take in its first Negro members. The Delaware Medical Society followed suit, as did the Florida State Medical Association in April, 1950.

These breakthroughs presaged action at the June, 1950, meeting of the American Medical Association in San Francisco. And action there was in the form of a resolution which for the first time officially recognized the existence of racial discrimination within the organization. The AMA's House of Delegates, after noting "that certain constituent and component societies of the American Medical Association have had or now have restrictive provisions as to qualifications for membership based on race and that this question is of deep concern to many interested parties," urged such bodies to "study this question in the light of prevailing conditions with a view to taking such steps as they may elect to eliminate such restrictive provisions."

Although this action was a step forward, it fell far short of the proposals made two years before by the New York County Medical Society. Consequently, the exponents of a more militant policy renewed the attack. However, they did not have enough support to overcome their segregationist opponents. In June, 1952, the AMA at its Chicago convention refused to go beyond a reiteration of its 1950 resolution.

In the meantime, the ferment within the association was producing some positive results. The 1950 edition of the *American Medical Directory,* published by the AMA, dropped the designation "colored" after the names of Negro doctors. A number of county medical bodies began to extend to Negro physicians and surgeons a measure of recognition long overdue. In 1949, the New York State Medical Society elected Dr. Peter M. Murray as one of its representatives to the national house of delegates, the first Negro to be chosen as a member of that policy-making body. From 1952 to 1960, Negro physicians were elected to the presidency of at least six county medical societies, including two large local units, New York County and Queens County, headed by Dr. Murray and Dr. John E. Lowry respectively.

During the fifties, agitation for racial equality within the AMA forced even some county and state affiliates in the South

to move forward. In 1951, Negroes were admitted to the Medical Society of Arlington County, Virginia. Similar action was taken by the Medical Society of the District of Columbia. One of the first cracks in the wall of the deep South came in November, 1952, when the Bibb County, Georgia, Medical Society offered full membership to Negro physicians. In 1953, the Pulaski County Medical Society, Arkansas, voted to accept Negro members, while the Alabama Medical Association adopted without a dissenting vote a report stating that all its county affiliated bodies could admit Negro physicians to membership.

The next year, the North Carolina and Virginia state medical societies voted to remove racially restrictive membership bars. Dr. Peter M. Murray, writing in the *New York State Journal of Medicine* on October 15, 1955, summarized the situation in the South as follows: "Negro physicians are now admitted to membership in some county societies in every state with the exception of two." The two states were Mississippi and Louisiana. When in May, 1956, the Clarkdale and Six Counties Medical Society accepted the first Negro physician for membership in Mississippi, Louisiana was the only Southern state of the seventeen still without any Negro members.

Despite these successes, most county medical societies in the South continued to exclude Negro physicians from membership. As the 1950's drew to a close, it became increasingly clear to desegregationist forces in the American Medical Association that more than verbal condemnation was needed to eliminate racially restrictive membership bars in Southern constituent societies. More and more did these elements contend that the 1950 and 1952 resolutions had to have "teeth" in them if antibias goals were to be achieved in the old Confederacy.

During the post-World War II period, doctors of both races also fought for an open-door policy for admission to specialty boards. Particularly notable was the fight to end racial discrimination in the American College of Surgeons. In 1945, the organization had only one Negro member, Dr. Louis T. Wright, nationally known surgeon at Harlem Hospital. At the time of Dr. Wright's election in 1934, it was expected that equally prominent Negro surgeons would be admitted to fellowship. But they were not, because Southern members and their Northern allies closed ranks. So influential was this combination in the organization's affairs that even application blanks were denied to colored physicians.

In April, 1945, Dr. George D. Thorne, a Negro member of the surgical staffs of Sydenham and Lincoln Hospitals in New York City, requested an application for membership in the American College of Surgeons. His request was turned down in a letter advising him that "fellowship in the college is not being conferred on members of the Negro race at the present time." The Thorne case became a matter of public concern. On May 28, 1945, Philip D. Schupler, a member of the New York State Assembly, demanded an investigation by Governor Dewey into the Jim Crow ruling of the American College of Surgeons barring Negroes from membership. Calling the Thorne case "an unusually disgraceful specimen of discrimination," Assemblyman Schupler declared that, if the state's Ives-Quinn Anti-Discrimination Law could not be invoked, then Governor Dewey should initiate an investigation into the matter and have legislation enacted to cope with the situation. State Senator Lazarus Joseph joined Assemblyman Schupler in protesting the action taken by the American College of Surgeons. Characterizing it as an affront to those who were fighting "all over the world to end discrimination," he urged

that "every man, regardless of race, creed, color or social background, . . . receive equal opportunity to enter a medical school, the American College of Surgeons, or any other organization."

Negro and white physicians were equally critical of the stand taken by the American College of Surgeons. In the May 20, 1945, issue of *New York Medicine,* official organ of the New York County Medical Society, an editorial commenting on the board's action denounced the ban on Dr. Thorne as "indefensible discrimination." Dr. Wright, sole Negro member of the organization, was asked by the New York newspaper *PM* what he thought of the Thorne case. On May 28, 1945, the daily quoted him as saying that the case "cannot be justified," that "it is a wrong thing." The previous year Dr. Wright had publicly protested the Negro ban by the American College of Surgeons. The protest, in the form of an article in the Pittsburgh *Courier,* had been sent to the organization's president.

As a result of mounting pressure, the segregationist forces in the American College of Surgeons began to give way. Dr. F. D. Stubbs of Philadelphia, a distinguished Negro surgeon, was elected to membership. Dr. John E. Perry, in his autobiography, *Forty Cords of Wood,* published in 1947, tells the rest of the story as follows:

> Quite recently a statement was published and alleged to have emanated from officials of the organization to the effect that they considered it un-American to withhold from any applicant the right of membership on account of race, creed, or color and four members of African descent were admitted. They were Peter Marshall Murray of New York, U[lysses] G. Dailey, Roscoe C. Giles and Carl G. Roberts of Chicago.

With the election of these four physicians, the doors of the American College of Surgeons swung open. Negro membership in the organization rose from six to more than a hundred by the close of the 1950's. The trend in most other national specialty

DR. F. D. STUBBS

boards was the same as racial bars for admission gradually gave way. In 1947, there were 93 board-certified Negro specialists in the country; in 1952, 190; and in the summer of 1958, about 350.

While efforts were being made to desegregate medical societies and specialty boards, integration was taking place in the nursing profession. In 1946, the American Nurses Association acted favorably on a resolution which called for admission to the national organization of all qualified nurses regardless of race, creed or national origin. As in the American Medical Association, so in the American Nurses Association, membership in the parent organization was dependent on membership in constituent bodies. Since Negro nurses encountered color bars for admission into Southern affiliates, the resolution provided that all nurses could join the national organization as individuals within a two-year period. In 1948, an intergroup relations program was set up to con-

centrate on bars to membership and other problems of Negro nurses.

The following year the American Nurses Association established a special committee to study the functions of the National Association of Colored Graduate Nurses as they related to the total integrationist program of the organization. The committee included members of the Negro body who were also members of the American Nurses Association. After frank and full discussion of the project, the proposals made by the ANA's special committee were accepted by the NACGN at its 1949 Louisville convention. In January, 1950, the NACGN's board of directors unanimously voted to recommend dissolution. At a special meeting of the membership held at St. Mark's Methodist Church in New York City, where the organization was founded in 1908, the recommendation was unanimously accepted.

On January 26, 1951, after forty-three years of activity, the National Association of Colored Graduate Nurses, serving about eleven thousand professional nurses and students, announced its dissolution. The following tribute was paid to it by the American Nurses Association:

> Steadily and purposefully the national nursing organizations have faced the fact that health knows no man-made barriers, does not recognize racial, religious or ethnic origins. . . . The A.N.A. congratulates the N.A.C.G.N. on its outstanding achievements in behalf of Negro nurses in this country.

From 1951 to 1961, the American Nurses Association made steady progress toward integrationist goals in the nursing profession. According to a review article, "Integration in Professional Nursing," published in the January, 1962, issue of *The Crisis,* the association's platform, code of ethics and by-laws, as well as those of its constituent bodies, emphasized equal rights.

By the end of 1961, only one state and a few districts still denied Negro nurses membership in the national organization. Negro nurses were elected to and served on its national board of directors and the boards of some state bodies. The association continued to give the Mary Mahoney Award to that individual who contributed the most to interracial relations in nursing. In 1960, the award was given to Mrs. Marie Mink, the first Negro nurse to become a member of the faculty of the University of Oklahoma. Policies were established by the association to create and maintain equal opportunities in employment. Through use of its official registries and guidance and placement services, Negro nurses were employed in hospitals, public health agencies, school services and the armed forces and as faculty members in colleges and universities.

Thus, the nursing profession, with its more than four hundred thousand trained personnel, integrated—the first profession in the United States to take this crucial step. And what were the results? On the positive side, gains were registered in various fields. From 1951 to 1961, there was a significant increase in the number of Negro graduate nurses employed in positions above staff level. Among the first hospitals to employ them in such a capacity on an integrated basis were Bellevue and Beth Israel hospitals in New York City. Most of the 1,152 schools of nursing in the country at the close of 1961 were open to Negro applicants. During the ten years following 1951, Negro nurses were on the faculty of many predominantly white institutions of higher learning and served also on several state boards of nursing.

All of these very important achievements were encouraging; but, when the first decade of integration came to a close in 1961, it was evident that much remained to be done. There were still problems of salary differentials based on race, inequities in job opportunities and advancement, segregated nurs-

ing schools, and often only token or no representation of Negro nurses in policy-making areas. In short, as an editorial in the September, 1961, issue of *Nursing Outlook* put it, ". . . much more still has to be done to accomplish all of the goals of N.A.C.G.N. . . . But if the next decade is as fruitful as the first, the future for full integration in nursing looks very bright indeed."

MEDICAL COLLEGES AND NURSING SCHOOLS

The post-World War II civil rights movement was accompanied by a campaign to establish the principle of equal rights in the education and training of Negro doctors and nurses. Particular emphasis was placed on cracking the tough segregationist opposition in the South.

At the beginning of the period, one-third of all the medical colleges in the country—twenty-six out of seventy-eight approved medical schools—were in Southern and border states. All twenty-six of these institutions were closed to Negro students. To eliminate racially discriminatory admission policies, the National Association for the Advancement of Colored People instituted a series of legal proceedings which resulted in a number of favorable Supreme Court decisions. Following these decisions, the University of Arkansas permitted the registration in 1948 of Edith Mae Irby, the first Negro admitted to a Southern all-white medical school. At the time, the only other medical college in the South where Negroes might enroll was Meharry. In the year 1947–48, Meharry had 234 students. If to these the one Negro student at the University of Arkansas was added, 235 Negro medical students were enrolled in thirteen Southern states, out of a total medical enrollment of 5,533. In 1947–48, of 1,268 graduates from Southern medical schools, only fifty-eight were Negroes; all

DR. JOSEPH L. JOHNSON

were graduates of Meharry. This represented about 4.5 per cent of all medical school graduates in the South, although about 25 per cent of the region's total population was Negro. On the basis of these figures, Dr. Joseph L. Johnson, dean of the Howard Medical School, concluded: "All things being equal and no racial discrimination existing, we might have expected 317 of the 1,268 doctors to be Negroes, instead of only 58." He urged that the medical schools of the South and the border states, including those of the District of Columbia, abandon racial restrictions in the admission of students.

Bowing to the Supreme Court's decisions, St. Louis University and the University of Texas decided in 1949 to follow the lead of the University of Arkansas by admitting Negro medical students. To quicken the pace of admissions, the National Medical Association in November, 1949, petitioned the Association of American Medical Colleges to go on record opposing racial bars in medical schools and unequal opportunities in pre-professional education. The Association of American Medical Colleges replied to the petition by saying it lacked jurisdiction in the matter.

Gradually, during the 1950's the doors of medical schools hitherto closed in the Southern and border states opened. In 1951, five medical colleges (Washington University, St. Louis; University of Louisville; Medical College of Virginia; University of Maryland; and the University of North Carolina) joined the other three in admitting Negro students. By 1960, six more were added to the ranks. Thus, within a decade or so, more than half of all Southern medical schools, fourteen out of twenty-six, were admitting Negro students, albeit on a token basis.

Partly as a result of these victories, the number and percentage of Negroes enrolled in predominantly white medical schools increased steadily during the post-World War II period. In 1947–48, 93 Negroes were in twenty white medical colleges. In 1955–56, the number of Negroes rose to 236 and the number of schools to forty-eight while many more claimed a readiness to accept colored applicants. Meanwhile, the percentage of Negro students in white medical schools increased from 15.8 per cent in 1947–48 to 31.0 per cent in 1955–56.

As these figures indicate, the main burden for training Negro doctors still rested on Howard and Meharry. Of the 588 Negro medical students in 1947–48, 495, or 84.2 per cent, were enrolled in these schools. In 1955–56, Howard and Meharry had 525 students, or 69.0 per cent of the 761 Negroes enrolled in the country's medical colleges.

As the cost of a medical education spiraled during the inflationary years following the Second World War, Negro students, especially those whose families were in low-income brackets, needed financial assistance. In 1946, a group of physicians in Chicago founded Provident Medical Associates, Inc., an organization interested in the medical education of Negroes and the conditions under which Negroes in medicine practiced. The body grew in size and influence; by 1952, it changed its name to National Medical Fellowships, Incorporated. By 1959, the organization had awarded a total of $745,230 in grants to 246 individuals. These fellowships, as well as those granted by other organizations, provided needy Negroes with money for their medical education.

The period from 1945 to 1960 also saw Negro medical school graduates pushing ahead in the important area of postgraduate education. More internships and residencies were opened to them than at any time in the past as an ever growing number of predominantly white hospitals dropped their racial bars. In 1947, of the 119 graduates of Howard and Meharry, only 49 served internships in eight white hospitals. In 1956, of their 129 graduates, 77 had internships in forty-six white hospitals. Thus, in less than a decade, the number of predominantly white institutions which had Howard and Meharry graduates increased almost 500 per cent. Moreover, in 1956, three out of every five graduates of Howard and Meharry served their internships in white hospitals. Whereas in the early 1930's Negro medical school graduates might be unable to secure internships, in 1956 there were more such approved posts than there were medical graduates. The same favorable situation prevailed in respect to residencies. In 1956, the number of residencies available to Negro doctors was sufficient to take care of all of them; and as in the case of internships, most of the residencies were in predominantly white hospitals.

In the fifteen-year period prior to 1960, Negro nurses also made significant gains in the field of education and training. As a result of pressure by Negro nurses and cooperation by dominant integrationist elements in the American Nurses Association, progress was made in opening the country's schools of nursing to all regardless of color. Some indication of the advances made can be gathered from a study financed by the Fund of the Republic in the mid-1950's. Entitled *Integration, North and South,* the study gives a list, admittedly incomplete, of events in the desegregation field during the period from 1954 to 1956.

Under "Health Facilities," the following white hospital schools of nursing and their locations were listed with the notation that they were accepting Negro applicants for the first time: Deaconess, Fairbault, Minnesota; Lutheran and St. Alexis, Cleveland, Ohio; Lancaster-Fairfield, Lancaster, Ohio; Ohio Valley School of Nursing, Steubenville, Ohio; School of Nursing, Burlington, Vermont; St. Joseph's, Bellingham, Washington; Tacoma General, Tacoma, Washington; Madison General, Madison, Wisconsin; Stamford, Stamford, Connecticut. The study also noted that, in Indiana, 100 per cent of the state's schools of nursing admitted qualified students in April, 1955, as compared to 80 per cent only two years earlier.

The extent of the gains made by integrationist forces after ten years of activity in nursing education was indicated in an editorial appearing in the September, 1961, issue of *Nursing Outlook.* It claimed that, in 1951, there were four all-Negro schools of nursing in the North and twenty-nine in the South. "Today, because of the many integrated schools, this need is no longer as great and many of the all-Negro schools, North and South, have closed their doors." Discussing the extent of integration in nursing education, the editorial stated flatly that the vast majority of the 1,152 schools of professional nursing in the country admitted all qualified applicants regardless of race and that a few of these schools were in the South. Concerning the employment of Negro nurses as faculty members, the editorial declared:

> Of the 172 colleges and universities that conduct baccalaureate programs in nursing and the 57 that conduct associate degree programs, we know that many of the predominantly white ones have, or have had Negro nurses on the faculties. Among these schools are Wayne State University, Teachers College of Columbia University in New York, University of California at Los Angeles, Syracuse University, University of South Dakota, University of Minnesota, New York University, Cornell University, Skidmore College, University of Oklahoma, Queens College, Adelphi College, Boston University and New York City Community College.

HOSPITAL FACILITIES

In 1947, an unusually provocative book appeared entitled *Let There Be Life: The Contemporary Account of Edna L. Griffin,*

DR. EDNA L. GRIFFIN

M.D. Written by Helen K. Branson, a reporter, it dealt with a young Negro physician of Pasadena, California. The incidents in the book, though presented in fiction form, were, according to the author's preface, based on actual happenings, changes being made "only in so far as necessary to preserve the professional confidence of the physician involved." The book opens with a story graphically illustrating one of the fundamental problems confronting the Negro patient and doctor: differential treatment in hospital facilities.

According to the account, Dr. Edna Griffin, recently arrived in Pasadena, called a hospital after a busy day's work to arrange for an emergency appendectomy for one of her patients, a poor, middle-aged Negro woman. Over the wire came the reassuring voice of the hospital attendant that within an hour everything would be ready—ward bed, operating room and required personnel. Having made the necessary arrangements, Dr. Griffin decided to drive to the sick woman's home to take her to the hospital. When the pain-wracked patient was told she was going to a white institution, she could hardly believe her ears. Reassured but still skeptical, she entered the doctor's car and before long arrived at the institution.

Leaving her patient, Dr. Griffin ran into the admitting room, where she met a surprised night clerk. Politely, he asked the Negro doctor if she was a member of the staff. Not yet, she answered, but her application was on file. Impassively, he told her that he could not be of much help. The hospital, he explained, was so overcrowded that its facilities had to be limited to staff personnel. He was sure she would understand. She replied that the only thing she understood was that her patient was suffering from acute appendicitis which might result in rupture. Sorry, he said, Negro patients had to have private rooms, and since there was not a single one available, his hands were tied.

Dr. Griffin dejectedly walked out of the admitting room to advise her patient that she would have to be taken home. The sick woman, growing steadily worse, could only respond by shaking her head to and fro as if to say, "I told you so; I know those lily-white hospitals." Eventually, physician and patient returned to the sick woman's home. After making her as comfortable as possible, the doctor left to telephone a Negro colleague for advice. He suggested that she do what he did in such emergencies: call an ambulance and send the patient to the Los Angeles County General Hospital. She protested that the hospital was twenty miles away and the patient, threatened with a ruptured appendix, might die on the way. Yes, he knew that, but there was nothing else that could be done.

Dr. Griffin ordered the ambulance and returned to the patient's home. The ailing woman, now in extreme distress, begged the physician to operate. So did the patient's husband, a poor colored worker. The doctor patiently explained she was in no position to operate. Besides, the ambulance was due to arrive momentarily. Just then the doorbell rang. The sick Negro woman was put on a stretcher, wheeled into the ambulance and taken away on what proved to be her last journey.

Dr. Griffin's experience was not unique. "The lack of adequate hospital facilities is perhaps the greatest single deterrent to the acquisition of adequate medical care by the Negro," Dr. John E. Moseley, director of the Cancer Prevention Center at Sydenham Hospital, wrote in *The Crisis,* May, 1949. "The lack is keenly felt both by the patient and doctor. It operates in devious ways to rob the patient of adequate diagnosis and treatment and to stifle the ambition and scientific advance of the physician." Two years before this was written,

the Commission on Hospital Care, a private body appointed by the American Hospital Association, likewise observed that the lack of adequate hospital facilities worked to the disadvantage of both Negro patients and Negro physicians. Because of discriminatory practices, the former were receiving inferior hospital care, and the latter were not being given the opportunity to develop professionally. Hence, the commission in its published report recommended that "adequate and competent hospital care should be available without restrictions to all people regardless of race, creed, color or economic status" and that "qualified Negro physicians should be admitted to membership on the medical staffs of hospitals on the same basis as are other physicians." The commission also approved the practice of employing more Negro nurses in hospitals.

During the post-World War II period, the struggle for equal rights in hospital facilities was part of the wider battle to desegregate medical colleges, nursing schools and professional bodies. The National Medical Association, the organized center of Negro medicine, was in the forefront of the fight to end discriminatory treatment in the country's hospitals. "The time is now ripe for a frontal attack upon what is perhaps the greatest of all the discriminatory evils, differential treatment with respect to hospital facilities," the NMA's official journal declared editorially in July, 1953. Pointing out that hospital discrimination and segregation were prevalent throughout the United States, sometimes "flagrant and contemptuous," sometimes "subtle and not acknowledged," the editorial urged that the evil be rooted out and destroyed forever.

In September, 1951, the journal editorially pressed for militant action in the manifold areas of health care. "It behooves us now to discard the timid and forced misgivings which many have had in the past about

DR. EMORY I. ROBINSON

'moving too fast,' 'being too radical' or 'attempting the impossible.' " Stressing the need to integrate "Negro personnel in all branches of the healing professions and their auxiliaries," the editorial opposed the perpetuation of the principle of a new system of separate hospitals because it might "pin down generations unborn with the curse of the segregation problem."

In line with this policy, the National Medical Association opposed the establishment of segregated veterans hospitals. To forestall what happened at the close of the First World War, the NMA's veterans committee, together with representatives of the National Association of Colored Graduate Nurses, the Medico-Chirurgical Society of the District of Columbia and the National Negro Publishers Association, met with General Paul R. Hawley, medical director of the Veterans Administration, in October, 1945, to discuss a program for complete integration of the administra-

tion's hospital system for both patients and professional personnel. Following the meeting, Dr. Emory I. Robinson, president of the National Medical Association, stated that the Veterans Administration should assist integration just as civilian hospitals were beginning to do. "We fully agree with General Hawley that there is no defense of segregation," Dr. Robinson declared. "Our Army has changed its policy and our Navy has changed its policy. The Veterans Administration cannot look back. It must look forward and must change its policy."

But to destroy the principle of segregation in the hospital system of the Veterans Administration was not easy. Despite the fact that veterans were legally entitled to medical care without discrimination, 24 of the 127 veterans hospitals operating in the beginning of November, 1947, had separate wards for Negro patients. Nineteen of them, all located in the South, refused to admit Negroes except in cases of medical emergencies. Yet, in spite of such setbacks, the civil rights forces refused to abandon the battle. Finally, in October, 1954, the agency ordered the end of segregation in all of its hospitals. Thereafter, the order was scrupulously carried out in all veterans hospitals, including those in Birmingham, New Orleans and Jackson.

The National Medical Association worked for the desegregation of veterans hospitals as part of a much broader program of hospital integration. In the summer of 1956, Dr. W. Montague Cobb, editor-in-chief of the association's journal, suggested the establishment of an organization to eliminate racially discriminatory treatment in the country's hospitals. Dr. Cobb, who was born in Washington, D.C., in 1904, received his A.B. degree from Amherst in 1925, his M.D. from Howard in 1929 and his Ph.D. from Western Reserve in 1932. Inspired by Dean Numa P. G. Adams, he returned to Howard Medical School in the

DR. W. MONTAGUE COBB

1930's to begin a noteworthy teaching career as professor of anatomy.

Dr. Cobb was a close friend of Dr. Louis T. Wright and, like him, was active in the affairs of the National Association for the Advancement of Colored People. In 1946, he represented the association in hearings before a Senate committee in support of national health insurance. Four years later, he was made a member of the organization's national board of directors. A vigorous advocate of civil rights, he refused to attend meetings of the American Association of Anatomists and the American Association for the Advancement of Science whenever those bodies met in Southern cities where Negro delegates were barred from staying in hotels and eating in restaurants with white delegates. His opposition was instrumental in making both organizations adopt resolutions against meeting in cities with segregated facilities.

In 1949, Dr. Cobb succeeded Dr. Ulysses

G. Dailey as editor of the *Journal of the National Medical Association.* Under his editorship, the size of the magazine was enlarged and its scope broadened. Articles on Negro medical history appeared, many of them written by Dr. Cobb, whose original research earned for him recognition as the country's principal historian in the field. Another of Dr. Cobb's innovations was the appearance in the journal of a section entitled "The Integration Battle Front," which consisted of pithy items of interest relating to the developing struggle for equal rights in medicine and health.

It was Dr. Cobb's foresight that created an organization whose purpose was "the elimination of segregation in the fields of hospitalization and health." This body, taking its name from an Egyptian physician of 5,000 years ago called Imhotep ("he who cometh in peace"), was sponsored by the

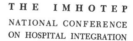

THE IMHOTEP
NATIONAL CONFERENCE
ON HOSPITAL INTEGRATION

sponsored by
THE NATIONAL MEDICAL ASSOCIATION
THE MEDICO-CHIRURGICAL SOCIETY OF THE DISTRICT OF COLUMBIA
THE NATIONAL ASSOCIATION FOR THE ADVANCEMENT OF COLORED PEOPLE

Imhotep
"He who cometh in peace"

MARCH 8-9, 1957

THE FIFTEENTH STREET PRESBYTERIAN CHURCH
15TH & R STREETS, N.W., WASHINGTON, D. C.

National Medical Association, the National Association for the Advancement of Colored People, the National Urban League and the Medico-Chirurgical Society of the District of Columbia. To achieve integration in hospital services, the organization proposed a threefold approach: the enactment of laws to render segregated practices illegal; the filing of court suits to end the use of public funds for the construction and/or maintenance of segregated projects; and the use of persuasion on the administrative front to achieve the elimination of discriminatory patterns.

Late in 1956, the newly formed association invited the American Medical Association, the American Hospital Association and other leading hospital agencies to send representatives to a meeting in Washington, D.C., March 8 and 9, 1957, to discuss discrimination in hospitals. In support of the projected meeting, the National Medical Association in its official organ declared:

> The Imhotep Conference [on Hospital Integration] will afford a golden opportunity to broaden understanding of the problem and unify action in respect to the elimination of one of the present major barriers to making the best in medical facilities available to all of the people of the nation.

Dr. Cobb presided over the first Imhotep Conference. It was held at the Fifteenth Street Presbyterian Church in Washington, D.C., with 175 registrants from twenty-one states and forty-nine localities. Representatives were present from sixteen societies of the National Medical Association, twenty-six chapters of the National Association for the Advancement of Colored People and four branches of the National Urban League. Thirty-two organizations engaged in or associated with hospital work were represented at the meeting, including the American Hospital Association, the American Medical Association, the American Nurses' Association, the National Health Council and the United States Public Health

Service. Significantly, neither the American Protestant Hospital Association nor the Catholic Hospital Association of the United States sent representatives to the conference.

Before the close of the decade, two other Imhotep national conferences on hospital integration were held, one in Chicago, May 23–24, 1958, and the other in Washington, D.C., May 22–23, 1959. The effectiveness of these meetings was vitiated by the refusal of such powerful organizations as the American Medical Association, the American Hospital Association and various Protestant and Catholic hospital bodies to participate officially and actively in the deliberations. That the Imhotep Conference continued to function in the face of this foot-dragging was only due to the courage and vision of Dr. Cobb and his associates.

Other organizations, Negro and white, joined the National Medical Association in the fight to desegregate hospital facilities. In Illinois, various labor unions, the Committee of Equitable Medical Care, the Cook County Physicians Association and the Illinois conference branches of the National Association for the Advancement of Colored People scored a notable victory when, in July, 1955, Governor William B. Stratton signed into law a measure depriving private hospitals of tax exemptions if they practiced racial discrimination in the admission of patients. The Cook County Physicians Association, representing several hundred Negro doctors in the Chicago area, supported the passage of the measure on the ground that discrimination in the admission policies of hospitals violated "the principle and spirit of American democracy" and "the humanitarian basis on which the practice of medicine has been established and should operate." In March, 1956, the united front of Negro organizations and labor unions had the satisfaction of seeing Chicago pass a law prohibiting segregation in all city-owned hospitals.

COOK COUNTY HOSPITAL, CHICAGO

The Cook County Hospital, Chicago, Illinois.

Similarly, in other parts of the country, hospital integration moved forward. In the winter of 1955, the last hospital in Denver to restrict admission dropped its racial bars. In Camden, New Jersey, segregation of patients in local hospitals ended in 1954. The following year, a Buffalo hospital for the first time named a Negro doctor chief of its staff. In Cincinnati, in the summer of 1955, a sixth hospital gave courtesy privileges to Negro doctors. In November, 1954, a Milwaukee hospital chose a Negro physician to head its staff, the first in the state to receive such an appointment.

In the meantime, at another Milwaukee hospital, the Capitol, a "saga of integration" was taking place. The Capitol was founded in 1945 by a doctor who, on returning from wartime service, found that, lacking local staff privileges, he could not hos-

pitalize his patients. Thus, he and five other physicians faced by the same predicament decided to build their own hospital. They constructed a two-story clinic which eventually had thirty-five beds. According to a story in the September, 1957, issue of *Hospital Management,* it was not long before six of the ten Negro doctors in Milwaukee barred by color from local hospitals applied to the Capitol for staff privileges. The Negro doctors were accepted. The hospital was completely integrated; and according to the account, no white patient ever objected to being treated by a Negro doctor or asked to be put into a private room to avoid a Negro patient.

Although progress was being made in desegregating hospital facilities during the postwar years, it did not proceed in a uniform manner or at a very rapid pace. Generally speaking, the movement was more pronounced in the North, where racial segregation and discrimination were extra-legal, than in the South, where the Jim Crow system was established by law. In 1960, the United States Civil Rights Commission, confronted by persistent charges from Negro and white organizations that "white" hospitals were denying staff privileges to Negro physicians and refusing to admit Negro patients or, if admitting them, providing segregated accommodations, launched an investigation. Personal interviews were held in key cities; questionnaires sent to 389 hospitals in thirty-four states. One hundred and seventy-five hospitals indicated they had no policy of discrimination; 60 admitted they had. Of the 64 Southern respondents, as many as 85 per cent reported some type of racial segregation or exclusion. Three of seven border states admitted the existence of such practices. On the other hand, only two of the 214 hospitals in the North and the West reported any type of racial segregation.

The movement toward hospital integration in the North was encouraged in the decade and a half prior to 1960 by the mass Negro exodus from the South and the concentration of the Negro population in the slum areas of the big cities. During World War II and after, Negroes by the hundreds of thousands left the South for the automobile assembly lines of Detroit; the shipyards of New York, Camden and the San Francisco Bay area; the steel fabricating plants of Pittsburgh, Gary and Chicago; and the aircraft factories of Los Angeles. Hoping to escape segregation Southern-style, they crowded into these and other densely populated urban centers only to find themselves imprisoned in tight pockets of segregated poverty and misery, Northern-style. As the years passed, it became increasingly evident that, for them, there was

no further escape, no safety valve for the outlet of racial tension. The end of the line had been reached, a factor of major importance in triggering the civil rights upheavals in the North during the first half of the sixties.

From 1940 to 1960, Northern and Western metropolitan areas experienced a tremendous increase in nonwhite population. During this period, the number of Negroes in New York rose almost two and a half times, to 1,100,000; in Chicago, more than 250 per cent, to 890,000; in Philadelphia, it doubled to 529,000; in Detroit, it more than tripled, to nearly 500,000; and in Los Angeles County, rose 600 per cent to almost 500,000. In the early sixties, Negroes constituted a majority of the population in Washington, D.C., and Newark; one-third or more in Detroit, Baltimore, St. Louis and Cleveland; a quarter or more in Chicago, Philadelphia, Cincinnati, Indianapolis and Oakland. In the North as a whole, the Negro population more than doubled, from less than 4,000,000 in 1940 to more than 9,000,000 in 1960. For the first time in the country's history, there were almost as many Negroes in the North as in the South.

This explosive increase in the number of Northern Negroes made the problem of *de facto* racial discrimination in hospital facilities more acute. Their sheer numbers and disease-producing slums made the need for hospital services greater. Since white political bosses needed the Negro vote to retain the boodle and patronage involved in the control of city governments, concessions had to be made to allay Negro discontent. Thus, the doors of Northern hospitals were pried open to more Negro patients, doctors and nurses. More beds were made available to Negroes as color bars were lifted in city-owned and privately operated hospitals. More Negroes were appointed to hospital staffs as progress was made against restrictive personnel policies.

Yet, despite the favorable trend, surveys throughout the 1950's showed that hospitals in the North were still resorting to ingenious devices to separate Negro from white patients and to exclude Negro physicians and nurses from hospital staffs. In 1950, the Southern California chapter of the National Council of Arts, Sciences and the Professions made a survey of hospital discrimination in Los Angeles County. A questionnaire was sent to thirty-two hospitals; seventeen responded. The survey showed that discriminatory hospital practices fell into two categories: discrimination against patients of minority groups and discrimination against physicians, nurses and technicians of minority groups. It was found that some hospitals practiced one type of discrimination; some, another; and some, both.

Eleven hospitals in the Los Angeles area, including those in Burbank, Pasadena and Long Beach, had racial segregation of patients, while six treated patients without discrimination. Eight hospitals were described as having "poor" records in integrating their staffs. Five others were said to be making definite progress along these lines. Of the 4,815 attending physicians on hospital staffs, 32 were Negro. In 1950, Los Angeles had 74 Negro doctors and a Negro population of 250,000: roughly one Negro physician to each 3,400 colored persons.

In 1956, the Detroit Commission on Community Relations issued a report on racial factors in hospital policies and practices. The report, for the year 1954, surveyed forty-seven hospitals in the Detroit area, with a total of 15,523 hospital beds. Of the 354,905 persons admitted, an estimated 52,557 were Negroes. According to the survey, four hospitals reported no Negro patient admissions; thirteen reported admission of emergency or accident cases. The remaining thirty had significant numbers of Negro patient admissions. The findings showed that twenty hospitals assigned beds on the basis of a discriminatory policy, with groupings of all-white, segregated or partially segregated; and twenty-seven, on the basis of a policy with groupings of integrated and partially integrated.

In eastern and southwestern Detroit and suburbs, the bed-assignment policy was uniform segregation except in government hospitals. In both these areas, as well as in three others that were studied, there were significant numbers of Negro residents. "In view of the distribution of Negro population in each of the five divisions of the Detroit study area," the report went on, "the Medical and Hospital Study Committee concludes that it is not the simple factor of geographic location of the hospital or other chance circumstance which accounts for the fact that 17 hospitals do not normally admit Negro patients and that 30 hospitals do admit significant numbers of Negroes." On the basis of its findings, the Detroit commission concluded:

1. A racially representative medical staff is vitally important if the hospital is to serve the entire community. . . . 2. Racial segregation has no place in present-day community hospital operation. The Negro citizen is legally, morally and financially entitled to equal accommodation and use of hospital facilities, despite customs, practice, or formerly expedient patterns of service.

In the meantime, the Committee to End Discrimination in Chicago Medical Institutions published a study embodying the results of its investigation of hospital facilities in a city with a Negro population of 590,000 at the time. Entitled "What Color Are *Your* Germs?", it was reproduced in the July, 1955, issue of the *Journal of the National Medical Association*. According to the brochure, though Chicago had six thousand doctors and sixty-five hospitals, it was "a dangerous town in which to fall ill," particularly for Negroes. Almost 50 per cent of them, when sick or injured, were taken care of in one institution, Cook County Hospital. Some went there because it was close to them. "But," the study noted, "a large percentage—patients with paid-up hospitalization policies and enough money to engage their own physicians and surgeons—go there because it's the only hospital that will accept them." Although some private hospitals in Chicago admitted colored patients, Negroes were accepted only when enough "Negro beds" were available.

The study cited incidents of Negroes being turned away by private hospitals in Chicago. The following is virtually a word-by-word account taken from the report. In February, 1954, a three-year-old Negro child became ill and was referred by the family doctor to a nearby institution for admission. The mother was told that the child was not sick enough to be hospitalized. The child died at home the next day. In October, 1953, a fifteen-year-old Negro boy was taken by his mother to a neighborhood hospital where his ailment was diagnosed as an intestinal obstruction. The mother, who could afford hospitalization, wished her son to be admitted. Instead, the youngster was sent to Cook County Hospital. Although taken immediately, he died there four hours later. In October, 1952, a fourteen-year-old Negro boy injured in an accident was brought to a nearby hospital. When the mother arrived, she was told that arrangements had already been made to take her son to Cook County Hospital. Hospitalization at the private institution was not even suggested, even though the family carried hospitalization insurance. The boy was admitted to the county hospital, where he was treated for internal injuries and shock.

The report concluded on this note:

The United States Public Health Service in its 1947 Chicago-Cook County Health Survey, recommended:

Hospital facility services shall be available to all patients on the basis of need and ability to pay, *without regard to race, color or creed and without segregation.*

What remains is for the people of Chicago to recognize that this is not exclusively a Negro health problem, but a *public* health problem. *It's up to you!*

Chicago hospitals discriminated against Negro physicians as well as Negro patients. The research department of the Chicago Urban League prepared a paper, "Integration in Hospital Appointments and in Hospital Care," for the workshop of the second Imhotep national conference, May 23–24, 1958. The paper contained a survey of Negro staff appointments in 1956 to predominantly white hospitals. Chicago ranked ninth in a list of fourteen communities. Of its 226 Negro physicians, only 16, or 7.1 per cent, served at predominantly white hospitals. Ahead of Chicago were Gary (82.4 per cent), Brooklyn, New York (70.6), Philadelphia (28.2), Los Angeles (24.8), Indianapolis (23.1), Boston (21.1), Detroit (15.6) and St. Louis (10.6). Below Chicago were Kansas City (5.4), Washington, D.C. (3.6), Atlanta, Nashville and New Orleans. The last three Southern cities, twelfth, thirteenth and fourteenth on the list, did not have a single Negro physician serving on the staff of a predominantly white hospital.

The segregationist record of these three cities of the old Confederacy reflected the rigidity with which the South clung to traditional lily-white policies and practices in respect to hospital facilities. In 1956, the Southern Conference of Methodists polled 2,400 Southern hospital administrators regarding their position on desegregation. Of these, 17 per cent were willing to accept it; 62 per cent were adamantly opposed to it; and 11 per cent felt that the most practicable way to solve the problem was by having separate hospitals. Eleven per cent were unwilling to indicate their positions.

Some four years before, *The Southern Patriot* conducted a similar poll. The publication, official organ of the Southern Conference Educational Fund, an organization headed by former New Deal administrator Aubrey Williams, mailed 2,414 ballots to hospital administrators in eighteen Southern states and the District of Columbia to find out whether they favored segregated, integrated or separate hospitals. The results of the poll showed that 71 per cent of those replying voted for hospitals with segregation. In the eleven states of the old Confederacy (Alabama, Arkansas, Florida, Georgia, Louisiana, Mississippi, North Carolina, South Carolina, Tennessee, Texas and Virginia), 335 hospital administrators, or 74.9 per cent, favored segregated hospitals; 51, or 11.4 per cent, desegregated; and 61, or 13.7 per cent, separate hospitals. In Georgia, Louisiana and Mississippi, there was not a single ballot cast for non-segregated hospitals. In seven states outside the old Confederacy (Delaware, Kentucky, Maryland, Missouri, New Mexico, Oklahoma and West Virginia) and the District of Columbia, 150 hospital administrators, or 62.7 per cent, were for hospitals with segregation; 74, or 31.0 per cent, without segregation; and 15, or 6.3 per cent, for separate facilities.

Significant as expressions of viewpoints were the replies received by The Southern Patriot to the alternative plans presented in its state-by-state poll. The following answers were received from three hospital administrators favoring segregation. One from Alabama: "It is my opinion that segregation is desired by both colored and white races. The Communist Party naturally is making an effort to create friction among all groups." Another from Mississippi: "We have separate buildings for Negroes and whites. The one for Negroes is perhaps the finest in the whole world. We wanted to use Negro doctors but could not get them. Did not have the courtesy of a reply from the only Negro physician I wrote." And

another from Oklahoma: "As superintendent of this hospital I would refuse hospitalization to a Negro in an emergency regardless. This problem has never arisen."

Those who favored integration had this to say. From Missouri: "We are here to take care of sick folk. The color of their skin or eyes makes no difference to us, as long as they pay their bills—and we don't really pay much attention to this." And from Kentucky: "I am in favor of no segregation. From what I've seen the public as a whole will accept it, the hospitals are just afraid to start it." There were others who believed that integration was coming, but that the South was not yet ready for it. A Virginia hospital administrator put it this way: "Better have separate hospitals. May be able to stop segregation in the South in 10 years, but not now." Said a Washington, D.C., hospital superintendent: "Our community is not yet ready for complete integration, but I believe [it] is coming. . . ."

It is quite possible that the Mississippi hospital administrator whose segregationist reply was presented in The Southern Patriot did not know, or might never have heard about Dr. Theodore R. M. Howard of Mound Bayou, a cotton town in the Mississippi delta founded and settled by Negroes after the Civil War. In 1942, Dr. Howard, a Negro, then only thirty-four, a surgeon at the George W. Hubbard Hospital of Meharry Medical College and one-time trainee at the Mayo Clinic, was appointed chief surgeon at Mound Bayou's Taborian Hospital. Under Dr. Howard's supervision, Taborian grew and, within four years, had seventy-six beds and two operating rooms. The hospital was so successful that on February 23, 1946, the Saturday Evening Post ran a feature article on it and its chief surgeon. The author of the article, Hodding Carter, described the hospital in glowing terms and quoted Dr. Theodore Howard as saying:

Mound Bayou's Taborian Hospital as seen from Dr. Howard's Clinic.

DR. THEODORE R. M. HOWARD

We've got a long waiting list. Even the demand for private rooms is twenty times the supply. Negroes want good care too. These days a good many of them can pay for the best of care. But in too many of Mississippi's too few hospitals Negroes have to bring their own sheets and spoons and someone to give nursing care. And, in many cases, the accommodations are dirtier than you'd believe.

When Dr. Howard made this statement, Mississippi's one million Negroes had less than one thousand hospital beds for them, despite the fact that, according to the best medical estimates, three thousand beds were needed to care for them adequately. In fact, there were not that many beds available for the state's one million whites. After 1946, Dr. Howard continued to build Taborian Hospital. His reputation, particularly in Negro medical circles, grew apace. In 1956, he was elected president of the National Medical Association.

Dr. Howard was also a leader in the

struggle for civil rights. When the white citizens councils of Mississippi were organized to thwart the intent of the Supreme Court's decision of 1954 to desegregate the schools, he became president of the regional Council of Negro Leadership. In that capacity, he fought the citizens councils and those plantation owners who subjected Negro professionals to every kind of reprisal, including forbidding tenants to go to Negro doctors, cancellation of insurance policies, and difficulties in securing credit.

When, in 1955, the Negroes Emmett Till, George W. Lee and Lamar Smith were killed in Mississippi and their slayers were unapprehended despite the intervention of the Federal Bureau of Investigation, Dr. Howard was quoted by the *Baltimore Morning Sun* of September 26, 1955, as saying before a membership meeting of the National Association for the Advancement of Colored People at the Sharpe Street Methodist Church in Baltimore: "We must find out why Southern investigators of the FBI can't seem to solve a crime when a Negro is involved." On January 18, 1956, FBI Director J. Edgar Hoover, in a letter to Dr. Howard, charged that the Negro physician's statements were false and irresponsible. The following day, Dr. Howard rejected the charge and declared that he would continue to "cry out against injustice and against that kind of administration of justice which permits murderers to go free to boast of their crimes."

Negro physicians who were active in the fight for racial equality in the South ran many risks. Dr. Albert C. Perry, Jr., a leader in the civil rights movement in Monroe, North Carolina, was sent to prison, and, therefore, lost his medical license. During the early postwar period, he and Robert F. Williams, a Negro mechanic, revitalized the Union County branch of the National Association for the Advance-

ment of Colored People. Williams, as president of the branch, and Dr. Perry, as vice-president, led a delegation of Negro children to an all-white municipal swimming pool after several colored boys had drowned in a river. Their request that one day a week be set aside for Negro children was rejected by local officials on the ground that it would cost too much to fumigate the pool after it had been used by Negroes.

As a result of his NAACP activities, Dr. Perry became one of the prime targets of the Ku Klux Klan. Finally, in 1957, the Klan struck openly, its hooded members staging a motorcade demonstration around Dr. Perry's home. There they were met by a group of forty Negroes, organized by Robert F. Williams, who routed the Klansmen with rifle fire. Shortly thereafter, Dr. Perry was accused of performing an abortion on a young white woman, a nurses' aide in a hospital where he was a staff member. Despite testimony given by white hospital associates concerning his religious scruples as a Catholic against abortion and despite his own steadfast denial of the charge, he was convicted; but the conviction was reversed by the North Carolina supreme court because of the systematic exclusion of Negroes from the jury. The Negro physician was given another trial, found guilty and sentenced to three years in prison. While he served his term, proceedings were instituted to revoke his license. Early in January, 1960, his license was cancelled by the North Carolina Board of Medical Examiners. By striking Dr. Perry's name from the state's register of licensed physicians, the board brushed aside the pleas of six Negro clergymen and the petition of 4,480 Negro residents of Union and neighboring counties.

During the post-World War II years, Federal government funds were used by Dixiecrat politicians to perpetuate their policy of racial segregation of hospital facilities.

"TITLE VI
CONSTRUCTION OF HOSPITALS

"PART A
DECLARATION OF PURPOSE

"Sec. 601. The purpose of this title is to assist the several States—

"(a) to inventory their existing hospitals (as defined in section 631 (e)), to survey the need for construction of hospitals, and to develop programs for construction of such public and other nonprofit hospitals as will, in conjunction with existing facilities, afford the necessary physical facilities for furnishing adequate hospital, clinic, and similar services to all their people; and

"(b) to construct public and other nonprofit hospitals in accordance with such programs.

"PART B
SURVEYS AND PLANNING

"GENERAL REGULATIONS

"Sec. 622. Within six months after the enactment of this title, the Surgeon General, with the approval of the Federal Hospital Council and the Administrator, shall by general regulation prescribe—

"(f) That the State plan shall provide for adequate hospital facilities for the people residing in a State, without discrimination on account of race, creed, or color, and shall provide for adequate hospital facilities for persons unable to pay therefor. Such regulation may require that before approval of any application for a hospital or addition to a hospital is recommended by a State agency, assurance shall be received by the State from the applicant that (1) such hospital or addition to a hospital will be made available to all persons residing in the territorial area of the applicant, without discrimination on account of race, creed, or color, but an exception shall be made in cases where separate hospital facilities are provided for separate population groups, if the plan makes equitable provision on the basis of need for facilities and services of like quality for each such group; and (2) there will be made available in each such hospital or addition to a hospital a reasonable volume of hospital services to persons unable to pay therefor, but an exception shall be made if such a requirement is not feasible from a financial standpoint.

In 1946, the Hill-Burton Act, with its "separate-but-equal" clause, was passed by Congress to provide grants-in-aid to individual states for the construction of hospitals. From 1948 to 1961, the South received a good slice of the $1,600,000,000 melon which the Federal government provided for the rebuilding of the American hospital system. In Georgia, of ninety hospitals, eighty-three were constructed with the help of Hill-Burton money.

The use of Federal funds to build segregated hospitals in the South was bitterly opposed. The National Medical Association and the Physicians' Forum urged the Federal government to withhold money from state agencies hiding behind the "separate-but-equal" provision of the Hill-Burton Act. In the June 7, 1952, issue of *The Nation,* Robert M. Cunningham, Jr., editor of *Modern Hospital,* hit at the use of Federal funds to build hospitals which evaded the anti-discrimination clause in the law "by using the false doctrine of 'separate-but-equal' facilities." About a decade later, the United States Civil Rights Commission in its published report recommended to President Kennedy that further Hill-Burton funds be denied hospitals that practiced racial segregation and discrimination under the guise of the so-called "separate-but-equal" principle.

During the postwar years, a few Southern and border state hospitals opened their doors to Negro physicians. Rarely was this done voluntarily. In 1946, Dr. W. Montague Cobb, on behalf of the Medico-Chirurgical Society of the District of Columbia, of which he was president, wrote to Guy Mason of the District's board of commissioners, protesting the segregation of Negro doctors at Gallinger Hospital, a city-supported institution. The protest was supported by the National Medical Association at its Louisville, Kentucky, convention attended by more than 1,200 physicians.

Aerial view of Gallinger Hospital, now called District of Columbia General Hospital.

With the help of Federal Security Administrator Oscar R. Ewing, an ardent supporter of racial equality, Gallinger Hospital agreed to admit Negro physicians to its staff. In 1948, after a twelve-year campaign, a hospital in Lynchburg, Virginia, granted limited staff privileges to Negro doctors. According to the arrangement, the physicians were restricted to two Negro floors of the hospital.

Negro physicians, in attempting to secure staff appointments to Southern hospitals, were handicapped by the segregationist policies not only of the hospitals themselves but also of county medical societies affiliated with the AMA. Since staff appointments required the accreditation of a physician by a local medical body and since most Negro doctors in the South were barred from such membership, their exclusion from hospital staffs was automatic. Thus, by the close of the 1950's, it was clear that, before Southern Negro physicians

could be integrated on hospital staffs, racial bars for membership in county AMA affiliates had to go.

Hospital segregation was widespread throughout the South. The "separate-but-equal" Negro hospitals were usually small and antiquated. Adequate facilities and personnel were lacking. Some white hospitals admitted Negroes to designated "colored" floors or wards. In these hospitals, there were few beds available, and waiting lists for admission were long. In other white hospitals, Negroes were unable to gain admittance, even in emergency cases. Under the circumstances, a news item—such as the one reporting that policemen in St. Louis were being instructed to take all serious emergency cases to the nearest city hospital instead of taking all white patients to City Hospital and all Negro patients to Homer G. Phillips Hospital—was hailed in the mid-1950's as a step forward.

THE HEALTH PICTURE

As in the period prior to the end of the Second World War, so after it the Negro people had a higher death and illness rate than whites largely because of color restrictions and dire want. During the affluent 1950's, Negro Americans were disproportionately represented in the one-fifth of the population classified as the hard-core poor and the one-fourth above them who lived on the verge of poverty. Jim Crow patterns in employment were among the many forces responsible for the depressed economic condition of the Negro masses.

Throughout the prosperous fifties, Negro youths suffered almost twice as much unemployment as white youths, and Negro adults compared to like segments of the white population were underemployed and underpaid. In 1949, the ratio of median nonwhite to white family income stood at 51.1 per cent. In 1952, it rose to a high of 56.8 per cent as a result of the Korean War prosperity. In 1959, it slid back to about the same level as ten years earlier, namely, to 51.7 per cent. Lower family income due to race was greatest in the South; in 1960, the median nonwhite family income was $2,687 less than that of the white family. Nowhere in the country was the dollar gap less than $1,500, despite the fact that there were more members in the Negro family working and more in the family group to support.

During the prosperous post-World War II period, the Negro people, in general, occupied the lowest rung of the economic ladder. In 1950, the median annual income of Negro men was $1,471 and of Negro women, $474. Thirteen years later it was $2,444 for Negro males and $953 for Negro females. Since these income figures include all Negro groupings, they conceal the much lower annual incomes of the bulk of the Negro people, the unskilled laborers and household servants in Northern and Southern cities and the cash tenants and sharecroppers in the Southern countryside. The last to be hired, the first to be fired, and the least likely to be promoted, Negro urban workers lived in what may be described as economic "dead-end streets." The same was true of Negro farmers, who, unable to meet the competition of the new agricultural machinery, were being cleared off their land. Living on subsistence or near-subsistence incomes, Negro workers and farmers made up a disproportionate part of the regions of poverty that disfigured the "affluent society."

What poverty does to the health of the poor has been graphically set forth by Dr. Robert Coles, research psychiatrist at Harvard University Health Services. Writing in *The Nation*, June 20, 1966, he observed:

> The everyday life of the poor is such that certain forms of medical and psychiatric illness are so widespread as to seem 'normal'; they are everybody's lot. . . . I no longer notice with surprise the terribly rotted teeth, the poor hearing, the eye-sight too long neglected, and hence hopelessly impaired. . . . I often find myself taking for granted the occurrence of parasitic diseases. Rat bites no longer seem rare and awful; rodents are everywhere, in the halls and in the apartments as well as in the littered alleys. Finally, there are to be found in the poor a host of diseases, deficiences and developmental disorders that even medical students in pursuit of variety and experience rarely see. They are illnesses and erosions of the body that go with poor diet. They are the neurological disorders brought on by untreated or poorly treated injuries or diseases. They are the serious congenital and metabolic flaws—in us they are quickly spotted and treated—that have been allowed unimpeded existence or growth.

During the post-World War II period, the millions of poor Negroes living in city ghettos or in rural slums lacked money to command private care and received precious little public medical assistance. Their low-income status helped swell the death rate among them. The National Health Assembly, which was convened in Washing-

DR. ROBERT COLES

ton, D.C., May, 1948, at President Truman's request, had this to say about economic conditions, medical care and higher Negro mortality rates:

> The Negro population tends, in general, to be at the bottom of the economic ladder and to receive care which is least adequate in terms of both quality and quantity. This is undoubtedly one of the important causes of the higher mortality rates among this racial group.

The same report gave another significant reason for the prevalence of higher Negro death rates, namely, racial discrimination in hospital and medical care.

> Still another factor in the situation—and . . . not restricted to the South—is the presence of community discriminatory patterns against minority groups. Community discriminatory patterns work to the disadvantage of all minority groups affected. But they are of particular importance as regards the Negroes. This group is already at a disadvantage because of its generally low economic status, but to these economic barriers are added other barriers which further reduce access to medical care. Hospitals in many parts of the country will not accept Negro patients . . . . and will not permit Negro physicians to use hospital facilities . . . . In various areas the medical care available to the Negro group is non-existent, or is far less than that available to the whites. . . .

Another by-product of racial discrimination in medical care tending to raise Negro mortality rates, not mentioned in the above quotation, was the lack of Negro doctors and doctors for Negroes. The gravity of the situation was stressed by National Medical Fellowships, Inc., which wrote in 1959: "Not only has the total number of Negroes increased faster than the Negro physician, but also the effective demand by Negroes for medical care has increased and is not being met adequately."

In the two decades of 1940 to 1960, the Negro population in the United States rose by 47.7 per cent, from 12,800,000 to 18,900,000, while the total number of Negro physicians increased by 10.5 per cent, from 3,800 to 4,200. In 1960, there was one Negro doctor for each 4,500 Negroes. In 1948, according to an authoritative source, there were 3,753 Negro doctors in the United States out of 193,432 licensed physicians. With an estimated Negro population of 13,818,504, there was one colored doctor to each 3,681 Negroes. In thirteen Southern states, the ratio was much higher than this, with one Negro physician to each 6,203 colored persons. In Mississippi, there was one colored physician to each 18,132 Negroes; and in South Carolina, one to 12,561.

Jim Crow practices combined with substandard living conditions made for higher mortality and morbidity rates among Negroes. In such categories as pulmonary tuberculosis, venereal diseases, communicable childhood illnesses, cardiovascular disorders and infant and maternal complications, the Negro death rate was higher than that of whites. Pulmonary tuberculosis, which in the nineteenth century was a universal disease affecting all races and social classes, was by the mid-twentieth, because of improvements in sanitation, nutrition and treatment, largely restricted to urban working-class districts. Since the bulk of the Negro population was concentrated in such areas, the Negro death rate and incidence from pulmonary tuberculosis were quite high. Compared to white rates, death rates for this disease in 1960 were roughly four times higher for Negroes, and the number of active cases was about three times higher. In 1959, tuberculosis was the number eight killer of Negro men and was ten times more prevalent among Negroes of twenty-five to thirty-four than among white males.

Syphilis was another disease undermining Negro American health. Its propagation was facilitated by poverty and ignorance. The disease thrived in an environment where large families were herded into limited quarters and family life was disorganized by the hopelessness and frustrations of day-to-day living. According to public health data for 1960–1961, the incidence of syphilis among Negroes was ten times greater than that among whites; and the death rate, almost four times greater. Although these figures may be exaggerated because of the disproportionate non-reporting of the whites, all available information tends to point to high Negro rates.

Communicable childhood diseases also raised Negro mortality rates. Compared to white, Negro death rates due to whooping cough, meningitis, measles, diphtheria and scarlet fever were particularly high. Although proper medical care could sharply reduce the fatal complications of these childhood diseases, Negro mortality rates from them were at least twice those of white rates. In the case of whooping cough, six times as many Negro children died of this disease in 1949–1951 as white, despite modern medical knowledge concerning immunization.

Similarly, for cardiovascular diseases, Negro death rates were higher than those of whites. Particularly elevated was the mortality rate of Negro females, possibly because of the increased burden placed upon them during the postwar period of maintaining the family group intact. In the boom years of the 1950's, the job market for Negro women steadily expanded due to the increased demand of the white middle classes for household servants. Meanwhile, employment for Negro men failed to show the same rate of expansion; and as a result, the responsibility of keeping the family together fell increasingly upon the female members. As poverty eroded Negro family life, the stress and strain upon the Negro woman became greater, making her more susceptible to cardiovascular disorders. Negroes were particularly hard hit by hypertension and hypertensive heart disease. In this area, the Negro mortality rate was about three times that of the white. Genetic predispositions are important in hypertension, but many other factors contribute to the condition, including psycho-social frustrations.

Deaths in childbirth and infancy likewise raised Negro mortality rates above those of whites. In 1959, maternal death rates were four times as high for Negroes; and infant mortality rates, roughly twice as high. Nonwhite babies dying within twelve months after birth per 100 were 6.3 in Albany, Georgia, as against 3.0 for white infants; in New Orleans, 5.4 as against 2.2; in Jackson, Mississippi, 4.4 as against 2.8; in New York, 4.3 as against 2.2; in Indianapolis, 4.2 as against 2.6; and in Birmingham, 4.0 as against 2.2. Mortality figures, however, tend to conceal prenatal and postnatal morbidity among Negro infants, since they tell us nothing about such problems as increased infection, anoxia and birth trauma, all of which may retard infants for life. In the overall picture of Negro health, these problems assume a particular

WHITNEY M. YOUNG, JR.

significance because of the large number of poverty-stricken Negroes lacking prenatal care, good food and expert delivery.

According to some authorities, mental illnesses appear to be relatively higher among Negroes than among whites. Statistical data show that, in 1950, one-third more Negro than white patients were in mental hospitals in the United States. Recent studies in New York City and New Haven found a shockingly high relationship between poverty and mental disorders. These studies revealed that mental illness was more severe and higher in incidence among the poor than among the affluent. On the basis of these findings, Whitney M. Young, Jr., in his book *To Be Equal* wrote:

> Since the number of Negroes who are poor is disproportionately high, we may infer that they constitute more than the average number of mentally ill in the population as a whole. Such a finding would hardly be surprising, considering the circumstances in which Negroes are forced to live.

Despite higher mortality and morbidity rates in significant disease categories, there were indications of an overall improvement in the Negro health picture. In 1940, the life expectation of Negroes was eleven years less than that of whites, fifty-three as against sixty-four. In 1960, the difference was only seven years, sixty-four for Negroes and seventy-one for whites. The dramatic improvement in the life expectancy of the Negro people was further evidenced by the fact that from 1900 to 1960 the life span of Negro Americans increased twofold, from thirty-two to sixty-four, and in terms of percentage gain was twice that of the white population. As in the days of slavery and immediately after, so in the first sixty years of the twentieth century, the irrepressible will of the Negro people to survive asserted itself. The hope for a vanishing Negro American—so tenaciously held in certain white supremacist circles—did not materialize. One of the sturdiest stocks in the world, colored Americans were more numerous and living longer than ever before. Their physical stamina and skill became the objects of public notice, particularly during the post-World War II years when the competitive field of professional sports was opened to them. The Jackie Robinsons of baseball, the Jim Browns of football and the Wilt Chamberlains of basketball rose to dominant positions in a world that was once exclusively white.

By 1960, the health gap separating the two races was narrowing. High Negro mortality and morbidity rates were in disease categories that were "treatable, predictable and unnecessary." Threats to life, especially from communicable diseases, could be reduced by improved living standards and better health facilities. In New York City's borough of Manhattan, where the Negro ghetto of Harlem is located, the tuberculosis death rate among nonwhites fell from 445.5 per 100,000 in 1910 to 62 per 100,000 in

1950. That tuberculosis, a totally unnecessary disease, could be controlled was further evidenced by the fact that from 1955 to 1960 the national nonwhite rate of new active cases declined by almost a third.

However, so long as Negroes in large numbers were ravaged by poverty and discriminated against in medical care, the chance of sharply reducing Negro mortality and morbidity rates from tuberculosis, syphilis, childhood diseases and infant and maternal complications was remote, and so was the likelihood of eliminating the racial health gap. Only through a higher standard of living and proper medical care could the Negro people bridge the divide completely.

Comprehensive health legislation was one way to make proper medical care available to the whole population, including the sorely disadvantaged Negro Americans. In the aftermath of the Second World War, progressive-minded men and women of both races looked to the Federal government for the adoption of a national health insurance plan. In August, 1945, Dr. Ernst P. Boas, chairman of the largely white Physicians' Forum, called for the support of the Wagner-Murray-Dingell Bill, which provided for comprehensive health coverage and strict enforcement of the principle of non-discrimination. In April, 1946, Dr. W. Montague Cobb, representing the more than half-million members of the National Association for the Advancement of Colored People, appeared before the United States Senate Committee on Education and Labor to speak on behalf of a national health bill embodying the recommendations of President Truman. In his statement, Dr. Cobb underscored the fact that poor health in the Negro sector of the population was "a hazard to the nation as a whole." He pointed out that Negro health could be improved by controlling the spread of communicable diseases. In closing, he said:

> . . . the N.A.A.C.P. regards S. 1606 as one of the most progressive and potentially beneficial pieces of legislation of recent years. It is sorely needed by the great majority of Americans, but it is most acutely needed by our 14 million American Negro citizens.

A similar stand on behalf of the people's health was taken by the National Medical Association. In 1946, its president, Dr. Emory I. Johnson of Los Angeles, testified in support of national health insurance. An editorial in the July, 1947, issue of the NMA's journal urged its readers to back the Wagner-Murray-Dingell Bill because it was the best measure that could be passed to improve the health of the American people and to further non-discrimination goals. This was in sharp contrast to the position of the American Medical Association, which spoke darkly about the introduction of "socialized medicine" from "the cradle to the grave."

However, nothing came of these progressive legislative proposals to make medical care accessible to the masses. Under the impact of the cold war, McCarthyism and the Eisenhower "return to conformity," the idea of a comprehensive health insurance system supported by tax dollars was shelved for almost a decade and a half. During the early 1960's, it was revived in the truncated form of medicare for the aged under Social Security, a measure strongly endorsed by the National Medical Association and bitterly opposed by the American Medical Association.

CHAPTER NINE

The Integration Battlefront

Freedom Now!

Not only must we redouble our efforts in the traditional areas, litigation, legislation and conciliatory conferences; we must also join in the direct action program assault on every form of social evil based on race. For this is the era of mass involvement and direct action. This we recognize, approve and applaud. But, my fellow physicians! We must do more than approve, we must participate.

Dr. Kenneth W. Clement, Presidential Address, 68th Annual Convention of the National Medical Association, Los Angeles, August, 1963.

For seven years we have invited them [representatives of the American Medical Association, American Hospital Association and other major hospital organizations] to sit down with us and solve the problem [of hospital integration] . . . ..By their refusal to confer they force action by crisis. And now events have passed beyond them. The initiative offered is no longer theirs to accept.

Dr. W. Montague Cobb, Seventh Imhotep National Conference on Hospital Integration, May 1963.

DURING the first half of the 1960's, the Negro drive for racial equality in medicine and health gathered momentum as more than a billion colored people in Asia and Africa pressed to enter modern society. Caught up by these powerful currents, the civil rights movement in the United States surged forward with its powerful roar—"Freedom Now!"

About a century ago, Dr. Martin R. Delany, the Negro abolitionist, addressing an audience of free Negroes in New York, said: "The white race are but one-third of the population of the globe—or one of them to two of us—and it cannot much

longer continue that two-thirds will passively submit to the universal domination of this one-third." In the aftermath of World War II, the prediction of Dr. Delany was realized as national liberation movements erupted in Asia and Africa to seal the fate of colonialism. In Africa, the freedom train began to roll when Libya in 1952, Morocco and Sudan in 1956, Tunisia and Ghana in 1957 and Guinea in 1958 became politically independent.

In 1960, these were joined by no less than sixteen other African states. During the next five years, eleven more achieved independence. By the mid-1960's, the Assembly of the United Nations had 56 African and Asian member states, 50.4 per cent of the total membership, as compared to only 11, or 21.6 per cent, in 1945, when the organization was founded. The emergence of the colored peoples of the world awakened in Negro Americans a new sense of pride, dignity, importance and belonging.

Inspired by the freedom struggles of the colored people abroad, Negro militants in America sparked a civil rights movement of their own to end Jim Crow, not in some distant future, but here and now. It was a grass-roots movement, a boiling over, a time of boundless energy and blazing courage, when the nobodies became somebodies and the impossible became possible. It was a time of youth, hope and enthusiasm. What generations of civil rights fighters had sought in vain to accomplish was now brought to fruition overnight. When the cry "communist-inspired" was used in an attempt to stop the movement, it was greeted with derision. Tear gas, fire hoses, electric prods, police dogs, clubs, billies, guns and jails broke before the indomitable will of a people who sang the new battle hymn of the republic, "We Shall Overcome." It was as if the entire history of the civil rights movement of the past one hundred years had been but a dress rehearsal for what came to be known as the "Negro Revolution."

CIVIL RIGHTS ACTIVITIES

This great popular upsurge of the sixties, so reminiscent of the earlier CIO crusade, began inconspicuously when a group of students sat down at a Woolworth's "white only" lunch counter in Greensboro, North Carolina. This first sit-in, which took place on February 1, 1960, opened the floodgates. The hosing down of Negro children during the massive demonstrations of the underprivileged and unemployed workers

of Birmingham; the march on Washington, D.C.; the sit-downs and lie-ins at construction sites in New York, Philadelphia and Cleveland; the impressive response to the call for school boycotts in a half-dozen Northern cities; the ghetto riots in New York, Rochester, Jersey City, Elizabeth, Paterson and Philadelphia; the Mississippi project with its freedom schools, political party and sharecroppers' union; the Selma to Montgomery march; and the Los Angeles upheaval forced the nation to take notice and caused the colored peoples of the world to protest the prevailing Jim Crow system in the United States. The Federal government stepped in and made concessions. But behind each of its moves toward racial equality, including the Civil Rights Act of 1964 and the Voting Rights Act of 1965, lay the sweat, pain and tears of countless boycotts, sit-ins, picket lines and mass demonstrations.

New organizations and new leaders sprang up to meet the challenge of the times: the Student Nonviolent Coordinating Committee, organized in 1960, and led by James Forman; the Southern Christian Leadership Conference, founded by the Rev. Martin Luther King, Jr., leader of the Montgomery, Alabama, bus boycott in 1956; and the Congress of Racial Equality, organized toward the close of World War II and headed by James Farmer. Based on grass-roots support, all three organizations employed the tactic of non-violent, militant civil disobedience. In the meantime, the older civil rights organizations—the National Association for the Advancement of Colored People, directed by Executive Secretary Roy Wilkins since 1955, and the National Urban League, led by Executive Director Whitney M. Young, Jr., since 1961—played their part in the movement by intensifying their activities along more traditional lines: court suits, new legislation and popular education.

JAMES FARMER

ROY WILKINS

With the deadline for social justice long overdue, Negroes in the medical and allied professions threw themselves into the battle to close the citizenship gap in the health field. As marches, sit-ins and other forms of direct action for equal rights rocked the nation, an ever growing number of the country's over five thousand Negro doctors became part of the irresistible ground swell. Like their brothers across the land, they staged sit-in demonstrations, threw up picket lines, and marched on city halls, state houses and even the national Capitol itself. They formed their own medical committees for civil rights, and all along the integration battlefront they fought for the immediate attainment of their objectives.

Militancy became the password of the movement. Reflecting the new spirit, Dr. Kenneth W. Clement, in his presidential address at the 68th Annual Convention of the National Medical Association in Los Angeles, August, 1963, observed:

DR. KENNETH W. CLEMENT

In this hour of the Negro's greatest struggle for his civil rights and his civil freedom, we need do well to remember that the cause of the Negro physician and his patient is one and inseparable. Not only must we redouble our efforts in the traditional areas, litigation, legislation and conciliatory conferences; we must also join in the direct action program assault on every form of social evil based on race. For this is the era of mass involvement and direct action. This we recognize, approve and applaud. But, my fellow-physicians! We must do more than approve, we must participate.

Meanwhile, Negro physicians were participating in the struggle for integration in medicine and health. On February 20, 1961, one year after the first sit-in at Greensboro, North Carolina, eight Negro physicians, members of the National Medical Association, were ordered out of the Biltmore Hotel, Atlanta, Georgia, for attempting to eat lunch in the hotel's cafeteria. When the eight, who were attending a conference held under the auspices of the Fulton County Medical Society, refused to leave and staged a sit-in demonstration, the police were summoned to arrest them. The Negro doctors were charged with trespassing, taken to police headquarters, booked, fingerprinted and released on bail after putting up their own one-hundred-dollar bonds.

Negro physicians also resorted to picketing. Concerning this form of direct action, the *Journal of the National Medical Association* in its July, 1963, issue declared editorially:

> . . . It is unthinkable that a physician could consider picketing beneath him as a dignified form of peaceful protest. The N.M.A. can already point with pride to the fact that in Atlanta, in Detroit and in Cleveland, leading physicians among its members have been participants in picketing demonstrations under various auspices.

This editorial appeared less than a month after the dramatic picketing of the American Medical Association convention in Atlantic City. On June 12, 1963, the Medical Committee for Civil Rights, a newly formed, biracial, national group of doctors and health personnel, sent out "An Appeal to the A.M.A." on the eve of its annual convention. The committee asked the American Medical Association "to speak out immediately and unequivocally against racial segregation and discrimination . . . wherever [they] exist in medicine and health services." Specifically, it urged the body to terminate "the racial exclusion policies of State and County medical societies" and to make available direct membership to Negro physicians thus denied, to "actively oppose the 'separate-but-equal' clause of the Hill-Burton Act" and to instruct its representatives on the Joint Commission on Accreditation of Hospitals to oppose accreditation of any hospital where patient services were not racially integrated.

The appeal was supported by leading Negro and white organizations, such as the American Jewish Congress, Congress of Racial Equality, National Association for the Advancement of Colored People, National Catholic Conference for Interracial Justice, Physicians' Forum, Southern Christian Leadership Conference, and Student Nonviolent Coordinating Committee. When the AMA's answer to the appeal was found to be "totally inadequate," the committee decided to move into the public arena "to convey the seriousness of the situation."

On June 19, 1963, a hundred years after the Emancipation Proclamation, a picket line of 20 health workers, headed by Negro and white physicians, paraded in front of Atlantic City's swank Traymore Hotel, where the American Medical Association was holding its 112th annual convention. The demonstration began only minutes after Dr. Edward R. Annis had stepped down from the dais after delivering his presidential address to the house of delegates. He was met by a Negro physician from New York City, Dr. John L. S. Hollo-

Physicians picket on the boardwalk in front of the AMA convention hotel in Atlantic City. Leading this demonstration are (from right to left) Dr. John L. S. Holloman, Jr., Dr. Robert Smith, and Dr. Walter Lear.

man, Jr., who, on behalf of the Medical Committee for Civil Rights, handed him a letter reiterating the committee's appeal to the AMA to speak out against segregation and discrimination, both in local and state medical societies and in health care facilities for Negroes. Dr. Annis accepted the letter; whereupon Dr. Holloman left the air-conditioned hall for the demonstration outside on the boardwalk. Falling in step behind him on the picket line were Dr. Robert Smith of Jackson, Mississippi, and Dr. Walter J. Lear of New York City, general coordinator of the committee and an authority on public health services.

Later that day, Dr. Percy E. Hopkins, chairman of the AMA's Board of Trustees, stated that the picketing was tending "to obscure the achievements in medical science being reported at [the] meeting" and that "a Negro physician—my friend Peter Murray of New York—served for 12 years

as a member of the A.M.A. policy-making House of Delegates . . . ." To these remarks, Dr. Holloman, who was co-chairman of the Medical Committee for Civil Rights, replied: "Dr. Murray's membership in the House was progress, but he's gone now . . . and so has the feeling of ten or fifteen years ago that allowed gradualism and tokenism in the breaking down of racial barriers."

Two weeks after the Atlantic City demonstration, physicians again picketed the American Medical Association in protest against its passive support of Jim Crow practices within the organization. This time the AMA's headquarters in Chicago was the scene of the demonstration. The picket line, called by the National Association for the Advancement of Colored People during its annual convention in Chicago, was led by Negro physicians and dentists, several of whom were members of

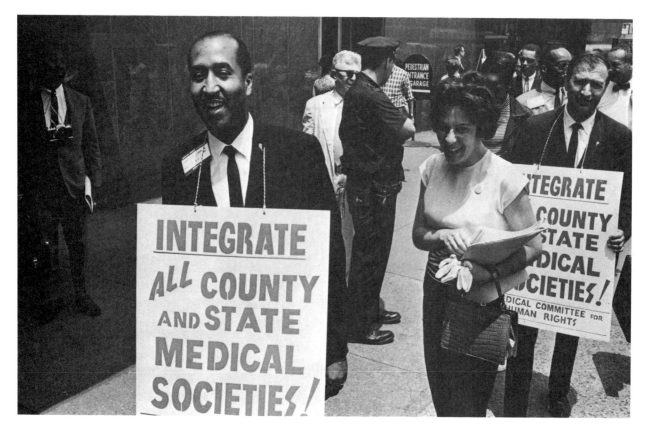

Dr. John L. S. Holloman, Jr., leads members of the Medical Committee for Human Rights in a biracial picket line outside the 114th annual convention of the American Medical Association in New York City.

the association's national board of directors and two of whom were officers of the National Medical Association. Subsequently, the NAACP's convention denounced the American Medical Association and the American Dental Association for failure "to keep pace with the rest of the Americas in the eradication of all vestiges of racial segregation and discrimination."

But the picketing of the American Medical Association in 1963 was pale compared to the demonstrations that greeted it in 1965 and 1966. On June 21, 1965, at its 114th annual convention in New York City, about 200 Negro and white demonstrators formed a picket line in front of the Coliseum, where the association was holding its scientific meeting. The demonstration was well organized. It began with one hundred people in a church near the convention hall. After receiving instructions, the group

moved out of the church and marched to the Coliseum. They were joined by another hundred. For two hours the demonstrators circled the building, carrying signs that demanded, "Integrate All County and State Medical Societies!" "End Discrimination in Medicine Now!" Handbills were distributed demanding positive and definitive action to end racial prejudice within the American Medical Association and throughout the health facilities of the nation. At the end of the picketing, the participants returned to their headquarters in the nearby church for a rally.

The picket line was even larger at the American Medical Association meeting in Chicago the following year. On June 27, 1966, about four hundred people picketed outside McCormick Place, where the scientific meeting was being held. Identifying their demonstration as a "witness to end racial exclusion" in medicine, the marchers—twice as many whites as Negroes—carried signs and distributed leaflets. When some of the demonstrators attempted to circulate the handbills inside the entrance hall of the building, they were ordered by security guards to stop and were threatened with arrest.

Both the 1965 and 1966 demonstrations were organized by the biracial Medical Committee for Human Rights, successor to the Medical Committee for Civil Rights. Among the national sponsors of the new organization were such outstanding white physicians as Nobel Laureate Albert Szent-Gyorgyi, Paul Dudley White, Leo Davidoff, Benjamin Spock, Albert B. Sabin, Howard A. Rusk, Leo Mayer, Louis C. Lasagna and Samuel Z. Levine, and such leading Negro physicians as Leonidas H. Berry, Paul Cornely and Albert B. Britton, Jr. The committee was presided over by Dr. John L. S. Holloman, Jr., who became national chairman in 1965, succeeding Dr. Aaron O. Wells. Both men were well-known Negro physicians practicing in New York City.

DR. AARON O. WELLS

Dr. Wells, first national chairman of the Medical Committee for Human Rights, has given the following description of its founding.

Members of the Medical Committee for Human Rights picketing outside the 1966 convention of the AMA.

One evening early last June [1964], I received an urgent call from a colleague and lifelong friend to attend a meeting, mostly of physicians, that had been called to answer a request for emergency medical aid for civil rights workers in Mississippi. The original appeal had come from persons working in the voter-registration summer project . . .. The first meeting I attended made a tremendous impression on me. I listened to determined and enthusiastic discussion from twenty to thirty persons who sought a program to meet the needs of volunteer workers. . . . In less than a week we decided the request could be met, and I volunteered to serve with the group, which at that time was so new it had no name. Four physicians were selected as an advance committee . . . to determine how our medical presence in Mississippi could be made most effective. They returned with an enthusiastic report, and we assigned medical teams to initiate the program. Before the first team entered Mississippi, this nucleus of dedicated persons found a name—the Medical Committee on [sic] Human Rights.

On July 16, 1964, the committee was formally launched in New York City at a meeting in Mt. Sinai Hospital attended by doctors from fifteen hospitals. The next day the members of the first medical team— a doctor, a registered nurse and a driver— left for Mississippi. The first team was followed by others; within five months, one hundred physicians, nurses, dentists and public health workers went to Mississippi to provide medical assistance for civil rights workers. They aided local physicians in examining and immunizing freedom workers, particularly in the smaller towns and rural areas, where medical facilities were limited. In emergency cases, they arranged with local doctors for first-aid treatment to civil rights workers and, when needed, hospitalization. Concerning the committee's contributions to the Mississippi Summer Project, Aaron Henry, chairman of the Council of Federated Organizations, said:

The contributions already made by the Medical Committee for Human Rights have been in several instances the difference between a successful campaign and failure. The presence of medical personnel is crucial in terms of confidence and general assistance in securing medical services for the civil rights workers. It is our desire, hope and request that this Committee will find it possible to remain on the scene in Mississippi as long as they are needed.

Early in August, 1964, two members of the Medical Committee for Human Rights, Dr. Aaron O. Wells and Dr. Charles Goodrich, were present when a third member, Dr. David Spain, arrived in Mississippi to examine the bodies of three young civil rights workers—one Negro, James Chaney, and two whites, Michael Schwerner and Andrew Goodman—murdered on June 21 near the town of Philadelphia, in Neshoba County. The three bodies had been discovered, two months after the tragic occurrence, buried under tons of red clay at a dam construction site. Dr. Spain, clinical professor of pathology at the State University of New York Downstate Medical Center in Brooklyn, who was requested by the Schwerner family to perform an autopsy on their son, described the body as follows:

The jaw was shattered, the left shoulder and upper arm reduced to a pulp. . . the skull bones were broken and pushed in toward the brain. In my extensive experience of 25 years as a pathologist . . . I have never witnessed bones so severely shattered, except in tremendously high-speed accidents, such as plane crashes.

Of the examination of the three bodies by the noted white New York pathologist, Dr. Wells wrote: "I cannot speak in detail of the actual examination, which was conducted by Dr. Spain, for the sight of those dreadfully mutilated young bodies put me in a state of emotional shock."

During the fall and winter, the Medical Committee for Human Rights kept the "Mississippi Story" alive in medical circles. Over four hundred people attended a meeting at the Albert Einstein College of Medicine in New York, where it was resolved to send thirty volunteer doctors and nurses to Mississippi as well as a donation of $2,500. In Los Angeles, at a meeting which attracted a "standing-room only" audience, including forty medical students, four students and a medical resident volunteered for service in Mississippi. In Pittsburgh, a letter was sent to physicians in the city and county to acquaint them with the committee's work and future program. The American Academy for Cerebral Palsy, which planned to hold its 1966 meeting in Biloxi, Mississippi, cancelled the assembly when the committee's presiding officer and others wrote letters protesting the locale of the meeting.

Originating in New York, the Medical Committee for Human Rights organized chapters in Los Angeles, Pittsburgh, New Haven, Washington and other large cities across the country. In April, 1965, it held its first national convention in Washington, D.C. On the opening day of the convention, the problem of the possible arrest of physicians for practicing medicine in states other than the one in which they were duly licensed was discussed. National Chairman Dr. Aaron O. Wells stated that the committee was consulting with legal counsel on the problem, but that, in the meantime, the committee's position was that doctors had an ethical obligation to render first-aid care. Dr. Arthur Falls, a Chicago surgeon associated with the Committee to End Discrimination in Chicago Medical Institutions,

DR. ARTHUR FALLS

reported that, if giving medical aid meant "going to jail," some of the group's members were "ready to go to jail."

The convention considered a number of important issues and passed several resolutions. James M. Quigley, assistant secretary of the Department of Health, Education and Welfare, disclosed that in the

James M. Quigley delivering an address before the first convention of the Medical Committee for Human Rights.

previous three and a half months the department had received about 150 complaints, most of them charging discrimination in hospital facilities. He urged the convention to work with the government to document fully complaints of this nature and to forward them to his department. James Forman, executive secretary of the Student Nonviolent Coordinating Committee, urged the development of medical care programs not only in Mississippi and elsewhere in the South but also in "Northern [Negro] ghettos." Appropriate resolutions were passed by the convention to implement these suggestions.

By the summer of 1965, the Medical Committee for Human Rights had expanded its program to include, in its own words, the "protection and care of student civil rights workers; development of rural health centers and mobile health units; health education; aid to community workers in developing health and medical programs; surveying medical needs and documenting discriminatory patterns in health services in the North and South, to provide a basis for change." Under the national chairmanship of Dr. John L. S. Holloman, Jr., the biracial committee increased its membership to three thousand and the number of its chapters to seventeen. At its second annual convention in Chicago, March, 1966, it drew up plans to go into poverty-stricken Appalachia to initiate pressure for better medical care.

In addition to the Medical Committee for Human Rights, the National Medical Association took part in the Mississippi Summer Project. On July 8, 1964, it joined the National Association for the Advancement of Colored People and the New York City Public Health Association in appealing to President Johnson "to take steps needed to ensure that the protective arm of the United States includes guaranty of emergency treatment for civil rights workers who may suffer injury from Mississippi racists."

The above appeal was occasioned by the shooting of a 16-year-old girl who attended a meeting in Moss Point, Mississippi, earlier in the week. At its 69th annual convention in Washington, August 2–6, 1964, the National Medical Association adopted a resolution directing its "component and constituent societies to recruit volunteers to render medical care in areas of the South where events determine the need . . .." An *ad hoc* committee of five, headed by Dr. Albert B. Britton, Jr., was appointed to recruit NMA volunteers to go to Mississippi. Members were urged to obtain reciprocal licenses before entering the state. With such licenses they could practice in Mississippi, thereby providing medical care not only for out-of-state civil rights workers, but also for resident Negroes.

In addition to sit-ins, picketing and the Mississippi Summer Project, Negro phy-

DR. ALBERT B. BRITTON, JR.

sicians engaged in mass demonstrations. They were part of the quarter of a million men, women, and children who marched on Washington for jobs and freedom in the summer of 1963. Almost two years later, they participated in the electrifying march from Selma to Montgomery, Alabama.

This demonstration came after weeks and months of a Negro voter-registration drive initiated by the Rev. Martin Luther King's Southern Christian Leadership Conference. For days, the nation witnessed on television the naked and brutal use of force by Selma policemen and Alabama state troopers as Negroes tried to exercise their right to march, petition and register to vote. Selma had become a battleground for civil rights. The large crowds and the repeated clashes with the police made the presence of medical personnel and equipment imperative. In February, 1965, the Medical Committee for Human Rights transferred from Mississippi to Alabama a small truck originally furnished by the National Council of Churches and subsequently outfitted as an ambulance, complete with a two-way radio. In addition, the organization enlisted the aid of a number of physicians to meet the medical needs of the participants.

On Sunday, March 7, 1965, the medical committee's ambulance, manned by three physicians, attempted to accompany the civil rights marchers as they left Selma for their long trek to Montgomery. The vehicle was stopped just short of the Pettus Bridge; on the other side of the bridge, the marching contingent was met by policemen and state troopers who used tear gas and billy clubs to force the demonstrators to return to Selma. When the injured were brought back across the bridge, they were attended by the physicians of the Medical Committee for Human Rights and two local Negro doctors, members of the National Medical Association.

Marchers stream across the Pettus Bridge, Selma, Alabama, beginning their five day, fifty-mile march to Montgomery.

This attack on "Bloody Sunday" made the civil rights forces more determined than ever to march from Selma to Montgomery, and additional provisions were made to take care of the medical aspects of the march. The Medical Committee for Human Rights recruited more physicians; and ultimately, about 120 of them, Negro and white, served until the march was over. Dr. David M. French, an associate professor of surgery at Howard University and a leading member of the Washington Chapter, arrived in Selma with authorization from Dr. Aaron

DR. DAVID M. FRENCH

O. Wells, chairman of the medical committee, to use drafts drawn on the national office to purchase all necessary medical supplies. When the only medical supply house in the area insisted on being paid in cash, personal appeals were made by the medical committee to doctors across the country, who raised funds in their communities and telegraphed them to Dr. French. In this way, cash was obtained and the necessary supplies purchased. Dr. Holloman joined Dr. French in Selma to assist in administering the medical coverage of the march.

In the meantime, Dr. W. Montague Cobb, president of the National Medical Association, advised the Rev. Martin Luther King of the NMA's willingness "to support the Selma effort in any way in which our assistance might be desired." Dr. Cobb received a reply from the Rev. Dr. King inviting him "to join in the March in Selma on Sunday, March 21, as a 'personal witness.'" The day before the demonstration began, Dr. Cobb arrived in the embattled city with NMA funds to help defray medical costs. The money was turned over to Dr. James E. Caple of Montgomery, president of the Alabama State Medical Association, a unit of the NMA. He and Dr. Edward A. Maddox, Jr., of Selma were in charge of the medical coverage of the march by NMA members. Thirty physicians belonging to the Alabama State Medical Association volunteered their services during the demonstration.

On March 21, 1965, the historic march began. Medical supplies, equipment and personnel were in readiness. A large medical van, supplied by the International Ladies Garment Workers Union, with complete X-ray and laboratory facilities as well as two beds for patient care, and the smaller ambulance belonging to the medical committee were the primary medical support vehicles for the march. Negro undertakers in Selma and Montgomery donated their own ambulances to be used in the evacuation of injured or sick persons either to the main ambulances along the line of march or to hospitals in Selma and Montgomery. The Dallas County Voters League, a Negro organization, furnished three mobile first-aid stations. During the five-day march, all these units provided the attending physicians with invaluable support. The doctors were assisted also by thirty-two nurses from the John A. Andrew Hospital of Tuskegee Institute and twenty-eight nurses from Dallas County and Montgomery.

Selma was chosen as the medical headquarters for the first half of the march, and the St. Jude Catholic Hospital on the outskirts of Montgomery, for the second half. The Catholic priest in charge of St. Jude set aside one wing of the hospital for the combined use of the Medical Committee for Human Rights and the physicians from Montgomery. On March 25, as the last of the marchers entered the plaza in front of the State Capitol in Montgomery, it was apparent to all that the medical arrangements had been well handled. Late that night, Mrs. Viola Liuzzo, a civil rights worker from Detroit, was murdered, adding proof, if such were needed, of the shame of Selma.

Dr. Paul Lowinger, a Detroit physician who served in the Selma to Montgomery march with the Medical Committee for Human Rights, submitted a letter to the *Journal of the American Medical Association* describing his personal and professional reactions to the historic demonstration in Alabama. Although the letter was accepted for publication by the *Journal's* editor on April 29, 1965, the physician was informed three weeks later that it would not be published. "In a con-

troversial issue such as this," the editor was said to have written, "it has been my policy to withhold judgment until after a latent period and a subsequent rereading of the original correspondence. Having allowed a sufficient time to lapse, it is my judgment not to publish this letter in the correspondence section of the J.A.M.A." Commented the physician, "One wonders about the events that occur during such 'a latent period.'" The question was also raised of "how controversial are the guarantees of the Federal Constitution and the U.S. Code?"

Negro physicians also contributed their services to the Meredith march through Mississippi. On June 5, 1966, James H. Meredith, who was the first Negro student to be admitted to the University of Mississippi, left Memphis, Tennessee, with a small

Dr. King leading the marchers to Montgomery, Alabama.

DR. ALVIN F. POUSSAINT

band of followers to march to Jackson, Mississippi, to encourage the Negro voter-registration drive. He had barely crossed the Mississippi border when he was felled by a shotgun blast. Quickly, a group of civil rights leaders met to announce their intention of continuing the Meredith demonstration through the heart of the delta country to the State Capitol in Jackson, a distance of 220 miles.

The Medical Committee for Human Rights was called upon to provide medical support for the marchers. Dr. Alvin F. Poussaint, a Negro psychiatrist and a leading member of the biracial group, was given the authority and the funds to make the necessary arrangements. He was well qualified for the task at hand. As Southern field director of the medical committee, he participated in the important work of the organization's clinic in Holmes County, Mississippi, which not only provided medical care for impoverished Negroes but also acted as a focal point for the dissemina-

tion of health education to many counties in the state.

Dr. Poussaint, supported by the Medical Committee for Human Rights, did an outstanding job in providing the marchers with the necessary medical and health care services. His achievements were especially noteworthy because the arrangements for the march were made on short notice and the demonstration itself covered a period of approximately three weeks—four times as long as the previous march from Selma to Montgomery. Dr. Poussaint and his team of nurses, as well as a group of volunteer doctors from various parts of the country, were in attendance all along the line of march. On June 26, 1966, the long trek came to an end in Jackson, where a crowd of fifteen thousand attended a rally demanding immediate and widespread changes in the treatment of Negroes. The throng cheered lustily as a Confederate flag was burned on the grounds of the State Capitol. There were cheers, too, for Dr. Poussaint when he stepped to the rostrum and said: "A new day is here, brothers, and we should begin to think, act, and feel that 'We Shall Overthrow' . . . the vicious system of segregation, discrimination, and white supremacy."

Negro physicians used not only direct action, but also litigation and legislation to eliminate racial discrimination and segregation in medicine and health. The National Association for the Advancement of Colored People provided counsel for Negro doctors, dentists and patients involved in court suits challenging the "separate-but-equal" clause of the Hill-Burton Act. In the meantime, on the legislative front, the National Medical Association was instrumental in securing the repeal of the "separate-but-equal" provision. Similarly, Negro doctors, working through their own and other organizations, helped pass the Civil Rights Act of 1964, which provided for the withdrawal of Federal funds from any public facility practicing discrimination.

Also successful was the three-year-old effort of the National Medical Association to enact a medicare bill for the aged under Social Security, a measure calculated to take care of the hospital needs of economically hard-pressed senior citizens, black and white alike. In August, 1962, the NMA placed itself on record as favoring such a measure. By this action, it became, in its own words, "a dissenter from the dominant organization of American medicine. . . ." In March, 1963, it reaffirmed its *de facto* "declaration of independence" by again endorsing medicare. Meanwhile, the American Medical Association assumed leadership in the fight against the adoption of such legislation. Its position was made clear in August, 1964, when its representative, Dr. Edward R. Annis, appeared before the Senate Finance Committee to urge rejection of a medicare bill under the Social

DR. JOHN A. KENNEY, JR.

Security Act as dangerous to "our free system of medicine and the quality of health care it provides." Following the election of President Johnson, the passage of medicare was given high priority. On May 4, 1965, Dr. W. Montague Cobb, president of the National Medical Association, accompanied by Dr. Kenneth W. Clement, past president, appeared before the Senate Finance Committee in support of a House resolution providing a hospital insurance program for the aged to be financed through Social Security. In his testimony, Dr. Cobb urged that "due anti-discrimination provisions be clearly written into [the resolution] so that possible litigation may be avoided." A few months later, medicare for the aged under the Social Security Act was passed.

OPERATION CLEAN-UP

For a decade and a half prior to 1960, Negroes in medicine were given a good dose of "tokenism" and "gradualism." Instead of keeping them quiet, the dose served only to make them more determined and militant. Under the momentum of the civil rights movement of the 1960's, they pressed forward in what they hoped would be "Operation Clean-Up!"

No longer were they willing to wait. They knew a resolution of their problems was long overdue, and they wanted something more than fine words. As Dr. John A. Kenney, Jr., President of the National Medical Association, put it in July, 1963, "The time has come in the problems that confront the physicians of the country, especially the Negro physicians, that something more than talk is absolutely necessary." About two months before, Dr. Cobb had expressed the same spirit of urgency and militancy when, calling for "equal justice in health care now," he told the Seventh Imhotep National Conference on Hospital Integration:

For seven years we have invited them [representatives of the American Medical Association, American Hospital Association and other major hospital organizations] to sit down with us and solve the problem. The high professional and economic levels of these bodies and the altruistic religious principles according to which they are supposed to operate seem to have meant nothing. By their refusal to confer they force action by crisis. And now events have passed beyond them. The initiative offered is no longer theirs to accept.

By the summer of 1963, sufficient tactical advances on the integration battlefront had opened the doors of almost every medical college in the country to Negro applicants. By then as many as nineteen Southern medical schools had provided for the admission of Negro students. Later, by the fall of 1963, two more in the South, Duke and Emory, and one in the border state of Maryland, Johns Hopkins, had followed suit. By the summer of 1966, four additional ones, Baylor, Louisiana State, Vanderbilt and the Medical College of Alabama, had jumped on the bandwagon. This brought to twenty-six the number of Southern medical schools that had dropped their racial bars since 1948, when the first Negro medical student was admitted to the University of Arkansas.

Despite the virtual elimination of discriminatory admission policies, Negro student enrollment in medical schools remained limited. From 1956 to 1962, the increase in the number of Negro medical students was no more than ten per year. In fact, the number of Negroes studying medicine at schools other than Howard and Meharry actually decreased, from 216 in 1956–57 to 164 in 1961–62. Subsequently, Negro student enrollment in white medical schools dropped by 80 per year—more than one-third. Concerning this decrease, the New York State Advisory Committee, in its May, 1964, report to the United States Commission on Civil Rights, noted:

In the city, as in the nation, the number of Negroes attending medical school is decreasing. There are more scholarships available to Negro medical students than there are students to use them. This Committee found no evidence that any medical school in the city does not admit and graduate Negro students on the same basis as white students. In fact, schools seeking a representative student body tend to give a slight preference to Negro applicants. . . .

Why then the present limited enrollment of Negro medical students? The committee found the answer in "the larger pattern of discrimination against and segregation of the Negro which has discouraged young men and women from attempting to fulfill educational prerequisites for a medical career."

By the late fifties, as a result of the hospital-building program under the Hill-Burton Act, there were five thousand more approved internships than there were students graduating from the medical schools of the country. During the first half of the 1960's, Negro medical graduates were no longer finding it difficult to secure internships and residencies at approved hospitals. In 1963, all of the 165 Howard and Meharry graduates were appointed as interns to as many as eighty-two different hospitals, a record number. Similarly, there was no difficulty in obtaining internships two years later, when 134 Howard and Meharry graduates of the class of 1965 were appointed to sixty-eight hospitals throughout the country. Significantly, few of these hospitals were in the South. By the mid-1960's, there was also an ample supply of residencies for Negro physicians. This was most important, for by then roughly 85 per cent of all interns went on to become residents because of the ever growing trend toward specialization in medicine.

Although Negroes were finding it easier to get internships and residencies at all-white hospitals, they were still faced with the problem, especially in the South, of being excluded from membership in local affiliates of the American Medical Association. As the decade of the sixties opened, most of the association's Southern constituent bodies, despite the parent organization's 1950 and 1952 resolutions, continued to deny Negroes membership privileges because of color.

To eliminate this and other racial inequities in the medical profession, representatives of the American Medical Association and the National Medical Association agreed to hold a series of discussions. The first took place on July 2, 1963, when leaders of both organizations met at AMA headquarters in Chicago. At this top-level meeting the conferees agreed to establish a continuing committee to meet with greater frequency than had similar joint committees in the past. At these meetings specific charges of discriminatory practices against Negro physicians were to be the basis for discussion. The agreement was received by Negro doctors with reactions ranging from an attitude of "wait and see" to a "waste of time." On August 7, 1963, the two groups held another meeting.

At the 68th annual convention of the National Medical Association in Los Angeles, August 12–15, 1963, Dr. Norman A. Welch, president-elect of the AMA, informed the Negro physicians present that progress was being made at the liaison meetings and that "the American Medical Association is aware that physicians of your race do have problems to overcome in your struggle for equal opportunities in the practice of medicine." Dr. Welch assured the delegates that the AMA was prepared to do what it could to help them solve these problems. He personally saw no barrier to the American Medical Association taking a stand on the repeal of the "separate-but-equal" provision of the Hill-Burton Act and going on record as opposed to racial discrimination in hospital staff appointments.

On December 19, 1963, a third liaison meeting of the two organizations was held. Among the AMA representatives were Dr. Norman Welch, president-elect; Dr. Percy Hopkins, chairman of the board of trustees; and Dr. F. L. Blasingame, former vice-president. Included in the NMA delegation were Dr. Kenneth W. Clement, president; Dr. W. Montague Cobb, president-elect; and Dr. John A. Kenney, Jr., past president. Dr. Edward R. Annis, president of the American Medical Association, presided over the three-hour session. Among the subjects discussed was a report by the National Medical Association on medical education, hospital staff appointments and county society membership. This was the last liaison meeting held by the two organizations; in fact, it was not until the summer of 1965 that proposals were made to reactivate the discussions.

As the year 1964 progressed, it became clear that, on the question of county society membership in the South, the American Medical Association would continue its ostrich-like policy of burying its head in the sands of the status quo. At its San Francisco convention in June, it adopted a resolution strong in words but weak in implementation. The resolution expressed unalterable opposition to "the denial of membership, privileges and responsibilities in county medical societies and state medical associations to any duly licensed physician because of race . . ." and called upon all individuals, as well as constituent bodies, "to exert every effort to end every instance in which equal rights, privileges or responsibilities are denied."

Following the San Francisco convention, militant AMA members, Negro and white, turned with renewed vigor to the elimination of color bars for membership in county and state medical societies. Fully aware that the national organization as constituted could do no more than verbally condemn any discrimination in Southern county and state medical bodies, they urged the adoption of a constitutional amendment to give the national organization the right to revoke the charters of recalcitrant local affiliates. A resolution to this effect was unanimously passed by the Medical Society of the County of New York on May 24, 1965. Introduced by Dr. Jerome A. Schack and Dr. John L. S. Holloman, Jr., the resolution called upon the state society to introduce at the AMA's June meeting the following amendment to its constitution and by-laws: "Membership in the American Medical Association of any constituent association shall be revoked if such constituent association shall allow any component society to deny membership to any individual on the basis of race, creed or color."

DR. JOHN R. FORD

The New York State Medical Society, however, refused to introduce the county resolution. Instead, it proposed a resolution calling for direct membership of Negro doctors in the AMA provided they had been barred because of color by local affiliates, a proposal which some felt was more appropriate to the spirit of the 1950's than to that of the mid-1960's. "That's just a piece of paper," observed a spokesman for the Medical Committee for Human Rights, according to the *Los Angeles Times* of June 22, 1965. "We're against it." In addition, the newspaper reported: "Direct membership [in the AMA] would not solve the problem, it was added. Only through county and [state] medical society membership can Negro doctors get the necessary hospital appointments in the South, the spokesman said." At its annual convention in New York, June 20–25, 1965, the American Medical Association continued its policy of fine words but no punitive action in regard to county medical society membership.

Pressure for positive action against racial discrimination on state and local levels continued to mount within the American Medical Association as preparations were made for its next convention. In March, 1966, a resolution asking the AMA to deny affiliation to any county or state society that continued to practice racial discrimination was introduced before the California Medical Association by two Negro physicians, Dr. John R. Ford of San Diego and Dr. Leroy Weekes of Los Angeles, as a substitute for one presented by the Marin County Medical Society recommending that Negro doctors who were not allowed to join state affiliates be made members-at-large of the national organization.

Meanwhile the State Medical Society of New York unanimously passed a resolution urging the AMA to adopt a constitutional amendment that would revoke the affiliation of any state medical body that allowed a component unit to restrict membership because of race. It also unanimously adopted a resolution giving a physician the right to appeal to the national organization if he were denied membership in a constituent association on the basis of racial discrimination. Other state medical societies joined the New York body in passing resolutions that would establish some mechanism by which Negro physicians would have the right of appeal. At the 115th annual convention of the AMA in Chicago, June, 1966, the various state resolutions were referred to a hearing committee, which condensed them into a report. Although the report ignored any disaffiliation ideas, it did suggest the establishment of an appeals procedure; for without such a mechanism, it acknowleged the virtual impossibility of following through on the 1964 resolution of unalterable opposition to the denial of membership in county or state societies because of race. The House of Delegates then voted that an appeals procedure be presented for its approval at the December clinical meeting in Las Vegas.

While Negro and white militants were striving on a national level to force the American Medical Association to intervene actively on behalf of Southern Negro physicians excluded from county affiliates because of color, the fight for such integrated bodies was taking place in the South itself. In the forefront of the struggle was a group of courageous Negro doctors who, for the most part, were members of the National Medical Association. As freedom rides, picket lines, mass demonstrations, sit-ins, kneel-ins and pray-ins swept the old Confederacy, Negro physicians in increasing numbers applied for admission to local AMA units. Sometimes the doors swung open; more often than not, they remained tightly shut. Progress was slow; by the summer of 1963, Negro doctors were

DR. WILLIAM R. ADAMS

admitted to only a scattering of county medical societies.

In one Southern state, Louisiana, no local affiliate of the American Medical Association would admit a colored physician, regardless of his professional qualifications. When Negro doctors in New Orleans applied for staff privileges to Charity Hospital, a tax-supported city institution, they were told to seek membership in the Orleans Parish Medical Society. What happened next can best be told by one of the participants, Dr. William R. Adams, who was quoted in a press dispatch as follows: ". . . when we made application there, we were turned down flatly, with no effort at subterfuge. We were told Negro physicians were not accepted." An official of the Orleans Parish Medical Society, commenting on the local group's refusal to admit Negroes, observed somewhat philosophically: "This is bound to be the situation in a community where all activities, including medicine, are segregated." Despite such rebuffs, the Negro physicians of New Orleans persisted in their efforts to become members of the local unit. Finally, in May, 1965, five of them were elected to membership. This action represented the first significant victory in the last Southern state to exclude Negro physicians from membership in county medical societies.

Typical of the determination of Negro doctors in the South to break down color bars for admission to local medical bodies was the case of Dr. Hiram B. Moore of South Pittsburg, Tennessee, a town of 4,500 people located just two miles north of the Alabama border. Late in 1964, Dr. Moore applied for membership to the Chattanooga and Hamilton County Medical Society. This was no new experience for him. On two other occasions his application for admission had been rejected.

Dr. Moore was a self-made man, highly respected in South Pittsburg for his ability

DR. HIRAM B. MOORE

to achieve what he set out to do. Born of poor parents, he worked his way through high school and college. After graduating from Meharry and serving an internship in North Carolina, he returned home to engage in the general practice of medicine. He soon assumed leadership among his people, organizing them as a political force. His voter-registration campaign was responsible for bringing 95 per cent of them to the polls. Elected to the town's housing and planning commissions, he fought for the rights of his people. When it was proposed that a sewer system be installed in the white section of the town, he argued that to be effective such a system would have to be built in the Negro section too since flies knew no barriers in the propagation of disease. He stuck to his point with such tenacity that the white commissioners eventually agreed.

Dr. Moore showed the same dogged resolution in his fight for admission to the all-white Chattanooga and Hamilton County Medical Society. When, in the fall of 1964, he presented his application for membership a third time, the society's House of Delegates voted unanimously to accept him. In reporting Dr. Moore's victory, the *Medical Tribune* of December 9, 1964, wrote:

> Now that he belongs to organized medicine's basic component, the county medical society, the winner of this year's "Outstanding General Practitioner" award of the National Medical Association can knock at and expect to enter other organizations that have been closed to him—Chattanooga's Erlanger and Memorial Hospitals, the Tennessee Academy of General Practice, the American Academy of General Practice, the Tennessee Medical Association and the American Medical Association.

Although Negro physicians were advancing inch by agonizing inch in their fight to enter Southern county medical societies, they were still far from able to mount a frontal assault on their adversary's position. In 1965, in the whole state of Louisiana, there was only one county society ready to accept them as members. In Mississippi the situation was little better: two local bodies admitted Negroes.

According to a newspaper report based on an authoritative source, in Georgia, sixty-eight of seventy-six county units denied membership to Negro physicians. In Alabama, sixty-six of seventy county societies discriminated against them. In Montgomery, Alabama, two of the city's eight Negro doctors, aided by the National Association for the Advancement of Colored People and the Imhotep National Conference on Hospital Integration, planned to sue the local medical society for admission. According to a press report, a suit was also to be filed against the medical society of Macon County, where forty of Alabama's eighty Negro physicians practiced.

For the Negro physician in many Southern communities, the crux of the problem facing him in the mid-1960's was membership in local AMA affiliates. Non-membership meant denial of hospital affiliation since doctors, as a matter of course, had to be accredited by their county societies before they could be eligible for hospital appointments. To Negro doctors in the South, such exclusion meant professional stagnation and economic deprivation. Without hospital connections, they were denied the opportunity of pursuing their medical education and training. Any hope they might entertain of doing research had to be abandoned. Moreover, if they wished to hospitalize their patients, they could do so only by referring them to staff physicians, thereby running the risk of losing them forever. Non-membership in local medical units imposed other economic disabilities. Without county medical society accreditation, Southern Negro doctors were automatically barred from participation in company and union-backed health care

DR. MIDDLETON H. LAMBRIGHT

plans, a new and rapidly developing area of medical practice.

In the North, where membership in local medical societies was open to all, the problem facing Negro physicians was chiefly one of participation in policy-making decisions. So deeply rooted was the spirit of *de facto* segregation that very few Negroes were admitted to positions of leadership and responsibility in Northern medical societies. Only in rare instances did they attain high elective posts. During the 1950's, Dr. Lorenzo R. Nelson was elected to head the Micosta-Osceola-Lake (Tri-County) Medical Society, Michigan; Dr. Peter M. Murray, the Medical Society of the County of New York; Dr. John E. Lowry, the Medical Society of the County of Queens, New York; and Dr. Joseph L. Carwin, the Stamford County Medical Society, Connecticut.

During the 1960's, Dr. Middleton H. Lambright was chosen to preside over the

DR. ARTHUR H. COLEMAN

Cleveland Academy of Medicine, Ohio; Dr. Elbert H. Pogue, the Union County Medical Society, New Jersey; and Dr. Clement M. Jones, the Hudson County Medical Society, New Jersey. Similarly, during the post-World War II years only a handful of Negro doctors were chosen to sit on the board of directors of local units.

By the mid-1960's, the question of Negro doctors' acquiring positions of leadership in Northern county medical societies came increasingly to the fore. The issue was put bluntly by Dr. Arthur H. Coleman, a San Francisco general practitioner and legal consultant to the National Medical Association, when he said recently: "I've taken the position that we still have *de facto* segregation in medical societies in the North. In San Francisco a Negro physician can enter the medical society but does not reach the decision-making level." To support his contention, Dr. Coleman cited the fact that no Negro had ever been nominated to a decision-making post in Oakland and that in San Mateo County, there was but one Negro on the board. In passing, it should be noted that in the San Francisco Bay area Negro physicians were considered to be much better off than their colleagues in many Northern localities.

"Operation Clean-Up" involved not only the desegregation of county medical societies but also the integration of hospital facilities. So numerous were the new discoveries in modern medical science that, by the early 1960's, it was clear to all that only through hospital affiliation could a doctor keep abreast of his field and improve his professional competence. It was also evident that the hospital, with all its diversified services, was central to the adequate care of suffering patients, no matter what their race, creed or economic status. Thus, hospital staff appointments for Negro physicians and equal hospital accommodations for Negro patients were prime objectives of the civil rights forces in medicine and health.

In this phase of the clean-up operation, the main target for attack was the Hill-Burton Hospital Construction Act of 1946. For more than a decade and a half, the "separate-but-equal" clause of the law was discreetly kept in the background while nearly two billion dollars of federal funds were poured into the rebuilding of the American hospital system. However, Negro citizens did not share equally with white Americans in the use of these Federally financed health care facilities. As the 1963 *Report of the United States Commission on Civil Rights* expressed it:

> . . . the evidence clearly shows that Negroes do not share equally with white citizens in the use of such facilities. As patients and medical professionals, they are discriminated against in their access to publicly supported health facilities. Commission investigation also shows that the federal government, by statute and administration, supports racial discrimination in the provision of health facilities.

As of March, 1964, 104 segregated hospitals and health facilities were built with Federal funds under the Hill-Burton Act, 84 of them for "whites only" and 20 for Negroes.

A two-pronged offensive was mounted to eliminate the "separate-but-equal" clause of the Hill-Burton Act. Court suits were instituted to declare the provision unconstitutional, and Congressional action sought to replace it with a specific anti-bias clause. In February, 1962, two hospitals in Greensboro, North Carolina, aided by Hill-Burton funds were sued by eleven Negro citizens who brought various charges of racial discrimination against the institutions. Argument centered about the "separate-but-equal" provision of the Hill-Burton Act, the plaintiffs contending it to be a violation of the Fifth and Fourteenth Amendments to the Constitution. The staff of the Legal Defense and Education Fund of the National Association for the Advancement of Colored People served as counsel.

Then, on November 1, 1963, one of the Greensboro cases, that involving the Moses Cone Hospital, came before the United States Court of Appeals in Richmond, Virginia. The court ruled that racial discrimination for both patient and staff was illegal in Federally aided hospitals and held the "separate-but-equal" provision of the Hill-Burton Act unconstitutional. On March 2, 1964, the Supreme Court of the United States sustained the decision by refusing to review the case, another historic landmark on the road to equal opportunity. On April 1, 1964, the United States Court of Appeals in Richmond, Virginia, reversed on appeal a lower-court decision in the case of *Dr. Hubert A. Eaton et al.* v. *the James Walker Memorial Hospital in Wilmington, North Carolina.* On May 18, 1964, the Public Health Service and the Department of HEW filed an order implementing the Moses Cone Hospital court decision banning discrimination in Federally aided hospitals.

DR. HUBERT A. EATON

Meanwhile, Senator Jacob Javits of New York and Representative John Dingell of Michigan voiced opposition on the floor of Congress to a continuation of the "separate-but-equal" clause of the Hill-Burton Act. Challenging the principle of racial discrimination and segregation in hospital facilities built with Federal funds, Senator Javits declared: "Negro M.D.'s meet obstacles in their practice and advancement every step of the way. Some hospitals still bar Negro patients altogether. Some limit their numbers and segregate them in basements and attics under 'the separate but equal' item." In September, 1962, Senator Javits' first bill to eliminate the clause was tabled by a vote of thirty-seven to thirty-three.

The following year Senator Javits' proposal for an anti-discrimination amendment to the Hill-Burton Act was rejected by a roll-call vote of 44 to 37. This came after a delegation of the National Medical Association had met with President Kennedy re-

JOHN DINGELL

JACOB JAVITS

questing his support for the Javits amendment. Shortly thereafter, the American Hospital Association voted to recommend the deletion of the "separate-but-equal" provision from the Hill-Burton Act. However, it was not until August, 1964, that the civil rights forces in Congress were able to overcome the opposition of powerful Southern senators and their Northern allies and secure the passage of a bill insuring equal health opportunities for all in Federally aided hospitals. This measure, which extended the Hill-Burton Act for five years, not only eliminated the "separate-but-equal" clause but specified that the state had to provide adequate facilities "for all persons residing in the state."

The NMA supported the insertion of an anti-bias clause and deplored the American Medical Association's failure to suggest such a provision in a proposed amendment to the measure. The signing of the bill by President Johnson was witnessed by a group of Congressional leaders and representatives of various organizations, including Dr. W. Montague Cobb, president of the National Medical Association.

Dr. Cobb was also the moving spirit behind the Imhotep National Conference, whose fight for hospital integration through the years was of inestimable value. Not only did the organization focus attention at its annual meetings on the problem of racial discrimination and segregation in hospitals, but it also strove to mobilize public support for hospital integration by direct action on the local level. At its fifth annual conference, May 26-27, 1961, Dr. Joseph L. Johnson called for the nationwide formation of local Imhotep committees composed of representatives of the local branches of the National Association for the Advancement of Colored People, the National Urban League and the National Medical Association. In preparing for its seventh annual conference in Atlanta,

Georgia, May 17–18, 1963, the organization's leadership called upon individuals and groups to write letters to editors of local newspapers protesting discriminatory conditions in local facilities. It also urged letters to state and Federal legislators asking that steps be taken to eliminate racial discrimination in hospitals.

Untiring efforts and ceaseless agitation on the part of the Imhotep National Conference, reinforced by the growing strength of the civil rights movement, began to have more effective results. In March, 1964, the board of trustees of the American Hospital Association accepted the logic of the Imhotep position by issuing a statement underscoring the need to make medical and hospital care available to all without qualifications of any kind.

On July 27, 1964, Anthony J. Celebrezze, Secretary of Health, Education and Welfare, convened an Imhotep-type conference in the nation's capital. The all-day meeting, attended by representatives of the American Medical Association, the National Medical Association, the American Dental Association, the National Dental Association, the American Hospital Association and the American Nurses' Association, discussed ways and means of speeding the elimination of racial bias in hospitals by voluntary action. High government officials, including the Associate Special Counsel to President Johnson, made it clear that the time had come to develop a cooperative program to eliminate racial discrimination in the nation's hospital facilities.

In the meantime, the Imhotep influence was felt by those hospitals that were managed or directed by religious bodies. At its sixth annual meeting in May, 1962, the Imhotep National Conference on Hospital Integration took special note of the paradox of racial discrimination in church-operated hospital facilities. Commenting on the contradiction, the *Journal of the National Medical Association* in September, 1962, said editorially: "Significant remedial action in this area may be anticipated if the matter is pursued with some vigor." It was so pursued by the Imhotep leadership, which appealed directly to church groups to eliminate the "un-Christian-like attitude" of racial bias in denominational hospitals. As the civil rights movement pushed ahead, advances were registered in the desegregation of a number of Catholic and Protestant hospitals. Particularly impressive was the progress made by Jewish institutions. By the close of 1964, member hospitals of the Council of Jewish Federation and Welfare Funds extended services to all patients and staff privileges to all doctors, regardless of race, creed or national origin.

Throughout the country, pressure, whether in the form of non-violent direct action or behind-the-scenes negotiations, was effective in bringing about a greater

ANTHONY J. CELEBREZZE

measure of desegregation in public and private hospitals. Yet, despite the progress made, Negro medical personnel and Negro patients still had a long way to go before hospital integration became a reality. In 1963, official and unofficial surveys revealed that staff privileges for Negro doctors were difficult to secure in cities across the nation. Some cities were better than others; but there were no "best" cities, because some discrimination was found in all.

According to a spot-check by *Medical Tribune* early in August, 1963, Indianapolis, Milwaukee and San Francisco were among the better cities. In Indianapolis, Negroes had fair representation on hospital staffs; as the general secretary of the Hoosier State Medical Association, an NMA affiliate, remarked: "I don't know of any hospital where a Negro physician can't get in." In Milwaukee, a Negro general practitioner stated that Negroes were able to obtain

DR. RAY TRUSSELL

appointments to most hospitals, and in San Francisco apparently all Negro physicians had staff appointments.

The *Medical Tribune* survey of August, 1963, showed other cities running the gamut from better to worse. A Negro internist in Los Angeles reported progress but observed that quite a few Negroes, especially board-qualified and certified surgeons, were not able to obtain appointments. In St. Louis, hospital staff appointments seemed to be opening up; the president of the NMA local affiliate viewed the future as "very hopeful, if the general situation keeps progressing as it is now." On the other hand, the future looked bleak in New Orleans, where Negroes were denied hospital staff appointments because of non-membership in the AMA local medical society. Across the state line in Mississippi, there were no Negro physicians in any of the state's public hospitals. The picture was different in Beaumont, Texas, where Negro doctors were admitted to all but one of the five local hospitals. The situation was described as even better in Dallas, Fort Worth and Houston.

The *Medical Tribune* spot-check of cities showed that, in the summer of 1963, Negro physicians in New York and Chicago, though making progress, were still having difficulty in obtaining hospital staff privileges. In New York City, Commissioner of Hospitals Dr. Ray Trussell was quoted as saying: "There is no question that discrimination is being practiced. While many Negroes have obtained hospital privileges recently, there still remains the question of various subtle practices that tend to limit him, once he has these privileges." One Harlem gynecologist estimated that there were less than fifty Negro physicians on all voluntary staffs combined, including those on the fringe areas of Negro-white neighborhoods. (In its *Report on New York City: Health Facilities,* May, 1964, the New York

State Advisory Committee to the United States Commission on Civil Rights wrote: "The most critical problem facing the Negro physician in New York City is that of securing an appointment to a hospital staff that carries admitting privileges for his patients with it.")

In Chicago, forty-three Negro physicians held sixty-six appointments at fewer than half of the city's sixty-nine private hospitals. A lawsuit, begun in 1961 against fifty-six hospitals, Blue Cross, Blue Shield and others, accomplished what was described as "the present astounding increase." (Early in 1964, the suit was suspended for a two-year period; and a "watch-dog commission" of seven members, including two Negro physicians representing the Cook County Physicians Association, was established. The commission was to investigate all charges made by the Negro doctors and to propose corrective action. If the plan proved effective, the suit was to be dismissed.)

Although Washington, D.C., was not included in the *Medical Tribune* survey, a 1963 study of private hospitals in the nation's capital showed the existence of the same pattern of racial discrimination in hospital staff appointments. This city, where the population was 54 per cent Negro, had 300 Negro physicians out of a total number of 2,200 practitioners. Of the Negro doctors, 72 were board-certified specialists. In the ten private hospitals located in the District of Columbia, 11 Negroes had staff privileges and 90 had courtesy privileges.

Two years after its first survey, the *Medical Tribune* conducted a second one on Negro integration in medicine. Published in the summer of 1965, the survey showed that, although some progress had been made in opening hospital staff appointments to Negroes, discrimination in the area was still nationwide, with conditions in some localities better than in others. In San Francisco, one of the "better" localities,

the problem was said to be one involving the participation of Negro physicians on hospital decision-making committees rather than admission to hospital staffs. In Philadelphia, it was reported that Negro doctors were being invited to join what were previously all-white staffs. In Milwaukee, Negroes were able to obtain staff appointments readily.

In St. Louis, however, the situation was not so favorable. The tendency there was to give Negro surgeons staff appointments but to keep Negro internists out. The reason for this, according to the report, was basically economic: the Negro surgeon had a quicker turnover of patients. In Los Angeles, one Negro physician noted "some progress" in hospital staff appointments. Another observed that some hospitals still continued to appoint Negroes on a quota basis. In New York, the consensus was that no significant progress was being made to integrate staff appointments at some of the city's best voluntary hospitals. In many of Chicago's hospitals, courtesy rather than regular appointments were general.

In the South, discriminatory practices in hospital staff appointments were far more overt. In New Orleans, Louisiana, Charity Hospital still refused to admit Negroes to its staff, though it accepted its first Negro intern. In Baton Rouge, the state's capital, two large hospitals agreed to open their doors to Negro doctors. In Natchez, Mississippi, for the first time one of the hospitals in the city accepted a Negro physician on its staff. In Huntsville, Alabama, the community's two Negro doctors were associated with local hospitals, while in Birmingham, one Negro physician was admitted to the University of Alabama Hospital and three were accepted by three of the city's larger hospitals. In Atlanta, Georgia, Grady Memorial Hospital, a municipal institution desegrated by court order, was reported to be ready to integrate all of its facilities. In addition, one of the city's newest hospitals completely integrated its staff positions.

Race prejudice and discrimination worked to the disadvantage not only of Negro physicians applying for staff privileges but also of Negro patients in need of hospital care. During the 1960's, despite the accelerated drive for equal rights and equal opportunities in hospital facilities, the evidence indicates that there was still much to be done along these lines throughout the country. In the South, the Negro people had fewer hospital facilities at their disposal than the white population. In Atlanta, Georgia, Negroes had the use of only 630 of 4,500 hospital beds, although they constituted 50 per cent of the population. In the Birmingham, Alabama, area, hospitals reserved 1,762 beds for whites and 574 for blacks, despite the fact that 40 per cent of the population was Negro.

Since Negroes did not share equally with white patients in the use of hospital facilities, such as were available to them were generally overcrowded. In a Texas hospital, built with Federal funds, Negro patients were forced to use beds in hallways and aisles, although in the "white" section, there were empty beds. In this particular hospital, there were no private rooms for Negroes and only one bathroom for Negro men and women. Given such conditions, Negroes in the South tended to shun "white" hospitals, holding out against them unless there was no alternative.

In the North, discriminatory policies and practices on the part of hospitals were more of a *de facto* character. Despite a Chicago ordinance to prevent racial discrimination in hospitals, the United States Commission on Civil Rights in 1963 found the situation there "especially acute." It discovered that nearly all Negroes in Chicago went to the Cook County Hospital, a public institution.

Even many able to pay went there because of the inability of Negroes to find sufficient accommodations elsewhere, though the city had as many as sixty-nine other hospitals. Three facilities in the metropolitan area with a predominantly Negro patient load had 329 beds, 214 of which were officially listed as "unsuitable" by the state agency administering the Hill-Burton Act.

In New York City, an official report published in 1964 indicated that most Negroes, even those with hospital insurance, were being cared for in wards rather than in semi-private rooms. According to the report, "more than half of the nonwhite participants in Blue Cross do not use semiprivate facilities although they are entitled to them." This, the study continued, might be "due to ignorance of their rights, lack of money to pay doctor's bills, or the fact that their physicians cannot get them into hospitals as semiprivate patients because the physicians lack admitting privileges and must send their patients through the clinics and into the wards."

The New York report further revealed that, although hospitals in the city claimed that patients were admitted and assigned beds without discrimination or segregation, charges were made that this was not always the case in privately operated institutions. The report quoted a highly placed white physician as saying: "There's no doubt that voluntary hospitals frequently find that they 'have no bed available' when a Negro patient wants to be admitted—except when the patient has a condition of special interest medically." On the whole, however, the report found that "apart from some instances of segregated patient placement, Negro patients in New York City receive nondiscriminatory attention."

In Los Angeles, according to a study published in 1963, Negro patients were being taken care of in the Los Angeles County General Hospital. Recently, how-

DR. LEROY R. WEEKES

DR. EARL B. SMITH

ever, more beds were being made available to Negroes in private hospitals. Dr. Leroy R. Weekes, author of the study, wrote:

> I know of no hospital in the Los Angeles area that refuses admission to Negro patients. I am not familiar with any hospitals which have certain sub-standard areas such as basements or attics specifically allocated to Negro patients. I am pleased to report that there are several hospitals which completely integrate their patients without any reference to race, color or creed.

However, he noted that some still practiced segregation, despite disclaimers to the contrary. In August, 1963, a Negro internist in Los Angeles told the *Medical Tribune* that, although public hospitals in the area placed patients at random, there was a type of segregation practiced in some large private hospitals by placing Negroes together in semi-private rooms.

In the May, 1965, issue of the *Journal of the National Medical Association,* Dr. Earl

B. Smith of Pittsburgh reported the existence of racial discrimination at the semi-private level in that city's hospitals. As he put it:

> There is still subtle and overt segregation of Negro patients at the semi-private level. We must admit that there are more persons in the city of Pittsburgh with semi-private insurance coverage than available semi-private beds. We advocate open hospital occupancy at all levels especially the semi-private without regard to race.

The article further revealed that in the last seven years there were complaints of discriminatory practices against Negro patients. "The Negro physician and the patient," wrote Dr. Smith, "have a dual obligation to correct these injustices."

Racial discrimination in patient placement also prevailed in St. Louis. The *Medical Tribune* of August 2, 1965, in its survey of integration of Negroes in medicine, quoted a general practitioner in St. Louis as saying that, in some of the city's large general hospitals, Negro "patients are concentrated in one wing predominantly or, when they request a semiprivate room in the largely white parts of the hospitals, are assigned a room with another Negro." The same source cited one fairly large private hospital on the edge of a Negro area as never having admitted a Negro patient.

In St. Louis as well as in other metropolitan areas throughout the country, Negro patients in increasing numbers were using county and municipal hospital facilities. Although vastly improved through the years, city and county hospitals still left much to be desired in the level of medical care. Because of inadequate funds, they were traditionally staffed by "low-qualified, low-paid personnel and part-time doctors."

In many metropolitan areas, the awareness was steadily growing that, if the level of hospital care was to be raised, integration of hospital facilities was essential. In Washington, D.C., where for years there had been a long, drawn-out fight over equal rights for Negro patients and Negro doctors, the Hospital Council urged all of its twenty-four major institutions to integrate their facilities. In a statement issued on December 10, 1964, the council urged among other things "that care should be provided to all in need of attention regardless of race, color, creed or national origin" and that practicing physicians be appointed to hospital staffs on the basis of qualifications and need rather than racial or other like considerations. The *Journal of the National Medical Association,* in its March, 1965, issue, described the statement as one that might be regarded "as both a precedent and a model for the cities of the nation."

Despite some promising signs, much still remained to be done to make equal rights and equal opportunities in medicine and health a reality. With the exception of medical colleges, the overwhelming majority of which were admitting or indicated a willingness to admit Negroes, racial restrictions continued to exist in other traditional areas.

In the South, Negro doctors were still barred from medical societies and hospital staffs. In the North, color prejudice was strong enough to exclude them from admission to a number of the larger and better private hospitals and from positions of leadership and trust in professional bodies. North as well as South, Negro physicians wanted to share with their white colleagues the opportunity to advance in all fields and not to be limited, as one Negro doctor facetiously put it, to radiology, anesthesiology and pathology because: "In radiology the patient is in the dark and can't see the doctor. In anesthesiology he's asleep. And in pathology he's dead and it doesn't make any difference."

Like Negro physicians, Negro patients suffered from a wide range of discriminatory practices. In the old Confederate states, they were still excluded from all-white hospitals or from the "white" sections of mixed hospitals. In the North and West, where *de facto* discrimination prevailed, they found themselves ingeniously placed in separate wards and semi-private rooms. Throughout the nation, they were forced to live in segregated areas where poverty and poor health went hand in hand and adequate medical care was woefully lacking.

During the early 1960's, statistical data from across the country revealed the same shocking racial disparities in health. In every section of the nation, Negro babies still had less chance to survive than white babies and less likelihood, if they did survive, to live as long as whites.

Thus, for those striving to achieve racial equality in medicine and health, there was still much unfinished business on the agenda.

CHAPTER TEN

No Time for Delay

I want to give notice that the National Medical Association in conjunction with other civil rights organizations will continue to fight with all its resources against all health institutions and facilities that discriminate against Negro physicians and their patients. Let the racists know that as long as they continue this nefarious practice, they will have no peace.

Dr. Lionel F. Swan, President's Inaugural Address, at the 72nd Annual Convention of the NMA, St. Louis, August, 1967.

The residents of the racial ghetto are significantly less healthy than most other Americans. They suffer from higher mortality rates, higher incidence of major diseases, and lower availability and utilization of medical services. They also experience higher admission rates to mental hospitals.

Report of the National Advisory Commission on Civil Disorders, March, 1968.

DURING the second half of the 1960's, the movement to eliminate racist attitudes and patterns of behavior in organized medicine and bring some measure of adequate health care to the racial ghettos made painfully slow progress. Whatever gains were registered in these areas, as well as in employment, voting, housing, education and slum clearance, came about as a result of continuous and unrelenting struggle. Yet, in spite of all efforts on the part of dedicated groups fighting for racial justice, the gains made were so few and far between that the condition of the Negro masses continued to deteriorate. Any hopes they might have entertained of escaping from their hard lot steadily diminished. A sense of futility took hold of black Americans locked into their ghettos. Gone was the feeling of euphoria and buoyancy so characteristic of the earlier civil rights crusade. Out of the stark realities of the late sixties came frustration and despair, time-bombs ticking away in the urban slums of the world's richest nation. There was no time for delay.

Notwithstanding the urgency of the situation, the country's white power structure continued to procrastinate. Token enforcement of civil rights laws and a crass indifference to the desperate plight of the needy signalized business as usual. As the gap widened between promise and fulfillment, a new militancy emerged in the nation's black communities. Triggered chiefly by the youth, the new trend was grounded in the belief that Afro-Americans, through their own group strength, could not only win human dignity but also control, politically and economically, the communities in which they lived. No longer satisfied to be "beggars in the white man's house," the black militants raised the slogan of "Black Power" with its corollaries of self-determination, self-pride, self-dignity and self-defense for the segregated ghettos of the nation.

Under the impetus of the new upsurge, black slum-dwellers, disenchanted by the token integration of the civil rights campaign, took to the streets in a series of demonstrations that shook the nation. In the summer of 1967 alone, nearly 150 racial ghettos erupted as outbreaks of varying degrees of intensity swept across the country, the uprising in Detroit being one of the bloodiest in recent American history. The murder of the Rev. Martin Luther King, Jr., on April 4, 1968 in Memphis, Tennessee, touched off a new round of explosions. The worst of these took place in Washington, D.C., where regular troops and National Guard units were called out by President Johnson to quell the disorders.

The radicalization of the Negro freedom movement—its transformation from a purely civil rights crusade largely benefiting middle-class elements to a movement designed to advance the socio-economic interests of the black masses—affected every segment of the black community, including Negro physicians. In a speech before the 72nd Annual Convention of the National Medical Association in

National Guardsmen, called in to quell disorders in the nation's capital following the assassination of the Rev. Martin Luther King, Jr., patrol the still-smoldering streets.

DR. JOHN L. S. HOLLOMAN, JR.

challenge the very basis of the system in which we all live, to restructure it so that all of its participants can in actuality enjoy peace, freedom and justice."

DESEGREGATING AT A SNAIL'S PACE

Qualitative changes in the black liberation movement were reflected in the increased militancy of Negro physicians on the desegregation front. In his presidential address at the NMA convention in St. Louis, August 9, 1967, Dr. Lionel F. Swan, who practiced medicine in the heart of Detroit's racial ghetto, hurled the following challenge at racist elements in the health field: "I want to give notice that the National Medical Association in conjunction with other civil rights organizations will continue to fight with all its resources against all health institutions and facilities that discriminate against Negro physicians and their patients. Let the racists know that as long as they continue this nefarious practice, they will have no peace. They

St. Louis, August 9, 1967, Dr. John L. S. Holloman, Jr., retiring president, said that in the aftermath of the summer outbreaks Negro physicians, despite their middle-class status, could "no longer deny [their] relationship to the mass of black Americans who are less fortunate, less educated, less affluent" than they. He urged his listeners to identify themselves with the Afro-American masses "who have not been able to break out of the ghetto." This was likewise the theme of Dr. Holloman's successor, Dr. Lionel F. Swan, whose "President's Column" in the organization's official journal made repeated references to the need of working closely with the poor of the ghetto, particularly its young people. To Dr. Leroy R. Swift, Chairman of the NMA Council on Talent Recruitment, the association had a special role to play relevant to black youth. In a committee report submitted January 31, 1968, he summarized that role as one that would prepare young black people "not merely to meet the challenges of this society, but to

DR. LIONEL F. SWAN

will have to go from court to court. They will have to fight for retention of their Federal funds, and I assure them that we shall never tire of the struggle."

Yet, despite pressure on the part of the National Medical Association, the Medical Committee for Human Rights and other organizations, the desegregation movement advanced at a snail's pace. Had there been the will to go beyond minimal or token enforcement of existing laws on the statute books, resolutions passed by professional bodies and official guidelines adopted by Federal agencies, restrictive racial policies in the medical and hospital fields would have become things of the past.

Although practically every medical school in the country had opened its doors to Negroes by the mid-1960's, few black students were able to qualify for admission because of the great difficulty of meeting high entrance requirements with an inferior educational background. How high the admission standards were could be gauged by the fact that in the academic year 1967–1968, the country's ninety-four medical colleges admitted only 9,702 of the 18,724 students who applied. Particularly hard hit by these high qualifications for admission were black youths whose educational impoverishment stretched back to inadequate instruction in both secondary and elementary school and to a home life circumscribed by material and cultural deprivation. Inferior schooling and a limited home environment arising out of traditional patterns of racial discrimination in American life resulted in the fact that there were proportionally fewer black students eligible for admission to medical schools than white. Only 6 per cent of college-age blacks were reported to be attending colleges in 1967. More than one-half of these were in predominantly Negro institutions, where the dropout rate averaged more than 50 per cent.

As the 1960's unfolded, the feeling grew that until the same kind of education was available to all, regardless of color, it would be necessary to provide Negroes with special courses, projects and services to permit them to reach the same scholastic level as their more fortunate fellow students. This feeling found expression in a joint statement issued in 1968 by the American Medical Association and the National Medical Association. The statement urged the development of special college courses for promising black students, summer programs of special study and additional scholarship aid at both college and medical school levels.

Other interested organizations made proposals relating to the admission procedures of the nation's medical schools, particularly in regard to the widely used Medical College Admission Test (MCAT) given to all applicants. While presumably "objective" and not the only criterion for admission, the test was geared to young people of the white, urban middle class, for it clearly favored students with precise language skills, a broad apperceptive base and a solid high school and college education. The need of further research on "the correlation between the MCAT and acceptance into medical school and also on the MCAT and performance" was recognized at a conference held in Atlanta, Georgia, in February, 1968. The three-day meeting, called by the Josiah Macy, Jr. Foundation of New York City and co-sponsored by the Association of American Medical Colleges and the Southern Regional Education Board, recommended that the research study be undertaken by the Association of American Medical Colleges and that students, regardless of color, who did poorly on the MCAT, receive instruction at training centers established by medical schools "to the end that, upon re-examination, their MCAT score would indicate that these students have become qualified candidates for admission to medical school. . . ."

The Medical College Admission Test, together with high entrance requirements for admission, kept the number of black students to a minimum. Of the approximately 33,000 students who attended the country's medical schools in the academic year 1967–1968, less than 800, or fewer than 2.5 per cent, were estimated to be black. During that year, there were only fifty-one Negro medical students in twenty-seven Southern medical colleges. In the North, the record was somewhat better as a number of medical schools made conscious efforts to enroll black students. Among these institutions was the Harvard Medical School, whose faculty in April, 1968, voted to set up "a special recruiting program to increase substantially the number of Negro students at [the] school." Subsequently, a petition signed by 278 Harvard medical students declared their complete support of the faculty's move. Despite Harvard's action and assertions by medical schools that they were ready to admit Negroes, black medical student leaders were skeptical. In January, 1968, the president of the Student National Medical Association, James A. Booker, Jr., flatly stated that "predominantly white medical schools are restrictive in the number of Negroes matriculating." And he added: "Paradoxically, there are more white medical students at Howard University alone than Negro medical students at all the medical schools in New York combined."

Special efforts were made during the second half of the 1960's to recruit Negroes for careers in medicine. The movement bore some fruit; in the fall of 1968, according to a survey made by the Association of American Medical Colleges, approximately three hundred black students were expected to enter the nation's medical schools, 50 per cent more than the number in the fall of 1963. Taking the lead in the drive to enlist black youth for medicine was the National Medical Association, which established a Council on Talent Recruitment as early as August, 1964, following the recommendations of Dr. W. Montague Cobb, then president of the organization. The council, under the chairmanship first of Dr.

Edward S. Cooper of Philadelphia and then of Dr. Leroy R. Swift of Durham, North Carolina, did yeoman service in raising funds for the project and motivating young people to careers in medicine. The Medical Committee for Human Rights was also engaged in talent recruitment. At its third annual conference in New York, early in 1967, Dr. Arthur Falls presided over a seminar that outlined ways and means of encouraging black youth to enter the health field. Similarly, the International Afro-American Museum, Inc., of Detroit, under the chairmanship of Dr. Charles H. Wright, worked to encourage the young to enter medicine. With the support of the Detroit Medical Society, an NMA affiliate, the organization made a film entitled "Opportunities for the Afro-American in the Field of Medicine," the aim of which was "to recruit black students for the nation's medical schools."

In June, 1967, the Josiah Macy, Jr. Foundation, in cooperation with National Medical Fellowships, Inc., held a four-day conference on Negroes for medicine. At the meeting, it was pointed out that one of the greatest potential sources for talent recruitment, particularly for medical schools, was the black woman. It was noted by the conference that, although women constituted well over 50 per cent of Negro college students, "less than 10 per cent of the Negro medical students [were] women." The potential of Negro women for medicine was recognized by The Woods Charitable Fund, Inc., of Chicago, which established a number of scholarships in the field. In June, 1968, in announcing these grants to seven young women to attend six medical schools, Dr. John C. Troxel, President of the National Medical Fellowships, Inc., said: "I am very pleased that increased attention is being given to opportunities for Negro women in medicine." Two of the seven women were to attend Howard University Medical College, an institution from which 278 women were graduated during the period from 1872

DR. LEONIDAS BERRY

through 1967. In fact, in 1967 a record-breaking number of women, twenty-one out of a class of ninety-nine, received their M.D. degrees.

The American Medical Association also joined in the drive to recruit black youths for careers in medicine. As a result of a series of liaison meetings between it and the National Medical Association in 1965 and 1966, the AMA agreed, in the words of Dr. Leonidas H. Berry, then president of the NMA and himself one of the negotiators, "to increase usage of Negro faces in doctor-recruitment literature and stories about medical careers." In a joint statement in 1968, both organizations urged all medical schools "to encourage members of their faculties to sponsor special projects involving Negro high school students in laboratory work or other enlightening pursuits to enrich their experiences." The statement went on to recommend to all medical societies, medical schools and related groups that they "expand their careers-programming

with students, parents and guidance counselors at schools of all levels. . . ."

Although the high cost of a medical education was still a serious factor tending to discourage black Americans from pursuing medical careers, it was no longer as decisive an influence as it had once been. To overcome this financial deterrent, private Negro and white foundations, the National Medical Association and the Federal government provided needy, qualified black students with scholarship awards covering tuition and other costs. That there were more grants available to Negroes than black applicants to accept them reflected the fact that medicine was becoming less and less attractive to promising young black people in comparison with other professions where the training period was shorter and not as arduous. Furthermore, the persistence of discriminatory patterns in medical bodies and hospital staffs did not help to make medical careers more inviting to young Afro-Americans.

Some advances were made in the closing years of the sixties to eliminate racial barriers and prejudice in medical societies. As in other areas, so here the movement forward was slow and came about only as a result of unremitting pressure. Despite an AMA agreement growing out of the AMA-NMA liaison talks of 1965-1966 to set up a special committee to urge local affiliates to comply with AMA antibias resolutions, and despite the establishment in 1966 of an appeals procedure within the AMA to hear individual cases of alleged discrimination, racial restrictions were still used to exclude Negroes from many AMA affiliates in the South. In 1968, it was estimated in civil rights circles that the number so barred in Alabama, Florida, Georgia, South Carolina, Mississippi and Louisiana came to nearly one thousand.

To prod the AMA leadership into positive action, members of the Medical Committee for Human Rights and supporters of the Poor People's Campaign established a picket line in front of the Fairmont Hotel on June 16, 1968, the opening day of the AMA's 117th annual convention in San Francisco. While fifty to one hundred pickets demonstrated outside the hotel against the AMA's record on racial discrimination and health services for the poor, inside two protesters ran up to the platform and seized the microphones just as the convention was getting under way. Pandemonium prevailed as the loud speakers were turned off and one of the demonstrators, a senior medical student at Stanford University and a member of the Medical Committee for Human Rights, castigated the AMA for racial and economic discrimination in medicine as well as a "backward delivery system of medical care." When he finished speaking, a representative of the Poor People's Campaign in the Bay area took the podium to denounce the AMA's discriminatory practices in health-care services for the poor. Eventually, order was restored but only after both demonstrators had spoken for about twenty-five minutes.

Meanwhile, copies of a statement by the Medical Committee for Human Rights were circulated to the nearly one thousand doctors and visitors in attendance. The statement noted that the country's health-care system faced "disintegration due in no small part to racial discrimination, economic discrimination, and archaic, poorly delivered and inadequate health programs." It held organized medicine partly responsible for this breakdown because it never felt "accountable to the American people for its actions. . . ."

Following the demonstration, Dr. Russell B. Roth, Vice-speaker of the House of Delegates, held an impromptu news conference. He was reported by the press as saying that he was in "no position to answer the scattergun charges" contained in the statement of the Medical Committee for Human Rights. "The bulk of these things," he continued, "are subjects of concern to our association. It is certainly a matter of attention to eliminate the last vestiges of discrimination in the AMA."

He went on to point out that a Massachusetts resolution calling for a constitutional change in the bylaws of the AMA to prohibit constituent bodies from practicing racial discrimination was being discussed in committee.

Two days later, the committee made its report to the House of Delegates. In a move obviously designed to sidetrack the Massachusetts resolution, the committee recommended the passage of a motion reiterating the older anti-bias statements of the AMA. Dr. Urban H. Eversole of Boston took the floor to warn his colleagues that previous policy resolutions had "failed to meet the problem head on without equivocation." Continuing, he said: "This session of the House of Delegates is the proper time to demonstrate to all American physicians, all students of medicine, and, in fact, to all America our sincerity by putting into our bylaws the rules by which we operate." In a surprising move, the house brushed aside the report of its own committee. A voice vote was taken on the Massachusetts resolution. There was no roll call asked or even a show of hands. Dr. Walter C. Bornemeier, Speaker of the House of Delegates, declared the Massachusetts amendment adopted. The approved resolution called for the drafting of new bylaws which would permit censure or, "in the event of repeated violations," expulsion of state medical societies practicing racial, religious or ethnic discrimination. The new bylaws were to be submitted for approval to the delegates at the December clinical convention. The AMA action was welcomed by Dr. T. G. G. Wilson, Chairman of the Medical Committee for Human Rights, as "a belated but gratifying recognition of the fairness" of his organization's demands for a constitutional amendment of the AMA's bylaws.

Similarly, the Southern Medical Association, reflecting the temper of the times, moved forward to eliminate the color line in medicine. At its annual convention in Washington, D.C., November 14–17, 1966, it invited all members of the Medical Society of the District of

Columbia, including its 150 Negro members, to attend the organization's meeting and join the association.

Some progress was also made to desegregate hospital facilities. But here, too, the movement—so essential to the professional development of Negro physicians and the well-being of black patients—proceeded slowly, despite the fact that the equal rights forces had the law of the land on their side. Under Title VI of the Civil Rights Act of 1964, government agencies could withhold Federal funds from hospitals that practiced racial discrimination. To implement the law, administrative guidelines were formulated by the Department of Health, Education and Welfare (HEW) in January, 1965.

Subsequently, reassuring statements were issued by high-ranking officials to the effect that the overwhelming majority of the nation's hospitals were complying with the Civil Rights Act. Dr. Leo J. Gehrig, Deputy United States Surgeon General, was reported in the *Los Angeles Times* of July 28, 1966, as saying that of the 6,681 general hospitals in the country that had applied for Medicare, as many as 6,439 had been certified under Title VI. Of the 219 that had been found in violation of the title, about 95 per cent, he asserted, were in the South. Less than a year later, in June, 1967, William H. Fleming, Regional Director of the HEW Office of Equal Health Opportunity with headquarters in Dallas, Texas, declared that most hospitals in the South were complying with Title VI and that there were only "pockets" of resistance to it. In June, 1968, Wilbur J. Cohen, Secretary of the Department of Health, Education and Welfare, stated that almost all of the country's seven thousand hospitals had been investigated or questioned in the past two years and that 98 per cent were in compliance.

Despite these optimistic and encouraging statements, civil rights leaders took a gloomier and more critical view of what was happening. At a press conference on December 16, 1965,

WILBUR J. COHEN

Dr. John L. S. Holloman asserted that most of the two thousand hospitals and health care institutions in the South discriminated in some way against Negroes. He said that only four of these hospitals, all in Mississippi, had been cut off from Federal-aid programs because of their refusal to sign Title VI compliance forms. Early the following year, the Commission on Civil Rights, after checking more than forty Southern communities, found that only a few had proceeded to desegregate completely their facilities. The *Los Angeles Times* of July 28, 1966, reported that at a meeting the day before in Atlanta, Georgia, a large number of Negro doctors and dentists charged that numerous hospitals in the South had been certified under Title VI only because they had signed compliance forms and not because they were desegregating their facilities.

The National Association for the Advancement of Colored People noted at its 1967 convention in Boston that there was "ample protection against discrimination by medical facilities using Federal funds, if the law [were] enforced." The following year, the Poor People's Campaign, organized by the Southern Christian Leadership Conference, included among its demands one calling upon the Federal government to enforce strongly civil rights legislation, as "it [applied] to hospital admissions and to staff privileges."

In the field of hospital desegregation, the enforcement of Title VI was at best minimal and was restricted almost exclusively to the South. For example, the Justice Department filed suits against such Southern facilities as the Marion County Hospital at Columbia, Mississippi (September, 1966), and the Orangeburg Hospital at Orangeburg, South Carolina (February, 1968). In both instances, the institutions were charged with racial discrimination in hospital facilities and medical care. Similarly, the Department of Health, Education and Welfare proceeded against several of the recalcitrant Southern hospitals. In December, 1966, the Public Health Service took the first formal steps to withhold Federal funds from seventeen hospitals in five Southern states. The following year, six of these facilities were declared ineligible for Medicare funds because of their failure to comply with the anti-discrimination provisions of the Civil Rights Act of 1964.

The National Medical Association, a leader in the fight for hospital integration over the years, vigorously opposed token enforcement of Title VI. Its position on the matter was made crystal clear by Dr. John L. S. Holloman at the interim meeting of the organization's Board of Trustees in St. Louis, February 11-12, 1967. In the preface to his formal report, the NMA president said: "The National Medical Association will continue to press for the full implementation of Title VI of the Civil Rights Act of 1964 and for the complete elimination of racial discrimination in all institutions and programs which receive federal financing assistance." In his report proper, Dr. Holloman urged a close watch, individually and collectively, of all health facilities. He

recommended that discriminatory practices be reported promptly to the NMA Committee on Medical Legislation, headed by Dr. John A. Kenney, Jr., for subsequent referral to the Office of Equal Health Opportunity, as well as any other proper agency.

The position of the American Medical Association on the implementation of the Civil Rights Act of 1964 was in sharp contrast to that of the National Medical Association. At the closing session of the 116th annual convention of the AMA in Atlantic City, June, 1967, the organization adopted a resolution that condemned the methods used by the Department of Health, Education and Welfare to enforce civil rights legislation in Southern hospitals. The resolution, as originally introduced by a Louisiana delegate, charged that the Office of Equal Health Opportunity, through its regional director in Dallas, was establishing a "race quota system" in Louisiana hospitals by asking them to furnish the names of their staff physicians and the number of white and nonwhite patients each staff member admitted to the hospital. Subsequently amended by another Southern delegate to include hospitals in Alabama and Georgia, the resolution was adopted by an overwhelming voice vote, despite the critical strictures of Dr. Leo J. Gehrig of Washington, D.C. He pointed out that the information being asked for was necessary to enforce the law since many Southern physicians were continuing to admit white patients to customarily white hospitals while sending black patients elsewhere. In a press conference in New York City, Dr. John L. S. Holloman, President of the NMA, strongly denounced the resolution as "an unwholesome retreat" and a distortion of the racial issue.

However, the stand of the American Medical Association on hospital desegregation was not a wholly negative one. On the positive side was the offer made in 1968 by the organization's Board of Trustees to work closely with the National Medical Association in investigating cases of racial discrimination, including those involving hospital staff privileges. The offer was accepted by the NMA House of Delegates at its August, 1968, convention in Houston, Texas, and was hailed by the association's incoming president, Dr. James M. Whittico, Jr., as a significant step forward. In commenting on *de facto* segregation in regard to hospital staffs, Dr. Whittico observed in his inaugural address: ". . . [The] picture is much better than it was 10 years ago as regards the admission of Negro physicians to 'white' hospitals; but still they are not being considered strictly on the basis of medical and moral qualifications."

Although headway was definitely being made to eliminate discriminatory practices in medicine, genuine and meaningful desegregation was still far from being realized. This was the gist of a survey based on interviews with Negro doctors in seventeen states and the District of Columbia, the results of which appeared in a series of five articles in the *Medical Tribune* in the fall of 1968. The findings of the publication's survey were summarized in its issue of October 14, 1968: "A new examination of the situation [the first was five years earlier] . . . shows almost uniform agreement that definite progress toward equal treatment is the rule in every region of the country—at least in a formal sense. The record is marred in some communities, however, by 'tokenism' in appointments and hospital staff privileges and in the admission policies of Negro patients by certain institutions. In addition, the relationship between white and black in a number of county medical societies that have admitted Negro physicians for the first time remains limited and 'correct,' rather than expansive and professionally casual."

HEALTH CARE IN THE BLACK GHETTOS

The struggle for desegregation in the medical and hospital fields was an essential part of the broader fight to bring to the poor of the black ghettos adequate systems for the delivery of health-care services. On the opening day of the White House Conference on Health that was held in Washington, D.C., on November 3, 1965, Dr. Alonzo S. Yerby, Hospital Commissioner of New York City, had this to say about the poor quality of medical care given to low-income groups in general and the Negro in particular: "Health care of the disadvantaged is piecemeal, often inadequate, underfinanced, poorly organized, and provided without compassion, or concern for the dignity of the individual. . . . Certain groups of the disadvantaged in America, notably the Negro, get even less than their share of health services, even though there is ample evidence that their needs are greatest."

That such was the case was also the considered opinion of the National Advisory Commission on Civil Disorders, whose report to President Lyndon B. Johnson in March, 1968, flatly stated: "The residents of the racial ghetto are significantly less healthy than most

DR. ALONZO S. YERBY

other Americans. They suffer from higher mortality rates, higher incidence of major diseases, and lower availability and utilization of medical services. They also experience higher admission rates to mental hospitals."

The battle to bring adequate health services to the nation's slums was complicated by the profound crisis that beset the nation's health industry in the late sixties. Medical manpower shortages and soaring medical costs were glaringly revealed as Medicare and Medicaid were implemented and a comprehensive health-care program, sponsored by the Office of Economic Opportunity, was launched. The lack of any clear-cut plan of operation, the multiplicity of overlapping government agencies, reductions in appropriations occasioned by an ever-widening and costly war in Vietnam and the intransigence of the top leadership of the AMA toward various aspects of the government's health program made a bad situation even worse. Under the circumstances, the movement to bring essential health services to the ghettos made tragically slow progress.

For years, competent authorities in the health field had predicted that American medicine would suffer from an inadequate supply of professionally trained personnel because of the rapid rise in population and the increasing demand for medical care services. By the second half of the 1960's, the medical manpower shortage was there for all to see. Even the American Medical Association came to recognize its existence when in June, 1967, on the eve of its 116th annual convention, the organization's Board of Trustees noted that the nation's shortage of doctors was reaching "alarming proportions." By the fall of that year, it was estimated that the physician shortage came to fifty thousand and that thousands of foreign doctors were being imported annually to help fill the American medical manpower gap. Equally critical were serious deficiencies in the supply of the country's auxiliary medical forces. A study conducted by the American Hospital Association and the Public

A large-scale recruitment program is under way to meet the nation's urgent need for trained nurses.

Health Service of more than one-half of the nation's registered hospitals indicated that approximately 275,000 additional nursing and technical personnel were needed in 1966 to provide optimum patient care.

Hardest hit by the critical shortage of physicians, nurses and technicians were those residents of areas where the black population was most heavily concentrated: the ghettos of the inner cities and the rural slums of the South. The *Los Angeles Times* of July 19, 1967, reported that the Negro district of Watts had only one-fifth as many doctors per capita as the rest of Los Angeles County. The National Advisory Commission on Civil Disorders cited in its report of March, 1968, a survey taken in Cleveland that indicated "there were 0.45 physicians per 1,000 people in poor neighborhoods, compared to 1.13 per 1,000 in nonpoverty areas."

Fewer doctors were also available to blacks living in the plantation regions of the Deep South. A team of medical men who made a study of conditions in six rural counties of Mississippi reported in mid-1967 that children living there were not only without proper food but also without access to doctors or dentists. Dr. Kenneth W. Clement, a past president of the National Medical Association, told the House Ways and Means Committee in March, 1967, that ". . . in Mississippi, Alabama, Arkansas, South Carolina and Georgia, from 22 per cent to 44 per cent of live births were to mothers unattended by physicians. . . ." In a thirty-five-page report to President Johnson in June, 1968, Secretary Wilbur Cohen of the Department of Health, Education and Welfare summarized the situation by referring to a maldistribution not only of physicians but also of hospitals "geographically and in relation to the poor, particularly the nonwhite poor."

The maldistribution of doctors geographically was matched by an imbalance racially. Although exact figures on the number of black physicians and medical school graduates are unavailable for the late sixties, various educated guesses, based on prior and first-hand knowledge, have been made. Writing in the *Journal of the National Medical Association*, November, 1967, Dr. Lionel S. Swan, President of the NMA, estimated the number of Negro doctors to be less than six thousand. Based on this estimate, Negroes constituted about 2 per cent of the nation's approximately 300,000 physicians, although they made up slightly more than 11 per cent of the 200 million people living in the country at the time. The same imbalance prevailed in respect to medical school graduates. Of the roughly 7,750 physicians who were graduated from American medical colleges in 1967, approximately 200, or about 2.5 per cent, were Negroes, most of whom came from Howard and Meharry.

For black students graduating from American medical colleges, the doctor shortage had one advantage: there were more internships available than applicants to fill them. As a result, Howard and Meharry graduates had no

trouble in securing such hospital appointments; in fact, averaging the years 1965 to 1968 inclusive, 139 of them received internships each year at seventy different hospitals across the nation. Similarly, Negro physicians found no difficulty in securing residencies; for here, too, there were far more posts than there were physicians to fill them.

The crisis in American medicine was reflected not only in the shortage of health personnel but also in constantly spiraling medical costs. According to a report submitted to President Johnson early in 1967 by Secretary John W. Gardner of the Department of Health, Education and Welfare, medical costs had risen since World War II at a rate about double that of the general cost-of-living index. The report further stated that charges for medical services reached an all-time high in 1966, when doctors' fees, which had been climbing at about 3 per cent a year since 1960, jumped to 7.8 per cent, while daily costs at hospitals shot up 16.5 per cent, their largest annual increase in eighteen years. Predictions were widespread in 1967 that medical costs, especially hospital charges, would continue to rise. According to a report in the *Los Angeles Times* of April 30, 1967, Walter J. McNerney, national president of the Blue Cross Association, estimated that daily rates at hospitals would increase by 12 per cent during the year, after which the annual rise was expected to "level off" at 7 to 8 per cent. About six months later, the Brookings Institution, after a survey of the impact of Medicare on the country's hospital facilities, predicted that hospital rates would reach $100 a day in the not too distant future.

From the standpoint of health, soaring medical costs spelled economic disaster for most black Americans. Relatively few Negroes were covered by existing hospitalization insurance programs. Individual rates were so high that only persons with above-average incomes could afford coverage. For individuals fortunate enough to work for companies that carried insurance, steady employment was necessary to ensure continued coverage. Because of low incomes and greater unemployment, few Negroes had hospitalization coverage. In Watts, Los Angeles, where the unemployment rate in 1965 was as high as 34 per cent, only 14 per cent of the men and 18 per cent of the women were covered by hospital insurance.

Maximum benefits under most hospital plans were so inadequate that financial ruin would result if extended treatment were required, particularly in a period of mounting medical costs. Moreover, in black communities the cost of keeping well had a way of rising even beyond that prevailing in white areas. In February, 1967, a subcommittee of the Senate's Small Business Committee was told that surveys conducted in New York and other large cities disclosed that ghetto residents paid substantially more for medicines than whites in the upper-income bracket.

Even if medical costs were not increasing, the mass of black Americans did not have the financial resources to purchase even a minimum of health care. About one-third of the country's black families earned less than $3,000 annually; very few reached the income level of more than $9,000 a year, which the Department of Labor estimated an urban family of four would need to maintain "a moderate living standard." Victims of unemployment and underemployment—"a sub-employment index" used by the Bureau of Labor Statistics in 1967 put the percentage of joblessness in poverty-stricken areas from 24.2 in Boston to 45.3 in New Orleans—the Negro poor were proportionally greater in number than the whites. According to the National Advisory Commission on Civil Disorders, in its report of March, 1968, ". . . the proportion of persons in the United States who are poor is 3.5 times as high among Negroes (41 per cent in 1966) as among whites (12 per cent in 1966)." President Johnson, in his budget message of January 29, 1968, estimated the number of persons in the poverty-income

bracket (set by the government at $3,350 a year for a family of four) at "less than 29 million," as compared with the 1963 estimate of 35 million.

In terms of health, poverty meant lack of medical care, improper diets, inadequate shelter and clothing and unsanitary living conditions. The correlation between indigence and ill health was underlined in a statistical profile of black ghetto life issued by the White House in November, 1967. In its section on health, the report read: "The life expectancy of nonwhites is lower in all adult age groups. Maternal and infant mortality rates are declining for all races, but remain much higher among nonwhites—four times greater on maternal deaths and twice as high on infant mortality. Nonwhites at all income levels pay fewer visits to doctors and dentists and are more likely to be treated in clinics. They suffer more disabling and chronic illnesses." The health gap between blacks and whites was also underscored in papers delivered by Paul M. Densen and Dr. James G. Haughton of New York City's Health Services Administration at a conference sponsored by Howard University in March, 1967. Both papers contended that health differences were not racially determined, the one by Dr. Haughton attributing racial disparities in health to such factors as limited accessibility to health facilities and the medical manpower shortage.

In the inner cities of the twelve largest metropolitan areas of the North, where more than a third of the country's black population lived, statistical data amply demonstrated the close relationship between poverty and poor health. In New York City, in 1964, two areas in Harlem that contained 25 per cent of Manhattan's population accounted for two-fifths of the borough's tuberculosis cases and roughly a third of its infant mortality. The Bedford-Stuyvesant area, which comprised 9 per cent of Brooklyn's population, was responsible for 34 per cent of its tuberculosis deaths and 22 per cent of its infant deaths. In 1965, the black ghetto of Watts in Los Angeles produced 44.8 per cent of the city's whooping cough, 42.8 per cent of its rheumatic fever, 44.6 per cent of its dysentery and 65 per cent of its reported tuberculin reactors, despite the fact that Watts, according to the 1960 census, contained only 17 per cent of the city's population. In 1966, the Negro infant death rate in San Francisco's ghetto neighborhoods was 57.8 per 100,000 population, as against a white rate of only 18.2. According to an article entitled "Health Hazards of the Slums," by Dr. Earl B. Smith in the *Journal of the National Medical Association*, March, 1967, the lower North Side, Hill and Homewood areas in Pittsburgh, which were 95 per cent black, had an infant mortality rate three times greater than that in the city as a whole.

Poverty and poor health were not restricted to the densely populated urban centers. In September, 1967, a 25-member national advisory commission, headed by Governor Edward T. Breathitt of Kentucky, reported to President Johnson that rural poverty affected an estimated 14 million Americans, many of whom were to be found in the plantation areas of the Deep South. The desperate economic plight of the rural poor of Mississippi was strikingly presented by Dr. Albert B. Britton, a Negro physician, in testimony before the Senate Subcommittee on Employment, Manpower and Poverty, April 10, 1967. Dr. Britton told the subcommittee that in 1960, "37 per cent of all nonwhite families [in Mississippi] and 10 per cent of all white families had an income of under $1,000." And he added that among nonwhite rural families "4 out of 5, or 81.3 per cent, lived on less than $2,000 a year, and more than half made do on less than $1,000 a year." Part of the tragic economic picture was the elimination of thousands of jobs on Mississippi plantations because of technological changes in cotton production. Press dispatches, citing a survey made by the Department of Labor in two Mississippi delta counties, reported in 1967 that 66 per cent of the people were unemployed, with Negro joblessness as high as 93 per cent.

What rural poverty meant in terms of hunger and disease was graphically revealed by a team of physicians who, in May, 1967, toured a six-county area of Mississippi "to survey the health and living conditions of a representative group of Negro children. . . ." In a report to the Field Foundation of New York City, the doctors told of seeing "children who are hungry and who are sick—children for whom hunger is a daily fact of life and sickness, in many forms, an inevitability . . . children who are getting *absolutely no medical care.*" They were especially distressed to find that diseases which might have been at one time correctable were now so bad as to be beyond medical help. It seemed unbelievable to them "that a nation as rich as ours, with all its technological and scientific resources, has to permit thousands and thousands of children to go hungry, go sick and die grim and premature deaths."

The Mississippi story of poverty, hunger and disease helped set in motion the Poor People's Campaign. Early in May, 1968, hundreds of indigent demonstrators from all parts of the country, organized by the Southern Christian Leadership Conference, met in Washington, D.C. They took up quarters in a shanty town called Resurrection City, built in the shadow of the Lincoln Memorial. The encampment was provided with health services by seven organizations, including the National Medical Association, the Medical Committee for Human Rights, the National Dental Association and the Medico-Chirurgical Society of the District of Columbia. To coordinate the activities of the various groups, the Health Services Coordinating Committee was formed on May 18, 1968. The committee, whose Executive Board was headed by Dr. Edward C. Mazique, worked closely with the Department of Public Health of the District of Columbia and the Howard University Medical College. More than three hundred doctors rendered medical and dental services on a

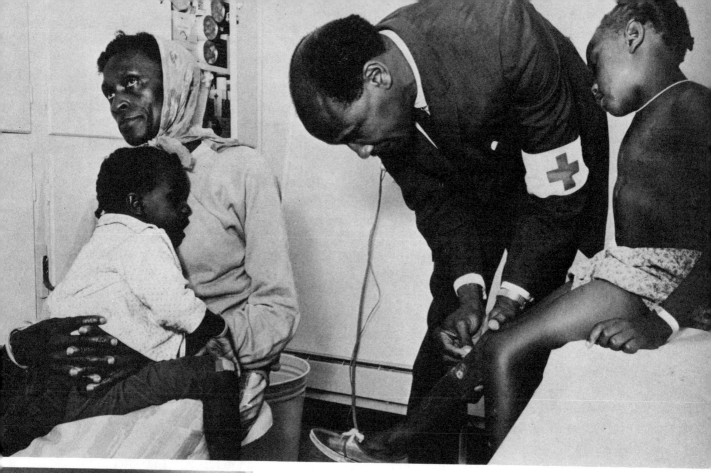

Over three hundred physicians, and many other volunteers from the Washington, D.C., area, participated in the medical services program during the Poor People's Campaign. In a medical aid station (below) set up at Resurrection City, in front of the Lincoln Memorial, a volunteer physician, Dr. Victor L. Assevero (above), treats a young patient. Left, Health Services Coordinating Committee volunteers inventory medical supplies at St. Stephen's Church.

twenty-four-hour basis to hundreds of impoverished demonstrators, many of whom were unaccustomed to medical attention of any kind. The coordinating committee continued to function until Resurrection City was closed down by the government on June 24, 1968, five days after a Solidarity Rally of tens of thousands of sympathizers and twelve days after the Poor People's Campaign submitted a list of twenty-two demands, four of which dealt with hunger and one of which called for changes in Federal programs providing health care.

As the 1960's progressed, it became increasingly evident that something had to be done and done quickly to meet the urgent health needs of the poor. The advent of Medicare and Medicaid was a step in this direction. Under these programs many elderly persons in dire economic circumstances received medical care they might not have had otherwise. Hundreds of thousands of the ghetto poor were among the nearly 20 million Americans who were enrolled in Medicare on July 1, 1968. In the two years prior to that date, Medicare funds amounting to $8.4 billion were spent to pay the hospital and medical bills of persons sixty-five and over. More than a million elderly citizens received post-hospital care at home and in nursing institutions, while a million and a half benefited from the out-patient diagnostic clinics attached to hospitals. In June, 1968, Secretary Wilbur J. Cohen of the Department of Health, Education and Welfare announced that approximately 7.5 million Americans sixty-five and over would benefit from Medicaid programs during the year.

The establishment of health-care centers in poor neighborhoods, open to all regardless of age, race, religion and ethnic origin, was one of the more creative government measures designed to deal with the problem of poverty and ill health. Sponsored by the Office of Economic Opportunity (OEO), the program was part of the much broader and highly publicized "war-on-poverty." Authorized by Congress in 1966 and endorsed by President Johnson in his State-of-the-Union Message the following year, the project to establish neighborhood health centers for the poor was directed by the OEO's Office for Health Affairs. Headed by Dr. Joseph T. English, the program made slow but steady progress. By March, 1967, health centers for the poor were established in New York, Chicago, Boston and Denver, the first in a program that, it was hoped, would expand to fifty cities in the next two years. By the end of April, 1968, the Office of Economic Opportunity had funded forty-two neighborhood health centers at a cost of nearly $90 million. Sixteen of the units were in full operation and eleven were providing limited services. Four more were scheduled to open in May. When all forty-two neighborhood health centers became fully operational, they were expected to be able to serve 900,000 persons, a modest number even in terms of the officially estimated "less than 29 million" poor Americans.

The neighborhood health units, sponsored by the Office of Economic Opportunity, were conceived as comprehensive medical-care centers to meet the needs of the poor. They were accordingly designed to provide services that would include medical and dental care, the treatment of mental ills, immunization, diagnostic tests, preventive health instruction, rehabilitation, drugs and ambulance service. In addition, the OEO-sponsored health projects were intended to serve as training centers to help meet the problem of joblessness among the poor. Unemployed school drop-outs, as well as older persons, were recruited by the clinics for training as nurse's aides, technicians, dieticians, medical clerks and social workers. However, the training program was hampered by sharp cutbacks in agency funds. The medical manpower shortage, particularly in rural areas, also impeded the progress of the OEO health-care program. Outside of the large urban centers, the agency was able to establish few clinics, the most notable being the Tufts Delta Medical Center in Bolivar

County, Mississippi, whose seven physicians and eighty auxiliary medical personnel were reported in March, 1968, to be serving about three hundred persons a week.

The health-care centers for the poor, though financed by the Office of Economic Opportunity, were run by private agents and not by the government. In some cases, the agent was the university medical school; for example, the University of Southern California Medical School in Watts, Los Angeles, and the Tufts University Medical School in Bolivar County, Mississippi. In Atlanta, the agent was the Fulton County Medical Society, which, in turn, subcontracted with the Emory University Medical School to run the center. Other agents included hospitals, health departments and associations formed by the community itself. In Kansas City, Missouri, OEO funds were given the local Human Resources Corporation, which arranged with municipal authorities to have the City Health Department administer the facility.

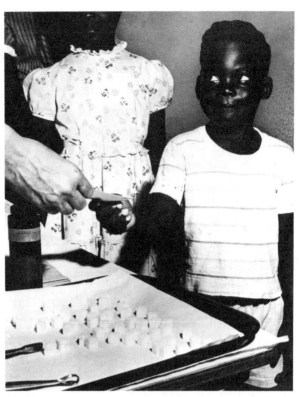

Modern mass immunization in clinics throughout the country is helping to wipe out the once-familiar diseases of childhood.

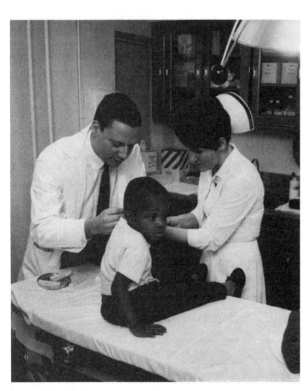

The OEO Columbia Point Center, under Tufts University in Boston, Massachusetts, includes a family health center for the poor.

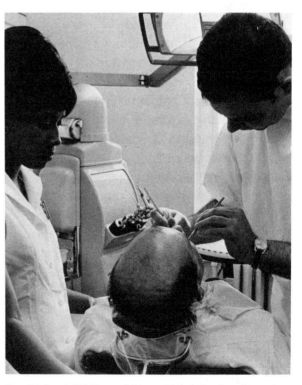

Dr. Richard Witlin and his assistant do dental work at the low-income clinic of the Beth Israel Hospital in New York.

The progress of the comprehensive health-care program, initiated by the Office of Economic Opportunity, was, like its other projects, hampered from the beginning by lack of funds. Despite the fanfare of the "war-on-poverty," actual OEO spending in any given twelve-month period hovered around the $2 billion mark, a sum considerably below the minimum of $10 billion a year suggested by one authority in the field.

Negro physicians actively participated in the development of OEO-sponsored health centers. In Brooklyn, New York, the Provident Clinical Society, an affiliate of the National Medical Association, received a grant to provide comprehensive medical care for some thirty thousand people in the poverty-stricken Bedford-Stuyvesant area. In Atlanta, Georgia, Negro doctors worked closely with the Fulton County Medical Society in planning for a health-care unit in the city's poor neighborhoods.

The National Medical Association supported fully the concept behind the comprehensive health-care program of the Office of Economic Opportunity, but it was critical concerning the implementation of the idea. An official policy statement, set forth by Dr. Lionel F. Swan, President of the NMA, and published in the January, 1968, issue of the organization's journal, accepted without reservation the concept of the multipurpose health-care center as "a logical means of bringing good medical care to the poor of our country." However, the association had certain qualifications in respect to the way the idea was being implemented, specifically the taking over of the neighborhood health units by medical schools, the soliciting of patients for particular clinics and proposals concerning transportation and housekeeping services.

Flowing from these reservations, a number of concrete recommendations were made to improve the operation of the OEO program. The statement proposed, among other things, that the medical school should serve as "ad-visor and consultant to the clinic, but not be in charge of the medical personnel"; that the workers employed by the centers should inform people of their right under Medicaid to go to any doctor or hospital of their choosing, "instead of the clinic only, with the city hospital as the back-up hospital"; and that lunches and baby-sitting services should be discontinued and transportation, if needed, be provided for indigent patients "not only to the comprehensive health-care clinic, but also to the office of any physician of [their] choice, or any other facility in the area." The statement concluded by saying that the NMA was interested in "the success of these urgently needed health facilities" and that success could be achieved "only if the community residents and their physicians [were] part of the planning and [were] made a part of the governing body of the facility."

The concept of a comprehensive system of medical care for the poor rested on the assumption that health care was not a commodity to be bought or sold but a fundamental right to which all Americans were entitled. When Dr. Milford O. Rouse, in his presidential address at the AMA convention on June 20, 1967, sharply challenged the assumption that "health care is a right rather than a privilege," his position was roundly condemned. The Medical Committee for Human Rights, the National Medical Association and the Physicians Forum promptly issued a joint statement denouncing the AMA for having taken "another step backwards, reaffirming its conservative and obstructionist policy when new ideas are urgently needed to guarantee the delivery of high quality medical care to all Americans," regardless of personal affluence. The statement went on to condemn AMA policies that helped impair the effective enforcement of Title VI, obstructed the passage of Medicare and Medicaid laws for years and hampered attacks on inadequacies in health-care delivery.

At the 73rd Annual Convention of the National Medical Association at Houston, Texas, August, 1968, President Lyndon B. Johnson told the assembled delegates that to the basic rights of employment, decent housing, education and freedom from discrimination should be added the right of every American "to as healthy a life as modern medicine can provide."

The bitter opposition of the top leadership of the AMA to the passage of Medicare, its subsequent refusal to "support or endorse" the legislation and its dogged resistance to any expansion of the program did not endear the organization to millions of Americans, black and white, who looked upon health care as "a right rather than a privilege." Slum dwellers in the big cities, who made up a substantial part of the medically indigent of the country, did not take kindly to the AMA position even when its leadership decided late in 1967 to call the organization's first national conference on health care for the poor. The meeting, held in Chicago in mid-December, was invaded by about 150 placard-carrying residents of a South Side ghetto, who demanded to be heard. The presiding officer, Dr. Milford O. Rouse, head of the AMA, was reported to have said: "You are interfering in our efforts to help the underprivileged." Several of the black demonstrators retorted: "We are the underprivileged." After Dr. Rouse agreed to permit the protesters to speak for five minutes, one of the group denounced a neighborhood hospital for discriminatory practices and a "hungry pursuit of the dollar," while another spokesman declared that, if the AMA were willing to condone such operations, "then we believe you need not waste your time sponsoring conferences on medical care for the poor and you can go on with business as usual."

NEIGHBORHOOD HEALTH CENTERS

As the national debate over the dearth of clinical resources in deprived areas rose in intensity in 1970, many student and community groups, as well as medical schools,

hospitals, health departments and group practice clinics, sought funds to develop facilities. In 1970 the Office of Economic Opportunity was funding sixty-four neighborhood health centers, of which twelve were new comprehensive health service projects.

In areas previously without medical services some progress has been attributed to the activities of the health centers. For example, in Bolivar County, Mississippi, infant mortality declined in 1970 to less than half the rate of 60 deaths per 1,000 live births at the time of the inception of the Tufts Delta Center in 1967.

Opposition to neighborhood health centers and internal difficulties have often impeded performance; nevertheless, neighborhood health centers have brought improved medical care to small numbers in the inner cities and rural areas. They have provided a measure of continuity of care as compared to treatment for acute emergencies and have placed new emphases on preventive medicine and total family care. Although token in number and mere symbols of what might be done with ample funds under a coordinated national plan, these facilities have forced a reevaluation of curricula and practices on the part of medical schools and hospitals.

Black Americans have brought a new set of values to the practice of medicine in the communities. They have pinpointed their priorities, have aided in planning and have brought hope to and developed cooperation among previously despairing ghetto people. In the course of community participation they have learned appropriate skills from the health professionals and in turn have taught the latter better ways of communication.

FAILURE OF MEDICAID

By 1970 expectations aroused among black and other poor Americans for improved medical care under Medicaid had proved an illusion. Although Medicaid was estimated to cost $6 billion to $7 billion in 1970—a sharp rise from 1966—only 8 million people had been covered by its services, and there has been no assurance that they received the full benefits of moneys expended.

In California, Governor Reagan announced a reduction of $140 million in Medi-Cal funds. Protesting the decision, the John Hale Society, an affiliate of NMA and the Black Students Caucus of the University of California School of Medicine in San Francisco were among thirty-one black organizations in the state to appear before the state legislature in December 1971 in support of Assemblyman Burton's proposal to restore the funds. Dr. Leonard Myers, president of the John Hale Society, charged that "the cut would force black doctors to subsidize the program and force the poor to use already inadequate welfare grants to pay for medical care."

The demand for health services has not abated, however. The *New York Times* reports that, in New York City, claims on Medicaid for the first half of 1970 totaled 87,455 at a cost of $98.6 million and, for the latter half of 1970, 46,722 claims were filed amounting to $56.9 million for state and federal reimbursement. Medicaid became operative on January 1, 1970, in the seven states that had not yet implemented Medicaid programs—Alabama, Arkansas, Florida, Indiana, Mississippi, New Jersey and North Carolina—when they received federal approval.

At its 75th annual convention in Atlanta in August 1970, the National Medical Association took no position on the national health bills and adopted a "wait and see" attitude. No other health legislation was adopted by the 91st Congress, except for the last minute Emergency Health Personnel Act. The President vetoed two important measures—the manpower bill which would have provided funds for training more doctors and the bill to provide grants for hospital construction and modernization. The veto of the latter was overridden by the Senate.

TOWARD THE FUTURE

Discrimination, less overt but more subtle than previously, persists despite moves toward greater acceptance of the black physician into the American medical establishment. Black physicians view the "welcome" signs from the medical societies with reserve.

"In our society with its legacy of hate and distrust and its history of turmoil and inequities, a black American can never be certain if he is being welcomed to the mainstream of American medicine," said Dr. Hubert A. Eaton of Wilmington, North Carolina, at a national conference on medicine in the ghetto. County medical societies which control hospital staff appointments have had to accept black physicians for fear of losing federal support for their hospitals, but these appointments are often token. Some segregated county societies remain adamant. Once black doctors obtain staff appointments, Dr. Eaton pointed out, they do not get committee appointments or promotions readily.

The overhaul of an outmoded, inequitable system of health care has become an overriding national issue, but is is by no means a national priority.

In August 1975 yet another proposed national health insurance bill died in the House. Congressmen were still hopeful, however, that compromise legislation might get through Congress before too long.

The expectation for achieving the basic reform of a national health plan federally financed to include the guarantee of free, equitable and accessible quality medical care in the poverty areas seems to lie in a continuing vigorous push ahead.

Appendices

Cesar's Cure for Poison*

TAKE the roots of plantane and wild hoarhound, fresh or dried, three ounces, boil them in two quarts of water to one quart, and strain it; of this decoction let the patient take one third part, three mornings fasting, successively, from which, if he finds any relief, it must be continued until he is perfectly recovered: On the contrary, if he finds no alteration after the third dose, it is a sign that the patient has not been poisoned at all, or that it has been with such poison that Cesar's antidote will not remedy, so may leave off the decoction.

During the cure, the patient must live on spare diet, and abstain from eating mutton, pork, butter, or any other fat or oily food.

N.B. The plantane or hoarhound, will either of them cure alone, but they are most efficacious together.

In summer you may take one handful of the roots and of the branches of each, in place of three ounces of the roots of each.

For drink, during the cure, let them take the following.

Take of the roots of goldenrod, six ounces, or in summer, two large handfuls of the roots and branches together, and boil them in two quarts of water to one quart, to which also may be added, a little hoarhound and sassafras; to this decoction, after it is strained, add a glass of rum or brandy, and sweeten it with sugar for ordinary drink.

Sometimes an inward fever attends such as are poisoned, for which he ordered the following.

Take one pint of wood ashes and three pints of water, stir and mix well together, let them stand all night and strain or decant the lye off in the morning, of which ten ounces may be taken six mornings following, warmed or cold according to the weather.

These medicines have no sensible operation, though sometimes they work in the bowels, and give a gentle stool.

The symptoms attending such as are poisoned, are as follow.

A pain of the breast, difficulty of breathing, a load at the pit of the stomach, an irregular pulse, burning and violent pains of the viscera above and below the navel, very restless at night, sometimes wandering pains over the whole body, a retching inclination to vomit, profuse sweats, (which prove always serviceable), slimy stools, both when costive and loose, the face of a pale and yellow colour, sometimes a pain and inflamation of the throat, the appetite is generally weak, and some cannot eat anything; those who have been long poisoned, are generally very feeble and weak in their limbs, sometimes spit a great deal, the whole skin peels, and lastly the hair falls off.

Cesar's cure for the bite of a rattlesnake.

Take of the roots of plantane or hoarhound, (in summer roots and branches together) a sufficient quantity; bruise them in a mortar, and squeeze out the juice, of which give as soon as possible, one large spoonful: If the patient is swelled, you must force it down his throat; this generally will cure; but if he finds no relief in an hour after you may give another spoonful which never hath failed.

If the roots are dried, they must be moistened with a little water.

To the wound, may be applied a leaf of good tobacco, moistened with rum.

---

*This snake-bite remedy, discovered by the Negro slave Cesar, was published in *The Massachusetts Magazine* in 1792.

The Memorial of 1844 to the United States Senate

Dr. James McCune Smith Refutes Secretary of State
John C. Calhoun's Remarks Concerning Negro Inferiority*

TO the Honorable the Senate of the United States, in Congress assembled:

The memorial of the undersigned, free colored citizens of the city and county of New-York, respectfully showeth, that

Whereas, in a letter, addressed to the Right Hon. Richard Pakenham, &c (bearing date April 18th, 1844,) the Hon. John C. Calhoun, Secretary of State for these United States, saith,

First, 'That in the States which have changed their former relations, (the States which have emancipated their slaves, meaning,) the African race has sunk into vice and pauperism;'

Secondly, That this 'vice and pauperism' is 'accompanied by the bodily and mental afflictions incident thereto—deafness, blindness, insanity and idiocy;' and that 'the number of deaf, dumb, blind, idiots and insane of the Negroes in the States which have changed the ancient relation between the races is one out of every ninty-six;' and, that, 'in the State of Maine, the number of Negroes returned as deaf, dumb, blind, insane and idiots, by the census of 1840, is one out of every twelve;'

Thirdly, 'And the number of Negroes, who are deaf and dumb, blind, idiots, insane, paupers and in prison, in the States that have changed, (the free States, meaning,) is one out of every six;'

Fourthly, While in all other States that have retained the ancient relations (the slave states, meaning,) between them (the races, meaning,) 'they (the slaves, meaning,) have improved greatly in every respect, in number, comfort, intelligence and morals;'

And whereas, in regard to these allegations,

First, Your memorialists have great reason to doubt the accuracy of the first; because,

Secondly, It appears in regard to the second allegation, which is the particular proof of the first, that in an examination of the census of 1840, it is found to be self-contradictory: to wit, in asserting the existence of the free colored persons insane, blind, deaf, dumb, in certain towns in the free States, in which towns, it appears by the same census of 1840, there are no free colored persons whatever of any condition:

For example, in

	Insane	Blind	Deaf & Dumb
MAINE			
In 8 towns containing no colored—there are reported,	27	1	2
NEW HAMPSHIRE			
11 towns containing no colored—there are reported,	12	0	3
VERMONT			
2 towns containing no colored—there are reported,	2	2	1
MASSACHUSETTS			
5 towns containing no colored—there are reported,	10	1	0
1 town Worcester, the white insane at the Asylum are returned as colored	133	0	0
NEW YORK			
19 towns containing no colored—there are reported,	29	8	5
PENNSYLVANIA			
11 towns containing no colored—there are reported,	20	6	6
OHIO			
33 towns containing no colored—there are reported,	48	9	5

*In 1841, over one hundred slaves aboard the slave-trader *Creole* rebelled and took the ship to the Bahamas, to the British port of Nassau. The refusal of Great Britain to return these slaves to the United States led Secretary of State John C. Calhoun to make some unfavorable remarks about the Negro in his correspondence with the British. In a meeting on May 3, 1844, it was resolved that a copy of the following memorial be sent to the Hon. Rufus Choate of the Senate, for presentation to that body. Dr. James McCune Smith, in behalf of the committee, then came forward and read the memorial.

INDIANA

4 towns containing no colored—there are reported,	6	9	7

ILLINOIS

9 towns containing no colored—there are reported,	18	0	3

MICHIGAN

12 towns containing no colored—there are reported,	12	2	5

IOWA

1 town containing no colored—there are reported,	2	0	4

	—	—	—
Showing total col'd inhabitants, 000 [*sic*]	186	38	36

By the same census, it appears that in the above, and other towns in the free States, there is—

An excess of colored insane over colored residents,	213
Error in the return of colored for white insane at Worcester, Mass.	133
Total,	346

The whole number of colored insane in the free States being stated to be 1,199 by the census of 1840; if from this number we deduct the 346 shown to be not colored persons, there remains 853 colored insane in the free States, or one in about 200, which your memorialists are satisfied is greatly beyond the actual proportion; because, so far as your memorialists have been able to ascertain, the proportion of the insane among the free colored is not greater than among the white population of the free States. It is stated, for example, by Dr. J. Ray, the physician of the Lunatic Asylum of the State of Maine, that there are not five colored lunatics or insane in that State. In the Lunatic Asylum at Blackwell's Island, in the county of New-York, there are but 17 colored insane, or about 1 to 1000 colored inhabitants of this county. In 1837, the same proportion existed in the free colored population of Philadelphia.

In regard to the deaf, dumb and blind, it will be seen that the census is likewise self contradictory, asserting that there are 74 free colored afflicted with these dispensations, in towns which contain no colored inhabitants.

Thirdly, In regard to the third allegation, which

asserts that one in every six of the free colored in the free States are either 'deaf, dumb, blind, insane, or in prison;' or, in other words, that there are 30,000 free colored supported at the public charge in the free States, your memorialists humbly think that they have furnished, in answer to the second allegation, sufficient facts to disprove the entire accuracy of this astounding assertion. And your memorialists further believe, that the same errors have crept into the census and other documents based thereon, in regard to the pauperism of the free colored, as they have shown to have crept into the census in regard to the insane, &c. Especially when your memorialists know, from the books of the alms-houses of New-York and Philadelphia, there are in these places one colored pauper to about 100 of the colored population, a proportion which is about the same as the pauperism of the free white citizens of these cities; and as these cities contain 37,000, more than one sixth part of the entire colored population of the free States; and as it is known that the proportion of paupers in this as well as in other classes is greatest in large cities, it is a fair inference that the third allegation, at least so much of it as relates to pauperism, cannot be accurate.

Fourthly, In relation to the fourth allegation, which is in substance, that the slaves have improved in morals, intelligence, comfort and number—reversing the order of the items; your memorialists would observe, that the natural increase of the slaves (which is greater than the natural increase of the whites or of the free colored) is a measure of their relative fecundity, not of their relative condition. Whilst the percentage of longevity, and the ratio of mortality, which are tests of relative condition, are greatly in favor of the free colored, the more remotely they may be removed in time from slavery. For the slaves who live beyond 36 years are only 15,49 [*sic*] per cent, while free colored in the free States who live beyond 36 years are 22,68, showing a balance of 7,19 per cent in favor of the condition of the free colored.

In the cities of New-York and Philadelphia, (by the city Inspector's reports,) it appears that a joint population of 37,000 free colored have diminished their ratio of mortality from 1 in 17 in Philadelphia, and 1 in 21 in New-York in 1820; to 1 in 40, in both places in 1843, being a distinct improvement in *condition* of at least 100 per cent in 23 years! There are no records of the mortality among the slaves!

In regard to *intelligence,* there are in the free States, to a total population of 170,000 free colored persons,

40,000 children of an age to go to school, one school to every 534 children, in addition to a large number of children attending white schools, and a number of colored students who are pursuing their studies at Oberlin Western Theological Seminary, and Dartmouth College; whilst the children of slaves are forbidden to be taught to read, under heavy penalties, in the States which have not changed the *ancient relations—death* being the penalty for the second offence. Your memorialists do not deem it irrelevant to state, in this connexion, that the proportion of adults above 20 years of age, who cannot read or write, is 1 in 1081, in the States which have changed the *ancient relations* (the free States) whilst the number of adults who cannot read and write is 1 in 144, in the States that have not changed the ancient relations (the slave States).

In regard to morals, believing that religion is the only basis of sound morals, your memorialists would state that there are to the 170,000 free colored people of the free States—

	Churches
Independent Methodists,	2
Baptist Association,	2
Methodist,	284
Baptist,	15
Presbyterian and Congregational,	3
Episcopal,	6
Lutheran,	1
Total, [*sic*]	318

Making about one church to every 543 of the free colored of the free States.

At the same time, granting that all the churches in the South are promiscuously attended by the slaves and whites, it appears, taking the eleven cities of Baltimore, Richmond, Petersburgh, Virginia, Norfolk, Charleston, Savannah, Mobile, New Orleans, Louisville, St. Louis and Washington, with a total population, of all classes, of 360,905; these cities contain only 167 churches; or one church to every 2,161 inhabitants; from which it follows that the free colored people of the North have a greater number of churches by nearly four fold, than have the entire population of these slave-holding cities. They have, also, 340 Benevolent societies; and 7 newspapers are printed by the free colored people of the free States.

For all of which reasons, your memorialists would humbly pray—

1st. That your honorable body would cause the Census of 1840 to be re-examined, and so far as possible, corrected anew, in the Department of State, in order that the head of that Department may have facts upon which to found his arguments.

2nd. That your honorable body would establish at Washington, a general office of Registration, with a proper officer at its head, who shall cause to be returned from each county in the United States, a yearly report of the sanitary condition of each class of inhabitants, as well as the births, deaths, and marriages.

3rd. That your honorable body will cause to be taken, in the Census of 1850, the number of adults who cannot read and write among the whites, the slaves, and the free people of color, in every county of the United States.

And your Memorialists will ever pray.

The Liberator (Boston), May 31, 1844.

David Ruggles' Water Cure Establishment

An 1847 Advertisement*

THE undersigned, gratefully appreciating the credit generously awarded by a discerning public to his success as a Hydropathic Practitioner, would respectfully inform the friends of Hydropathy that his establishment is pleasantly situated near Bensonville, on the west banks of the Licking Water, or Mill River, about two and a half miles from the centre of the town. It is thirty-six by seventy feet; three stories high, with a piazza on the south side. There are separate parlors, bathing and dressing rooms, for ladies and gentlemen. There are also twenty lodging rooms, each of which is well ventilated and conveniently furnished for the accommodation of two persons. Among the variety of baths in the establishment are the plunge, douche, drenchee, and spray baths. The ladies' plunge is six by ten feet, three and a half deep; the gentlemen's, eight by twelve, three and a half deep. There are also two cold douches, one of which is situated a mile, and the other half a mile from the establishment. The former has a fall of twenty-two feet, the latter eighteen. The scenery in this vicinity is picturesque and romantic. There are a variety of pleasant walks passing near and to springs of pure water. The walks are sufficiently retired to allow water-cure patients to appear as they should, plainly dressed, enjoying their rambles, without being exposed to public gaze and observation. Since daily experience, for the last three years, has strengthened his opinion, that the condition of the skin clearly indicates the character of many diseases, and the *ability* or *inability* of an invalid to bear the water treatment in its various forms; also the necessity of applying the dry woollen [sic] blanket, or the wet sheet to promote evaporation of a sweat, when either may be necessary; and from results which have attended his application of the treatment, he hesitates not to say, that the *electric* sympton of the skin indicates *vitality* or *power,* and that an invalid, whose skin is not attended with this sympton, cannot be safely or successfully treated with water. Among the complaints which are here successfully treated, are pulmonary affection, liver complaints, jaundice, acute or chronic inflammation of the bowels, piles, dyspepsia, general debility, nervous and spinal affections, inflammatory or chronic rheumatism, neuralgia, sicatica, lame limbs, paralysis, fevers, salt rheum, scrofulous and erysipelas humors.

All patients who visit this establishment for a course of treatment, should furnish themselves with three comfortables, three woollen blankets, one linen and three cotton sheets, two pillow cases, six crash towels, some well worn linen, to cut for fomentations, an old cloak or mantle, and a syringe.

Terms for treatment and board are $5.50 per week, for those who occupy rooms on the third floor; on the first and second floors, $6.00 per week, payable weekly; washing extra. A patient, who, from choice or necessity, occupies a room alone, on the third floor, will pay $8.00 per week; on the first and second floors, $8.50 per week. Invalids who are so feeble as to need extra attention and fire in their rooms, (except for swathing purposes,) will procure their own nurses and fuel, or pay an extra price.

D. RUGGLES

Northampton, Aug. 1847

N.B. The afflicted, desirous of being examined in regard to their complaints, and of ascertaining the adaptedness of the water-cure in their particular case, should call on Tuesdays and Fridays.

*This advertisement for David Ruggles' Water Cure Establishment was placed in many issues of Frederick Douglass' newspaper the *North Star*.

Successful Negro Physicians of the Mid-Nineteenth Century

A Chapter from a Book Written by Dr. Martin R. Delany in 1852

THERE are a number of young gentlemen who have finished their literary course, who are now studying for the different learned professions, in various parts of the country.

Jonathan Gibbs, A.B., a very talented young gentleman, and fine speaker, is now finishing his professional studies in the Theological School at Dartmouth University. Mr. Gibbs also studied in the Scientific Department of the same Institution.

William H. Day, Esq., A.B., a graduate of Oberlin Collegiate Institute, is now in Cleveland, Ohio, preparing for the Bar. Mr. Day is, perhaps, the most eloquent young gentleman of his age in the United States.

John Mercer Langston, A.B., of Chillicothe, Ohio, also a graduate of Oberlin College, a talented young gentleman, and promising orator, is completing a Theological course at the School of Divinity at Oberlin. It is said, that Mr. Langston intends also to prepare for the Bar. He commenced the study of Law previous to that of Theology, under Judge Andrews of Cleveland.

Charles Dunbar, of New York city, a promising, very intelligent young gentleman, is now in the office of Dr. Childs, and having attended one course of Lectures at Bowdoin Medical School in Maine, will finish next fall and winter, for the practice of his profession.

Isaac Humphrey Snowden, a promising young gentleman of talents, is now reading Medicine under Dr. Clarke of Boston, and attended the session of the Medical School of Harvard University, 1850-51.

Daniel Laing, Jr., Esq., a fine intellectual young gentleman of Boston, a student also of Dr. Clarke of that city, one of the Surgeons of the Massachusetts General Hospital, who attended the course of Lectures at the session of 1850-51, at the Medical School of Harvard University, is now in Paris, to spend two years in the hospitals, and attend the Medical Lectures of that great seat of learning.

Dr. James J. Gould Bias, a Botanic Physician, and talented gentleman of Philadelphia, is a member of the class of 1851-52, of the Eclectic Medical School of that city. Dr. Bias deserves the more credit for his progress in life, as he is entirely self-made.

Robert B. Leach, of Cleveland, Ohio, a very intelligent young gentleman, is a member of the medical class for 1851-52, of the Homeopathic College, in that City. Mr. Leach, when graduated, will be the *First Colored Homeopathic* Physician in the United States.

Dr. John Degrass, of New York City, named in another place, spent two years in Paris Hospitals, under the teaching of the great lecturer and master of surgery, Velpeau, to whom he was assistant and dresser, in the hospital — the first position — for advantages, held by a student. The Doctor has subsequently been engaged as surgeon on a Havre packet, where he discharged the duties of his office with credit. . . .

Dr. John P. Reynolds has for a number of years been one of the most popular and successful physicians in Vincennes, Indiana. We believe Dr. Reynolds was not of the "regular" system, but some twenty-three or four years ago, studied under an "Indian physician," after which, he practised very successfully in Zanesville, Ohio, subsequently removing to Vincennes, where he has for the last sixteen years supported an enviable reputation as a physician. We understand Doctor Reynolds has entered into all the scientific improvements of the "eclectic school" of medicine, which has come into being in the United States, long since his professional career commenced. His popularity is such, that he has frequently been entrusted with public confidence, and on one occasion, in 1838, was appointed by the court, sole executor of a very valuable orphans' estate. . . .

Dr. McDonough, a skillful young physician, graduated at the Institute, Easton, Pennsylvania, and finished his medical education at the University of New York. The Doctor is one of the most thorough of the young physicians; has been attached to the greater part of the public institutions of the city of New York, and is a good practical chemist.

Of course, there are many others, but as we have taken no measures whatever, to collect facts or information from abroad, only getting such as was at hand, and giving the few sketches here, according to our own recollection of them, we close this short chapter at this point.

Dr. Martin R. Delany, *The Condition, Elevation, Emigration, and Destiny of the Colored People of the United States, Politically Considered* (Philadelphia, 1852), 134–137.

The First Graduation of the Howard Medical School*

THE first annual commencement of the Medical Department of Howard University was held on March 3, 1870, in the lecture-room of the Medical School. Three years before, the Board of Trustees of the University, on January 8, 1867, had appointed a committee, consisting of Dr. Silas L. Loomis, Dr. Hiram Barber, and Rev. D. B. Nichols, to consider the presentation of a plan for the organization of a Medical Department for the University. On January 14, the committee reported that seven professorships should be established: in chemistry, materia medica, and jurisprudence, anatomy, physiology, obstetrics, surgery and practice of medicine. . . . By vote of the Faculty, the first formal session of the Department was to begin on October 28, 1868.

The session continued during the autumn and winter of 1868-1869, with eight students in attendance; seven of these were studying medicine and one was studying pharmacy. The report of the Dean . . . stated that seven of these students were colored and one was white. . . .

The report of the President, General O. O. Howard, for the year 1869, stated that "the Medical College has taken a permanent stand among the medical institutions of the country. With facilities rarely enjoyed by such schools in their incipiency, it is believed that by proper effort, it can be made a great success and the means of most extensive usefulness."

.   .   .   .

The second session of the Medical Department was announced in a two-page leaflet containing a picture of the University building, a list of instructors and information concerning fees and requirements. . . .

During this session, there were 24 medical students, and 49 clinical students in attendance, a total of 73 students.

On March 3, 1870, the session ended, and the commencement was held in the lecture-room of the building at 6 o'clock in the evening, before a large assembly. . . . The Dean, Dr. Silas Loomis, . . . paid tribute to the interest, unity, and generosity of the Trustees of the University in voting for the Medical Department "everything asked for and required. . . . He called attention to the charter of the University, which was broad enough to include the youth of both sexes and all races. The speaker . . . called attention also to the high standards of the school. "Most colleges," said he, "graduate their students in two years, but Howard University, in keeping with the suggestions made at the Medical Convention at St. Louis, insisted that its students should take a course of three years' duration." . . . He concluded that in the field of the practice of medicine, they might meet difficulty because of prejudice, but he would urge them to "strive to make a mark for themselves and their diplomas an honor to the University."

The President of the University, General Howard, conferred the degree of Doctor of Pharmacy upon Mr. James T. Wormley, a son of James Wormley, then a wellknown caterer in the city. . . . General Howard stated that Mr. Wormley had had considerable experience in the Medical Department of the Army during the Civil War. In conferring the degree, the President called attention to Mr. Wormley's "good record and the fidelity which had marked his course. . . ."

Mr. James T. Wormley has, therefore, the honor of being the first graduate of the Medical Department of Howard University, his graduation occurring on March 3, 1870. One degree, however, was conferred in 1869. This was an honorary degree of M.D., which was conferred upon Professor Alexander T. Augusta, who held the M.B. degree from the Trinity Medical College, Toronto, Canada.

The first graduates of the Medical School proper came after the third session of the Medical Department, since the course was a three years' course.

Thus there went forth the first graduates of the Medical Department to "sail life's rugged sea." Since this period, hundreds have been added to the number who are rendering large service in various parts of the world.

*This is an excerpt from an article by Dr. Charles H. Wesley in *The Howard Alumnus*, March, 1927, p. 137.

The Struggle for Equal Rights in Medicine in the District of Columbia

An Act to Incorporate the Medical Society of the District of Columbia, 1819

BE IT enacted by the Senate and House of Representatives of the United States of America, in Congress assembled, that Charles Worthington, James H. Blake, John T. Shaaff, Thomas Sim, Frederick May, Joel T. Gustine, Elisha Harrison, Peregrine Warfield, Alexander McWilliams, George Clark,, Henry Huntt, Thomas Henderson, John Harrison, Benjamin S. Bohrer, Samuel Horseley, Nicholas W. Worthington, William Jones, James T. Johnson, Richard Weightman, George May, Robert French, and such persons as they may from time to time elect, and their successors, are hereby declared to be a community, corporation, and body politic, forever, by and under the name and title of the Medical Society of the District of Columbia; and by and under the same name and title they shall be able and capable in law to purchase, take, have and enjoy, to them and their successors, in fee or for lease, estate or estates, any land, tenements, rents, annuities, chattels, bank stock, registered debts, or other public securities within the District, by the gift, bargain, sale, demise, or of any person or persons, bodies politic or corporate, capable to make the same, and the same, at their pleasure, to alien, sell, transfer or lease and apply to such purposes as they may adjudge most conducive to the promoting and disseminating medical and surgical knowledge, and for no other purpose whatever: *Provided nevertheless,* That the said society, or body politic, shall not, at any one time, hold or possess property, real personal or mixt, exceeding in total value the sum of six thousand dollars per annum.

SEC. 2. *And be it further enacted,* That the members of the said society, above designated, shall hold, in the City of Washington, four stated meetings in every year, viz: on the first Mondays in January, April, July and October; the officers of the society to consist of a President, two Vice-Presidents, one Corresponding Secretary, one Recording Secretary, one Treasurer and one Librarian, who shall be appointed on the second Monday in March, one thousand eight hundred and nineteen, and on the annual meeting in January forever thereafter, (not less than seven members being present at such meeting), and the society may make a common seal, and may elect into their body such medical and chirurgical practitioners, within the District of Columbia, as they may deem qualified to become members of the society; it being understood that the officers of the society now elected are to remain in office until the next election after the passage of this act.

SEC. 3. *And be it further enacted,* That it shall and may be lawful for the said Medical Society, or any number of them attending, (not less than seven), to elect by ballot five persons, residents of the District, who shall be styled the Medical Board of Examiners of the District of Columbia, whose duty it shall be to grant licenses to such medical and chirurgical gentlemen as they may, upon a full examination, judge adequate to commence the practice of the medical and chirurgical arts, or as may produce diplomas from some respectable college or society; each person so obtaining a certificate to pay a sum not exceeding ten dollars, to be fixed on or ascertained by the society.

SEC. 4. *And be it further enacted,* That any three of the examiners shall constitute a board for examining such candidates as may apply, and shall subscribe their names to each certificate by them granted, which certificate shall also be countersigned by the President of the society, and have the seal of the society affixed thereto by the Secretary, upon paying into the hands of the Treasurer the sum of money to be ascertained, as above, by the society; and any one of the said examiners may grant a license to practice, until a board, in conformity to this act, can be held; *Provided,* That nothing herein contained shall authorize the said corporation in any wise to regulate the price of medical or chirurgical attendence, on such persons as may need those services.

SEC. 5. *And be it further enacted,* That after the appointment of the aforesaid medical board, no person, not heretofore a practitioner of medicine or surgery within the District of Columbia, shall be allowed to practice within the said District, in either of said branches, and receive payment for his services, without first having obtained a license, testified as by this law directed, or without the production of a diploma, under the penalty of fifty dollars for each offense, to be recovered in the county court where he may reside, by bill of presentment and indictment; one-half for the use of the society, and the other for that of the informer.

SEC. 6. *And be it further enacted,* That every person who, upon application, shall be elected a member of the Medical Society, shall pay a sum not exceeding ten dollars, to be ascertained by the society.

SEC. 7. *And be it further enacted,* That the Medical Society be, and they are hereby empowered, from time to time, to make such by-laws, rules and regulations, as they may find requisite, to break or alter their common seal, to fix the times and places for the meetings of the board of examiners, filling up vacancies in the medical board, and to do and perform such other things as may be requisite for carrying this act into execution, and which may not be repugnant to the constitution and laws of the United States: *Provided,* That nothing herein contained shall extend to prohibit any person during his actual residence in any of the United States, and who, by the laws of the state wherein he doth or may reside, is not prohibited from practicing in either of the above branches, from practicing in this District; *Provided always,* That it shall and may be lawful for any person, resident as aforesaid, and not prohibited as aforesaid, when specially sent for, to come into any part of this District, and administer or prescribe medicine, or perform any operation for the relief of such to whose assistance he may be sent for.

SEC. 8. *And be it further enacted,* That Congress may, at any time, alter, amend, or annul this act of incorporation of said society at pleasure.

H. CLAY,
Speaker of the House of Representatives.

DANIEL D. TOMPKINS,
Vice President of the United States and President of the Senate.

JAMES MONROE.

Approved February 16, 1819.

Constitution and By-Laws of the Medical Society of the District of Columbia, Washington, D.C., 1924.

A Plea for Racial Equality

Memorial of the National Medical Society of the District of Columbia to the Senate and House of Representatives of the United States, 1870

WHEREAS it has been stated in a published circular, that the persons endeavoring to form a medical society on the basis of "equality before the law," have maliciously and falsely attacked the Medical Society of the District of Columbia, we deem it but just to the public, as well as ourselves, to make the following statement of facts:

Within the past few years some colored physicians, regular graduates of medical colleges, and of untarnished character and reputation, having held positions as surgeons in the Union army during the rebellion, have settled in this city, and secured to themselves a large professional practice.

There being only one medical society in the District where all licenses to practice must be obtained, and all advantages flowing from medical and professional discussions were to be enjoyed, it became the duty of these colored physicians to obtain license and membership, in order to keep up their medical education, and derive all the advantages from weekly professional discussion.

The Medical Society of the District of Columbia has, on two different occasions, refused to elect these colored physicians to membership, acknowledging that the color of the candidates was the reason for so doing; and some of its members have refused to consult with them, because they were not members of the Society.

This was in June, 1869. Hoping that discussion of the subject would aid in securing justice, we were content to await the result.

January 3, 1870, by a vote of 26 to 10, the Society refused to consider a resolution offered by Dr. Reyburn, which read as follows, viz:

"Resolved, That no physician (who is otherwise eligible) should be excluded from membership in this Society on account of his race or color."

Some of the present officers of the Society have

refused to consult with the colored physicians, but instead thereof, have taken charge of patients who were under their care, without giving them the customary notice of their dismissal, in direct violation of the ethics of the profession.

These colored physicians have applied to the Society for membership, but were rejected by a large majority, although the Board of Examiners reported favorably on them. At the last election of officers in the Society, held January 3, 1870, the chairman of this board was removed, and a gentleman, late of the Confederate army, well known for his opposition to the admission of colored physicians, was elected in his place, thus insuring their future defeat. Other gentlemen who served during the war in the Confederate army are now prominent in the control of its affairs.

At the same meeting, a white candidate, a gentleman of high professional standing, and occupying an important position, was objected to, solely on the ground that he was believed to be in favor of the admission of colored members.

Again, the circular published by the committee of the Society, states that their weekly meetings are "social reunions." These meetings are conducted under strictly parliamentary rules, from the opening to the adjournment, and only professional questions, essays, and papers, are brought forward for discussions, and gentlemen are even required to obtain permission of the President to retire from the meeting. If these meetings, held in compliance with the charter of the Society, are only social reunions, then the meetings of all bodies not strictly parlimentary are social reunions.

Other colored men will soon graduate from medical colleges in the United States and throughout the world, and their rights should be protected and guaranteed within this District.

It is a fact worthy of note, that this is the only country and the only profession in which such a distinction is now made. Science knows no race, color, or condition; and we protest against the Medical Society of the District of Columbia maintaining such a relic of barbarism.

We, for the reasons stated, and in accordance with the spirit of the times, ask Congress to grant a charter to a new Society, which will give all rights, privileges and immunities to all physicians, making only the presentation of a diploma from some college recognized by the American Medical Association, and good standing in the profession, the qualifications necessary for membership.

Robert Reyburn, M.D., *President,* John G. Stephenson, M.D., Alex T. Augusta, M.D., D. W. Bliss, M.D., Silas L. Loomis, M.D., W. G. H. Newman, M.D., R. J. Southworth, M.D., Jos. Taber Johnson, M.D., John Edwin Mason, M.D., *Committee.*

C. Adams Gray, M.D., *Secretary.*

The New Era (Washington), January 27, 1870.

The AMA and the Negro Physician

Minutes of the 1870 AMA Convention

THE Association convened at Lincoln Hall on Tuesday, May 3, at 11 A.M., and was called to order by the President, GEORGE MENDENHALL, M.D., of Ohio, assisted by Vice-Presidents LEWIS A. SAYRE, M.D., of New York, FRANCIS GURNEY SMITH, M.D., of Pennsylvania, and JOHN S. MOORE, M.D., of Missouri. . . .

The Committee of Arrangements, through their Chairman, THOS. ANTISELL, M.D., of the District of Columbia, welcomed the delegates in the following remarks:—

Mr. President and Members of the American Medical Association:

. . . .

"You have met here in pursuance of your resolution to make it your partial home, and by such step you propose to make your sittings here more truly professional and business-like in character; here you are met for cultivating medical knowledge and for promoting the usefulness, the honor, and the interests of the medical profession—to aid in its elevation, purification, and progress. The mission of the Association is in the bond of brotherhood, to encourage scientific emulation, and point out new paths which may lead to the advancement of the medical standards in theory and practice; in fine, to search out and adopt TRUTH—Truth, the search for which is the most untiring of all the instincts of man. Viewed in this light, it is no doubt good for the Society that some of its sessions should be free from the constant struggle between sense of duty of performance and the friendly importunity of hospitality. It is understood that you have met here for work, and your Committee have felt that they are not only not authorized, but that they have been strictly forbidden to take any action in a social direction.

"It is from meetings such as this, meetings of representatives from all parts of our widely populated country, representing the extremest views of medical life and practice, the interests of the colleges, the hospitals, the polished cautious physician of the city, and the daring self-reliant doctor of the country, the general practitioner of private circles, the specialist of a great metropolis, the representatives of medicine in either branch of the public service, the time-honored Nestors of the profession, and the ambitious and pushing neophytes ready to jostle them in the struggle for existence;—it is from such a conglomeration of sentiment that we hope to obtain as a happy result of our intercommunion, *the unity of the profession.* To attain that desirable result, your brethren at home have deputed you here and expect from you the active exercise of all the talents which you possess, to preserve and strengthen that unity of thought and action which is growing up among us.

"This congress presents one feature which no medical association in any part of the globe possesses to any extent similar, namely, the immense area of territory here represented. No other society possesses the true basis, the data of climatology in its widest sense like this; a territory extending from bleak and ice bound oceans and eternal winter, to the balmy subtropical winds and waters of regions of perennial spring, and in width extending along a parallel of one-eighth the circumference of our globe. Surely a society representing so much territory has much in its power to communicate upon the external causes of disease, and here ought to be studied, with more beneficial results to the physical geography, topography, and meteorology, of zymotic and malarious disease.

"In thus welcoming you who have met for deliberation in our national metropolis, we trust that American medicine will in these reunions set her distinctive marks of freedom from the prejudices of the past, the *idda tritres* that out of such reunions may grow increased good fellowship, increased *ésprit du corps,* increased respect from the public toward our calling, higher modes of thought, purer springs of action, increased individual respect for our brethren, increased peace within our profession, increased strength without."

. . . .

Dr. ANTISELL rose to a question of privilege. He said, grave charges had been preferred against the Committee of Arrangements. . . .

First. A charge that the majority of the Registration Committee had refused to register the delegates presenting credentials from several societies, colleges, and hospitals in the District of Columbia which claimed the right to representation.

Second. Direct charges against the Medical Society and the Medical Association of the District of Columbia, accompanied by a protest against the admission of delegates from those bodies.

Third. Direct charges, which had been lodged with the Committee of Registration, against the National Medical Association of the District of Columbia, accompanied by a protest against the registration of delegates from that Society and from such other institutions as were supplied with medical officers who were members of that Society.

In regard to the first charge, your Committee find on investigation that the Registration Committee have duly registered all the delegates from all the medical institutions claiming representation in the District of Columbia in accordance with the usages and by-laws of the Association, except the Medical Society of the Alumni of Georgetown College, the National Medical Society, the Howard Medical College, the Freedman's Hospital, and the Smallpox Hospital, these being the institutions included in the charges already mentioned in the third specification.

It remains, therefore, only to consider the second and third specifications, and your Committee ask leave to report on these separately. In relation to the second we unanimously recommend the following resolution:—

Resolved, That the charges offered by Dr. REYBURN, as a minority of the Committee on Registration, against the Medical Society and the Medical Association of the District of Columbia, are not of a nature to require the action of the American Medical Association, the first charge referring to a duty imposed on the Society by an act of Congress, and the second referring to a matter which does not come in conflict with any part of the code of ethics.

Resolved, That so far as relates to the Medical Society of the Alumni of Georgetown College, it has been shown to us that the Society has sixty resident members, and is therefore entitled to six delegates instead of as requested by the Committee.

In regard to the third proposition relating to the National Medical Society, Howard Medical College, the Freedman's Hospital, and the Smallpox Hospital, we recommend the following:—

Resolved, That the duties of the Committee of Arrangements, so far as relates to the registration of members, is purely clerical, consisting in the verification of the certificates of delegates and a report on the same. If credentials in proper form are presented from any society or institution possessing such form as would place it *prima facie* in the list of institutions enumerated in the constitution of the Association as entitled to representation, but against which charges have been made or protests presented, the names of the delegates presenting such credentials, together with the charges or protests in the possession of the Committee, should be reported to the Association for its action.

Resolved, That the charges lodged with the Committee of Arrangements against the eligibility of the National Medical Society of the District of Columbia have been so far sustained that we recommend that no member of that Society should be received as delegates at the present meeting of this Association.

> N. S. DAVIS,
> H. F. ASKEW,
> J. M. KELLER.

Dr. ALFRED STILLE presented a report from the minority of the Committee, as follows:—

The undersigned members of the Committee on Ethics, while subscribing to the greater portion of the report of the majority, feel it their duty nevertheless to dissent from the final resolution recommending the exclusion of the members of the National Medical Society of the District of Columbia from the present meeting of this Association; they offer, therefore, in lieu of that resolution the following:—

Whereas, The institutions excluded from representation by the action of the Committee on Credentials, viz: The National Medical Society, the Howard Medical College, the Freedman's Hospital, and the Smallpox Hospital, are regularly organized as the constitution of the Association requires: *And whereas,* the physicians so excluded are qualified practitioners of medicine who have complied with all the conditions of membership imposed by this Association: *And whereas,* in the judgment of the undersigned no sufficient ground exists for the exclusion of such institutions and physicians from this Association: therefore,

Resolved, That the institutions above named are entitled to representation, and that the physicians claiming to represent them are entitled to seats in the American Medical Association.

> ALFRED STILLE,
> J. J. WOODWARD.

Dr. T. C. MADDOX, of Maryland, moved to accept the report of the majority.

Dr. COX moved to substitute the report of the minority.

Dr. E. L. HOWARD, of Maryland, moved to lay the minority report on the table, and called the ayes and noes on the motion.

The question having been asked who from the District of Columbia had a right to vote, the President decided that all from the District of Columbia should be allowed to vote who had been favorably reported upon by the Committee on Ethics.

Dr. COX appealed from the decision of the Chair.

The vote was put by the Permanent Secretary, who announced that the Chair was sustained by ayes 115, nays 90.

The Permanent Secretary then called the roll on the motion to lay the minority report on the table, and announced the vote. Ayes 114, nays 82, as follows:—

.   .   .   .

A motion was then made that the majority report be adopted. . . .

On motion of Dr. G. S. PALMER, of Maine, it was

Resolved, That the majority of the Committee on Ethics be respectfully requested to inform this Association on what principle the delegates of the Medical Department of Howard University were excluded from membership in this Association.

After much discussion, Dr. DAVIS promised to give, in writing, the reasons for the action of the majority of the Committee.

.   .   .   .

Dr. JOHN L. SULLIVAN, of Massachusetts, offered the following:—

Resolved, That no distinction of race or color shall exclude from the Association persons claiming admission and duly accredited thereto.

On motion of Dr. L. A. SAYRE, of New York, the vote on this resolution was suspended temporarily, as the Committee on Ethics were now prepared with their report as to the reasons for excluding certain delegates.

Dr. N. S. DAVIS, on behalf of those who made the majority report, presented the following:—

In reply to the resolution of the Association, calling upon the majority of the Committee on Ethics for the reason why they in their report excluded the delegates from the Medical Department of Howard University, they respectfully state that there is nothing in their report which directly excludes delegates from the said university, or any other medical institution in the District of Columbia, except the National Medical Society.

The resolution on this subject, reported by the Committee, is in these words:—

"*Resolved,* That the charges lodged with the Com-

mittee of Arrangements against the eligibility of the National Medical Society of the District of Columbia have been so far sustained that we recommend that no members of that Society should be received as delegates at the present meeting of the Association."

It will be seen that the only parties excluded from admission as delegates at the present meeting are the members of the National Medical Society. If the Medical Department of Howard University had chosen to send any delegates who are not members of that Society, there is nothing whatever in the report to prevent them from being received.

In the papers referred to your Committee on Ethics were a list of charges with specifications in the usual form against the recognition of the National Medical Society. These charges may be clearly stated as follows:—

1st. That said National Medical Society recognizes and receives as members medical men who are not licentiates, and who are acting in open violation of sections 3, 4, and 5 of the law of Congress constituting the charter of the Medical Society of the District of Columbia.

2d. That a large part of the members of the National Medical Society are also members of the Medical Association of the District of Columbia, and are openly and freely violating the rules and ethics of the Association to which they have subscribed.

3d. That they have, both in its capacity as a society and by its individual members, misrepresented the action of the Medical Society and the Medical Association of the District of Columbia, and used unfair and dishonorable means to procure the destruction of the same, by inducing Congress to abrogate their charter.

Each and all of these charges were, in the opinion of the majority of our Committee, fully proved by the members of the National Medical Society themselves, who appeared voluntarily before your Committee as witnesses. Therefore, if we have any regard to the maintenance of the laws of the land, or the ethics of our medical organizations, the undersigned could not come to any other conclusion than was expressed in the last resolution recommended by the majority of the Committee on Ethics.

(Signed)   N. S. DAVIS,

H. F. ASKEW,

JAMES M. KELLER.

A motion was made to refer the report to the Committee of Publication, on which much discussion ensued, fully participated in by Drs. Reyburn, Antisell, W. P. Johnson, J. J. Woodward, Busey, and others, when the previous question was called and sustained, and the report was referred to the Committee of Publication.

The resolution of Dr. Sullivan, which had been temporarily postponed, was then taken up, and after some further discussion, on motion of Dr. E. L. Howard, of Maryland, it was laid on the table —ayes, 106; nays, 60.

Dr. H. R. Storer, of Massachusetts, offered the following:—

Resolved, That inasmuch as it has been distinctly stated and proved that the consideration of race and color has had nothing whatsoever to do with the decision of the question of the reception of the Washington delegates, and inasmuch as charges have been distinctly made in open session to-day attaching the stigma of dishonor to parties implicated, which charges have not been denied by them, though present, therefore

The report of the majority of the Committee on Ethics be declared, as to all intents and purposes, unanimously adopted by the Association. . . .

On motion, the Association adjourned to meet at San Francisco, on the first Tuesday in May, 1871.

WM. B. ATKINSON,
Permanent Secretary.

WM. LEE,
Assistant Secretary.

Transactions of the American Medical Association, Vol. XXI, 1870.

Resolutions on Restrictive Membership Provisions, 1950

Dr. J. Morrison Hutcheson, Virginia, presented the following resolutions, which were referred to the Reference Committee on Miscellaneous Business:

Whereas, This House of Delegates recognizes that certain constituent and component societies of the American Medical Association have had or now have restrictive provisions as to qualification of membership based on race and that this question is of deep concern to many interested parties; and

Whereas, It is desirable that the attitude of not only the entire membership of the American Medical Association but of the whole medical profession be accurately reflected on this issue; and

Whereas, It is the policy of the American Medical Association to broaden the scope of educational facilities and raise the ethical levels of practice of all physicians in order to improve the quality of medical care for the American people; therefore be it

Resolved, That these facts be brought to the attention of all component and constituent societies appreciating that membership is a component and constituent society responsibility; and be it further

Resolved, That constituent and component societies having restrictive membership provisions based on race study this question in the light of prevailing conditions with a view to taking such steps as they may elect to eliminate such restrictive provisions.

Proceedings of the House of Delegates of the American Medical Association, June 26–30, 1950.

AMA-NMA Liaison Activities, 1966*

After one or two years of moratorium on conferences, forced by an impasse, our administration reactivated the liaison conferences between AMA and NMA, again seeking to remove a senseless social embargo which still exists against licensed and practicing physicians based upon a criterion of race in some societies and tokenism in others.

I am happy to report to you that three such meetings were held during our tenure, breaking all previous records for the number of meetings in one

*An excerpt from the address delivered by Dr. Leonidas H. Berry as outgoing president of the National Medical Association, August 9, 1966. Reproduced by permission of author.

year. The first meeting was held at the AMA Headquarters, September 25, 1965. On April 1, 1966, the NMA Liaison Committee was the luncheon guest of the entire AMA Trustee Board, at which time problems of discrimination were further discussed. On Sunday, August 7, 1966, the liaison groups assembled for conferences, with NMA Liaison Committee and the NMA Trustee Board serving as luncheon hosts during our convention at the Pick-Congress Hotel in Chicago. What has been accomplished by these conferences, other than frequent meetings? Some would say very little. I would say probably more than ever before in the same length of time and enough so that I strongly recommend continuation of this type of communication.

First, we agreed on a program of joint recruitment in medical careers and AMA officials agreed to increase usage of Negro faces in doctor-recruitment literature and stories about medical careers. Second, frequent meetings of liaison groups were agreed upon as mutually desirable. Third, there was an agreement that AMA Trustee Board and House of Delegates would appoint Negro members of AMA and NMA to top-level national committees and councils of AMA—and 25 or more names of volunteer candidates, with their curricula vitae, were submitted. Fourth, President James Z. Appel, who with AMA Board Chairman, Dr. Percy Hopkins, were the AMA leaders in our deliberations, extended a special invitation for your President to attend AMA convention ceremonies and other affairs as a special guest of the AMA.

Fifth, a special committee of the AMA Board of Trustees was appointed to contact local societies to urge compliance with the AMA resolutions previously passed on racial discrimination by their House of Delegates and to devise means of achieving voluntary improvement in racial discriminatory practices in societies, in hospitals, and in patient care. Sixth, finally, of considerable significance, we believe is the action of the AMA House of Delegates at their June '66 convention in passing a resolution to amend their constitution permitting their Judicial Council to hear and consider the charges of any doctor alleging racial discrimination in any area of the United States. Considering the AMA's stand of nearly 100 years, that their organization could have no responsibility in the matter of the practices of racial discrimination in their local component societies, this would seem to be a crack in the iceberg. To be sure, our liaison conferences could only have a small share of credit for this resolution. Much more important were the AMA delegations who presented resolutions calling for expulsion of racially discriminating societies and perhaps of considerable importance was the interracial picket line of 250 people protesting racial discrimination at the June '66 convention.

The Colored Man in Medicine

An Address Delivered by Dr. L. T. Burbridge
at New Iberia, Louisiana, January 1, 1895

HAD I been called upon to select a subject upon which to address you on this occasion, I doubt my ability to select one more appropriate to my thoughts and feelings, and more suitable to this audience and this occasion than the one given me by its promoters, viz.: The Colored Man in Medicine. Although I am as yet but a young disciple of the healing art, I believe in common with most young practitioners who have had ample leisure to reflect upon the hopes and possibilities of the medical profession so far as the colored man is concerned, there is for him a bright and promising future. I, therefore, thank you for the privilege of addressing you on this subject and on such an auspicious occasion, an occasion (if you will allow me to say) when the heart of every true and loyal colored man should turn in thankfulness to God for his great deliverance from the greatest curse that ever afflicted any Christianized people. Thank God we to-day are living under entirely different circumstances to those existing previous to the time this day is intended to commemorate. Under the blessings of freedom we enjoy a purer air, a more lofty existence than before, and the sunlight of peace, prosperity and intellectual growth is shedding softened rays upon our pathway, lighting up the darker places and beckoning us on to a future as bright and promising as any ever enjoyed by any other people. May it shine more and more unto the perfect day.

Having been so recently released from bondage, burdened with all the ignorance and superstition which that state implies, it would appear that the colored man had had short time in which to prepare himself for the learned professions. Not so however. With his characteristic power of imitation, and his readiness to adapt himself to the study of scientific medicine with the same zeal and earnestness he had manifested in working his old master's crops, naturally quick of perception and kind and sympathetic in disposition, he made rapid strides in the most difficult of sciences, and the medical history of the last few years furnishes ample testimony to his success.

Had I statistics at my command I could furnish some interesting figures of the growth and progress of the colored man in medicine. It is sufficient to say, however, that thirty years ago, there were few if any Negro M.D.'s to be found, while to-day there is scarcely a Southern town and a large proportion of the Northern towns and cities that cannot boast of one or more colored physicians, regular graduates of authorized Medical Colleges. While this is true we are compelled to admit that there is a field for many more. It is estimated that there is one white physician to every 300 of his people, while there is only one colored doctor to every 20,000 of his people. This furnishes an idea of our need, for we feel assured that when the colored physicians become more numerous so as not to be a rare object then he will be more respected by all classes of people. Then too we feel proud to state that the practice of the colored doctor is by no means confined solely to his own race. For even here in the historic old State of Louisiana, whose fertile vales have often echoed to the cry of the oppressed, the Negro physician enjoys in many instances a small, but growing white patronage. This in itself is a confession of a recognition of skill and ability, wrung as it were from the lips of the oppressor. And what has been the reception of the Negro physician from his white professional brother? Has he been laughed at, and scoffed upon as being unworthy of any consideration as a scientific man? By no means is this true. While we admit that in all cases he has not been received with open arms due, more perhaps, to petty prejudices and jealousies than any doubt of his medical skill, still on the whole he has received many marks of respect and appreciation, and many kindnesses in the loan of books and instruments from his white professional contemporaries, for which he has been duly grateful. And in many instances the white physicians have not hesitated to avail themselves in consultation over grave cases of his sound common sense and superior medical and surgical skill. The outlook, I say then, is hopeful yet the path of the Negro doctor is by no means strewn with flowers. Isolated, as many of them are, from a daily intercourse with colored men of their own profession and despairing of any assistance from the opposite race, often their only recourse is their books and journals. Under such circumstances the Negro physician sometimes finds himself confronted with a deep and seemingly impassible gulf over which it seems impossible to leap and around which he can see no way. Turning back is not to be thought of, go ahead he must. Then it is that his self-reliance and manhood, if he has any, show themselves. If he stops to reflect he will remember that others have passed the same way, and why should he not do likewise? So summoning all his skill and strength for the effort he makes the leap, lands safely on the other side and has won. . . .

These are not the only difficulties that confront a Negro doctor, but he meets serious drawbacks in the lack of race pride, and confidence which some of his people manifest toward him. It seems that many of our good people have not as yet learned to appreciate the merits of the doctors of their own race. There are those who not only fail to give their own patronage, but take every reasonable opportunity of throwing obstacles in the way of their progress. This, I am glad to say, is rather the exception than the rule, still it is an exception that occurs entirely too often for the comfort of the doctors, and for the welfare of the race he represents. The advent of the colored man into medicine worked an era of better sanitary protection, and better medical attention generally for his people than they had ever enjoyed before, because of the competition it excited. It would appear then that the colored physician instead of arousing their animosity, should be an object of their confidence and respect. The colored physician does not ask patronage on the score of color, and on the other hand he does not want to be denied work on that account. He does not ask that allowances be made for his deficiencies because he is a Negro, and on the other hand he does not want to be denied the privileges that skill and ability should demand for any medical man whether he be white or black. A recognition of skill and competency is all that he asks regardless of color. In other words he wants to be treated as a man—one who has fully prepared himself to do the work as thoroughly and skillfully as any other man of whatever nationality. The Negro physician realizes the fact that this is his only hope for successfully overcoming the many discouraging features of his work, and with this fact in view he has ever bent diligently to the accomplishment of the task set before him. One has not to go far to judge of his success.

Here in your own thriving town you have a specimen of a diligent, hard-working, aspiring Negro physician, Dr. Jefferson, who has been with you now about two years, deserves much credit for the success with which his efforts have met in this community. This, I judge, he has won not from the fact that he is a colored physician, but from the manifest skill and ability with which he has undertaken, and accomplished difficult work. So it is that in spite of opposition, in spite of discouragements, in spite of the numerous obstacles which arise to impede his progress, the Negro doctor is steadily moving onward.

In November last the colored doctors of Florida, and adjacent states, met and formed a Colored Medical Association. At this meeting papers were read and discussed that would have done credit to any medical association of this country, and the daily papers in commenting upon this association spoke of its action as being highly creditable to the colored medical profession, and to the Negro race at large. Is not this encouraging, and does it not bid us to look hopefully forward to the future?

The advantages offered to the colored man for a medical education are good. Meharry, New Orleans and Shaw Medical Colleges, in the South are doing good work, and in the North but few if any doors are closed against the colored aspirant; while England, France and Germany all extend to him a welcoming hand. . . . I repeat that the colored medical profession is yet in its infancy. If in thirty years they have accomplished so much what may we not hope for a century? When we reflect that our white professional brother has not one, but many centuries back of him, does not that encourage us to look for brighter things for the Negro physician? May we not hope that the day will come when the Tulane and Vanderbilt Medical Colleges will open their doors to all regardless of color, where the white and black doctors of the South will travel side by side in the same railway coach, when there will be no white or black medical associations, but all be united in one band of harmonious fellow workers with but one object, and that the relief of suffering humanity? We smile at the thought, but history has repeatedly chronicled greater and more wonderful revolutions than these, and so will it again. Then with a firm reliance on self, and an unwavering trust in God, the great harmonizer and peace-maker, we press manfully onward in our struggle for truth and right, believing that in the fullness of time all things will end well. . . .

The Afro-American Encyclopaedia (Nashville, Tenn., 1895), 70–74.

The Flexner Report*

INTRODUCTION

THE present report on medical education forms the first of a series of papers on professional schools to be issued by the Carnegie Foundation. . . .

When the work of the Foundation began five years ago the trustees found themselves intrusted with an endowment to be expended for the benefit of teachers in the colleges and universities of the United States, Canada, and Newfoundland. It required but the briefest examination to show that amongst the thousand institutions in English-speaking North America which bore the name college or university there was little unity of purpose or of standards. A large majority of all the institutions in the United States bearing the name college were really concerned with secondary education.

Under these conditions the trustees felt themselves compelled to begin a critical study of the work of the college and of the university in different parts of this wide area, and to commend to colleges and universities the adoption of such standards as would intelligently relate the college to the secondary school and to the university. . . .

At the beginning, the Foundation naturally turned its study to the college, as that part of our educational system most directly to be benefited by its endowment. Inevitably, however, the scrutiny of the college led to the consideration of the relations between the college or university and the professional schools which had gathered about it or were included in it. The confusion found here was quite as great as that which exists between the field of the college and that of the secondary school. Colleges and universities were discovered to have all sorts of relations to their professional schools of law, of medicine, and of theology. In some cases these relations were of the frailest texture, constituting practically only a license from the college by which a proprietary medical school or law school was enabled to live under its name. In other cases the medical school was incorporated into the college or university, but remained an *imperium in imperio*, the

college assuming no responsibility for its standards or its support. In yet other cases the college or university assumed partial obligation of support, but no responsibility for the standards of the professional school, while in only a relatively small number of cases was the school of law or of medicine an integral part of the university, receiving from it university standards and adequate maintenance. . . .

Meanwhile the requirements of medical education have enormously increased. The fundamental sciences upon which medicine depends have been greatly extended. The laboratory has come to furnish alike to the physician and to the surgeon a new means for diagnosing and combating disease. The education of the medical practitioner under these changed conditions makes entirely different demands in respect to both preliminary and professional training.

Under these conditions and in the face of the advancing standards of the best medical schools it was clear that the time had come when the relation of professional education in medicine to the general system of education should be clearly defined. The first step towards such a clear understanding was to ascertain the facts concerning medical education and the medical schools themselves at the present time.

. . . .

The attitude of the Foundation is that all colleges and universities, whether supported by taxation or by private endowment, are in truth public service corporations, and that the public is entitled to know the facts concerning their administration and development, whether those facts pertain to the financial or to the educational side. We believe, therefore, that in seeking to present an accurate and fair statement of the work and the facilities of the medical schools of this country, we are serving the best possible purpose which such an agency as the Foundation can serve; and, furthermore, that only by such publicity can the true interests of education and of the universities themselves be subserved.

. . . .

The significant facts revealed by this study are these:

---

*In 1909, Abraham Flexner prepared a report entitled *Medical Education in the United States and Canada*. This report strongly influenced the setting of standards for medical colleges and led to the closing of all Negro medical colleges with the exception of Howard and Meharry. The complete report is long and detailed, and only the following sections are presented here: excerpts from the Introduction; Chapter XIV, on medical education of the Negro; and a review of each Negro medical college. The wording of the material, including the author's use of the word "negro," is reproduced exactly as it appears in the original report, which was published in 1910.

(1) For twenty-five years past there has been an enormous over-production of uneducated and ill trained medical practitioners. This has been in absolute disregard of the public welfare and without any serious thought of the interests of the public. Taking the United States as a whole, physicians are four or five times as numerous in proportion to population as in older countries like Germany.

(2) Over-production of ill trained men is due in the main to the existence of a very large number of commercial schools, sustained in many cases by advertising methods through which a mass of unprepared youth is drawn out of industrial occupations into the study of medicine.

(3) Until recently the conduct of a medical school was a profitable business, for the methods of instruction were mainly didactic. As the need for laboratories has become more keenly felt, the expenses of an efficient medical school have been greatly increased. The inadequacy of many of these schools may be judged from the fact that nearly half of all our medical schools have incomes below $10,000, and these incomes determine the quality of instruction that they can and do offer.

Colleges and universities have in large measure failed in the past twenty-five years to appreciate the great advance in medical education and the increased cost of teaching it along modern lines. Many universities desirous of apparent educational completeness have annexed medical schools without making themselves responsible either for the standards of the professional schools or for their support.

(4) The existence of many of these unnecessary and inadequate medical schools has been defended by the argument that a poor medical school is justified in the interest of the poor boy. It is clear that the poor boy has no right to go into any profession for which he is not willing to obtain adequate preparation; but the facts set forth in this report make it evident that this argument is insincere, and that the excuse which has hitherto been put forward in the name of the poor boy is in reality an argument in behalf of the poor medical school.

(5) A hospital under complete educational control is as necessary to a medical school as is a laboratory of chemistry or pathology. High grade teaching within a hospital introduces a most wholesome and beneficial influence into its routine. Trustees of hospitals, public and private, should therefore go to the limit of their authority in opening hospital wards to teaching, provided only that the universities secure sufficient funds on their side to employ as teachers men who are devoted to clinical science.

. . . .

The development which is here suggested for medical education is conditioned largely upon three factors: first, upon the creation of a public opinion which shall discriminate between the ill trained and the rightly trained physician, and which will also insist upon the enactment of such laws as will require all practitioners of medicine, whether they belong to one sect or another, to ground themselves in the fundamentals upon which medical science rests; secondly, upon the universities and their attitude towards medical standards and medical support; finally, upon the attitude of the members of the medical profession towards the standards of their own practice and upon their sense of honor with respect to their own profession.

. . . .

The object of the Foundation in undertaking studies of this character is to serve a constructive purpose, not a critical one. Unless the information here brought together leads to constructive work, it will fail of its purpose. The very disappearance of many existing schools is part of the reconstructive process. Indeed, in the course of preparing the report a number of results have already come about which are of the highest interest from the constructive point of view. Several colleges, finding themselves unable to carry on a medical school upon right lines, have, frankly facing the situation, discontinued their medical departments, the result being a real gain to medical education. Elsewhere, competing medical schools which were dividing the students and the hospital facilities have united into a single school. In still other instances large sums of money have been raised to place medical education on a firmer basis.

In the preparation of this report the Foundation has kept steadily in view the interests of two classes, which in the over-multiplication of medical schools have usually been forgotten,—first, the youths who are to study medicine and to become the future practitioners, and, secondly, the general public, which is to live and die under their ministrations.

. . . .

It is hoped that both the purpose of the Foundation and its point of view as thus stated may be remembered in any consideration of the report which follows, and that this publication may serve as a starting-point both for the intelligent citizen and for the medical practitioner in a new national effort to strengthen the medical profession and rightly to relate medical education to the general system of schools of our nation.

CHAPTER XIV

THE MEDICAL EDUCATION
OF THE NEGRO

The medical care of the negro race will never be wholly left to negro physicians. Nevertheless, if the negro can be brought to feel a sharp responsibility for the physical integrity of his people, the outlook for their mental and moral improvement will be distinctly brightened. The practice of the negro doctor will be limited to his own race, which in turn will be cared for better by good negro physicians than by poor white ones. But the physical well-being of the negro is not only of moment to the negro himself. Ten million of them live in close contact with sixty million whites. Not only does the negro himself suffer from hookworm and tuberculosis; he communicates them to his white neighbors, precisely as the ignorant and unfortunate white contaminates him. Self-protection not less than humanity offers weighty counsel in this matter; self-interest seconds philanthropy. The negro must be educated not only for his sake, but for ours. He is, as far as human eye can see, a permanent factor in the nation. He has his rights and due and value as an individual; but he has, besides, the tremendous importance that belongs to a potential source of infection and contagion.

The pioneer work in educating the race to know and to practice fundamental hygienic principles must be done largely by the negro doctor and the negro nurse. It is important that they both be sensibly and effectively trained at the level at which their services are now important. The negro is perhaps more easily "taken in" than the white; and as his means of extricating himself from a blunder are limited, it is all the more cruel to abuse his ignorance through any sort of pretense. A well-taught negro sanitarian will be immensely useful; an essentially untrained negro wearing an M.D. degree is dangerous.

Make-believe in the matter of negro medical schools is therefore intolerable. Even good intention helps but little to change their aspect. The negro needs good schools rather than many schools,— schools to which the more promising of the race can be sent to receive a substantial education in which hygiene rather than surgery, for example, is strongly accentuated. If at the same time these men can be imbued with the missionary spirit so that they will look upon the diploma as a commission to serve their people humbly and devotedly, they may play an important part in the sanitation and civilization of the whole nation. Their duty calls them away from large cities to the village and the plantation, upon which light has hardly as yet begun to break.

Of the seven medical schools for negroes in the United States,[1] five are at this moment in no position to make any contribution of value to the solution of the problem above pointed out; Flint at New Orleans, Leonard at Raleigh, the Knoxville, Memphis and Louisville schools are ineffectual. They are wasting small sums annually and sending out undisciplined men, whose lack of real training is covered up by the imposing M.D. degree.

Meharry at Nashville and Howard at Washington are worth developing, and until considerably increased benefactions are available, effort will wisely concentrate upon them. The future of Howard is assured; indeed, the new Freedmen's Hospital is an asset the like of which is in this country extremely rare. It is greatly to be hoped that the government may display a liberal and progressive spirit in adapting the administration of this institution to the requirements of medical education.

Meharry is the creation of one man, Dr. George W. Hubbard, who, sent to the south at the close of the war on an errand of mercy, has for a half-century devoted himself singly to the elevation of the negro. The slender resources at his command have been carefullly husbanded; his pupils have in their turn remembered their obligations to him and to their school. The income of the institution has been utilized to build it up. The school laboratories are highly creditable to the energy and intelligence of Dr. Hubbard and his assistants. The urgent need is for improved clinical facilities—a hospital building and a well equipped dispensary. Efforts now being made to acquire them deserve liberal support.

The upbuilding of Howard and Meharry will profit the nation much more than the inadequate maintenance of a larger number of schools. They are, of course, unequal to the need and the opportunity; but nothing will be gained by way of satisfying the need or of rising to the opportunity through the survival of feeble, ill equipped institutions, quite regardless of the spirit which animates the promoters. The subventions of religious and philanthrophic societies and of individuals can be made effective only if concentrated. They must become immensely greater before they can be safely dispersed.

---

[1] Washington, D. C.: Howard University; New Orleans: Flint Medical College; Raleigh (N. C.): Leonard Medical School; Knoxville: Knoxville Medical College; Memphis: Medical Department of the University of West Tennessee; Nashville: Meharry Medical College; Louisville: National Medical College.

NEGRO MEDICAL COLLEGES

District of Columbia

HOWARD UNIVERSITY MEDICAL COLLEGE. Organized 1869. An integral part of Howard University.

Entrance requirement: A high school course or its equivalent.

Attendance: 205, most of whom are working their way through. Practically all the students are colored.

Teaching staff: 52, 22 being professors, 30 of other grade.

Resources available for maintenance: The school budget calls for $40,000, of which $26,000 are supplied by student fees, most of the remainder by government appropriation. Though the school has been changed from a night to a day school, the fees raised from $80 to $100, and the admission requirements stiffened, the attendance has nevertheless increased.

Laboratory facilities: The laboratory equipment includes anatomy, pathology, histology, bacteriology, and chemistry. There is no organized museum, though the school possesses a number of specimens, normal and pathological, charts, models, etc.

Clinical facilities: Clinical facilities are provided in the new, thoroughly modern, and adequate government hospital of 278 free beds, with its dispensary, closely identified with the medical school. A pavilion for contagious diseases alone is lacking.

Date of visit: January, 1910

General Considerations

OF the medical schools in Washington, Howard University has a distinct mission—that of training the negro physician—and an assured future. The government has to some extent been the patron of the institution, and has done its medical department an incalculably great service by the erection of the Freedman's Hospital. Sound policy—educational as well as philanthropic—recommends that this hospital be made a more intimate part of Howard University, so that students may profit to the uttermost by its clinical opportunities. Its usefulness as a hospital in its immediate vicinity will be thereby increased; and its service to the colored race at large will be augmented to the extent to which it is used to educate their future physicians. . . .

Kentucky

LOUISVILLE NATIONAL MEDICAL COLLEGE (Colored). An independent school, organized 1888, now affiliated with the colored State University.

Entrance requirement: Less than high school education.

Attendance: 40.

Teaching staff: 23, of whom 17 are professors.

Resources available for maintenance: Fees, amounting to $2560.

Laboratory facilities: Nominal.

Clinical facilities: A small and scrupulously clean hospital of 8 beds is connected with the school.

Date of visit: January, 1909.

General Considerations
[This college not mentioned in this section.]

Louisiana

FLINT MEDICAL COLLEGE (Colored). Organized in 1889, it is a department of New Orleans University, which is managed by the Freedman's Aid Society of the Methodist Episcopal Church, North.

Attendance: 24.

Teaching staff: 15, of whom 6 are professors. All are practitioners.

Resources available for maintenance: Tuition fees, $1300 (estimated), and small appropriations voted by the Freedman's Aid Society constitute the income. The entire budget, including that of the hospital adjoining, is less than $10,000 annually.

Laboratory facilities: There is scant equipment in anatomy, chemistry, pathology, and bacteriology. The rooms are in poor condition.

Clinical facilities: The school controls a hospital of 20 beds, with an average of 17 patients monthly, and a dispensary with an average daily attendance of one or two.

Date of visit: January, 1909.

General Considerations

Flint Medical College is a hopeless affair, on which money and energy alike are wasted. The urgent need in respect to the medical education of the negro is concentration of resources slender at best on a single southern institution. Much the most favorably situated for this purpose is Meharry Medical College at Nashville.

North Carolina

RALEIGH: *Population,* 20,533.

LEONARD MEDICAL SCHOOL Colored. Organized 1882. An integral part of Shaw University.

Entrance requirement: Less than four-year high school education.

Attendance: 125.

Teaching staff: 9, of whom 8 are professors, one of other grade.

Resources available for maintenance: Mainly fees and contributions, amounting to $4721, practically all of which is paid to the practitioner teachers.

Laboratory facilities: These comprise a clean and exceedingly well kept dissecting-room, a slight chemical laboratory, and a still slighter equipment for pathology. There are no library, no museum, and no teaching accessories. It is evident that the policy of paying practitioners has absorbed the resources of a school that exists for purely philanthropic objects.

Clinical facilities: These are hardly more than nominal. The school has access to a sixteen-bed hospital, containing at the time of the visit three patients. There is no dispensary at all. About thirty thousand dollars are, however, now available for building a hospital and improving laboratories.

Date of visit: February, 1909.

General Considerations

. . . .

A word as to the colored school at Raleigh. This is a philanthropic enterprise that has been operating for well-nigh thirty years and has nothing in the way of plant to show for it. Its income ought to have been spent within; it has gone outside, to reimburse practitioners who supposed themselves assisting in a philanthropic work. . . . Raleigh cannot, except at great expense, maintain clinical teaching. The way to help the negro is to help the two medical schools that have a chance to become efficient,—Howard at Washington, Meharry at Nashville.

Tennessee

KNOXVILLE MEDICAL COLLEGE Colored. Established 1900. An independent institution.

Entrance requirement: Nominal.

Attendance: 23.

Teaching staff: 11, of whom 9 are professors.

Resources available for maintenance: Fees, amounting to $1020 (estimated).

Laboratory facilities: None. The school occupies a floor above an undertaker's establishment.

Clinical facilities: None. It was stated by a student that twice between October 1 and January 28 "a few students were taken to the Knoxville College Hospital."

There is no dispensary.

The catalogue of this school is a tissue of misrepre-

sentations from cover to cover.

Date of visit: January, 1909

UNIVERSITY OF WEST TENNESSEE, MEDICAL DEPARTMENT Colored. Organized 1900.

Entrance requirement: Nominal.

Attendance: 40.

Teaching staff: 14, all of whom are professors.

Resources available for maintenance: Fees, amounting to $2000 (estimated).

Laboratory facilities: There is meager equipment for chemistry, pharmacy, and microscopy. Otherwise the rooms are bare.

Clinical facilities: The students have access to eight or ten beds, twice weekly, in a small hospital close by.

There is a dispensary, without records, in the school building.

Date of visit: November, 1909.

MEHARRY MEDICAL COLLEGE Colored. Organized 1876. The medical department of Walden University.

Entrance requirement: Less than a four-year high school education.

Attendance: 275.

Teaching staff: 26, of whom 12 are professors, 14 of other grade.

Resources available for maintenance: $23,946, representing income from endowment of $35,000, subscription from the Freedman's Aid Society, and fees, the last item being $20,310.

Laboratory facilities: The school possesses fair laboratories for chemistry and physiology and highly creditable laboratories for bacteriology, histology, and pathology, the outfit including animals, microscopes, microtome, and pathological material in excellent order. A separate frame building, well kept, is devoted to anatomy. The equipment and general conditions reflect great credit on the zeal and intelligence of those in charge of the school and its several departments.

Clinical facilities: These are restricted. The school has access to Mercy Hospital, 32 beds.

Date of visit: January, 1909.

General Considerations

. . . .

Of the three negro schools in the state, two are without merit. The third—Meharry—is a most creditable institution. The reader is referred to chapter xiv, "The Medical Education of the Negro," for a fuller discussion of its needs and deserts.

The Interracial Committee of Montclair, New Jersey

Report of a Survey of a Hospital Committee*

INTRODUCTION

Our instructions were to find out and report the facts concerning the hospitalization of the colored population particularly in Montclair, and next in adjacent territory. It was the further suggestion of the chairman, Dr. Weirs, that we ascertain what is being done in this connection in other places and parts of the United States. We make our presentation only as a preliminary report. It is far from complete.

REPORT OF NATIONWIDE SURVEY

We felt that it would be a good thing to get the crystalized sentiment of one hundred physicians in various parts of the country. To that end, one hundred questionnaires were mailed out. We have not been able to tabulate all the answers, but we felt that the answers to questions 3, 4, 5, 6, 7, 8, 19 and 20 would help largely in determining the existing sentiment. Of the seventy-eight who answered questions 3, 4, 5, 6, 7, 8, 19 and 20 we give the following tabulated results:

Number 3. Are Negroes admitted to hospitals on the same basis as whites? Thirty-three answered "yes." Forty-five answered "no." Thirty-nine of these lived in the north and thirty-eight in the south and one in the far west.

Number 4. Are the existing facilities adequate? Thirty-four answered "yes, for patients." Forty-four answered no. Thirty-nine of these answers were from the north, thirty-eight from the south and one from the far west.

Questions 5, 6, 7, 8 have to do with acceptance of Negro doctors in the general hospitals, both publicly owned and semi-private, for practice on their patients. Four answered that conditions were satisfactory. Sixty-two said "no," they were not permitted such privileges. Twelve answered somewhat indefinitely, showing that in some instances they were admitted to courtesy privileges with a staff position here and there. Thirty-nine of these answers were from the north and thirty-eight from the south and one from the far west.

Question 19 seeks to learn whether the doctors endorse a program of hospital construction for the Negro race or favor efforts to get admission into the existing institutions. Forty-nine favored the development of Negro hospitals. Nine opposed, and twenty favored both a program of hospital building for the [Negro] race and at the same time seeking opportunities in existing hospitals. That gives us sixty-nine out of the seventy-eight who answered who do favor Negro hospital construction. Of this number forty-four have residence in the north and thirty-four in the south. Of the twenty who favor both propositions seventeen have residences in the north, one in the far west, California, one in Virginia and one in Atlanta and two in Washington, D. C. Of those in the north, nine live in New Jersey, two in New York, one in Pennsylvania, one in Chicago and three in Boston.

Question 20 referred to the color of the hospital staff. It is interesting to note that those answering, regardless of the section of the country, are very nearly unanimous in their choice of a mixed staff of white and colored physicians—seventy for and eight against. Only one of the eight was directly opposed to whites. The other seven were opposed not to white

*The material in this appendix contains part of a report prepared by Dr. John A. Kenney, Sr., on behalf of The Interracial Committee of Montclair, New Jersey. Dr. Kenney, a graduate of the Leonard Medical School, was chairman of a subcommittee organized "to find out and report the facts concerning the hospitalization of the colored population particularly in Montclair . . . and ascertain what is being done in this connection in other places and parts of the United States." Because of the length of the report, only part is reproduced here. A more detailed presentation can be found in the *Journal of the National Medical Association*, July-September, 1931, pp. 97–107.

Dr. Kenney's work in Montclair centered around the problem of the Negro in medicine. When he founded his private Kenney Memorial Hospital, Negro doctors in north Essex County did not have privileges at any private hospital in the area. However, when constantly increasing expenses for modern equipment made it impossible to support the hospital with its small number of beds, there was not a doctor on its staff who was not affiliated, in one way or another, with one or more of the white hospitals in the area. Dr. Kenney's hospital, besides providing needed medical care for Negroes, made two tremendous contributions to the Montclair area: it offered Negro doctors and nurses the type of clinical experience available to white physicians in white hospitals; and, because its staff was biracial, it helped significantly to break down some of the racial barriers that existed in medicine.

physicians but to the principle of Negro hospitals.

The response to the canvass has been very gratifying. Forty-seven answered the first communication. Fifty-three follow-up letters were sent out bringing thirty-one more replies, making seventy-eight in all. This is very unusual and reflects the general interest throughout the nation in this hospital question.

The questionnaires were sent into twenty-four states. Twelve were sent to southern states and twelve to the north and west.

STATISTICAL INFORMATION

The population of the United States according to the latest census reports is 122,775,000. The Negro population is nearly 13,000,000, or just about one-tenth of the whole. The number of physicians for the entire population is 83,000, making one physician to each 1,400 persons. The total number of Negro physicians in the United States is between 3,500 and 4,000, making one physician to each 3,200 of its population. The number of approved hospitals in the United States according to the 1930 survey is 6,719. The non-approved is 540, making a total of 7,259 hospitals with a hospital bed capacity of 9,555,869, or one hospital bed to each 137 of the population. The total number of hospitals expressly for Negroes is around 225, furnishing one hospital bed to each 1,941 of the Negro population. According to Dr. B. C. H. Harvey, dean of medical students of the University of Chicago, the Negro medical students in the north are about one in thirty thousand of the colored population while as for the total population the ratio is one in six thousand. He further shows that there are about five times as many white doctors for the white people as there are colored doctors for the colored people.

The health standard of a people is judged very largely by its hospital status. Measured by the above means you are prepared to be told that compared with the white race as a whole the Negro health standard is low. . . . The mortality of Negroes in the cities of the United States has been given as 180 per cent of the mortality among the whites. . . . Statistics along this line in general show the death rate of Negroes to be as much as two, and in some instances three and four, times that of whites. According to United States Life Tables of 1920, the expectation of life for whites was fifty-five years and for Negroes forty-one years.

These figures would indicate that there is a very high Negro morbidity and mortality rate and that there is necessity for concentration upon efforts to improve the Negro health conditions.

It has been shown that 450,000 Negroes are seriously sick all the time. The cost of this illness is $75,000,000 a year; sickness and death cost annually $100,000,000; $500,000 more is lost annually in wages because of illness; and a billion dollars is spent yearly in medicine, most of which is for patent medicine.

There are 664 hospitals approved by the American Medical Association for 5,584 internes per year. There were 4,565 medical graduates in 1930. Thus there were 1,019 more positions for internes than there were graduates to fill the places.

On the other hand, for the Negroes we have about 80 to 90 internships available per year with an average of 117 graduates in medicine annually, thus showing a deficit of some 35 or 40 internships for the Negroes against a surplus of 1,019 for the whites.

THE SURVEY OF ESSEX COUNTY HOSPITALS

. . . Working under the auspices of the Hospital Committee of the Interracial Committee of Montclair, I recently mailed a questionnaire to each of the twenty-five hospitals in the county in order to have first-hand information concerning their practices regarding Negro patients, doctors, internes and nurses. This was done in an effort to determine the necessity for a hospital for our group in this section. Thus far we have answers from nine hospitals. We have also questioned formally about twenty-five colored physicians in this section. The answers from the nine hospitals and from fourteen physicians indicate that practically all the hospitals furnish ward service to Negro patients. Very few (two of those who answered) will admit Negro patients to semi-private or private rooms. None admit Negro doctors to their visiting or to their courtesy staffs, and only two indicated that they might consider applications to the courtesy service. None have Negro internes. Only one indicated that the question of Negro internes would be at all considered. None have or would even consider the question of Negro nurses, either as pupils or as graduates in service, or for private patients.

THE NEED OF HOSPITAL SERVICE FOR NEGROES

Some years ago, when I was at Tuskegee Institute, a woman called on me because she was in need of operative treatment. The lady for whom she worked wanted her to go to another city for the operation and offered, if she would do so in the service of a certain surgeon that she knew, [to] defray all the expenses. The patient went to this city to investigate conditions. It so happened that the day she visited the hospital, a colored female patient had been operated on in the operating room of the main building; and in the process of transferring her while still under ether from the operating room to a little building in the back yard of the hospital, she was left lying on her stretcher in the yard. When the prospective patient saw this, she returned to Tuskegee for me to perform the operation, saying that otherwise she would not have it at all. She thus properly declined her madam's offer. This condition is not at all unusual or out of the ordinary.

Dr. H. D. Dismukes, of Kimball, West Virginia, writes, "White hospitals allow no Negro doctors to practice in them or visit their patients in a professional capacity. . . ." The Bluefield Sanatorium, which he is now suing for breach of contract, would take Negroes in, operate on them as quickly as possible, place them in an ambulance while still under anesthesia and take them across town to a Negro hospital to convalesce.

Dr. Carl G. Roberts, of Chicago, former president of the N.M.A., in his contribution to the Hospital Number of the *Journal, N.M.A.,* July-September 1930, states: "A few years ago a survey was made of the local hospital situation and it was ascertained that less than one per cent of the hospitals accepted or even tolerated Negro patients. This one per cent included the municipal and charity institutions, as well as the three colored hospitals. It was not an unusual occurrence for the victim of a serious accident to be denied first aid at the nearest private hospital, and to die while being transported over a long distance to the county institution. In a large Protestant hospital in Evanston, adjacent to Chicago, a colored woman was subjected to a laparotomy by a member of the staff. Before recovering from the anesthetic, she was carried out to the ambulance and transported across the city to a small colored sanitarium, because the hospital in question did not accept any colored patients in the rooms or wards. So distressing did the situation become, especially as to the denial of first aid to seriously injured victims of unavoidable accidents, that a law was passed by the state legislature compelling hospitals to give first aid to emergency cases, regardless of race.

"The discriminatory tactics of the local hospitals added immeasurably to the difficulties of the colored medical student, curtailing his clinical opportunities and prohibiting his presence as an interne, with one or two notable exceptions."

In his hospital investigations in the south under the American Medical Association, Dr. A. B. Jackson found some very striking examples of this. We quote him as follows, "In one little city we visited, which presents a real typical condition which we find in the south, Negroes are placed in the basement of the white hospitals—if they have the money to pay for it—and they have to hire their own nurse, as it is most unorthodox for a southern white woman to nurse a Negro. . . ."

Another place . . . he describes as "just a dumping ground employed by white surgeons to drop Negro patients whom they operated on at the local white hospital, and shipped thereto in an ambulance while still under the effects of anesthesia." He further says, "This surgical crime we found committed throughout the south with such a degree of regularity that we began to accept it as a custom." He tells of an instance in which the daughter of a Negro president of a North Carolina college was injured in an automobile accident and was turned away from a hospital though she was torn, crippled, and bleeding. He speaks of many such cases with which they met, but puts particular attention upon two others. One was in Arkansas where a wealthy Negro suffered a stroke of apoplexy. The man who rushed him to the nearest hospital looked like a white man, therefore, all arrangements were made acceptably for his admission, but when the transfer began and his identity was made known, he was refused; and he had to be taken to a Negro hospital which was nearly one hundred miles away. The other instance was that of a farmer's wife stricken with appendicitis followed by rupture and peritonitis. The village white doctor wrote an urgent note appealing to the nearest hospital to operate on her at once. There she was carried but refused treatment. The next hospital was forty miles away. With his wife groaning with pains, her husband carried her there. Here too they met the same fate. An hour later, helped by some strange men, she was lifted from the truck and carried into a private home of some strangers, where the next day she died.

There is just one other instance of this same kind of gross immorality that I shall cite, which was reported by Dr. P. M. Murray of New York. A Fisk University student, the son of Dr. George S. Moore, Clinical Director of the United States Veterans Hospital at Tuskegee, in an automobile accident sustained fracture-dislocations of a neck vertebra with compressed spinal cord. This happened between Athens and Decatur, Alabama. In this terrible condition he was refused admission to any hospital in that territory on the ground that there were in the hospital no facilities for colored patients. After a wait of several hours an ambulance was secured, and he was carried some thirty miles from Decatur and admitted to a hospital in Huntsville where his father said everything possible for him was done; but death followed as a result of pneumonia from the exposure to which he was subjected after the accident.

It is a rather strange thing even in the north that if I get sick and apply for a bed in the general ward of some of the hospitals with white people I'll be admitted, but if I have saved money enough to give me a little more comfort and privacy in a room to myself I am told "no." I ask in seriousness and sincerity what is the special brand of psychology here? That actually goes southern practices one better. When I was riding on a Pullman through North Carolina and certain passengers objected to my presence, the conductor offered me a private room. As I was well and strong and had no desire for a private room I thanked him but decided to stay where I was. That was in North Carolina.

It is paying us a compliment out of all proportion to our merits to say that the white nurses, internes and doctors need hospitals for their training and for their practice to keep them abreast of the times, but that Negroes have so much more intelligence and native capacity that they can practice the same system of medicine and surgery without it, that they don't need it. That would be a mighty fine compliment, if true.

One argument from the other side is that all the white doctors have not hospital connections. That is true, but those who are eligible, in the rotation of service, may get there sometime. With us the door of hope is shut in our faces. Listen to this: "Do you admit Negro doctors to your visiting or to your courtesy staffs?" "No." "Will you consider such admission, and if so under what conditions?" "No." However, we do not take such answers as final.

CONCLUSION

Our limited general survey tends to substantiate known conditions; viz, that in the country as a whole, hospital facilities for Negroes are very inadequate and that opportunities for hospital training and advancement for Negro physicians are very meagre. . . .

Negro doctors, internes and nurses are pretty generally excluded from the facilities of the existing institutions. Two or three applications for courtesy privileges are now pending. The outcome of these is watched with interest.

Precedents there are in sufficient number to warrant local institutions in going as far as they are inclined to do in granting professional privileges to our group.

For the satisfactory solution of the problem, a community hospital that will give unprejudiced facilities to [every] racial group seems inevitable.

The following two recommendations are made:

1. That the Committee's activities be continued.

2. That a technical survey of hospital conditions as affecting the Negro population of Essex County, N. J., be made. In a conversation with Dr. McEachern of the American College of Surgeons he suggested such a survey would cost about $500.

A conference with Dr. Michael Davis, director of medical activities of the Rosenwald Fund, drew from him the tacit understanding that the fund might be willing to cooperate with the proper local agencies and through them make the survey. Dr. Paul Keller, Medical Director of Beth Israel Hospital in Newark, favors such a survey.

The Essex County Health Council and the County Medical Society are now interested in this matter to the extent that a joint committee has been appointed to consider it. We, with a small committee, by invitation have been before the Executive Committee of the County Health Council, which visit resulted in the appointment of the above-mentioned joint committee.

We have earnestly and diligently sought to find a program that seems reasonable for intra-racial harmony and that at the same time should command interracial support. The following is presented and we move its adoption:

"There is no general formula that will fit all sections and conditions. In the final analysis each section and each community must and will decide for itself what is best.

"But in general for the fifteen per cent of the Negro population north of the Mason-Dixon Line, untiring, never ceasing, sane and sensible efforts must be made to get representation for qualified members of our group in the existing public hospitals.

"Since such a program will very necessarily be slow, and as an aid to it and to that larger group who will never come directly under its benefits, we recommend that wherever needed hospitals be established, with the basic idea of supplying this deficiency, that they are not to be considered in principle or in practice segregated units for Negroes only, but for any and all peoples who may apply for treatment. Nor should such hospitals be held as excuses for curtailing any privileges which Negro patients and doctors and nurses now enjoy in the existing institutions; nor shall they be used to block any movement for greater racial privileges in other hospitals. They should have mixed boards of white and colored citizens, and a mixed staff of white and colored physicians and surgeons. They should be exponents of true interracial efforts."

The chairman of the committee desires to express his appreciation for the kindly consideration and very helpful attitude shown by Rev. Edgar Swan Wiers, Chairman of the Interracial Committee of Montclair.

Next he is greatly indebted to the Hospital Committee as a whole and to its individual members, all of whom have been very cooperative.

The committee extends its thanks to all who have in any way aided it in its task and particularly the seventy-eight out of one hundred physicians in twenty-four different states of the union who answered the questionnaires sent.

On motion of Mr. Ernest S. Suffern, and duly seconded, the recommendations of the committee were unanimously endorsed and a vote of thanks extended to the committee.

Signed,
Dr. L. W. Halsey,
Mr. F. D. Greene,
Mrs. George E. Bell, Secretary,
Dr. John A. Kenney, Chairman,
Hospital Committee of the
Interracial Committee of Montclair

May 26, 1931

APPENDIX TO THE REPORT

EXHIBIT A

The Interracial Committee of Montclair, N. J.,
Hospital Committee

Dr. L. W. Halsey,   Mrs. George E. Bell, Sect'y
Mr. F. D. Greene,   Dr. John A. Kenney, Chr.

Dear Doctor:

We are making a study of the subject of Negro hospitalization. In order that we may have something concrete to aid us in our local and general endeavors, we are desirous of knowing what the hospital situation is in your city. By answering any or all of the questions appended you will be rendering the cause a great service.

Thanking you in advance for this or any other information or suggestions pertinent to the subject of our attention.

Very truly yours,
The Hospital Committee of the
Interracial Committee of Montclair

Questionnaire

1. Are there any special arrangements for the hospitalization of the Negro race in your section or community?

2. If so, please detail what they are.

3. If not, are Negroes admitted to the hospitals on the same basis as the whites?

4. Are the existing facilities adequate?

5. To what extent are Negro doctors admitted to public, or municipally owned hospitals for the care of their patients?

6. Are any Negro doctors on the public hospital staffs?

7. Do any of the hospitals admit Negro doctors to their staffs?

8. Do any of them grant courtesy privileges to the Negro doctors?

9. What is the attitude of the Negroes in your community toward race hospitals?

10. Are there any race hospitals in your community?

11. If so, under what auspices are they conducted?

12. To what extent are they supported or patronized by the Negro public?

13. To what extent are they supported or patronized by the Negro doctors?

14. What opportunities are there for training Negro medical internes?

15. What facilities are there for colored young women to fit themselves for the profession of nursing?

16. Are colored nurses employed in the hospitals in your section?

17. To what extent are they employed in the homes? White? Colored?

18. If your hospital facilities are not adequate for the accommodation of Negro patients, doctors, internes, and nurses, what plans are under way to remedy this serious defect?

19. Guided by the sentiment of your locality would you endorse a program of hospital construction for the Negro race, or would you favor efforts to get admission to the existing institutions?

20. If your answer is in favor of Negro hospitals, would you support a mixed staff of white and colored physicians or of colored only?

EXHIBIT B

The Interracial Committee of Montclair, N. J.,
Hospital Committee

Dr. L. W. Halsey,   Mrs. George E. Bell, Sect'y
Mr. F. D. Greene,   Dr. John A. Kenney, Chr.

May 9, 1931

To the Board of Managers:

Dear Sirs:

In an address at a public meeting of the Interracial Committee of Montclair last year the present chairman of the Hospital Committee made the statement that there is no hospital in the State of New Jersey except the Kenney Memorial Hospital, private, where the Negro doctors may treat their patients. Many persons in the audience were surprised and later approached the speaker and asked if it were really true.

This Hospital Committee was appointed to develop the facts concerning Negro hospitalization. To that end the enclosed questionnaire is submitted to you. Will you kindly aid the work of this committee by furnishing the information sought?

The Committee extends, in advance, its thanks to you for your assistance in the matter.

Very truly yours,
John A. Kenney,
Chairman Hospital Committee

JAK/B

A Survey of Facilities in Essex County for Negro Hospitalization.

1. Name of Hospital.
2. Address.
3. Name and title of executive officer.
4. Does your hospital serve Negro patients?
5. Are they admitted to wards?
    a. To semi-private rooms?
    b. To private rooms?
6. If admitted are they segregated or are they admitted to your general service the same as other patients?

7. How many beds in your institution?
8. Daily average of patients for 1930.
9. What per cent of these were Negroes?
10. Are Negro doctors admitted to your visiting staff? Courtesy staff?
11. If not, would you consider their admission?
12. Do you admit Negro internes?
13. If not, would you consider their admission?
14. Do you use Negro graduate nurses?
15. Are Negro graduate nurses permitted to serve patients in your hospital?
16. Have you a nurses' training school?
17. Do you train Negro nurses?
18. If not, would you consider such training and on what basis?
19. Do you consider the existing hospital facilities adequate for Negro patients?
    a. For Negro doctors?
    b. For Negro internes?
    c. For Negro nurses?
20. If not, would you support a program of expansion in your institution giving greater liberality to these groups?
21. Would you endorse and support, morally and financially, either or both, a program for the establishment of a community hospital primarily for the Negro population, with the idea of giving greater opportunities to Negro physicians, internes and nurses as well as to patients?

Name and title of official answering this questionnaire.

NOTE: If such a hospital is established while its basic idea is for the Negro race it must not be considered a segregated unit for Negroes only, but for any and all peoples who may apply. Nor must it be an excuse for curtailing any privileges which Negro patients and doctors now enjoy in the existing institutions; nor shall it be used to block any movement for greater racial privileges in other hospitals. It should have a mixed Board of white and colored citizens of prominence and a mixed staff of physicians and surgeons. It should be an exponent of true interracial enterprise.

Care and Treatment of Negro Veterans at Tuskegee*

by Dr. Eugene H. Dibble, Jr.

IT is with deep sincerity that I express my gratitude for the honor and privilege of appearing before you, as Manager of the Veterans Administration Facility at Tuskegee, Alabama, to acquaint you briefly with the work we are endeavoring to do at Tuskegee in the care and treatment of Negro veterans. I want to say that we at Tuskegee are proud to be able to take part in the efforts of our Government to care for and to rehabilitate, where possible, the lame, halt and diseased defenders of our Country.

The scope of the work of the Veterans Administration is well known to you gentlemen; but, I feel it is not amiss to remind you that there has been a steady increase in the number of beds made available for the care and treatment of veterans, as well as continuing efforts to utilize all the resources of Science in the treatment of their manifold disabilities. In an address delivered by the Administrator before the Academy of Medicine in April, reviewing the development of the Veterans Administration and the increase of its facilities for hospitalization of veterans since the end of the fiscal year, June 30, 1940, the Veterans Administration had 60,000 beds, the Administrator stated, 35,000 of them are set apart for sufferers from mental and nerve disabilities; 20,000 of these beds are reserved for general medical and surgical cases; and over 5,000 of them have been set apart for victims of tuberculosis.

In the care and treatment of disabled ex-service men the Veterans Administration is constantly improving its equipment and technics. As new equipment is developed and proved, provision is made for its use at appropriate facilities, and, where necessary and feasible, those employees responsible for the use of such new equipment are given special courses of instruction in treatment technics; and, when new drugs and medicines are discovered and their use approved by the proper medical authorities, they are made available to the various facilities.

Since more than 400,000 Negroes were enrolled in the armed forces of the United States during the First World War, the problem of providing adequate care and treatment for the disabled Negro veteran, as well as furnishing the care and attention needed by white comrades-at-arms, became acute immediately following the end of the war. Facilities for their care were few and widely scattered. As you remember, many veterans were kept in base hospitals in the various cantonments. In most instances, such hospitals were located at great distances from the bona fide homes of the patients, the accommodations were more or less emergency in nature and extent, and such hospitals were not generally suitable for prolonged periods of hospitalization, which were necessary to rehabilitate many of the battle casualties.

But our government met this problem forthrightly and as speedily as was practicable. On August 9, 1920, the Bureau of War Risk Insurance, the Rehabilitation Division of the Federal Board for Vocational Education, and certain hospitals caring for veterans under the direction of the United States Public Health Service were transferred and combined into an independent bureau under the President, to be known as the Veterans' Bureau, with a Director at its head. During the same year, a committee of experts was appointed to make a survey of the needs of the country for hospital facilities for disabled veterans and to submit appropriate recommendations to the Secretary of the Treasury. Included in the recommendations of this committee was one which stated that since approximately three hundred thousands of the Negroes who served in the war were natives of the Southern States, a hospital should be provided specifically for their care and attention and to be located in that section of the country.

Tuskegee, Alabama was selected as the most suitable place for the Negro hospital, it being in the deep South and near the approximate center of the Negro population of the United States. Tuskegee, already made famous by Tuskegee Institute, founded by the late Booker T. Washington, was immediately acclaimed as an ideal location. In addition to the great institution endeavoring to educate Negro Youth, there would be another dedicated to the rehabilitation of disabled Negro World War Veterans.

Veterans Hospital No. 91 was dedicated on February 12, 1923, and formally opened for the admission of patients on June 15, 1923. The original bed capacity was 600. Three hundred for neuropsychiatric cases and 300 for sufferers from tuberculosis. The

---

* This speech was delivered by Dr. Dibble, Manager of the Veterans Administration Facility at Tuskegee, Alabama, at the State Service Office School of Instruction in Atlanta, Georgia. It was later published in the *Journal of the National Medical Association*, September, 1943. Reprinted by permission of the author.

bed capacity was increased to 807 in 1929; to 1,136 in 1933; and to 1,498 in 1937. Upon the completion of the remodelling of three wards, then in process, there were added sixty beds for general medical and surgical cases, making a total bed capacity of 1,558. Facilities for the treatment of the various types of diseases and disabilities have likewise undergone changes or modifications. The number of beds available for neuropsychiatric patients was increased to 1,087; general medical and surgical beds were increased to 411; and the Tuberculosis Unit was abolished, the procedure requiring that such patients as are found to be suffering from tuberculosis to be transferred to the Facility at Oteen, North Carolina, or to another suitable Facility, with the exception of tuberculosis patients who are also afflicted with neuropsychiatric disorders, which group is housed in a special ward at the Tuskegee Facility.

The Facility reservation, consisting of 486 acres, more or less, is located approximately one mile from Tuskegee Institute, and approximately one and seven-tenths of a mile from the town of Tuskegee, Alabama. Fifty-five acres comprise the area occupied by the buildings, lawns, shrubs, roadways, etc.; 110 acres are under cultivation; and the remainder is given over to trees, woodlands, right-of-ways, etc. The number of major buildings is 37, of minor buildings and structures, 26, making a total of 63 buildings of the reservation. Situated as it is on one of the rolling hills surrounding Tuskegee, and with its large expanse of lawn and shrubs and winding roads, we believe our Facility to be very beautiful, particularly in the spring and early summer; and I take this opportunity to invite all of you to pay us a visit and give us an opportunity to show you around our station.

The personnel force of the station consists of 645 employees—38 physicians, 2 dentists, 77 nurses, 269 hospital attendants, 93 dietetic employees, the remainder consisting of administrative officials, technicians, clerical employees and various types of custodial employees, including mechanics, laborers, guards, janitors, maids, chauffeurs, laundry helpers, etc. This force has undergone a steady increase, due to increased activities and number of patients, from 176 on duty June 30, 1923 to the present number.

The Facility at Tuskegee has been designated as an N.P.—General Medical Facility; and our patients fall into these two main types. The neuropsychiatric cases may be divided as follows: Functional disorders, such as dementia praecox

and manic depressive types, 60 percent, and neurological disorders, such as various types of brain diseases and diseases of the spinal cord, 10 percent. Among the general medical cases, cardiovascular and cardiorenal cases predominate.

The treatment of the Negro veteran follows the same pattern as that of the white veteran, except for certain modifications which must be made to meet conditions arising from his heredity, environment and socio-economic status. For instance, their immunity to certain types of parasitic diseases and disproportionate lack of resistance to others make it necessary that careful study be given to the use of viruses in the treatment of Negroes; each case must be carefully studied to determine whether the veteran can safely be told of his physical or mental condition as revealed upon examination; and, since the economic status of the larger number of these Negro veterans is very low, and inasmuch as the average age of the veteran is forty-five and jobs are becoming less and less available to him, efforts must be made to rehabilitate him thoroughly before he is discharged; for, in most cases, to discharge him during convalescence, which might require weeks or months, would impose a grave burden on his family, already overtaxed by the struggle for existence. A patient discharged under these conditions, finding himself first a burden on his family and then unable to obtain gainful employment after his recovery, usually fails to make the proper social and occupational adjustment; it is from this group that most of our "borderline" cases come. Therefore, as stated before, we have not only the problem of curing the disease with which the veteran is suffering, but the responsibility of rehabilitating him to the point where he will be able to make the proper adjustments when he returns to his home.

The treatment of our large group of mental patients consists primarily of occupational therapy, including a well-organized recreational program. The occupational assignments are made chiefly to the woodworking shop, paint shop for the renovation of Government property, farm, landscape section, and to the sewing room where bath hammocks and pajamas are made. Large groups are also regularly assigned to the Laundry and to the Dietetic Sections, as well as to the Utilities Division and as Messengers.

The bath hammocks made by the patients are used in connection with prolonged baths for acutely disturbed patients; the pajamas are placed in stock and used by the patients; and the vegetables and hogs from the farm are utilized in our Dietary Department.

For the regressed and deteriorated types of patients, we have a habit training unit operated on kindergarten methods. In this unit the patients are taught simple rules of conduct, to perform simple tasks, to coordinate their efforts, and personal neatness and simple rules of hygiene and sanitation. From this group, the patient is promoted to the next class where he is taught basket weaving, rug making, etc. When he has reached the proper stage of improvement he is able to perform activities in connection with outside occupational therapy projects. Later, if his progress continues, he is able to return to his home for a trial visit or discharge.

Our Library also plays a large part in our rehabilitation program. We are extremely fortunate in having on duty a qualified and enthusiastic Librarian who is unusually energetic and cooperative in arranging bibliotherapy activities for our patients. Books are carefully selected for those coming to the Library and for distribution on the wards. The Librarian has organized a Press Club, a Debate Club, a Philatelic Club, a Book Review Club, and many other groups composed of patients. These activities afford a splendid method for self-expression for the patients, restore self-confidence, and generally greatly benefit them.

We are modestly proud of the work which has been done for the blind patients at our station. The Librarian has developed an extensive class in Braille and Moon-Point by which blind patients have been taught to read and, in many cases, to write. Through the daily classes, the reading of Braille and Moon-Point books and the use of Talking Books, the blind patients have been enabled to keep up with the current events of the day and to understand and appreciate such literature as has been prepared for the blind. These activities for the blind patient have changed him from the most hopeless, despondent, indifferent and unhappy of patients into a person of cheerful disposition and one imbued with a zest for living. The isolation and helplessness of blindness have been dissipated through the magic of Braille, of Moon-Point, of Talking Books. He has again contacted the living world about him, he is able to thrill to its pulsation, and to react to its changes, as other men. More than 200 blind patients have been taught to read and write Braille during the eleven years the program has been in existence.

Our recreational activities are planned to reach the masses, as nearly as possible. Hence, seasonable games are provided, such as baseball, volley ball, soft ball, croquet, tennis, hiking, swimming, dancing, singing, bus rides and other entertainment features, when feasible. Movies are provided twice weekly. In addition, there are daily radio programs and games for indoors, such as billiards, pool, checkers, dominoes and card games.

Another important feature of our treatment of neuropsychiatric patients is the use of trial visits, in order that the patient might make an attempt at social readjustment when he has improved to a proper degree. However, in carrying out this phase of our program, we must depend to a large extent upon the assistance of social workers and service officers. In every instance, before we release a patient for a trial visit, we obtain a full social service report relative to his home conditions. Many times the home location is rural and relatives and friends are not fully cognizant of the purpose of the investigation and refuse to give, or only partially cooperate in giving the social worker the desired information. When this condition arises, the local service officer can be, and is, of tremendous assistance, because he can explain the situation to the persons concerned and remove doubts or suspicions from their minds. We have had many occasions to seek the aid of service officers under these circumstances, and, it must be said, they have not once failed to come to our side and give us the required assistance.

On quite a few occasions when patients have been sent home for trial visits, it has been found that their failure to adjust properly has been due to the attitude of their families and neighbors. The fact that at the time the patient was taken to the hospital he was highly disturbed mentally—insane—has fixed in their minds a belief that he should still be regarded as insane and unfit socially. This places a burden on us to use every available means to educate the people generally to the stage where they can appreciate the efforts of the Administration and the purpose of the trial visit. They must be made to know that a goodly number of mental patients entirely recover from their mental illnesses, in the same sense that general medical or surgical patients recover, and that they should be given sympathy, understanding and assistance in their steps toward readjustment.

As indicated in the classification of our patients, we have a relatively large group of patients suffering with syphilis of the brain and spinal cord.

For a number of years, we were unable to treat these patients by means of the modern and accepted method—malaria therapy—as Negro patients did not respond to the tertain strain of malaria fever, which was then in use. However, in 1932, through the exhaustive study and research of our Assistant Clinical Director, it was found that by the use of the quartan strain of malaria—a foreign strain to which the Negro patient had not developed an immunity—gratifying results could be obtained. The patients readily responded with chills and fever, and beneficial results began to be achieved. Since that time, we have been highly successful with malaria therapy, having treated more than five hundred cases, with a large proportion of complete recoveries and returns to gainful employment. The same strain of malaria is still in use at this Facility; and, with its effectiveness definitely established, we have furnished blood to many other Veterans Administration Facilities and to numerous State institutions.

The development of the quartan strain of malaria for use in treating neurosyphilis among Negroes is one of our most interesting accomplishments; and we are justly proud that we have been able to rehabilitate so many patients through this more modern method of therapy, as compared with previous results through the use of chemotherapy, tryparsamide and bismuth injections.

We have also used insulin shock treatment for dementia praecox; but it is too early to make a definite report of the success of this form of therapy.

Although statistics are apt to prove highly disinteresting, at the risk of boring you, in closing I wish to quote the following statistical data which will give you a picture of our patient turnover for the period May 1, 1939 to April 30, 1940:

Patients admitted direct for treatment	1949
Patients admitted for examination & observation	59
Admitted by transfer from other facilities	63
Returned from trial visit or leave of absence	270
Total gains during the year	2274
Patients discharged direct	1783
Discharged upon completion exam. & observation	36

Transfers to other facilities	90
Deaths	182
Discharged while on trial visit or leave of absence	423
Total losses during the year	2514
Patients transferred to Oteen, N. C.	47
Patients transferred to Hines, Illinois	17
Patients transferred to Mountain Home, Tenn.	25
Transferred to Sun Mount, New York	1

Finally, I wish to thank you for the privilege granted me to come before you to acquaint you with the work we are attempting to do at Tuskegee in the care and treatment of Negro veterans. I would like to say that our relations with the various State Service Officers, and particularly with Captain C. Arthur Cheatham, State Service Officer for Georgia, have been most cordial; and we have been immeasurably aided in our efforts by their cooperation and assistance. The kindliness of these officers in dealing with Negro veterans and their wholehearted efforts to assist them in gaining admission to the hospital, have earned the gratitude of every veteran whom I have contacted, and certainly, that of us who are striving at Tuskegee to do our part in the care and rehabilitation of the Negro veteran.

Of those men who served in the first World War, numbers are being treated in private hospitals, others in their homes and the balance in Veterans Hospitals. Negro veterans are treated in many of the Veterans Administration Facilities throughout the country, with particularly large units for Negroes at various Facilities, such as, Columbia, South Carolina; Lake City, Florida; Waco, Texas; etc.; however, the largest number of Negro veterans treated by one institution will be found at and in the Veterans Administration Facility at Tuskegee, Alabama.

I cannot speak of our Facility at Tuskegee without expressing my sincere gratitude and that of our Staff for the interest and the sympathetic cooperation of the Administrator of Veterans Affairs, of the Medical Director, and of the other officials at the Central Office of the Veterans Administration without whose interest and kind cooperation our program would be rendered far more difficult, if not impossible, of accomplishment.

Legal Developments in Medical Civil Rights[*]

THE HILL-BURTON ACT[**]

Basic Objectives

In 1946 Congress enacted the Hospital Survey and Construction Act, permitting State-Federal cooperation in providing needed community health facilities. This law, sponsored by Senators Lister Hill and Harold H. Burton, came to be known as the Hill-Burton Act. It authorized matching Federal grants, ranging from one-third to two-thirds of the total cost of construction and equipment, to public and nonprofit private health facilities.

"Separate but Equal" Facilities

The Hill-Burton Act originally directed the Surgeon General to require an assurance from all applicants that the facility or any addition would be available to all persons residing in the area without discrimination on account of race, creed, or color.

Part A—Declaration of Purpose

Sec. 601. The purpose of this title is to assist the several States—

(a) To inventory their existing hospitals (as defined in section 631 (e)), to survey the need for construction of hospitals, and to develop programs for construction of such public and other nonprofit hospitals as will, in conjunction with existing facilities, afford the necessary physical facilities for furnishing adequate hospital, clinic, and similar services to *all their people*. . . .

However, the law permitted an exception to this requirement in localities where separate health facilities were planned for separate population groups if the facilities and services were of like quality for each group.

(f) That the State plan shall provide for adequate hospital facilities for the people residing in a State, without discrimination on account of race, creed, or color, and shall provide for adequate hospital facilities for persons unable to pay therefor. Such regulation may require that before approval of any application

for a hospital or addition to a hospital is recommended by a State agency, assurance shall be received by the State from the applicant that (1) such hospital or addition to a hospital will be made available to all persons residing in the territorial area of the applicant, without discrimination on account of race, creed, or color, but an *exception* shall be made in cases where *separate* hospital facilities are provided for *separate* population groups, if the plan makes equitable provision on the basis of need for *facilities and services of like quality for each such group;* and (2) there will be made available in each such hospital or addition to a hospital a reasonable volume of hospital services to persons unable to pay therefor, but an exception shall be made if such a requirement is not feasible from a financial standpoint.

Thus Congress, by statute, incorporated the "separate but equal" concept into the Hill-Burton Act. Eight years later, in 1954, the Supreme Court issued the first of a series of decisions declaring "separate but equal" public facilities unconstitutional. The racial policies governing the administration of the program, however, did not change until late 1963.

During the first 17 years of the Hill-Burton program, approximately 70 separate health facilities (less than 1% of all Hill-Burton projects) were constructed either for white or for Negro patients. All of the other Hill-Burton projects were classified as "nondiscriminatory" facilities.

"Nondiscriminatory" Facilities

Sponsors of health facilities not constructed as "separate but equal" were required by statute to assure that the facilities would be made available to all persons without discrimination on account of race, creed, or color. Nearly all of some 7,000 Hill-Burton projects were of this so-called "nondiscriminatory" type.

The nondiscriminatory requirement of the Act, as interpreted by the General Counsel of HEW, meant that:

1. No person could be denied admission as a patient because of race, creed, or color to that portion of the facility constructed with Federal funds. However, he could be denied admission to other portions of the facility.
2. No patient could be denied any service essential to his medical care.

[*] The material contained in this appendix has been adapted from the pamphlet *Equal Opportunities in Hospitals and Health Facilities,* published by the U.S. Commission on Civil Rights in March, 1965.
[**]Hospital Survey and Construction Act (79TH CONG., 2D SESS.—CH. 958—AUG. 13, 1946). Italics have been added by the author for emphasis.

3. Patients could be segregated within the facility by race, creed, or color.
4. Professionally qualified persons could be denied staff privileges, and internes and residents could be denied training on account of race, creed, or color.

The General Counsel based his ruling on the language of the Hill-Burton Act, his interpretation of the legislative history, and the statutory provision prohibiting the Surgeon General from interfering in the internal administration of any facility receiving grants.

CURRENT POLICY DEVELOPMENTS

Simkins v. Cone*

In 1963, the doctrine of equal access to health facilities was significantly advanced by the *Simkins* decision which resulted from a case brought in the Federal District Court in North Carolina by Negro physicians, dentists and patients—all of whom alleged discriminatory practices by two Greensboro hospitals. Both hospitals had been constructed with Hill-Burton funds under the "separate but equal" provision. However, while one hospital excluded Negroes altogether, the other admitted a few Negro patients but imposed special restrictions not applicable to whites. The Negro plaintiffs asked the Court to:

1. Order the hospitals to cease denying Negro physicians and dentists the use of staff facilities on the ground of race.
2. Restrain the hospitals from denying and abridging admission of patients on the basis of race.
3. Restrain the hospitals from refusing on the basis of race to permit patients to be treated by their own physicians and dentists in the hospitals.
4. Declare the "separate but equal" provision of the Hill-Burton Act and implementing regulations of the Surgeon General unconstitutional under the Fifth and Fourteenth Amendments.

The Department of Justice intervened in the proceeding and joined with the plaintiffs in asking that the "separate but equal" provision of the Hill-Burton Act be declared unconstitutional.

The District Court decided against the Negro plaintiffs, but on appeal the Fourth Circuit Court

reversed this decision and granted the relief sought by the plaintiffs. The U. S. Supreme Court refused to review the case, and thus left intact the ruling of the Fourth Circuit.

After the Circuit Court handed down its decision in the case on November 1, 1963, the Public Health Service (PHS) suspended approval of all new applications for "separate but equal" facilities. Following the Supreme Court's refusal to review the case in March 1964, Secretary of Health, Education, and Welfare Anthony Celebrezze announced new non-discrimination requirements to implement that *Simkins* decision. Regulations implementing these new requirements were filed by PHS on May 18, 1964 affecting all pending and future applications and providing that:

> before a construction application is recommended by a State agency for approval, the State agency shall obtain assurance from the applicant that all portions and services of the entire facility for the construction of which, or in connection with which, aid under the Federal Act is sought, will be made available without discrimination on account of race, creed, or color; and that no professionally qualified person will be discriminated against on account of race, creed, or color with respect to the privilege of professional practice in the facility.

The Civil Rights Act of 1964

Title VI**
Nondiscrimination in Federally-Assisted Programs

On July 2, 1964, the President of the United States signed the Civil Rights Act of 1964. Title VI of the Act prohibited discrimination in Federally-assisted programs and provided that:

> no person in the United States shall, on the ground of race, color, or national origin, be excluded from participating in, be denied the benefits of, or be subjected to discrimination under any program or activity receiving Federal financial assistance.

The Act also directed each Federal agency administering a program to issue regulations affecting the requirements of Title VI. On January 3, 1965, the regulations of the Department of Health, Education, and Welfare implementing Title VI became effective. On approving these regulations the President stated:

> This Nation's commitment to the principle of equality of treatment and opportunity for all

---

Simkins v. *Moses H. Cone Mem. Hosp.*, 323 F.2d 959 (4th Cir. 1963), *cert. denied*, 376 U.S. 938, 84 S.Ct. 793 (1964).

**78 Stat. 252, Sec. 601 (1964). Pub. Law 88–352.

Americans will be well served by the new regulations assuring that Federal programs are available to all citizens without regard to their race, color or national origin.

Discriminatory practices by Hill-Burton-aided facilities based on race, color, or national origin are forbidden by Title VI regulations. Discriminatory practices based on creed are forbidden by other departmental directives. The following are examples of those practices which are now prohibited:

1. A hospital refuses to admit a patient or after admission subjects the patient to segregation or separate or different treatment because of his race.
2. A hospital discriminates in the selection of residents, interns, student nurses or other trainees.
3. A nursing home admits all patients, but discourages use of the recreation room or specifies certain hours for use to patients of one race.
4. A health facility denies to professionally qualified persons the privilege to practice in the facility or denies the privilege on the ground that the doctor is not a member of a medical association which refuses to ac-

cept him as a member on the ground of race, creed, color, or national origin.

The Title VI regulations do not effect health facilities completed and no longer receiving any Federal financial assistance on or after January 4, 1965. However, these completed facilities are still subject to the more limited 1946-63 regulations. Desegregation beyond the requirements of the 1946-63 departmental regulations may be accomplished through:

a. Voluntary desegregation of the facilities
b. State or municipal action by statute, ordinance, or administrative rule
c. Federal or State court action to apply the ruling of the *Simkins* case.

Medical facilities which have not received financial assistance under the Hill-Burton program may still be subject to Title VI requirements because of their participation in other Federal assistance programs. For example, a hospital providing medical care for indigent patients which is under contract with a county welfare agency receiving Federal financial assistance may not discriminate; the hospital is held to the same standard of equal opportunity as any Hill-Burton facility.

Policy on Nondiscrimination

Whereas, Regular membership in the American Medical Association is limited to "those members of a state association who hold the degree of Doctor of Medicine or Bachelor of Medicine and who are entitled to exercise the right of membership in their state association, including the right to vote and hold office, as determined by their state association"; and

Whereas, This limitation makes it possible for a constituent or state association to deny for reasons of color, creed, race, religion or ethnic origin the privileges of membership in the American Medical Association to otherwise qualified persons; and

Whereas, Such denial is inconsistent with the ideals of the American Medical Association and contrary to a long-established policy of the Association; and

Whereas, The American Medical Association cannot in good conscience continue to allow a condition to exist that makes it possible for a constituent association to circumvent or thwart its policies in regard to eligibility for membership; therefore be it

Resolved, That the Bylaws of the American Medical Association be amended to state clearly that membership in the American Medical Association or any

of its constituent associations shall not be denied or abridged on account of color, creed, race, religion or ethnic origin; and be it further

Resolved, That the Bylaws of the American Medical Association be amended to provide that in addition to receiving ". . . appeals filed by applicants who allege that they, because of color, creed, race, religion or ethnic origin, have been unfairly denied membership in a component and/or constituent association . . . ," determining facts and reporting its findings to the House of Delegates, the Judicial Council, shall, if it determines the allegations are indeed true, admonish, censure or, in the event of repeated violations, recommend to the House of Delegates that the state association involved be declared to be no longer a constituent association of the American Medical Association; and be it further

Resolved, That the Council on Constitution and Bylaws be directed to prepare amendments consistent with the above provisions for consideration by the House of Delegates in Miami, December 1-4, 1968.

Adopted June 1968

A Victory over Racism in Medicine

Dr. Hubert A. Eaton's Account of His Successful Struggle to Integrate the Staff of the James Walker Memorial Hospital, Wilmington, North Carolina

IN 1954, the city of Wilmington, located in the southeast corner of North Carolina, had a population of approximately 45,000 people. There were six Negro physicians and at least fifty white physicians practicing there, whose seriously ill patients were treated in the city's two hospitals. The James Walker Memorial Hospital, predominantly for white patients, maintained about twenty-five beds reserved for Negro patients. These beds were located in a building completely separate from the main hospital building, so that it was necessary for Negro patients to be taken out-of-doors in all kinds of weather in order to reach the operating room, delivery room, X-ray department or any of the hospital's other primary facilities. No Negro physicians were allowed staff privileges there.

The second hospital in Wilmington, Community Hospital, provided treatment for Negro patients only and had a biracial medical staff. In 1943, Dr. Hubert A. Eaton, son of Dr. Chester A. Eaton, a graduate of Leonard Medical School, had come to Wilmington to enter private practice. Shortly after his arrival, he joined the medical staff of Community Hospital.

In 1954, while searching the real estate records in the County Court House for business reasons, Dr. Eaton discovered a block plan for the property on which the James Walker Memorial Hospital was located. He was shocked to find the word "free" written across these two city blocks. He had always been told that this was a private hospital and was astonished to learn that the institution was paying no city or county taxes. It was at that moment that he made the decision to apply for staff privileges at the James Walker Memorial Hospital. His letter of application led to the litigation which, years later, helped put an end to the system of segregation and discrimination against Negro patients and physicians in tax-supported hospitals throughout the nation.

Approximately two months after his initial letter of application was mailed to the James Walker Memorial Hospital, Dr. Eaton persuaded two colleagues, Dr. Daniel C. Roane and Dr. S. James Gray, also to make application for staff privileges at the hospital and to join him in litigation, which by that time seemed inevitable. The three physicians employed Conrad O. Pearson of Durham, North Carolina, and Robert R. Bond of Wilmington, as their lawyers. At that time, Mr. Pearson was chief NAACP lawyer for the state of North Carolina, and Mr. Bond was a local attorney.

It required approximately one year, from March of 1955 to March of 1956, to gather information, plan, research the case and prepare the complaint which was filed in the Wilmington office of the Eastern District of the United States Federal Court. It was not until twenty-three months later, in February, 1958, that the first hearing was set on the motions made by the various parties.

In June of 1958, the Federal district judge ruled that "no state action was involved in this matter" and allowed a motion to dismiss, which had been filed by lawyers for the defendant, the James Walker Memorial Hospital. The case was appealed to the United States Court of Appeals for the 4th District, and on November 29, 1958, this court affirmed the decision of the district judge.

On December 3, 1958, a letter was sent by Drs. Eaton, Gray and Roane to the NAACP Legal Defense and Educational Fund stating that funds for further prosecution of their case were exhausted and requesting that the NAACP defense fund appeal the case to the United States Supreme Court. Their request for help was granted, and a petition for writ of certiorari to the United States Court of Appeals for the 4th District was filed during the October, 1958, term by Attorneys Thurgood Marshall, Jack Greenberg, Conrad O. Pearson and Robert R. Bond. In May of 1959, the Supreme Court issued a denial of certiorari; the lawyers representing Dr. Eaton had exhausted all legal remedies of their case and had lost. Significantly, however, three Supreme Court justices—Warren, Douglas and Brennan—entered dissents, which are very rarely entered on a denial of certiorari. And, thus, it was evident that these three justices felt very strongly about the case.

Although Dr. Eaton had lost his case, he was not discouraged. His lawyers felt that they knew where their errors had been made; and they decided to let the matter rest until early in 1960, at which time they planned to make new demands on the hospital concerning its policies of discrimination and segregation and pursue the matter further based on circumstances as they existed at that time.

On April 6, 1960, Drs. Eaton, Roane and Gray made application once again to the James Walker Memorial Hospital for staff privileges. After this second application, Dr. Eaton and his fellow litigants received a letter signed by the hospital administrator enclosing applications for courtesy staff privileges, which they filled in and returned. Five months after filing their letters of application, they received a letter from the hospital advising them that their applications had not been approved.

At about this time, two local citizens joined the three physician plaintiffs as parties in the second suit against the hospital—Mrs. Vernetta E. Hussey, whose physician was Dr. Roane, and Leland M. Newsome, whose physician was Dr. Eaton. In the ten years during which this case was under litigation, no local white physicians, either individually or as a group, expressed any concern about the inhuman treatment which their Negro patients were subjected to at the James Walker Memorial Hospital.

In July, 1961, ten months after the physicians were denied courtesy privileges for the second time, a second suit was filed. The first hearing on this case took place in September, 1962, in Wilmington. A few months later, District Judge Algernon Butler ruled against the plaintiffs, as had Judge Don Gilliam in the first suit.

In April of 1963, notice of appeal was filed by Attorney Michael Meltsner, who with Jack Greenberg argued the *Eaton* vs. *James Walker Memorial Hospital* case before the United States Court of Appeals in Richmond, Virginia. This session was attended by Drs. Eaton and Roane. On April 1, 1964, Dr. Eaton received a letter from Attorney Conrad Pearson stating that the James Walker Memorial case had been reversed and remanded. This decision brought to a successful conclusion almost ten years of litigation.

C O P Y

Foster F. Burnett, M.D.
Founder

Hubert A. Eaton, M.D.
Director

BURNETT-EATON CLINIC
410 North Seventh Street
Wilmington, N.C.

November 5, 1954

Mr. Horace E. Hamilton, Superintendent
James Walker Memorial Hospital
Wilmington, North Carolina

Dear Mr. Hamilton:

I am writing this letter as an application to the medical staff of the James Walker Memorial Hospital for courtesy privileges. I am interested in using the facilities of your hospital to treat private patients--medical, obstetrical, and surgical.

I have been a practicing physician in Wilmington, North Carolina, for the past twelve years and a surgeon for the past ten years. I hold the following degrees: B.S., Johnson C. Smith University; M.S. and M.D., the University of Michigan. I served one year of internship at the K. B. Reynolds Hospital, Winston-Salem, North Carolina. At present, I am a member of the surgical staff and medical staff of Community Hospital.

Should a formal application blank be required, kindly forward one to me by return mail. Should you desire references, please indicate such in your reply.

Very truly yours,

HAE:et

H. A. Eaton, M.D.

Foster F. Burnett, M.D.   Hubert A. Eaton, M.D.
                                                                Director

BURNETT-EATON CLINIC
410 North Seventh Street
Wilmington, N.C.

C
O
P
Y

March 10, 1955

Dr. J. Watts Farthing
303 N. 10th Street
Wilmington, North Carolina

Dear Dr. Farthing:

     I am writing this letter to you as President of the Medical Staff
of the James Walker Memorial Hospital. On November 5, 1954, I applied
to Mr. Horace E. Hamilton, Superintendent of James Walker Memorial Hospital, requesting courtesy staff privileges. I indicated to him that I
was interested in using the facilities of James Walker Hospital to treat
private patients in the medical, obstetrical, and surgical services. I
set forth my qualifications and requested that a formal application blank
be sent to me.

     On January 17, 1955, I had received no answer from Mr. Hamilton; so
I wrote him another letter asking that he please refer to my letter of
November 5, 1954. I indicated at this time that, if I did not hear from
him within the next thirty days regarding the matter, I would refer the
item to my lawyer.

     Approximately thirty days after sending this letter to Mr. Hamilton,
I had not received an answer; therefore, I referred the matter to Attorney
R. R. Bond. Attorney Bond had a telephone conversation with Mr. Hamilton
on or about February 17, 1955, but received a "no comment" to his inquiry
regarding this matter.

     Upon the advice of my lawyer, I am writing this letter to you, as
President of the Medical Staff, requesting courtesy staff privileges at
the James Walker Memorial Hospital. I have also written to Attorney Allan
A. Marshall, President of the Board of Managers of James Walker Hospital.
I am writing these additional letters to satisfy myself that I have exhausted
all avenues of approach regarding this situation.

     I trust that you and the proper authorities at James Walker Hospital
will give this matter your immediate and full attention and courtesy me
with a reply. As a licensed practitioner and as a legal resident of Wilmington and New Hanover County, it is my opinion that I have every right
to use the facilities of James Walker Memorial Hospital for the treatment
of my patients.

                                              Very truly yours,

                                              H. A. Eaton, M.D.

HAE:et

C O P Y

                                         J. Watts Farthing, M. D.
                                         303 North Tenth Street
                                         Wilmington, North Carolina
                                         March 15, 1955

Dr. Hubert A. Eaton,
410 North Seventh Street,
Wilmington, N. C.

Dear Dr. Eaton:

          Your letter of March 11, 1955 was not
received until today, March 15, 1955. As President
of the Medical Staff of the James Walker Memorial
Hospital the matters mentioned in your letter have
not been brought to my attention since they do not
fall within the province of the Medical Staff.
Appointment to the Medical Staff of the Hospital
cannot originate within or through the Medical Staff
itself. Formal application must be filed through
the Superintendent of the Hospital. This has been
the procedure required for many years, to my own
knowledge since 1938 when I, myself, applied.

                    Sincerely yours,

                    J. Watts Farthing, M. D.

JWF/db

Board of County Commissioners
New Hanover County
Wilmington, North Carolina

Attention: Mr.

Gentlemen:

Enclosed herewith you will find copies of the following correspondence:

1. A letter from Dr. H. A. Eaton to Mr. Horace E. Hamilton, Superintendent of James Walker Memorial Hospital, dated November 5, 1954.

2. A letter from Dr. H. A. Eaton to Mr. Horace E. Hamilton, Superintendent of James Walker Memorial Hospital, dated January 17, 1955.

3. A letter from Dr. H. A. Eaton to Dr. J. Watts Farthing, President of the Medical Staff of James Walker Memorial Hospital, dated March 10, 1955.

4. A letter from Dr. H. A. Eaton to Attorney Allan A. Marshall, President of the Board of Managers of James Walker Memorial Hospital, dated March 10, 1955.

A perusal of the above listed correspondence will indicate that for the past five months, I have been attempting to secure courtesy staff privileges for the use of the James Walker Memorial Hospital's facilities in the treatment of my private patients. I have made application to every person in authority, whom I thought would ordinarily be charged with the administration of the hospital, but so far, I have received no answer other than a letter from Dr. Farthing, President of the Medical Staff, to the effect that the Medical Staff had nothing to do with applications for the use of the hospital's facilities. Dr. Farthing's letter stated further, that such applications should be made to the Superintendent of the hospital. Since my very first letter of application in the series listed above was directed to the Superintendent of the hospital, it would seem that my application was filed in the correct office in the first instance.

It is apparent to me, after the elapse of five months, that the persons to whom I have applied, do not intend to take any action upon my application. Since white doctors with qualifications equal or similar to mine are allowed courtesy staff privileges in the James Walker Memorial Hospital, I am compelled to arrive at the conclusion that I am being discriminated against solely because of my race and color. Consequently, I am bringing this matter to your attention and am requesting that you take immediate steps to see that my application is fairly considered by the proper persons.

#2 Board of County Commissioners

It is a matter of public record that this institution is tax exempt and further, that contributions are made to it by the Board of County Commissioners and by the City Council from public funds. My position is that so long as this hospital takes advantage of tax exemptions and receives contributions from the public funds, it has no right to discriminate against a physician solely because of his race cr color.

This letter is addressed to you as the highest governing body in New Hanover County in connection with the hospital in question, and as the last source of redress that I have before resorting to legal action to assert what I deem to be my constitutional rights in this matter.

An early reply from you will be greatly appreciated.

Very respectfully yours,

H. A. Eaton, M.D.

C. O. PEARSON
ATTORNEY AND COUNSELLOR AT LAW
Post Office Box 1428
Durham, N.C.

September 1, 1956

Judge Don Gilliam
United States District Court
Eastern District
Raleigh, North Carolina

RE: Civil Action #700
     Eaton et al vs. James Walker Memorial Hospital

Dear Judge Gilliam:

We filed a complaint in the Wilmington District sometime during March 1956, seeking a declaratory judgment to
establish the rights of Negro physicians to have courtesy
staff privileges at the James Walker Memorial Hospital.
The defendants filed a motion to dismiss under Rule 12, and
we would like to be heard as soon as possible on this motion
either in Chambers or at the convenience of all Counsel.

We have prepared a brief on the motion to dismiss, and
I am enclosing the original for your file.

With every good wish, I am

                                    Very truly yours,

                                    C. O. Pearson
                                    ATTORNEY AND COUNSELLOR AT LAW

COP/pm
Enclosure-1

cc: Mr. Cicero P. Yow
     Wilmington, North Carolina

     Mr. John Bright Hill
     Wilmington, North Carolina

     Hogue and Hogue
     Wilmington, North Carolina

Wilmington, North Carolina
December 3, 1958

N.A.A.C.P. Legal Defense and
   Educational Fund, Inc.
107 43rd Street
New York, N.Y.

RE: Eaton et al vs. James Walker Memorial Hospital et al
     United States Court of Appeals for the Fourth Circuit
     Appeal Case No. 7731

Gentlemen:

This action was commenced by H. A. Eaton, S. J. Gray, and
D. C. Roane as private individuals to secure rights to practice
in the James Walker Memorial Hospital, Wilmington, North Carolina,
after we had been denied such rights solely on the basis of race,
to wit: solely because we are Negroes.

We first went through administrative channels and then to
the City and County. After receiving no relief, suit was filed
in the local United States District Court with Attorneys Robert
R. Bond of Wilmington, North Carolina, and Conrad O. Pearson of
Durham, North Carolina, as Counsel.

With respect to the merits of our case, we refer you to our
Counsel.

We have taken this case through the Fourth United States
Court of Appeals; and, at this point, our funds for prosecuting
this case further (to wit: through the United States Supreme
Court) are exhausted.

Accordingly, we are appealing to you to assume all further
legal and financial responsibility in the further prosecution of
this case.

                                    Respectfully yours,

                                    H. A. Eaton, M.D.

                                    S. J. Gray, M.D.

                                    D. C. Roane, M.D.

C
O
P
Y

April 6, 1960

Mr. Emory Grubbs, Superintendent
James Walker Memorial Hospital
Wilmington, North Carolina

Dear Mr. Grubbs:

This letter comes as an application for courtesy staff privileges at the James Walker Memorial Hospital. You are, of course,
aware that such a request was made on a previous occasion and was
denied in accordance with the Hospital's policy of not admitting
Negro physicians to such privileges. It seems to me, however, that
there has occurred a sufficient change of circumstances that you
may wish to reconsider my application at this time. Over five years
have passed since my first application; and I believe that North
Carolina, along with the rest of the nation and the world, now takes
a different view of race relations. Moreover, I am increasingly impressed with the realization that, as a practicing physician, I am
not able to give the best medical care possible to my patients because
I am barred from the most excellent facilities of the James Walker
Memorial Hospital. If my patients desire to use your facilities,
they cannot continue to employ me because I cannot treat them in your
hospital.

The Negro citizens of this area are becoming increasingly vocal
concerning their dissatisfaction with this condition, and I believe
that you will concede that anybody so suppressed would react in a
similar manner. Of course, the urgency of this situation is far
greater than it was when the Hospital was built and now becomes
vastly more urgent year by year.

I have been a practicing physician in Wilmington, North Carolina,
for almost seventeen years. For the past fifteen years, I have been
a member of the active Surgical Staff of Community Hospital. I hold
the following degrees: B.S., Johnson C. Smith University; M.S. and
M.D., University of Michigan. I served one year of internship at the
R. B. Reynolds Hospital, Winston-Salem, North Carolina. At present,
am Chief of the Medical Staff at Community Hospital.

I am hopeful that your Board of Managers will reconsider and
olish their policy of denying competent Negro physicians the use
the Hospital's excellent facilities.

Very truly yours,

H. A. Eaton, M.D.

JAMES WALKER MEMORIAL HOSPITAL

Wilmington, North Carolina

September 7, 1960

Dr. H. A. Eaton
411 North Seventh Street
Wilmington, N. C.

Dear Dr. Eaton:

Your application dated April 28, 1960, for membership to the
Courtesy Staff of James Walker Memorial Hospital, has been
referred through the proper channels and reviewed.

This is to advise you that your application was not approved.

Very truly yours,

E. N. Grubbs
Director

ENG:s

OFFICE OF THE DIRECTOR
REPLY TO UNDERSIGNED

JAMES WALKER MEMORIAL HOSPITAL

Wilmington, North Carolina

April 26, 1960

Dr. Hubert A. Eaton
411 North Seventh Street
Wilmington, N. C.

Dear Dr. Eaton:

In reply to your letter of application for Courtesy Staff
Privileges, we are enclosing our regular application blank
which you may fill in and return at your convenience. Upon
receipt of this form properly filled in, it will be handled
in the usual manner.

Very truly yours,

E. N. Grubbs
Director

ENG:s

Encl. 1.

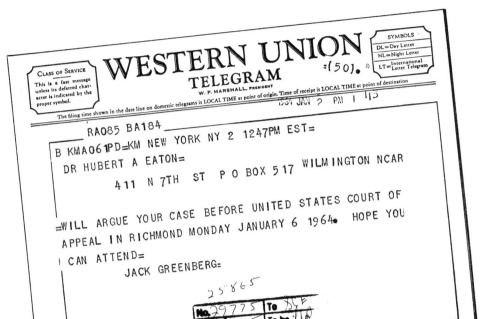

WESTERN UNION
TELEGRAM =(50).

CLASS OF SERVICE
This is a fast message unless its deferred character is indicated by the proper symbol.

W. P. MARSHALL, PRESIDENT

SYMBOLS
DL=Day Letter
NL=Night Letter
LT=International Letter Telegram

The filing time shown in the date line on domestic telegrams is LOCAL TIME at point of origin. Time of receipt is LOCAL TIME at point of destination

1964 JAN 2 PM 1 45

RA085 BA184

B KMA061PD=KM NEW YORK NY 2 1247PM EST=

DR HUBERT A EATON=

411 N 7TH ST P O BOX 517 WILMINGTON NCAR

=WILL ARGUE YOUR CASE BEFORE UNITED STATES COURT OF
APPEAL IN RICHMOND MONDAY JANUARY 6 1964. HOPE YOU
CAN ATTEND=
        JACK GREENBERG=

THE COMPANY WILL APPRECIATE SUGGESTIONS FROM ITS PATRONS CONCERNING ITS SERVICE

UNITED STATES COURT OF APPEALS
FOR THE FOURTH CIRCUIT

No. 9058.

Hubert A. Eaton, Daniel C. Roane,
Samuel James Gray, Vernetta E. Hussey
and Leland M. Newsome, on behalf of
themselves and others similarly situated,
Appellants,

versus

Emory Grubbs and the Board of
Managers of James Walker Memorial
Hospital, a body corporate,
Appellees.

APPEAL FROM THE UNITED STATES DISTRICT COURT FOR
THE EASTERN DISTRICT OF NORTH CAROLINA, AT WIL-
MINGTON. ALGERNON L. BUTLER, DISTRICT JUDGE.

(Argued January 6, 1964.   Decided April 1, 1964.)

Before SOBELOFF, Chief Judge, and HAYNSWORTH, BORE-
MAN, BRYAN and J. SPENCER BELL, Circuit Judges, sitting en banc.

Jack Greenberg (Constance Baker Motley, Michael Melts-

C. O. PEARSON
ATTORNEY AND COUNSELLOR AT LAW
POST OFFICE BOX 1428
DURHAM, N. C.

PHONE: 681-7993

April 1, 1964

Dr. Hubert A. Eaton
P. O. Box 517
Wilmington, North Carolina

Dear Dr. Eaton:

I received a telegram today from Mr. Maurice S. Dean, Clerk of United States Court of Appeals. The James Walker Memorial Hospital Case has been reversed and remanded.

I wish to extend my congratulations to you and your associates for following this matter through and I am sure that this case will have a great deal of influence on health problems affecting all people in the South. I say again congratulations.

Sincerely yours,

C. O. Pearson

COP:eaf

C
O
P
Y

April 6, 1964

Attorney C. O. Pearson
P. O. Box 1428
Durham, North Carolina

Dear Conrad:

Thank you very much for your letter, dated April 1st, congratulating us on the James Walker Memorial Hospital decision. This has been a long fight; and, even though we will be moving into a new hospital here in the next three years, this decision is good for many reasons. It not only takes the bad precedence out of the picture with regard to the first decision, but it gives us a moral boost and additional motivation to continue our fight against discrimination in all areas of life.

We wish to thank you for the help and assistance which you rendered from time to time in this case since it was first filed in 1955.

Sincerely yours,

Hubert A. Eaton, M.D.

HAE:hf

Are Negro Schools of Nursing Needed Today?

*Integration is a two-way street—good Negro and white schools of nursing should open their doors to all races; poor ones should close theirs**

by M. Elizabeth Carnegie

ARE Negro schools of nursing needed today? This is a rhetorical question to which my answer is no. According to the latest available figures from the National League for Nursing, there are 1,128 schools (29 are closing) of professional nursing in the United States. Of this number, 22 are predominantly Negro schools. Six of these 22 schools have a policy to admit students regardless of race, but only one (Harlem in New York) has white students enrolled. Of these 22 schools, only 9, on December 31, 1963, were accredited by the National League for Nursing; 3 of the 9 are colored divisions of white schools in a southern state.

Below is a list of predominantly Negro schools and their accreditation status according to type of program (DI—diploma; DE—degree; AD—associate degree):

Accredited by NLN

Tuskegee Institute, Tuskegee, Ala.	DE
Freedmen's Hospital, Washington, D.C.	DI
Gray Hospital, Atlanta, Ga.	DI
Medical Center, Columbus, Ga.	DI
University Hospital, Augusta, Ga.	DI
Provident Hospital, Chicago, Ill.	DI
Dillard University, New Orleans, La.	DE
Homer G. Phillips Hospital, St. Louis, Mo.	DI
Harlem Hospital, New York, N.Y.	DI

Not Accredited by NLN

Florida Agricultural and Mechanical College, Tallahassee	DE
Albany State College, Albany, Ga.	DE
Provident Hospital, Baltimore, Md.	DI
Agricultural and Technical College of North Carolina, Greensboro	DE
Lincoln Hospital, Durham, N.C.	DI
Community Hospital, Wilmington, N.C.	DI
Kate Bitting Reynolds Hospital, Winston-Salem, N.C.	DI
Winston-Salem College, Winston-Salem, N.C.	DE

Columbia Hospital School for Negro Women, Columbia, S.C.	DI
Prairie View College, Prairie View, Tex.	DE
City of Memphis Hospitals, Memphis, Tenn.	DI
Hampton Institute, Hampton, Va.	DE
Norfolk Division, Virginia State College, Norfolk	AD

Since national accreditation is the main criterion for determining the quality of a school of nursing, it can be assumed that slightly more than half, or 59 percent, of the Negro schools are inferior. Also, only two of these 22 schools are located in the two states (Alabama and South Carolina) in which none of the white schools indicates that it accepts Negro students.[1] But even in these two states, laws have been changed recently to permit Negroes to attend institutions of higher education, and both have state-supported universities with nursing programs.

Why then, are these schools maintained? Why do those located in states that have mixed schools, generally, continue to operate as Negro schools? Could it be that those white schools, who say that they admit Negro students, have a quota for Negroes? (The charter of the New England Hospital for Women and Children School of Nursing in Boston, where the first Negro nurse, Mary Mahoney, was graduated in 1879, provided for the admission of *one* Negro and *one* Jewish student each year.[2]) Could it be that most of the southern states are still clinging to the concept of "separate but equal" education? Could it be that the state boards of nursing in southern states who approve these inferior schools, year in and year out, have dual standards of education—one for Negroes and one for whites? Could it be that the accredited Negro schools are not opening their doors to white students, thereby voluntarily maintaining segregated schools? Or, is it as Alida Dailey, director of nurses at Harlem Hospital School of Nursing in New York, explained in her reply to Dr. Channing Tobias, director of the Phelps-Stokes Fund, at the fortieth anniversary luncheon of the National Association of Colored Graduate Nurses in 1948: "The pattern is not of

*Reprinted, with permission, from *Nursing Outlook,* 1964. The answer to the question posed by the title of this article is the opinion of the author—not necessarily that of *Nursing Outlook.*

our choosing—many [white nursing schools in the North still] exclude the colored student."[3] Has the number of Negro schools in the North and South decreased in the past few years because of integration in the North which made them no longer necessary?

Double Standards?

In 1924 the Hospital Library and Service Bureau conducted a survey of the Negro schools of nursing in the country to determine management of these schools—control of budget, amount of white cooperation, number of students, number of instructors, entrance requirements, length of course, working hours per week, division of service, post-graduate courses, housing, and recreation. As to the quality of these schools, one white director of a southern school commented: ". . . The type of training the average colored nurse receives in this part of the country is far inferior to that given to white nurses. Even the best training for colored nurses hardly approximates the poorest training given to white nurses. From another standpoint, their educational background is not so good. . . ."[4] This is a typical situation and this director deserves credit for admitting it. The average white director in a school such as this exhibited no concern for the low standards. In fact, as late as the forties, on my visit to practically all of the schools in the South, where there were white directors, in most instances, their attitude toward the Negro nurses and students ranged from apathy to hostility. Yet they held the top positions, exerting no effort to train future leaders among the Negro nurses. In this type of situation, it is understandable that the average Negro nurse and student may have developed the traits of victimization Allport refers to in his book, *The Nature of Prejudice* —obsessive concern, withdrawal and passivity, hostility, and even self-hate.[5]

Under the aegis of the Rosenwald Foundation, Nina D. Gage, director of the Hampton Institute School of Nursing in Virginia and Alma C. Haupt, associate director of the National Organization for Public Health Nursing, made a survey in 1932 of Negro schools of nursing in six southern states— Alabama, Georgia, Louisiana, Mississippi, Tennessee, and Texas. They reported:

> The schools of nursing themselves are of many varieties—some so poor at to make one question how they can possibly meet the standards of a State Board of Nurse Examiners. . . . In . . . one, two shabby houses were used as a hospital of 35 beds and a nurses' home for 12 students. A colored nurse is superintendent of

nurses and the sole member of the faculty. A three-year course is given, every subject being taught by the one nurse. . . . No public health subjects are included in the curriculum, . . . but the students are frequently sent out to homes as private duty nurses, and the wages thus earned help to run the hospital.[6]

Twelve years after the Gage and Haupt survey and during the early part of World War II, Estelle M. Osborne, then consultant for the National Council for War Service and Rita E. Miller, then part-time consultant for the U.S. Public Health Service, made a survey at the request of Surgeon General Thomas Parran to determine the status of Negro nursing schools in the country and elicit trends relating to the employment and professional participation of Negro nurses. They found that conditions in the schools, especially in the South, had not changed to any great extent. Although they made specific recommendations for upgrading the educational situation in the poorer schools, no formal steps were taken at that time to implement the recommendations.[7]

The Cadet Nurse Corps program during World War II was designed to increase the number of nurses for the war effort. All schools of nursing that were approved by their respective state boards of nursing were eligible to participate in the program which financed the education of students. To qualify for inclusion in the program, the schools had to meet certain minimum requirements. This alone helped to upgrade many of the poorer schools. ". . . Of the 1,125 schools that participated in the program of the Cadet Nurse Corps . . . 76 were rated *very poor* and 256 *poor*. Thus almost 30 percent fell below the grade of *fair*, in which category 646 schools were placed. Only 147 schools, or 13 percent of the total, were rated good or excellent [by the USPHS consultants]."[8] Of the 28 all-Negro schools, 21 had been approved for Cadet Nurse Corps funds.[9] Although the Cadet Nurse Corps program had a nondiscriminatory clause, the administrators of the funds did nothing to encourage integration, but followed the pattern of "separate, but equal."

Since the war, many of the poor schools have improved their educational standards. More Negro nurses have furthered their education and have replaced the whites in administrative and faculty positions in Negro schools. But, even with the general upgrading of Negro schools of nursing, there are still today 13 schools that do not have national accreditation, although they have approval of their respective state boards of nursing. Some of these schools, admittedly less than good, have never attempted to participate in the National League for Nursing's school improvement program, or any other program through which they might raise their standards. How can their graduates be expected to compete with graduates of good schools of nursing for positions, to say nothing of their ability to give quality nursing care.

In 1949 the National Committee for the Improvement of Nursing Services reported on a survey of schools of nursing in the United States, Hawaii, and Puerto Rico, and 97 percent of the schools responded. The findings were published and made available to those interested in improving nursing service to the people.[10] The survey included general characteristics, organization, student health, curriculum, library, clinical experience, instructional personnel, performance on state board examinations, budget, and measurement of student ability and achievement. These schools were ranked in three groups according to the way they met the criteria for a good school of nursing. Group I included those which had met the criteria, or had the potential. This group comprised 25 percent of the total schools; Group II, the middle 50 percent; and in Group III were those schools with the lowest national standards. It is significant that only 10 of the then 28 Negro schools qualified for placement in Group I—2 in the North and 8 in the South.

The state board of nursing is the legal body which determines admission requirements, approves a school of nursing after it has met certain minimum requirements, and examines its graduates to determine if they are safe to practice nursing. All schools of nursing require applicants to be high school graduates in the upper third of their class, but I know of one Negro school in the South that admitted a class of students, none of whom was in the upper third of her high school graduating class and this was acceptable to the state board. Considering the inferior elementary and secondary education of Negroes in the South, one can understand the dilemma this school must have been in, but is this a reason to perpetuate inferior education at the expense of the health of the public? Embree, writing in *Brown America* reveals the inadequacies of public school education in the South:

> Many of the schools run for only three or four months with teachers paid but $25 or $30 a month for these short terms. Studies of eight southern states show average expenditure of $44.31 per capita for whites and only $12.50

for Negroes. In certain states with huge black populations, the discrepancies are even greater. . . . The inadequacy of these provisions for either race is seen when one compares them with the average expenditure throughout the United States as a whole which is $87.22 per school child. . . . To the visitor . . . colored schools seem not a system but a series of incidents: bizarre, heroic, pathetic. . . .[11]

Another personal experience. One Negro graduate in a southern state failed miserably on the state board examination for licensure three times. On the fourth take, which was supposed to have been denied a nurse without supervised study, she was given the grade of 70 percent (lowest passing grade) in every subject. To me it was obvious that the board "gave" this graduate a license.

Fifteen Schools Close in the Fifties and Sixties

During the past ten years, 15 schools for Negro nurses came to grips with the problem of continuing and solved their problems by closing their doors. Only 3 of these schools (Lincoln, St. Philip, and Meharry) had national accreditation when they closed.

Mercy-Douglass, Philadelphia—This school, which had been in existence since 1907 (as Mercy Hospital School of Nursing until 1948 when it merged with Douglass Hospital), closed in 1961. For a while, it made its clinical and housing facilities available to Tuskegee Institute School of Nursing in Alabama. By the time Mercy-Douglass decided to discontinue its program, all schools of nursing in Pennsylvania, by state law, had opened their doors to Negro students. This school, which had served a need for 54 years, no longer needed to continue as a segregated institution.

Lincoln School for Nurses, New York—A school established expressly for Negro nurses, Lincoln had been in operation in New York City from 1898 to 1961. It was founded by a group of white philanthropists for the purpose of training colored women to care for the colored sick people. At that time, and as late as the forties, Negroes were denied admission to white schools in New York. This nationally accredited school graduated 1,864 nurses not only from New York, but from every state and such foreign countries as the British West Indies, Canada, and Africa. The charter had been changed to permit Lincoln to accept white students, but when it closed, only one white student had completed the course.

Lincoln filled a need as a pioneer school when

Negroes were denied admission to other schools. When this was no longer the situation in New York, the board and alumnae believed there was no need for a segregated school in New York.

Meharry Medical College School of Nursing, Nashville, Tennessee — Established in 1900, as George W. Hubbard Hospital School of Nursing, Meharry discontinued its nursing program in 1961 after its national accreditation status had been threatened, mostly because of the high incidence of state board failures. At the time of closing, 92 percent of the students were from the southern region as opposed to 52.4 percent in 1944 when the majority of Negroes from the North who wanted to study nursing were forced to enroll in southern Negro schools.[12]

Because of the poor primary and secondary education of the southern Negro students, their academic performance as nursing students was poor. Even before admission, the aptitude test results on the whole showed that at least 40 percent of the students had weaknesses in verbal ability, general information, arithmetic processes, and mechanical aptitude.[13] It was understandable, therefore, that these students were poor achievers in the nursing school.

St. Philip, Richmond, Virginia—"Nursing Students Few; School Will Be Closed," was the headline of a news story in the March 19, 1960, issue of the *Richmond Times-Dispatch*. St. Philip closed in 1962 after 42 years of service.

Here again was a nationally accredited school in the South that had outlived its usefulness—Negro students from the North no longer needed to apply for admission. (When I was on the faculty there in 1942, about 80 percent of the students were from the North.) The enrollment had decreased more than 50 percent since 1954, according to President R. Blackwell Smith of the Medical College of Virginia which operated St. Philip. Also, the Medical College of Virginia School of Nursing had been accepting Negro students for several years before St. Philip closed.

St. Mary's Infirmary, St. Louis, Missouri—Four years after the 1954 Supreme Court decision, St. Mary's, a Catholic school, was closed. Although the school had been in existence since 1933, it had been unable to attain accreditation.

Catholic schools of nursing represent 40,000, or one-third, of the student nurse population of this country and, according to a 1961 survey, 191 of the 309 schools admit Negro students.[14] At the forty-eighth annual convention of the Catholic Hospital Association of the United States and Canada in June, 1963, a resolution was adopted by the Conference of Catholic Schools of Nursing to make a determined effort to recruit Negro students to Catholic schools of nursing. The council further recommended that "admission policies related to age, race, creed, marital status, and sex should be evaluated in the light of social change."

LaMar School, University Hospital, Augusta, Georgia—Opened in 1894, this school had graduated 905 nurses when it closed in 1957 because of its graduates' high incidence of failure on state board examinations and lack of demand for the graduates in the community. (In 1962, however, the University Hospital began again to admit students to its Negro division. Again the division was called the LaMar School, but since then this name has been dropped.)

Hampton Training School for Nurses, Dixie Hospital, Hampton, Virginia — Organized in 1891, this school survived until 1956, without ever having participated in any type of school improvement program.

St. Agnes, Raleigh, North Carolina—Established in 1896, this school closed in 1959 because the hospital closed. It had never attained national accreditation.

Brewster-Duval, Jacksonville, Florida—Opened first as Brewster Hospital School of Nursing in 1901 under the direction of the Women's Home Missionary Society of the Methodist Episcopal Church, this school closed in 1954 and was reopened in 1961 as Brewster-Duval Hospital School of Nursing, but closed again in 1963. It had applied for national accreditation but never met the criteria.

Piedmont Sanatorium, Burkeville, Virginia—Established as a 2-year course in a tuberculosis sanatorium in 1918, the school closed in 1960. To qualify for state approval, the students had to spend their entire third year at another school for clinical instruction in medical, surgical, obstetric, and pediatric nursing.

Gilfoy School, Mississippi Baptist Hospital, Jackson—Opened in 1911, this school, with two programs, one for whites and one for Negroes, stopped admitting Negro students in 1960.

Kansas City General Hospital No. 2., Kansas City, Missouri—This school, established in 1911, was one of two schools—the other, No. 1, was for white students. In 1957 the Negro nursing school (No. 2) merged with the white school.

L. Richardson Memorial Hospital School of Nursing, Greensboro, North Carolina—Opened in 1927, this school was closed in 1953.

States	Negro Schools		White Schools		Total
	Accept Whites	Do not Accept Whites	Accept Negroes	Do not Accept Negroes	
Alabama	—	1	—	12	13
Alaska	—	—	—	—	—
Arizona	—	—	6	—	7 (1 no data)
Arkansas	—	—	1	5	6
California	—	—	55	3	60 (2 closing)
Colorado	—	—	10	—	10
Connecticut	—	—	19	—	19
Delaware	—	—	5	1	6
Dist. of Col.	1	—	5	—	6
Florida	—	1	9	7	18 (1 closing)
Georgia	—	4 *	1	14	19
Hawaii	—	—	3	—	3
Idaho	—	—	3	1	4
Illinois	1 (SL)	—	68 (SL)	—	70 (1 closing)
Indiana	—	—	23	—	23
Iowa	—	—	24	—	24
Kansas	—	—	19	—	20 (1 closing)
Kentucky	—	—	15	—	15
Louisiana	1	—	2	9	12
Maine	—	—	6	—	6
Maryland	—	1	17	2	20
Massachusetts	—	—	57 (SL)	—	57
Michigan	—	—	30	3	33
Minnesota	—	—	24	—	26 (2 closing)
Mississippi	—	—	1	10	11
Missouri	1	—	23	4	28
Montana	—	—	5	—	6 (1 closing)
Nebraska	—	—	13	1	14
Nevada	—	—	1	—	1
New Hampshire	—	—	10	—	11 (1 closing)
New Jersey	—	—	38 (SL)	—	38
New Mexico	—	—	2	—	2
New York	1 (SL)	—	116 (SL)	—	124 (7 closing)
North Carolina	—	5	1	28	34
North Dakota	—	—	9	—	9
Ohio	—	—	55	2	58 (1 closing)
Oklahoma	—	—	9	1	11 (1 closing)
Oregon	—	—	5	—	5
Pennsylvania	—	—	107 (SL)	—	109 (2 closing)
Puerto Rico	—	—	9	—	9
Rhode Island	—	—	7	—	7
South Carolina	—	1	—	13	15 (1 closing)
South Dakota	—	—	9	—	11 (2 closing)
Tennessee	—	1	6	11	18
Texas	—	1	19	14	34
Utah	—	—	6	—	6
Vermont	—	—	5	—	6 (1 closing)
Virginia	1	1	3	22	29 (2 closing)
Washington	—	—	16 (SL)	—	17 (1 closing)
West Virginia	—	—	13	1	14
Wisconsin	—	—	21	1	23 (1 closing)
Wyoming	—	—	1	—	1
Total	6	16	912	165	1128 (29 closing)

* Three of these programs (University Hospital in Augusta, Medical Center in Columbus, and Grady in Atlanta) are Negro units of schools that also have white units. They are not truly integrated schools.　　SL. State Law. State has a fair educational practice act, therefore, schools accept students regardless of race.

Good Samaritan Hospital School of Nursing, Charlotte, North Carolina—This school was opened in 1881 and closed in 1960.

Good Samaritan Waverly Hospital School of Nursing, Columbia, South Carolina—Opened in 1910, this school closed in 1953.

Five New Schools Opened Between 1953 and 1961

In spite of the trend toward integration of schools of nursing specifically and educational institutions generally, five schools, exclusively for Negroes, were established in the South between 1953 and 1961—four in colleges and one in a hospital: Agricultural and Technical College of North Carolina at Greensboro in 1953; Winston-Salem College, Winston-Salem, North Carolina, in 1953; Norfolk Division, Virginia State College, in 1956; City of Memphis Hospitals, Memphis, in 1956; and the Albany State College, Albany, Georgia, in 1961. None of these programs has national accreditation. With all of them being located in states where some white nursing programs accept Negroes for admission, one wonders why they were established, and why, if they do not meet the criteria for a good school of nursing,

the state boards permit them to continue.

These schools are drawing on well-prepared Negro nurses for faculty—nurses who could be making significant contributions in good schools of nursing. This is a dissipation of the all-too limited supply of qualified faculty.

The Old Ones Remain

Of the old schools of nursing for Negroes, 9 are nationally accredited and 13 are not.

With the exception of Tuskegee Institute, Alabama, and Prairie View College in Texas, these schools are located in metropolitan areas where there are also mixed schools of nursing in operation. In some instances, areas where clinical facilities are limited, students from both the white and Negro schools use the same ones and often the same instructors. A case in point: Negro students from Florida A and M University and white students from Florida State University, both in Tallahassee, use the same facility, the W. T. Edwards Tuberculosis Hospital in Tallahassee, for instruction. Both are state schools wasting the taxpayers' money by operating separately. Last year Florida State University admitted Negro students to other departments. Could they not work toward the end of amalgamating the two schools of nursing? This should happen *with all deliberate speed.*

Prairie View College, even though not in a metropolitan area where white schools are located, should discontinue its unaccredited nursing program which has been in operation since 1918. The school is isolated in a rural setting and the students and faculty are kept in transition to and from hospitals for clinical experience, as far away as 60 miles. One questions the need for this school when 19 formerly all white schools in the state are now admitting Negro students.

The two schools for Negro nurses in the North—Harlem in New York and Provident in Chicago—have *no* reason to be segregated. Even those in border states, where integration has been achieved, have no excuse. These are Freedmen's in Washington, D.C.; Provident in Baltimore; Hampton and Virginia State College in Virginia; and all schools in North Carolina.

One could argue that, with the serious shortage in the supply of nurses, all schools are needed to meet the demand for them. This would seem logical, but when the statistics are examined, we find that since 1941 the number of schools of nursing in the country has decreased, yet the total number of students has increased. In 1941, there were 1,303 schools with an average of 67 students per school. In 1957, there were 1,118 schools with an average of 101 students per school. This means that even though 118 schools closed, enrollment rose: In diploma schools alone, the mean enrollment rose from 83 in October, 1949, to 109 in October, 1961.[15] The intense national nurse recruitment effort, alone, indicates that existing schools have the facilities to accommodate more students. So it would seem that with 912 of the 1,099 schools (82 percent) in the country that have a policy to admit students regardless of race, Negro applicants could be accommodated easily.

Integration Begins with the Schools

I firmly believe that there is no need for all-Negro schools of nursing today. Most of the all-Negro schools are weak, and weak schools perpetuate an injustice to the student, the patient, and the community. These weak schools should be closed immediately, and the nine nationally accredited schools should move as fast as they can toward either amalgamating with white schools that are also good, or opening their doors to white students, making integration a two-way process.

Our nation is currently engaged in a great effort to assure equal opportunity and human dignity for all its citizens. Segregated schools of any kind can no longer be tolerated in a society based on democratic principles. The man in the street knows that recruits are needed from all races and ethnic groups to meet the nurse shortage and that disease knows no color line.

Dodson, speaking at the biennial convention of the American Nurses' Association in Atlantic City in 1952, had this to say: "Nursing has made great progress in intergroup relations. But we will not reach our goal until all Negro nurses are integrated in our organizations, our services, and our schools."[16] Much progress has been made in all three areas since 1952, but I believe that integration in education is basic to integration in *all* other areas.

References

1. NATIONAL LEAGUE FOR NURSING. *State Approved Schools of Professional Nursing, 1963.* New York, The League, 1963.
2. NATIONAL ASSOCIATION OF COLORED GRADUATE NURSES. *A Salute to Democracy at Mid-Century.* New York, The Association, 1951.
3. SHAPIRO, CHARLOTTE, The Negro nurse in the U.S.A. *RN* 11:34, Nov. 1948.
4. EDUCATIONAL FACILITIES FOR COLORED NURSES. *Trained Nurse Hosp.Rev.* 74:260, Mar. 1925.
5. ALLPORT, G. W. *The Nature of Prejudice.* Boston, Beacon Press, 1954.
6. GAGE, NINA D., AND HAUPT, ALMA C. Some observations on Negro nursing in the South. *Public Health Nurs.* 24:674, Dec. 1932.
7. NEWELL, HOPE. *The History of the National Nursing Council.* New York, National Nursing Council, 1951, p. 50.
8. BROWN, ESTHER LUCILE. *Nursing for the Future.* New York, Russell Sage Foundation, 1948, p. 109.
9. NEWELL, *op. cit.,* p. 30.
10. WEST, MARGARET, AND HAWKINS, CHRISTY. *Nursing Schools at the Midcentury.* New York, National Committee for the Improvement of Nursing Services, 1950.
11. EMBREE, E. R. *Brown America.* New York, Viking Press, 1931, p. 126.
12. GUNTER, LAURIE M. The effects of segregation on nursing students. *Nursing Outlook* 9:74, Feb. 1961.
13. *Ibid.*
14. SHANAHAN, T. J. Negroes in nursing education. *Hosp.Progr.* 42:100, July 1961.
15. CUNNINGHAM, ELIZABETH V. *Today's Diploma Schools of Nursing.* New York, National League for Nursing, 1963, pp. 5-7.
16. DODSON, DAN W. No place for race prejudice. *Amer.J.Nurs.* 53:164, Feb. 1953.

The Medical Committee for Human Rights*

by Dr. David M. French

THE Medical Committee for Human Rights is an organization with a most interesting beginning. It came into being as a result of the 1964 summer activities of the Council of Federated Organizations (COFO) in the state of Mississippi. It is my feeling that the major stimulus behind the pilgrimage of physicians to Mississippi that summer was the fact that many of these physicians were closely related to the youngsters who were working with the Student Non-Violent Coordinating Committee. Most of these children had previously been considered fairly normal college students; but during that summer of 1964, they had decided to depart from tradition and, at the risk of losing their lives, contribute their efforts to an unprecedented type of service.

It is within reason to assume that these students were so firm in their convictions that they could not be easily dissuaded; and for this reason their parents or relatives, as the case may be, felt that the second best thing, perhaps, would be to join them in their activities. With this in mind, a number of professional men, including physicians, dentists, lawyers and people in the social sciences, went to Mississippi in hopes that they might provide an overall protective blanket for their offspring.

These professional men, however, were caught up in a web of activity, performing actual services in the support and treatment of civil rights workers; and they found themselves suddenly in direct contact with conditions which they perhaps had heard about but which had never really deeply impressed them. These were the health conditions of the Negroes living in a state of peonage in the rural areas of Mississippi. As the summer wore on, these physicians came to know each other well; and they desired to work together in a concerted effort to do some lasting good, not only in Mississippi but also in other areas of the deep South.

The vast majority of these physicians of whom I speak lived in the metropolitan area of New York. There were also numerous individuals from Pittsburgh, Boston, Detroit, Chicago and other areas throughout the North. The group of physicians from New York City decided to band itself together and raise funds to support a more coordinated activity and set up a central office. Early meetings were held at Mount Sinai Hospital in New York and in the offices of John L. S. Holloman, Jr., a Negro practitioner in the community. From this early beginning, the Medical Committee for Human Rights came into being. It was probably formally established in the fall of 1964 at the annual national convention of the American Public Health Association, which was held at the Hilton Hotel in New York City.

Many of the individuals who had become involved with the medical committee and the COFO activities of 1964 were from the academic ranks of Northern medical schools and already had membership or direct interests in the American Public Health Association (APHA). As a result, the association lent its unofficial sanction to the early activities of this organization. A booth was set up in the lobby of the Hilton Hotel, along with other booths demonstrating various activities of members within the APHA. And, in addition, a goodly portion of the program in several of its sections was related to this new aspect of public health interest, namely, that associated with the health needs of underprivileged people in the rural South. At the close of the APHA convention, many individuals returned to communities outside the New York City area; and there was a notable expansion of chapters in Northern urban centers.

It was felt that a constitutional convention should be held to formally organize a national program. The newly formed chapter in Washington, D.C., which had come into being in the fall of 1964, offered to hold the national convention in the city of Washington. The early meetings of the Washington Chapter were all held at the Howard University Medical School, and it was deemed advisable to try to utilize Howard University as the site of the first annual constitutional convention of the Medical Committee for Human Rights. The cooperation of the university and medical school officials was immediate, and plans were made rapidly to bring about this first convention.

It was felt that it would be especially fitting that Howard University be the site of this organizing convention since, through its law school, it had spearheaded the legal attack which historically could

---

*This material was generously contributed by Dr. David M. French, Associate Professor of Surgery and Chief of Pediatric Surgery at Howard University College of Medicine and Chairman of the Medical Committee for Human Rights, 1966–67.

be considered the beginning of the modern rapid advancement of desegregation in the United States. The 1954 school desegregation case, won in the Supreme Court of the United States, was largely planned and carried out through the auspices of faculty members of the College of Law of Howard University, in association with lawyers from the legal department of the NAACP. This first national convention of the Medical Committee for Human Rights, in April, 1965, was well attended by representatives from many cities in the United States, as well as several in Canada, and was considered a great success: it resulted in a general agreement of articles of confederation, which were compiled and became the legal basis for the future function of the organization.

Constitution of the
Medical Committee for Human Rights

Article I
Name and Objects

Section 1. *Name.* The name of this organization shall be the Medical Committee for Human Rights.

Section 2. *Objects.* The purposes and aims of the organization shall be to engage in study, education and other activities or programs consistent with the scientific and humanitarian responsibilities of health personnel and to provide professional support and assistance to improve the health conditions and human rights of all people, especially those who are deprived by virtue of economic circumstances, social class, minority group membership or systematic patterns of racial discrimination and to improve the facilities for medical care for such persons and for civil rights workers who might otherwise be deprived of adequate medical care; provided, however, that this organization shall not engage in any activity which is not exclusively charitable, scientific, educational, religious and/or literary. No part of the activities of this organization shall be devoted to carrying on propaganda or otherwise attempting to influence legislation, and the organization shall not participate or intervene in any political campaign on behalf of any candidate for public office. No part of the net income of this organization shall inure to the benefit of any private individual, and in the event of dissolution all of the assets of this organization remaining after the payment or satisfaction of its liabilities shall be distributed only to an organization or organizations whose purposes are exclusively charitable, scientific, educational, religious and/or literary.

Article II
Membership

Section 1. *Membership Pre-requisites.* Any person who is in accordance with the principles and policies of the Medical Committee for Human Rights may become a member of this organization by application to the local Chapter, if such local Chapter is available, or, if not, by application to the Governing Council, by accepting membership in writing under and in accordance with the terms of this Constitution and by paying annually in advance the requisite membership dues as prescribed by the Governing Council.

One of the things which served to bring about this final crystallization into a national body undoubtedly was the strategic role played by the medical committee during the Selma to Montgomery civil rights march, which had taken place in March, 1965. The Southern Christian Leadership Conference, in conjunction with the Student Non-Violent Coordinating Committee, had undertaken a project in November, 1964, based in Selma, Alabama, to increase voter registration in Dallas County and the adjoining counties, if possible. This project, which had modest beginnings, gradually increased in size and activities over the next several months; and by January, 1965, it was a quite forceful and active organizational attempt. However, there was great resistance from the white power structure in that area, and open confrontation and hostile interchanges were continuously occurring between the two groups.

The Medical Committee for Human Rights had continued to function after the COFO summer project of 1964 through two nurses located in Jackson, Mississippi. The National Council of Churches had provided the medical committee with a small Ford van-type truck, which had subsequently been outfitted as an ambulance, complete with a two-way radio. This unit was transferred to Alabama in February of 1965 for use by the increasing number of individuals who were gathering in Selma as a result of the project's national publicity. The large number of participants and the repeated clashes with the police and the local white populace, frequently resulting in injury, as well as the normal sicknesses which occur among crowded groups of people, made it necessary for the medical committee to keep some physicians on hand at all times in order to meet the medical needs of the participants.

The culmination of this super-charged atmosphere occurred on Bloody Sunday in early March of 1965. At that time the medical committee ambulance, manned by three physicians, had attempted to accompany the civil rights marchers in their effort to cross the Alabama River as they left Selma to march to Montgomery. As is now history, these marchers were met on the other side of the Pettus Bridge, were gassed, beaten, trod upon by horses mounted by policemen and, through physical violence, were turned back to Selma and not allowed to complete their mission. The physicians in the ambulance were prevented from crossing the bridge and attending the injured. When the injured were brought back across the bridge, however, they were treated by the physicians of the Medical Committee for Human Rights and two local Negro doctors, who pitched in during this emergency situation. It should be mentioned also that the two local Negro physicians—members of the National Medical Association—were quite active in doing everything they could at this time.

This first attempt of the marchers to leave Selma was given prominent national publicity. And from all over the United States, even from Hawaii, and from Europe, individuals who were eager to participate in, observe or report on this affair came into the small city of Selma. The Medical Committee for Human Rights found it necessary to recruit more physicians; and, ultimately, approximately 120 medical committee physicians served over the next several weeks until the culmination of the march at the State Capitol in Montgomery, Alabama.

From the very beginning of the increased activity, the medical committee was readily joined by Negro physicians who resided in the state. In all, approximately fourteen physicians closely cooperated with the committee in an effort to give the medical care needed by the large numbers of people who ultimately became involved in this civil rights activity. All of these cooperating physicians were Negro members of the National Medical Association.

It should be pointed out that the large number of people who congregated in this small town of Selma, Alabama—whether they were white or black—were *persona non grata* from the point of view of the white community. For this reason, they had no choice but to look to the Negro community for room, board and sustenance in all respects. No one was welcome in the white hotels or motels; and the only individuals who were able to utilize them during this activity were representatives of the U.S. government—primarily the Department of Justice—who supposedly were above refusal by the white populace.

During the final two weeks before the actual march from Selma to Montgomery, legal action was undertaken which resulted in an injunction, issued by Federal Judge Frank Johnson in Montgomery against the governor and the legislature of the state of Alabama, making it possible for the marchers to move on to Montgomery. During this final period of time, much planning was going on; and the medical committee was readily accepted in the strategy sessions by the Southern Christian Leadership Conference and the Student Non-Violent Coordinating Committee. At the same time, members of the Medical Committee for Human Rights (Washington Chapter), including Dr. Fred Solomon, were actively negotiating with members of the Justice Department, as well as with the White House itself, in an attempt to convince the Federal government to take positive steps to prevent violence and possible waste of human life during the anticipated march from Selma to Montgomery.

The Federal government showed great concern in this matter but was unwilling to do more than alert the Air Force Bases in Selma and Montgomery to prepare their medical teams to meet any emergency —should it occur. The government was unwilling to bring these servicemen frankly into the open and thereby commit itself to support of the civil rights march. During the last week before the actual march, when I arrived in Selma, Alabama, the medical committee had come to be looked upon by all to provide, in some miraculous fashion, all of the necessary items and support to assure the protection of health and to meet the needs of possible emergency. But there was not one among us who did not recognize how little we could do should a concerted and well-organized effort in the direction of violence take place during this long march through the heartland of Alabama.

Before leaving Washington, D.C., for Selma, Alabama, Dr. Fred Solomon and I spent approximately ten days in trying to force the executive branch of our Federal government to take a positive stand. As I told them, my duty as a physician in trying to preserve human health and life is best carried out by prevention of any injury or episode that might possibly lead to death. This I did not feel could be carried out with any force less than the military forces of the United States government.

Before my arrival in Selma, Dr. Aaron Wells, then the national chairman of the Medical Committee for Human Rights, had been in charge of all medical committee activities and had sat in on all the planning sessions which were held daily by Hosea Williams, an assistant to the Rev. Martin Luther King. It should be pointed out that medical preparations for the march included planning for the food and its sanitary preservation and issuance during the march; the provision of sanitary latrines for use by the marchers; the provision of adequate water to be supplied through hostile country; and, in addition to this, having a plan for the treatment and evacuation of wounded individuals, which might conceivably be needed under the circumstances. The Southern Christian Leadership Conference was able to obtain many of these items. They were able to obtain the use of trucks donated by a large rental service. They were able to obtain drivers and the carrying in of materials and supplies with the cooperation of the truckers' union. All of the items necessary for the overall medical support were eventually obtained prior to the march.

At the last moment, the governor of Alabama obtained permission from the state legislature to request the President of the United States to provide, through the Armed Forces of the United States, the necessary protection and support for the marchers. I had sent a telegram to Governor Wallace (along with a copy to Al Lingo, the Director of Public Safety for Alabama) in which I outlined what I thought were the minimal needs to meet the requirements of the injunction passed by the Federal judge, which included the protection and provision of basic health needs by the state of Alabama for the three hundred marchers. This telegram, which was sent to Governor Wallace at approximately 10 o'clock in the morning, apparently caused a great flurry of activity. On that same evening, the national newscast which we were accustomed to observing in a local Negro motel was cancelled in favor of a statewide television broadcast from the combined houses of the legislature of the state of Alabama.

In this program, Governor Wallace reiterated his pleas against the march and went ahead to read my telegram, which had been sent in the name of the national chairman of the Medical Committee for Human Rights. He read this telegram in support of his contention as to how dangerous the march would be and how great would be the needs of these marchers. He stated in his telecast that studies made that day revealed that the cost for such protection would be about $300,000, which he considered a prohibitive amount to withdraw from the state treasury. On this basis, he requested that the state legislature empower him to request that the President of the United States step in and provide this protection. There was an overwhelming vote in support of this plea by the governor; and President Johnson, who was about to step in his helicopter to spend the week on his ranch in Texas, had to cancel his plans in order to spend some time that evening laying the necessary groundwork for the military protection of the marchers.

The following morning (Saturday) the President of the United States, over a nationwide broadcast, revealed his plans for the activation of the Alabama National Guard, to be supervised in its activities by regular army units, which he would call in from several places in the United States. This activity was in actual function by that Saturday evening. The military guardsmen of the state of Alabama, with their stars and bars insignia on the shoulder patch of every man, were, in fact, on duty. Included among them was Wilson Baker, Director of Public Safety of the town of Selma, who, on being federalized into activity, joined a number of other native Selma individuals under the command of the President of the United States.

On that same evening, the President's troubleshooter from the Department of Justice arrived and consulted with me concerning the medical planning. I stated that I had seen the soldiers but as yet had not been contacted as to what type of medical support they anticipated. He stated that the injunction handed down by the Federal judge required that the marchers provide their own medical care. Nevertheless, the commanding officer of the National Guard and Mr. Baker were brought that same evening into my office in the basement of the First Baptist Church in Selma. They consulted with me, exhibiting what seemed to be a great spirit of cooperation, and offered every assurance that violence leading to a need for medical care would be prevented. Additionally, Mr. Baker was able to supply us with information that made it possible for us to obtain a large water tank on wheels, which was used throughout the march to supply drinking water for the marchers.

The International Ladies Garment Workers Un-

1965 MAR 18 PM 3 56

ZVA187 SA119
NSB168 SSG124 NS SEA054 PD SELMA ALA 18 1152A CST
DR FRED SOLOMON COLLEGE OF MEDIKINE
HOWARD UNIVERSITY WASHDC
TO MEET HEALTH AND SAFETY NEEDS OF 5,000 MARCHERS SUNDAY 21
OF MARCH OVER 12 MILES OF U.S. HWY 80, OF 300 MARCHERS MONDAY
22, TUESDAY 23, WEDNESDAY 24, AND THURSDAY MARCH 25 ON SAME
HWY TO MONTGOMERY; OF 5,000 - 10,000 DEMONSTRATORS WHO NEED
SAME FACILITIES WITHIN MONTGOMERY, THURSDAY 25 ON FINAL 4 MILES
TO STATE CAPITOL
      STATE RESPONSIBILITY CAN BE MET ADQUATELY OLY BY PROVIDING
THE FOLLOWING MINIMUM NEEDS:
    1. SIX EQUIPPED AMBULANCES
    2. TWO MOBLE AID STATIONS
    3. NINE 300 GALLON WATER TRAILERS
    4. PORTABLE TOILET FACILITIES

    5. TWO RUBBISH DISPOSAL TRUCKS AND CONTAINERS
    6. MOBILE RADIO COMMUNICATIONS FOR COORDINATION
    7. ADEQUATE MEDICAL PERSONNEL - PHYSICIANS, NURSES &
AIDMEN
    8. STATE CONTROL, PROTECTION, AND COORDINATION OF ALL
ABOVE MEDICAL AND PUBLICHEALTH ACTIVITIES
      ORIGINAL GOVERNOR WALLACE COPIES MR HOSEA WILLIAMS, SCLC,
334 AUBURN AVE. ATLANTA, GA. MR RANDOLPH BLACKWELL, SCLC, 334
AUBURN AVE. ATLANTA, GEORGIA COL. ALBERT T. LINGO, EXEKUTIVE
OFFICER OF ALABAMA STATE TROOPERS, STATE CAPITOL, MONTGOMERY
ALABAMA   DR FRED SOLOMON, COLLEGE OF MEDICINE, HOWARD UNIVERSITY,
WASHINGTON D.C.
      AARON O WELLS MD MEDICAL COMMITTEE FOR HUMAN RIGHTS HOSEA
WILLIAMS COORDINATOR OF MARCH ON MONTGOMERY SOUTHERN CHRISTIAN

ion called out a medical van outfitted with complete X-ray and laboratory facilities, as well as two beds for patient care. This van and the truck given to us by the National Council of Churches and outfitted by us for medical use became the primary medical support vehicles during the march. Local Negro undertakers in Selma and Montgomery provided their own ambulances for use as shuttle vehicles along the line of march for the purpose of evacuating possible wounded or sick people either forward to the large advance van supplied by the garment workers' union or back to the smaller van belonging to the medical committee. They were also available for immediate evacuation to the hospitals of either Selma or Montgomery. This medical plan was basically the one used throughout the march, and it worked quite successfully.

During our original reconnaissance search for camp sites, we chose as the last camp site prior to entry into the town of Montgomery the grounds of Saint Jude's, a Catholic institution devoted primarily to the service of Negroes. The Catholic priest in charge of that institution was approached and deserves a hero's medal for the positive stand he took. The Bishop of Mobile had come out in the press only days before against involvement by priests or nuns of the Catholic Church and had expressed his wishes that no one within his diocese should function in any way in relation to this march. In spite of this order, this brave priest not only allowed us to camp on the grounds of Saint Jude's but cleared one wing of the Saint Jude's Hospital and made it available for the combined use of the medical committee and the doctors from Montgomery.

Two days before the march began, we were joined by Dr. Holloman from New York, who was to become the national chairman of the medical committee the following year and who helped considerably in the administration of this march, which, by this time, covered miles of territory and involved many people.

To support the march, I was authorized by Dr. Wells in New York to buy all necessary medical supplies using drafts drawn on the national office of the Medical Committee for Human Rights. We soon learned, however, that the only medical supply house available in that area, which was located in Montgomery, under no circumstances would accept a check of any type from any of us. They were quite obviously hostile to our purpose in buying the supplies. However, they did not absolutely refuse to serve us; they simply insisted that we pay cash for whatever we bought. This problem was ultimately solved by personal appeals made by members of the medical committee to our fellow physicians in various parts of the United States, who took it upon themselves to raise funds in their communities and telegraph them to me in Selma. The entire cost of the medical aspects of the march was supported by these contributions.

Following the successful completion of the march from Selma to Montgomery, the Medical Committee for Human Rights decided to open a permanent Southern field office in Jackson, Mississippi. Dr. Alvin Poussaint was chosen to become the Southern field director. Dr. Poussaint, a trained psychiatrist, decided to devote several years of his life to running this office and developing a larger scope of medical activity in the deep South. From his own office in Selma, he was able to administer the opening of a secondary office in Alabama and another office which functioned for a short period of time in Bogalusa, Louisiana. The staff of the Southern office was enlarged so that, at one time, seven nurses were employed.

The major activities of the medical committee in the states of Mississippi, Alabama and Louisiana were in support of a clinic in Holmes County, Mississippi, which was opened under the financial support of the Winnick Fund, administered through the National Council of Churches. This clinic not only provided medical care but also served as a center from which emanated activities devoted to health education in many of the counties of Mississippi. Similar activities were carried out in Selma and, to a far lesser extent, in Bogalusa. In this fashion, the name of the medical committee became legend among the impoverished Negroes of Mississippi, Alabama and Louisiana as many people obtained medical attention which had never previously been available to them or their ancestors.

By late 1965, the Medical Committee for Human Rights had come to include seventeen chapters in as many states, including a chapter in Atlanta, Georgia. It is interesting to note that the Atlanta Chapter had its beginnings in the Atlanta headquarters of the Fulton County Medical Society, the local chapter of the American Medical Association. During the summers of 1965 and 1966, not only were there Southern field programs in progress, but in southern California the student groups sponsored by the medical committee had activated a program among the low-paid Latin American hired hands in the valleys of southern California.

In June of 1966, immediately following the President's Conference on Civil Rights—which was held in Washington, D.C., and was attended by a number

In the United States District Court for the Middle District of Alabama, Northern Division

HOSEA WILLIAMS, JOHN LEWIS and AMELIA BOYNTON, on behalf of themselves and others similarly situated,

                Plaintiffs,

UNITED STATES OF AMERICA,

                Plaintiff-Intervenor,

      vs.

HONORABLE GEORGE C. WALLACE, as Governor of the State of Alabama; AL LINGO, as Director of Public Safety for the State of Alabama; and JAMES G. CLARK, as Sheriff of Dallas County, Alabama,

                Defendants.

FILED

MARCH 17, 1965

R. C. DOBSON

                Clerk

By..

              Deputy Clerk

CIVIL ACTION NO. 2181-N

PRELIMINARY INJUNCTION

This cause coming on to be heard under the motions of the plaintiffs and the plaintiff-intervenor, United States of America, for a preliminary injunction and also upon the motion of the defendant Governor Wallace for a preliminary injunction, and due notice having been given to all parties, and the Court having considered the testimony offered in support of and in opposition to said motions and being fully advised in the premises, and for the reasons set forth in the memorandum opinion of this Court entered on this date and pursuant thereto, it is

ORDERED, ADJUDGED and DECREED that, pending further order of this Court, George C. Wallace, as Governor of the State of Alabama, Albert J. Lingo, as Director of Public Safety for the State of Alabama, and James G. Clark, Jr., as Sheriff of Dallas County, Alabama, their successors in office, agents, representatives, employees, and other persons in active concert and participation with them be and each is hereby restrained and enjoined from:

(1) Arresting, harassing, threatening, or in any way interfering with the efforts to march or walk, or the marching or walking, by the plaintiffs, members of their class, and others who may join with them, along U.S. Highway 80 from Selma, Alabama, to Montgomery, Alabama, said march, as presently approved by this Court, to commence in Selma, Alabama, not earlier than Friday, March 19, 1965, and not later than Monday, March 22, 1965, and to terminate in Montgomery, Alabama; and

(2) Otherwise obstructing, impeding, or interfering with the peaceful, nonviolent efforts by said plaintiffs, members of their class, and others who may join with them, in protesting and demonstrating by assembling and by marching along U.S. Highway 80 from Selma,

Alabama, to Montgomery, Alabama, as said march is proposed in plaintiffs' plan filed with this Court and served on the defendants on March 16, 1965, and to the extent that said plan is presently approved by this Court.

It is further ORDERED, ADJUDGED and DECREED that, pending further order of this Court, the defendants George C. Wallace, as Governor of the State of Alabama, Albert J. Lingo, as Director of Public Safety for the State of Alabama, and James G. Clark, Jr., as Sheriff of Dallas County, Alabama, their successors in office, agents, representatives, employees, and all others acting in concert with them, be and each is hereby restrained and enjoined from failing to provide police protection for the plaintiffs, members of their class, and others who may join with them, in their march, as presently scheduled and presently approved by this Court, to commence not earlier than Friday, March 19, 1965, and not later than Monday, March 22, 1965, along U.S. Highway 80 from Selma, Alabama, to Montgomery, Alabama.

It is further ORDERED, ADJUDGED and DECREED that the motion for preliminary injunction filed by the defendant Governor Wallace, the motion by the plaintiff-intervenor, United States of America, for relief in addition to that herein specifically granted, and the motion of the plaintiffs for relief in addition to that herein specifically granted be and each is hereby denied.

It is further ORDERED that jurisdiction of all matters herein involved be and the same is hereby specifically retained.

Done, this the 17th day of March, 1965.

      /s/ Frank M. Johnson, Jr.

UNITED STATES DISTRICT JUDGE

of representatives from the medical committee—Mr. James Meredith decided to undertake his march from Memphis, Tennessee, to Jackson, Mississippi, in an effort to inspire Negroes of the rural South to register to vote. As is now history, he was shot on the outskirts of Hernando, Mississippi; and following this, a greatly enlarged march was organized to go through the heart of the delta land of Mississippi (some 220 miles) all the way to Jackson.

The medical committee was again called on to give the medical support for this march; and Dr. Alvin Poussaint was given the authority and the funds to organize this activity. He and his team of nurses, as well as a group of volunteer physicians from various places in the United States, were constantly with the marchers along the entire course of the march into Jackson.

Dr. Poussaint, supported actively by the medical committee, performed an unusually outstanding job. He was able to provide the many medical needs which, in this instance, covered a period of approximately three weeks—much longer than the previous march from Selma to Montgomery—and which, in addition, had to be planned and organized on a moment's notice due to the nature of the origins of the march. There was none among the marchers who did not agree that the comforting presence of the medical committee was instrumental in maintaining the morale necessary for the completion of this long and arduous march.

TITLE 3—THE PRESIDENT
Proclamation 3645
PROVIDING FEDERAL ASSISTANCE IN THE STATE OF ALABAMA

By the President of the United States of America A Proclamation

WHEREAS, On March 17, 1965, the United States District Court for the middle district of Alabama entered an order in the case of Williams et al., Plaintiffs, United States of America, Plaintiff-Intervenor v. Wallace et al., Defendants, Civil Action No. 2181-N, approving an exercise by the Plaintiffs and the members of the class they represent of their right to march along United States Highway 80 from Selma to Montgomery, Alabama, commencing in Selma, Alabama, not earlier than Friday, March 19, 1965, and not later than Monday, March 22, 1965, and terminating in Montgomery, Alabama, within five days from commencement; and

WHEREAS, in relation to such judicial order and march the Governor of the State of Alabama has advised me that the state is unable and refuses to provide for the safety and welfare, among others, of the plaintiffs and the members of the class they represent; and

WHEREAS, as a consequence of such inability and refusal of the State of Alabama, and by reason of recent events in and about Selma and Montgomery, Alabama, there is a substantial likelihood that domestic violence may occur in connection with such march, with the consequence of obstructing the execution and enforcement of the laws of the United States, including the aforesaid judicial order:

NOW, THEREFORE, I, Lyndon B. Johnson, President of the United States of America, under and by virtue of the authority vested in me by the Constitution and laws of the United States, including Chapter 15 of Title 10 of the United States Code, particularly Sections 332, 333, and 334 thereof, do command all persons engaged or who may engage in such domestic violence obstructing the execution and enforcement of the laws to cease and desist therefrom and to disperse and retire peaceably forthwith.

IN WITNESS WHEREOF, I have hereunto set my hand and caused the seal of the United States of America to be affixed.

Done at Johnson City, Texas, this twentieth day of March in the Year of our Lord Nineteen [SEAL] hundred and sixty-five, and of the Independence of the United States of America the one hundred and eighty-ninth.

LYNDON B. JOHNSON
March 20, 1965
1:28 a.m.

By the President:
DEAN RUSK,
Secretary of State.

[F.R. Doc. 65–3022; Filed, Mar. 20, 1965; 7:40 p.m.]

Executive Order 11207
PROVIDING FEDERAL ASSISTANCE IN THE STATE OF ALABAMA

WHEREAS, on March 20, 1965, I issued proclamation No. 3645, pursuant in part to the provisions of Section 334 of Title 10, United States Code; and

WHEREAS, the likelihood of domestic violence and obstruction of the execution and enforcement of the laws of the United States referred to therein continues:

NOW, THEREFORE, by virtue of the authority vested in me by the Constitution and laws of the United States, including Chapter 15 of Title 10 of the United States Code, particularly Sections 332, 333, and 334 thereof, and Section 301 of Title 3 of the United States Code, it is hereby ordered as follows:

SECTION 1. The Secretary of Defense is authorized and directed, for the period commencing with the signing of this order and ending as soon as practicable after the termination of the march referred to in the above-mentioned proclamation, to take all appropriate steps, including the provision of assistance to the law enforcement agencies of the State of Alabama, to remove obstructions to the execution and enforcement of the laws of the United States in that state, including the order of the court referred to in the above-mentioned proclamation, and to suppress domestic violence in any way related to the said march.

SEC. 2. In furtherance of the authorization and direction contained in Section 1 hereof, the Secretary of Defense is authorized to use such of the Armed Forces of the United States as he may deem necessary.

SEC. 3. I hereby authorize and direct the Secretary of Defense to call into the active military service of the United States, as he may deem appropriate to carry out the purposes of this order, any or all of the units or members of the Army National Guard and of the Air National Guard of the State of Alabama to serve in the active military service of the United States until relieved by appropriate orders. The Secretary of Defense is further authorized to recall any unit or member so relieved if he deems such recall appropriate to carry out the purposes of this order. In carrying out the provisions of Section 1, the Secretary of Defense is authorized to use the units, and members thereof, called or recalled into the active military services of the United States pursuant to this section.

SEC. 4. The Secretary of Defense is authorized to delegate to the Secretary of the Army or the Secretary of the Air Force, or both, any of the authority conferred upon him by this order.

LYNDON B. JOHNSON
March 20, 1965
1:30 a.m.

THE WHITE HOUSE

[F.R. Doc. 65-3023; Filed, Mar. 20, 1965; 7:45 p.m.]

The National Medical Association Speaks Out for Medicare

The Testimony of Dr. W. Montague Cobb, President of the NMA,

before the Committee on Finance of the United States Senate

Dr. COBB. Thank you, Senator.

Mr. Chairman, I am Dr. W. Montague Cobb, president of the National Medical Association and professor and chairman of the department of anatomy in the Howard University College of Medicine. With me is Dr. Kenneth W. Clement, a surgeon of Cleveland, Ohio, and the immediate past president of the National Medical Association, and a member of the last advisory council on disability to the Social Security Administration. May I express on behalf of the National Medical Association our appreciation of this opportunity to convey to you our views in support of H.R. 6675 which we consider one of the most vital bills now before the Congress.

We of the NMA are most keenly mindful of the heavy responsibilities imposed by the high status which public opinion has accorded the medical profession in the United States of America. We realize that the esteem in which the profession is held can be maintained only through rendering the service which our Nation anticipates. The mercurial speed of scientific advance and technological improvements in medicine in recent years has presented manifold problems in making properly available to all our citizens the benefits of this progress.

In some areas we have made enormous strides. We now devote unprecedented sums to the prosecution of medical research. Chiefly with the aid of the Hospital Survey and Construction Act of 1946 and its subsequent amendments and extensions, we have practically rebuilt our hospital system, so that our facilities are without parallel in the history of the world. Court decisions and the Civil Rights Act of 1964 have guaranteed that our federally aided facilities must be equally available to all citizens without bias of any kind.

In the provision of adequate personnel for the healing professions, knotty problems remain, because population increases constantly and geometrically, while physicians, dentists, nurses, pharmacists, and the various specialized technical associates are graduated in limited numbers but once or twice a year. Nevertheless, large plans now being implemented are significantly increasing our educational facilities in the health fields, and, we are coming to sense the importance of prevention, as against the cure, of illness by our espousal of public health programs of ever broader scope and intensity.

Our greatest problem now lies in finding ways to pay the costs of the medical care that modern knowledge has made possible. The principle that in our society every citizen, rich or poor, should be able to obtain the medical care he needs is not debated. The problem of financing has been accentuated by the fact that costs of medical care have risen astronomically in recent times and may continue to do so. Hospital stays, diagnostic procedures and many drugs have zoomed upward in expense, and the application of future discoveries and advances is likely to raise costs even further. Moreover, because we have in large measure been able to conquer or control the diseases and conditions which produced mortality in early life, a major portion of our armamentarium for restoring and maintaining health must today be directed at the later years of the lifespan and for the benefit of the elderly members of our population, a segment which steadily increases in numbers and in population percentage.

For the past two decades legislation considered by the Congress has reflected a recognition of a deep concern for this problem of the costs of medical care. The many volumes which recorded the testimony of experts and interested persons on the subject reveal that every possible aspect has been at some time examined. There has also accumulated a certain experience with some types of plans and legislation. Most of all, unflagging public interest in the problem is at peak.

The National Medical Association firmly believes that more than 20 years of study, observation and experience are enough, and that the time has come for broad definitive action.

We are of the opinion that from the long period of attention given the problem has emerged the recognition that our senior citizens, those aged 65 years and over, are in most need of financial assistance for medical care, and that the most effective and logical way to provide this assistance would be through the social security system.

Those of us who can remember the depths of the

great depression which began in 1929, know that the social security system, which arose as one of the preventives of future privation, has proved a bulwark to the Nation's economy and the welfare and inner sense of dignity of our citizens. No one would think of abolishing social security. Rather our efforts have been toward extending its coverage so that no one would have to want in old age or suffer the indignity of sublimated "pauper's oaths."

The National Medical Association strongly endorses H.R. 6675, the Social Security Amendments of 1965 as passed by the House of Representatives.

We have not come hastily to this position. Our 5,000-member organization, formed in Atlanta in 1895 because of exclusion practices against Negro physicians, has gained in its 70 years a pervasive and national knowledge of the health needs and problems of those in poor economic circumstances.

In April 1946, through our late president at that time, Dr. Emory I. Robinson of Los Angeles, the National Medical Association endorsed S. 1606, a bill for a national health program, familiarly known as the Wagner-Murray-Dingell bill, before the Committee on Education and Labor of the U. S. Senate.[1]

In 1949 at our Detroit convention our house of delegates tabled a motion to rescind this endorsement. In 1961 at our New York convention our house of delegates unanimously adopted a resolution to support the extension of social security coverage to self-employed physicians. We here endorse the provisions for this purpose in H.R. 6675.

In 1962 our house of delegates at our Chicago convention formally endorsed the principle of providing medical care for the elderly under the social security system. This action was reaffirmed by the house at our Los Angeles convention in 1963 and our Washington convention in 1964, and further through action of our board of trustees in interim session in Cincinnati in February 1965. Our immediate past president, Dr. Kenneth W. Clement of Cleveland, who sits on my left, testified on behalf of the NMA in favor of H.R. 3920 before the Committee on Ways and Means of the U. S. House of Representatives on January 22, 1964.[2]

This statement of Dr. Clement's is of considerable length and detail and renders such elaboration unnecessary at this time.

Briefly, the National Medical Association considers that H.R. 6675 would provide medical assistance to the elderly on the most rational and equitable basis possible. As a prepayment plan it would permit our citizens to provide medically for their later years during their productive work period. The nationwide and uniform coverage afforded would protect against the exhaustion of meager life savings, liens on previously unmortgaged real estate and the indignities of means tests.

Because of the greater incidence of illness, the longer hospital stays and lowered income of the elderly, these citizens are an understandably high risk group to private insurance companies and they cannot afford the high premium rates of private insurance policies which are often found canceled when most needed.

Public assistance programs in the past have proved limited in scope, varying in coverage among the several States, and largely available only after aged individuals have expended their financial resources.

H.R. 6675 significantly improves the health care for the aged over past bills which our association supported; by the addition of supplementary voluntary health insurance which would include payment for physicians and other related services, at a cost which the aged would be able to pay.

This addition is recognized by the association as desirable and necessary. It is in keeping with present methods of providing for payment of physicians' services; it is modest in cost; it is significantly broad in coverage; and it satisfies a recognized unmet need in the basic social security program for meeting the cost of institutional health and other related services.

The National Medical Association finds no peril or threat in these programs to the private medical practitioner, or to the free enterprise hospital system in this country. Adequate safeguards are written into the bill, including prohibitions against unwarranted interference by the Government and allowing for the desirable participation of consumers and providers of health care through the advisory councils, etc.

As H.R. 6675 presently stands, no physicians' service would be paid for through the social security hospital insurance trust fund and provisions for private insurance company participation in this and the supplemental voluntary health insurance program is afforded.

The assertion that this is socialized medicine is, therefore, pure nonsense.

Payments to pathologists, physiatrists, radiologists, and anesthesiologists are removed in the present bill as reimbursable hospital cost items. However, we are for restoring them. Their inclusion would make

---

[1] Hearings on national health program, S. 1606, before the Committee on Education and Labor, U. S. Senate, pt. 2, pp. 787–794, 1946.

[2] National Medical Association testimony, H.R. 3920, JNMA, vol. 56, pp. 213–221, 1964.

the above criticism no more valid, for the precedent for including them is far more established in practice than excluding them.

Senator HARTKE. Let me ask you a question, you say radiologists should be covered but we have been told that anesthesiologists are in a different category.

Do you have any comment on that?

Dr. COBB. Yes, sir, pathologists and radiologists have no natural contact with the patient. They examine specimens or take a picture at some other point.

The physiatrist provides a service of physical therapy of some kind but it is at the request and direction of another physician. In that sense it is in a hospital service. The anesthesiologist has an even more intimate contact with the patient because he is responsible both preoperatively and postoperatively for some degree of care of the patient.

But it is, there is, a gradation in the degree, and you might say to a certain degree that matter is moot, but you can't dispense with it, and it is our feeling that it might be lumped in the inescapable services of the hospital costs.

Senator HARTKE. Thank you, sir.

Dr. COBB. Moreover, the services provided in general by this group of physicians calls for a specified contractual relationship with the hospital, and, the patients they "treat" are largely captive in nature and unrelated to any real free elective choice. Certainly the free choice exercised by patients of physicians located outside of, but practicing in, the hospitals is denied those using the service of this group.

In past testimony in favor of the enactment of H.R. 3920, the National Medical Association recognized a continued need for public assistance programs and their improvement in the area of health care.

This the association reaffirms and finds worthy those provisions in H.R. 6675, which improve these programs; namely, the consolidation of five titles of the Social Security Act into a new title, title XIX, which would set minimum benefit requirements, in in-patient hospital services, outpatient hospital services, other lab and X-ray services; and the provisions for the needs of funds to meet the deductibles that are imposed by the new basic program of hospital insurance.

The recently passed House bill provides for deductibles and coinsurance. This is an understandable inclusion, with the intent to dissuade abuse and overuse of these plans. Initially the funds from which benefits are paid deserve such protection. It is the hope of the National Medical Associa-

tion, that these deductibles will remain under close scrutiny and should future experience dictate, lowered and ultimately removed.

H.R. 3920, in the amendment section dealing with public assistance and medical assistance for the aged, sets forth new eligibility requirements which could have the effect of making more deserving of medical care [those] in the aged group eligible for [the] same, by removing the deterrents inherent in means tests, real estate liens, and residency requirements.

The residency requirements in the several States have never taken adequately into consideration the necessary increasing mobility of the American people, including the aged.

The National Medical Association supports these amendments and other improvements in the Kerr-Mills law contained in H.R. 3920.

The principle is now firmly established in law that health care supported in whole or in part by public funds must be administered without discrimination as to race, creed, color, or national origin. We strongly urge that due antidiscrimination provisions be clearly written into H.R. 6675 so that possible litigation may be avoided.

Since the last general increase in cash benefits for social security beneficiaries, significant general price increases have occurred affecting clothing, food and shelter, merely reducing the purchasing power of the benefits.

The provisions of H.R. 6675 which increase the general cash benefits by approximately 7 percent are welcome. The National Medical Association supports this increase for it will contribute to the physical, mental, and social well-being of the aged.

The elderly, like the young, need a sense of affection and security. They have a yearning so beautifully expressed by Charles Matheson in his well-known hymn:

> O love that will not let me go,
> I hide my helpless self in Thee,
> I give Thee back the life I owe,
> That in thine ocean depths its flow,
> May richer, fuller be.

Like this love, the benefits of H.R. 6675 cannot be taken away. The sense of security thus imparted will help to sustain our elderly in their waning years. Can we deny this small assurance to those on whose shoulders we stand?

Thank you, Mr. Chairman.

U.S., Congress, Senate, Committee on Finance, *Hearings, on H.R. 6675, Social Security*, 89th Cong., 1st Sess., 1965, pp. 323–328.

The Disadvantaged and Health Care*

by Dr. Alonzo S. Yerby

THE term "disadvantaged" is a contemporary euphemism for the poor. We employ euphemisms to shield ourselves from the harshness of reality. Yet to speak of the poor as disadvantaged has its own advantage for it implies a correctable state—an improvement over the biblical warning that we shall have the poor with us always.

In the context of the American dream the poor are those most newly arrived at the bottom of the ladder, and all that is needed is to grasp the rungs firmly and begin the climb. Recently, we have begun to recognize the fact that among the poor there are subgroups who never seem to reach beyond the lower rungs of the ladder and who, all too frequently, slip and fall to the bottom again. We have identified, among these bottom-dwellers, third-generation welfare recipients and others who are somehow cut off from the upward mobility which characterizes much of American society.

Dr. George James[1] in describing the characteristics of the poor stated:

> The heads of poor families are much more likely to be over 65 than the average of all families. They are much more likely to have had an education restricted to eight years, and they are much more likely to be unemployed. In numbers there are more white poor people than there are nonwhite, because white persons are an overwhelming majority of the population. The Negro is *twice as likely* to be poor than his white fellow citizen. To be a Negro, born in a rural area, and not to have gone past eighth grade in school, is a prescription for poverty.

Today the average Negro child is born into a family that is substantially poorer than the average white family. In part, this is because the Negro family head has less education than the white, earns less even at the same levels of education, and has less chance of fulltime employment.[2]

Certain health differences have been found to characterize all of the poor. Several decades ago, the U. S. Children's Bureau pointed out that infant mortality rates rise as family income decreases. Today, children in poor families rarely see a dentist and are less likely to have received adequate preventive health care. Adults in poor families have several times as much disabling heart disease, arthritis, or mental illness than families earning $7,000 or more per annum. Negroes, as a subgroup of the disadvantaged, suffer even greater handicaps. President Johnson in his now famous speech "To Fulfill These Rights," presented on June 5, 1965, at Howard University, stated that the infant mortality of nonwhites in 1940 was 70 per cent greater than that for whites, and 22 years later (1962) it was 90 per cent greater.

Dr. Leona Baumgartner,[3] in a recent editorial, referred to a New York City study which showed that:

> . . . in 1955 the perinatal rates of nonwhite families in which the father was in a professional, managerial, or technical occupation was significantly higher (49.3 as compared to 34.0) than for white families in which the father was in the laboring class. If occupation of the father is a reliable index of socio-economic status, then this finding would indicate that the most advantaged nonwhite family has a poorer chance of having a live and healthy baby than the least advantaged white family.

An unpublished analysis of all births occurring in New York City in the years 1961-1963 revealed the following perinatal mortality rates** for different occupational and ethnic groups:

	White	Negro	Puerto Rican
Professional, managerial or technical	16.7	24.2	22.5
Clerical and sales workers	20.8	31.5	24.4
Craftsman and operatives	20.9	32.9	24.3
Laborers and service workers	25.9	36.6	27.8

** These rates are obtained by employing fetal deaths of more than 28 weeks' gestation and infant deaths at less than seven days for the years 1961-1963 as numerator and live births for 1962 multiplied by three added to fetal deaths of more than 28 weeks' gestation for all three years as denominator.

---

*This paper was delivered at the White House Conference on Health, November, 1965. At that time, Dr. Yerby was commissioner of hospitals, Department of Hospitals in New York City. He is now with the Harvard University Faculty of Public Health as professor and head of the Department of Health Services Administration. Copyright 1966 by the American Public Health Association, Inc., and reproduced by permission of author and association.

While the rates for Negro babies with fathers in the professional, managerial, and technical occupations are slightly lower than that for white babies with fathers in the laboring or services occupations, it is interesting to note that the Negro rates are not only higher than the white rates in each occupational class, but they are also higher than the rates for the Puerto Ricans. Clearly, in terms of health, there is a special disadvantage to being a Negro in the United States which transcends being poor.

Existing Inequities

Statistics such as these can but suggest the inequities of health care. They do not convey the implications, both now and in the future, of the small Negro boy in Mississippi who told the late Michael Schwerner that he did not like going to the doctor because he did not like to go in the back door. Nor do they describe the woman 8½ months pregnant who, after waiting three hours, was turned away from a prenatal clinic in New York City without seeing a doctor because the hospital did not serve the district in which she lived.[4]

Health care of the disadvantaged is many things. It is frequently inadequate, sometimes quite poor, provided with little dignity or compassion, and rarely related to the total needs of the individual or family. These things are certainly not true of health care in general in the United States. Why are there such differences? How did it come to be this way?

The tradition of the "Poor Law" medicine for the poor stretches back to colonial days. Town physicians were appointed to care for the poor as early as 1689.[5] Later, physicians were sometimes permitted to bid for the post, and it is safe to assume the lowest bidder was not necessarily the most able or conscientious.

Our next refinement was the almshouse which served as a depository for the sick, for orphans, widows, the unemployed, the aged, and the insane. In the latter part of the nineteenth century, exposés of the shocking conditions in many almshouses led to reforms in which children and later the mentally ill were excluded from these institutions. Discoveries of the nature of contagion led to separate institutions for persons with communicable diseases. Hospitals began to be commonplace as the nineteenth century drew to a close, and some of them, for example, Bellevue in New York City, could trace their beginnings to an almshouse.

As Benjamin Franklin stated, the early hospitals in America were developed by people who "did charitably consult together" to relieve the "dis-temper'd poor." Sheps[6] has concluded that it was not surprising that such institutions for the poor were an activity set apart from the main stream medical care of the community as a whole. He reminds us that such venerable institutions as the Massachusetts General Hospital and the New York Hospital did not provide for private patients until 1900.

Social Legislation

The almshouse and the town physician remained the mainstay of the needy sick until the great depression of the 1930's. Many states, beginning with New York, established special programs of aid to permit localities to provide relief, including medical care, to those in need. These programs were superseded by the Federal Emergency Relief Act of 1933. This was closely followed by the Social Security Act of 1935.

It is significant that this legislation established the principle of federal aid for specific categories of persons. Need alone was not acceptable as qualifying a person for aid under the federally aided state welfare programs. Unemployment was considered to be a temporary condition and needy able-bodied adults and intact families were excluded. The Poor Law tradition of aiding selected groupings of unfortunates, such as orphans, the aged, and the blind was thus incorporated into what was otherwise the landmark of social legislation in the United States. The Social Security Act has been amended frequently since 1935, but not to the sweeping extent of the 1965 amendments. Here for the first time in the United States the principle of social insurance for health care has been enacted into law. Yet, even this far-sighted legislation, in its Title XIX, preserves and extends categorical aid for the needy and the medically needy. Health care is conditioned on both need and other attendant difficulties, such as disability, old age, blindness, or family breakdown. The Poor Law tradition lives on.

Title XVIII of Public Law 89-97 provides a significant measure of protection against the economic consequences of serious illness for the aged who are disadvantaged by small fixed incomes and a high incidence of incapacitating illnesses. Many of us who supported the passage of this legislation had hoped that it also would provide an opportunity to improve the organization and the quality of health services for the aged. As a result of compromises and concessions, few important safeguards remain in the Medicare Law. Out of deference to the fears and sensitivities of the providers of services, fiscal intermediaries were interposed between them and the Social Security Administration. This ill-conceived device may, on the one hand, weaken the present position of the voluntary non-profit health insurance industry and, on the other hand, dilute and restrict legitimate public control over this essential public program.

The pervasive stigma of charity permeates our arrangements for health care for the disadvantaged and whether the program is based upon the private practice of medicine or upon public or non-profit clinics and hospitals, it tends to be piecemeal, poorly supervised, and uncoordinated. Those who provide the services tend to focus their attention on the episode of disease or even the symptom, defending their actions on the grounds that they are poorly paid by the public welfare agency, or that their mission of teaching and research must come first.

Uncoordinated Medical Care

In most of our large cities the hospital outpatient department, together with the emergency room, is the basic source of care for the poor. Today's outpatient departments still retain some of the attributes of their predecessors, the eighteenth century free dispensaries. They are crowded, uncomfortable, lacking in concern for human dignity and, worse yet, *no longer free*. To these unhappy circumstances has been added a steady proliferation of specialty and subspeciality clinics, so that it is not uncommon for a hospital to boast of 30 or more separate clinics meeting at different hours, five or six days a week. Fragmentation of patient care is inevitable and some hospitals admit patients directly to specialty clinics without a medical evaluation.

The chronically ill older patient, who frequently suffers from several disease conditions, or poor families with several small children are seen in several clinics which frequently meet on different days. Even if the clinical record is excellent and readily available, it is difficult if not impossible for any one physician to know the patient as a person and to coordinate his care. Recently the staff of a large teaching hospital clinic complained to the New York City Welfare Department that delays in providing carfare were interfering with the treatment of a family with seven children who were under care in nine different clinics. No one had considered coordinating the care of these children or scheduling the visits to afford some relief to the overburdened mother.

Clinic patients, particularly welfare patients with no fees to pay, frequently seek care from more than one institution at the same time. Sometimes, this has been the result of multiple referrals by

several different agencies, each unaware of the patient's existing relationship with other sources of treatment. Sometimes, this is due to deliberate shopping on the part of the patient who is seeking help for his unrelieved complaints, or a modicum of personal attention. A recent study in New York City revealed that many welfare patients who "shopped" the clinics of several hospitals were amazingly sophisticated in their choice of good clinics and sources of extra attention for their many personal and social needs.[7]

All too often, however, one sees the unhappy, sometimes tragic end-results of such uncoordinated piecemeal medical care. The failures are, as a rule, not failures of individual physicians or nurses or other personnel, but rather failures of the system—a system lacking in adequate communications, continuity, follow-up, or the fixing of responsibility. When many are responsible for management of a patient, often no one is responsible.

Inpatient hospital care for the poor is usually better organized and more effective. Traditionally a place for the teaching of medical students, the wards of our voluntary and public hospitals are often the source of some of the finest medical care to be had. Yet there, too, inequities appear. Rising costs, inadequate reimbursement, personnel shortages, failure to attract well-trained house staffs are plaguing many hospitals. Public hospitals are particularly hard hit by the nursing shortage compounded by conditions of employment which are not competitive with other hospitals. As a result, the quality of care of the disadvantaged in many large public hospitals has reached critical levels.

A recent review of a 400-bed municipal hospital revealed that the total complement of registered nurses for the hospital was 46, with only 31 actually available for direct patient care on a regular basis. On one 4:00 p.m. to 12:00 midnight shift, there were three professional nurses and one supervising nurse on duty in the entire hospital. This shortage of professional nursing is reported to have resulted in diabetic patients not getting insulin injections; critically ill patients not getting antibiotics; and patients developing bed sores for lack of nursing care.

Since the shortage of professional nurses is felt throughout the United States and its impact will be increased when Medicare benefits become available, the nursing care of the poor can hardly improve without a massive national effort to train, recruit, and retain nurses. The Nurse Training Act of 1964, which provides $283 million in aid over the next five years to nursing schools, could bring the total nurses in practice to 680,000 by 1970. However, this would be 190,000 nurses short of the number considered necessary by the Surgeon General's Consultant Group in its 1962 report.

While little progress has been made in improving health care services for the disadvantaged, here and there are bright spots and signs of movement. My predecessor, Dr. Ray Trussell, with the firm support of Mayor Wagner, aligned the 13 unaffiliated municipal hospitals in New York City with strong voluntary teaching hospitals and medical schools. This act resulted in dramatic improvement in medical staffing and made it possible for each institution to maintain its accreditation. Recently, I extended the affiliation contract arrangement to cover nursing services as a pilot project in one municipal hospital. Working through New York City's Interdepartmental Health Council, it has been possible for standards to be set that apply to all medical institutions which provide care for needy patients for whom the city has assumed responsibility. In addition, we are now building in the lower East Side of Manhattan our first multipurpose health institution which will provide preventive services, ambulatory care, inpatient care, mental health care, day care for the aged, and welfare services — a pattern that we believe should be duplicated throughout the nation.

Within this framework, I have found it possible to develop and begin the application of standards for outpatient care of welfare recipients, and to use a group practice prepayment (the Health Insurance Plan of Greater New York) plan to provide comprehensive care to almost 13,000 aged welfare recipients.

Summary

Health care of the disadvantaged is piecemeal, often inadequate, underfinanced, poorly organized, and provided without compassion or concern for the dignity of the individual. It remains as a legacy of the Poor Law, little changed in concept or application, while discoveries in medicine and other health sciences have advanced with lightning speed. Certain groups of the disadvantaged in America, notably the Negro, get even less than their share of health services, even though there is ample evidence that their needs are greatest.

We can no longer tolerate a two-class system of health care. In another, but strikingly similar context, the Supreme Court of the United States has ruled that separate is not equal. Let the word go forth from this White House Conference on Health that America is prepared to assure all of its citizens equal access to health services as good as we can make them, and that the poor will no longer be forced to barter their dignity for their health.

References

1. James, George. Poverty as an Obstacle to Health Progress in Our Cities. A.J.P.H. 55,11:1757–1771 (Nov.), 1965.
2. Fein, Rashi. An Economic and Social Profile of the Negro American. Daedalus (Fall), 1965.
3. Baumgartner, L. Health and Ethnic Minorities in the Sixties (editorial). A.J.P.H. 55,4:495 (Apr.), 1965.
4. Report of the Conference on Prenatal Clinic Care in New York City. Maternity Center Association of New York. (May 9), 1963.
5. Rosen, George. Society and Medical Care. McGill M. J. Vol. XVII (Dec.), 1948.
6. Sheps, Cecil. Hospitals, Health Services and Patients. J. M. Educ. 40:50–61 (Jan.), 1965.
7. Goodrich, Charles. Personal communication.

A Congressman

Speaks on

Medical Civil Rights*

Representative Joseph Y. Resnick

NOT long ago, in response to a call from Dr. Martin Luther King, Jr., I and fourteen of my colleagues flew to Selma, Alabama, to investigate first-hand the situation down there and to see in what way we could be of help. Travelling down to Selma we stopped in Atlanta, and while I was waiting to change planes I remembered the story of the Negro minister who had served many years in Alabama, active in the civil rights movement. When he felt his life was in danger he decided he had better go to New Jersey, where a fine church and congregation was offered to him in one of the better suburbs. One day, after living a comfortable life in New Jersey for about three years, the Lord came to him and said, "Son, we need you in Alabama." The minister replied, "Lord, it's so nice here in New Jersey, I'd like to stay. My children have friends to play with. I have a nice automobile, life is pretty good, everybody likes me, nobody throws rocks at my windows or burns crosses on my lawn and, besides, I served my time." But the Lord once again said, "Son, we need you in Alabama." Finally the minister replied, "Let me think about it for twenty-four hours." The next day the minister said, "Alright, Lord, I have decided I will go back to Alabama . . . on one condition . . . and that is that you come with me." There was a pause

* This speech was delivered by Representative Joseph Y. Resnick of New York before the annual convention of the Medical Committee for Human Rights, Washington, D.C., April 23, 1965. Reprinted by permission of author.

as the Lord thought that one over for a minute, and then he said, "O.K. But only as far as Atlanta."

When I arrived in Selma, Alabama, it seemed to me that the Lord truly did go only as far as Atlanta. I wondered just what it meant in practical terms when Negroes were deprived of their voting rights. What did this actually cost them? One insight into this problem was provided by the new "liberal" mayor, for whom the Negroes voted because he promised that he would see that maybe the garbage in Negro neighborhoods would be collected, and that possibly sometime in the future, not necessarily in the near future, mind you, the city of Selma would consider paving the streets in the Negro section. As one of the Negro ministers put it, "The only place in Selma where everybody is equal is at the Tax Collection window."

Surely the right to have one's garbage collected has nothing to do with the principles of states' rights, integration or even the moral and intellectual superiority of Governor George Wallace and others like him. The only frequently heard comment we got from the hostile whites in Selma (and we mean *no* friendly ones) was "What are you down here for, why don't you straighten out Harlem, and crime in the subways?" And I would reply, "We have our problems in the North, but the one essential difference between us is that we know our racial problems and are willing to face them. We know that the Negro is being deprived of his rights, not only as a citizen but as a human being. You won't acknowledge that this is happening." As I said in an interview following hearings which were held, "It was almost as if we were talking Greek and they only understood Chinese. There was absolutely no communication between the two groups, and they could not understand what the fuss was all about and what was wrong." But some of us *do* understand the fuss. People like you in the Medical Committee for Human Rights, your commitment is complete, and so is your identification with the major domestic problem of our time. By providing necessary services, such as on-the-spot medical attention for civil rights workers in the South, you have undertaken a role that is difficult, not universally popular, and dangerous to life and limb. But it is a role that honors you and the medical profession because you are fulfilling your oath by doing what is right and what is necessary regardless of the consequences. You are proving everyday that idealism still burns brightly in American life. I salute you and ask the American people to support you in your work.

Viewed in its historical perspective, the civil rights movement today can give us cause for satisfaction. The pace of progress is being quickened. We have recently seen the passage of sweeping legislation in this field. And when it became apparent that a major loophole remained, the President hastened to demand, in eloquent terms, a new law that would assure the Negro of his right to vote.

We in Congress are confident that an effective voting rights law will soon be passed. And I, for one, will fight for the provision that will outlaw, once and for all, the poll tax—in any kind of election, local or state.

We are now entering upon a new phase in the effort to obtain equality for all of our citizens. Recent and current civil rights activities on the legislative front have led some people to believe that we have come about as far as we can by legislation, that now all that remains in order to reach the promised land is to allow nature to do its work with the passage of time.

I happen to believe that in the field of civil rights history has made it abundantly clear that the passage of *laws* accomplishes more than the passage of *time*. Look at what did *not* happen between 1865 and 1954; and look at what *has* happened since 1954.

What next? What unfinished business will remain after the voting bill is passed? Well, first of all, every citizen, white and Negro, must dedicate himself to the task of checking up and mopping up—in every state, city, and village—to guarantee universal compliance with existing laws in this field. Secondly, we must support every effort to expand the American economy and to make enough jobs for everyone. For full employment is an absolutely essential ingredient in the proper social development of our underprivileged classes. Third, new laws may be needed to overcome our major remaining problems. Laws to end discrimination in housing, laws to curb organized terrorism. Laws to make murder and other crimes against civil rights workers punishable by the Federal government. Laws to prevent local and state police forces from being used as instruments of brutality and suppression against peaceful citizens engaged in legal activities. Laws to desegregate public and private health facilities. And, finally, laws that will prevent our responsible professional people, who are engaged in work that affects the public interest, from practicing discrimination within their own ranks.

Let me give you one example of what I mean, which will interest you particularly as members of the medical profession. The American Medical Association is the nation's largest and most important medical organization. It is the number one medium of exchange for ideas and information. It inspects medical schools and publishes lists of approved schools which all states follow in issuing medical licenses. It advises official state agencies. It approves hospitals for internship and medical practice. Its relationship with state medical boards has given it the power of a quasi-public institution. The A.M.A. has been granted this great responsibility because it is widely believed that the organization represents the American doctor. But you know that this is not quite true. There are many Negro doctors whom the A.M.A. does not represent because a number of its county and state societies do not accept qualified Negro physicians as members—purely on the basis of race. The national governing body of the A.M.A. has consistently refused to take corrective measures.

The A.M.A. has the power to act against local chapters that practice racial discrimination. Their leadership has denied this, but the fact is that on at least two separate occasions resolutions have been introduced in their house of delegates which would have imposed sanctions on chapters which practice racial discrimination. These resolutions were voted on and failed, but the important fact is that—as this vote proved—the A.M.A. does indeed have the power to control the membership practices of local chapters, *if* it wishes to use it. So far they have refused. What a contrast between *your* reaction as individual doctors to the civil rights struggle, and that of the A.M.A. In the field of civil rights they have chosen to remain a "Reluctant Dragon." Personally I believe that your position is more typical of the general attitude of doctors than the A.M.A.'s, but America cannot wait for the A.M.A. to wake up to today's facts of life.

As I have pointed out, the extension of the activities of the A.M.A. has made it a quasi-public organization. Assuming its activities to be essential and in the public interest, this organization cannot be allowed to practice discrimination either as a body or within its component parts. Consequently, I introduced legislation last month that would deprive any professional group—such as the A.M.A. —of its tax exempt privileges if it practices or tolerates discrimination in the acceptance of qualified members.

I hope that all professional organizations will take note of this and put their own houses in order if the situation requires it.

How odd, unfair, and illogical it is that Negroes on every level of American society should be denied the opportunity to enter the mainstream of our national life. After all, he is our oldest ethnic minority. When the Mayflower deposited its first white settlers on the shores of the New World, the Negro was already established in Jamestown. But, despite his early arrival, he had had a tough time trying to "make it" as an American. Why? Other minorities have made it. After all we are a nation of minorities, a nation of immigrants. My own parents came here from Russia not too many years ago. Many of you in this distinguished audience, I am sure, are also first generation Americans. And for most of us, somehow the great American dream came true. Our parents managed to survive poverty. We went out and got an education. And finally we were able to earn a decent living from respected trades, businesses or professions. The Negro has not had these doors open to him and after so many years still finds himself, with some notable exceptions, of course, near the bottom of the social and economic ladder. I have heard this phenomenon discussed frequently. What is it, people ask, that permitted the Irish, Germans, Jews, Greeks, etc., to be woven into the fabric of American life with reasonable harmony and success—while this same opportunity was denied to the Negro? Worst of all, the Negro's failure to achieve equality is sometimes turned against him in a grotesque

attempt to prove that he is inherently *incapable* of achieving equality. Why has equality eluded the Negro, and where does the problem have its roots? Unlike all our other immigrants, the Negro was forcefully taken from his home and brought here as a slave. Not even as an indentured slave, who might one day buy his freedom, but a slave with no rights and no hope of ever attaining freedom for himself or his descendants.

Slavery is an ancient institution in human history, but Negro slavery as practiced in the United States made its own history. It is unique in its crushing dehumanizing impact. It dropped an iron curtain between the Negro and his past. It simply did not recognize the slave as a human being.

Consider the Negro in his African homeland. It was once thought that he was just a simple savage with no culture, sharing a uniform background and society with all other Negroes. We know that this is not true. The huge continent of Africa encompassed many different kinds of societies, cultures, and political structures. Human activity was richly varied. There were highly organized social and political structures, some of them quite democratic. Negroes lived under orderly governments, with established legal codes and highly organized social systems, usually centered upon the family. They had well-developed schools as pottery makers, weavers, woodcarvers, goldsmiths, and ironworkers. They were kings and fishermen, princes and farmers, hunters, husbandrymen, artists, musicians and sculptors. And there were the storytellers, the human history books.

When the African was taken from his home and sold into slavery in America, he ceased to be an African. Indeed, he almost ceased to be a human, because it is a fact that in this land of liberty, founded by the persecuted minions yearning to breathe free, was practiced the most totalitarian, dehumanizing form of slavery known to man.

The Negro was stripped of his name, his clothing, his language, his religion, his leaders, his stories and legends. All of his past and virtually every feature of his culture were all but wiped out. He was left without family, friends, and possessions.

Practically everything that distinguishes a man from a beast was taken from him. There is no precedent for it in all recorded history. Slavery was an old institution with broadly established rules which recognized certain basic rights of the slave. Spain and Portugal, for example, had centuries of experience with slavery. The Africans they brought as slaves to Latin America were protected by an old established body of slave law known as "Las Siete Partidas." The Latin American Negro was not stripped of his heritage. All of his rights were spelled out. As a result, the Negro in Latin America has developed a totally different personality than his counterpart in the United States, and he has become a vital, productive and integral component of Latin American society.

American slavery was totalitarian. The slave was property, no different legally from a barn or a horse. It was almost impossible for him to become a free man. He existed in a closed system where the emphasis was on mere survival, very much, as a matter of fact, like the Nazi concentration camps. And it is interesting to note that psychologists have detected striking similarities in the psychological damage inflicted upon the enslaved Negro and the concentration camp inmate. The slave had no family life. Marriage was not legally recognized. His children and women could be taken from him and sold elsewhere. He was not taught to read or allowed to go to church. His ancient legends and history reached a dead end. Slavery of this form placed the Negro in a dependent role, lowered his need for achievement, and deprived him of his ancient heritage as a source of inspiration and orientation. It caused a mutation in his psychological and personality development and resulted in the creation of a caricature that has plagued him since emancipation.

For all practical purposes, he became a person without a past. Important elements of a Negro's African culture *were* retained—and yet lost at the same time because they were soon absorbed into the total American culture. For, as the Negro historian Benjamin Quarles points out, "The Negro was destined to place his stamp upon the distinctive American contributions to the fields of music, dance, literature, and art. Negro creations were destined to become national, rather than racial."

How different all this is from the stories of our other American immigrants. They left the old country, but always brought a lot of it with them. They brought language, name, religion, holidays, family, books and customs. It gave them stability in the raging tides of a strange new country. We can just imagine an immigrant father comforting his son who came home with angry tears because the others called him offensive names. "Look, son," his Irish father might have said, "the Irish were a brave and proud people when the mists of history were just rising. Your own ancestors fought beside Irish kings." And then for good measure, he could finish by reading some of the works of the great Irish poets.

The Italian father might have taken his son to the library and shown him shelves of books about the glories of Rome. Or to the museum to look at Roman art and sculpture.

And the Jewish father might have sat down with his son and talked reverently about a civilization that reached back over five thousand years and gave the world so many men of accomplishment.

Pride, that was the vital ingredient. Every child was taught and still is taught, in the natural course of growing up, to have pride in his history, his people, and the old homeland, wherever it was. And how could the Negro father comfort his child, even after emancipation, when a somewhat normal domestic life was more possible? There was no "old country"; he did not even know what part of Africa his forebears came from. There was no history to be proud of. There was no past. And there was not even a present, because the Negro was a victim of another cruel trick. Even his accomplishments in the United States were ignored. He was deprived of his American hero-figures as well as his ancient ones. The writers and publishers of our history books have committed unpardonable sins of omission. They have been biased—perhaps innocently and unconsciously. To them the Negro has never been an individual, capable of human accomplishments worth recording. When he has been written about at all in our history books, with perhaps one or two exceptions, it has been in terms of his "problem," or slavery. Always collectively. One would never know that there have been outstanding Negro patriots, artists, and inventors. What have we read about slave rebellions or about Negro participation in the Revolutionary War? How many of us have ever heard of Crispus Attucks, Ira Frederick Aldridge, Paul Laurence Dunbar, Charles Richard Drew, or Norbert Rillieux? We owe much to these great Americans, who would most certainly be well known to all of us had they been white. But they were Negroes, and consequently have been condemned to obscurity by the writers of our history books.

I would like to suggest to our major textbook publishers that they form a committee to read through all our textbooks and, where necessary, rewrite them to restore to Negroes their proper place in American history.

Because he was deprived of his past, because he virtually started from scratch on American soil, the Negro among all immigrants is the only 100 per cent American product. He has every right to be proud of himself, and to say, "Look at me, I am an

American. I eat apple pie and pizza like everybody else. And my holidays are the red, white and blue holidays like July 4th and Thanksgiving."

There is no question about it. He is an important part of the picture. But one thing is still missing. The Negro is an immigrant, and as an immigrant he is entitled to one privilege that he does not yet have but which most other ethnic groups already enjoy.

Almost every American minority picks one day during the year when its members get dressed up, have a parade or a party, and let the world know what it's missing by not being Irish, Italian or Polish or what have you. These days are important not only because the group has an excuse to stick out its chest in pride. They are days when Americans remind themselves and everyone else that ours is a pluralistic culture. At the tulip festival in Michigan each year the Dutch are saying, "We never forget that we are Dutch and proud of it—but Dutch-Americans." Such a day becomes the focus for magazines and broadcast media to zero-in on the particular group and publicize its contributions, cul-ture, and national heroes. And so it seems to me that it would be a wonderful thing if America's Negroes proclaimed such a day for themselves. It might be called "Negro Heritage Day." It should be a beautiful day in spring, when the memory of the bitter winter is still there, and when everyone is looking forward to the bright promise of summer. It should be a day when the buds on the trees are beginning to swell, to help us forget how barren they so recently looked. It would be a day of singing, and partying, and dancing, and celebrating in the home, in our streets, and in our parks. It would be a day when a Negro's white neighbors and friends would join in the celebration, just as all America joins in the celebration of St. Patrick's Day. It would be a day for America to express its gratitude that the Negro came to our shores and joined us in forging the greatest nation the world has ever known. A day when each Negro would proclaim at the top of his voice, "We are proud of our heritage. We are proud to be Negroes. We are proud to be Americans."

Presidents of the NMA and the NACGN

Presidents of the National Medical Association

1895–1897   DR. ROBERT F. BOYD
Nashville, Tennessee

1898–1900   DR. H. T. NOEL
Nashville, Tennessee

1900–1902   DR. O. D. PORTER
Bowling Green, Kentucky

1903   DR. F. A. STEWART
Nashville, Tennessee

1904   DR. CHARLES V. ROMAN
Dallas, Texas

1905   DR. JOHN E. HUNTER
Lexington, Kentucky

1906   DR. R. E. JONES
Richmond, Virginia

1907   DR. NATHAN F. MOSSELL
Philadelphia, Pennsylvania

1908   DR. W. H. WRIGHT
Baltimore, Maryland

1909   DR. P. A. JOHNSON
New York, New York

1910   DR. MARCUS F. WHEATLAND
Newport, Rhode Island

1911   DR. AUSTIN M. CURTIS
Washington, D.C.

1912   DR. H. F. GAMBLE
Charleston, West Virginia

1913   DR. JOHN A. KENNEY, SR.
Tuskegee Institute, Alabama

1914   DR. A. M. BROWN
Birmingham, Alabama

1915   DR. F. S. HARGRAVES
Wilson, North Carolina

1916   DR. ULYSSES G. DAILEY
Chicago, Illinois

1917   DR. D. W. BYRD
Norfolk, Virginia

1918   DR. GEORGE W. CABANISS
Washington, D.C.

1919   DR. D. A. FERGUSON
Richmond, Virginia

1920   DR. J. W. JONES
Winston-Salem, North Carolina

1921   DR. JOHN P. TURNER
Philadelphia, Pennsylvania

1922   DR. H. M. GREEN
Knoxville, Tennessee

1923   DR. J. EDWARD PERRY
Kansas City, Missouri

1924   DR. JOHN O. PLUMMER
Raleigh, North Carolina

1925   DR. MICHAEL O. DUMAS
Washington, D.C.

1926   DR. WALTER G. ALEXANDER
Orange, New Jersey

1927   DR. CARL G. ROBERTS
Chicago, Illinois

1928   DR. C. V. FREEMAN
Jacksonville, Florida

1929   DR. T. SPOTUAS BURWELL
Philadelphia, Pennsylvania

1930   DR. L. A. WEST
Memphis, Tennessee

1931   DR. W. H. HIGGINS
Providence, Rhode Island

1932   DR. PETER M. MURRAY
New York, New York

1933   DR. G. HAMILTON FRANCIS
Norfolk, Virginia

1934   DR. MIDIAN O. BOUSFIELD
Chicago, Illinois

1935   DR. JOHN H. HALE
Nashville, Tennessee

1936   DR. W. HARRY BARNES
Philadelphia, Pennsylvania

1937   DR. ROSCOE C. GILES
Chicago, Illinois

1938   DR. LYNDON M. HILL
Atlanta, Georgia

1939   DR. GEORGE W. BOWLES
York, Pennsylvania

1940   DR. ALBERT W. DUMAS, SR.
Natchez, Mississippi

1941   DR. A. N. VAUGHN
St. Louis, Missouri

1942   DR. H. E. LEE
Houston, Texas

1943   DR. T. MANUEL SMITH
Chicago, Illinois

1944–1945   DR. EMORY I. ROBINSON
Los Angeles, California

1946   DR. WALTER A. YOUNGE
St. Louis, Missouri

1947 DR. J. A. C. LATTIMORE
        Louisville, Kentucky
1948 DR. C. AUSTIN WHITTIER
        San Antonio, Texas
1949 DR. C. HERBERT MARSHALL
        Washington, D.C.
1950 DR. HENRY H. WALKER
        Nashville, Tennessee
1951 DR. JOSEPH G. GATHINGS
        Washington, D.C.
1952 DR. WHITTIER C. ATKINSON
        Coatesville, Pennsylvania
1953 DR. A. PORTER DAVIS
        Kansas City, Kansas
1954 DR. MATTHEW WALKER
        Nashville, Tennessee
1955 DR. AUGUST C. TERRENCE
        Opelousas, Louisiana
1956 DR. THEODORE R. M. HOWARD
        Mound Bayou, Mississippi
1957 DR. A. M. TOWNSEND, JR.
        St. Louis, Missouri
1958 DR. RELLIFORD STILLMON SMITH
        Macon, Georgia
1959 DR. EDWARD C. MAZIQUE
        Washington, D.C.
1960 DR. JAMES T. ALDRICH
        St. Louis, Missouri

1961 DR. VAUGHAN C. MASON
        New York, New York
1962 DR. JOHN A. KENNEY, JR.
        Washington, D.C.
1963 DR. KENNETH W. CLEMENT
        Cleveland, Ohio
1964 DR. W. MONTAGUE COBB
        Washington, D.C.
1965 DR. LEONIDAS H. BERRY
        Chicago, Illinois
1966 DR. JOHN L. S. HOLLOMAN, JR.
        New York, New York
1967 DR. LIONEL SWAN
        Detroit, Michigan
1968 DR. JAMES M. WHITTICO, JR.
        St. Louis, Missouri
1969 DR. JULIUS W. HILL
        Los Angeles, California
1970 DR. WILEY T. ARMSTRONG
        Rocky Mountain, North Carolina
1971 DR. EMERSON C. WALDEN
        Baltimore, Maryland
1972 DR. EDMUND C. CASEY
        Cincinnati, Ohio
1973 DR. EMERY RANN
        Charlotte, North Carolina
1974 DR. BERNAL CAVE
        New York, New York

1975 DR. JASPER F. WILLIAMS
        Chicago, Illinois

Presidents of the National Association of Colored Graduate Nurses

1908–1910 MISS MARTHA FRANKLIN
            New Haven, Connecticut
1910–1912 MRS. MARY TUCKER
            Philadelphia, Pennsylvania
1912–1913 MRS. MARY CLARK LEMUS
            Richmond, Virginia
1913–1914 MRS. ROSA WILLIAMS BROWN
            Palm Beach, Florida
1914–1916 MISS CARRIE SHARPE
            Petersburg, Virginia
1916–1923 MRS. ADAH B. THOMS
            New York, New York
1923–1926 MISS PETRA A. PINN
            Wilberforce, Ohio

1926–1929 MISS CARRIE E. BULLOCK
            Chicago, Illinois
1929–1930 MRS. HALLIE AVERY WEST
            Memphis, Tennessee
1930–1934 MISS MABEL C. NORTHCROSS
            St. Louis, Missouri
1934–1939 MRS. ESTELLE M. R. OSBORNE
            New York, New York
1939–1947 MRS. F. FOULKES GAINES
            Chicago, Illinois
1947–1949 MRS. ALIDA C. DAILEY
            Montclair, New Jersey
1949–1951 MRS. MABEL KEATON STAUPERS
            New York, New York

Bibliography

A Guide to the Literature

A DEFINITIVE work on the history of the Negro in medicine in the United States must await further research in the field. Scholarly investigation is of prime importance, not only in respect to the archives of the National Medical Association and its affiliated units but also in respect to the documents and publications of such government bodies as the Freedmen's Bureau, the Public Health Service, the Children's Bureau, the Department of the Interior and the Department of Health, Education and Welfare. In addition, the catalogues, files and special announcements of Howard, Meharry, Leonard, West Tennessee and other Negro medical schools should be intensively researched. Similarly, the bulletins, reports and press releases of philanthropic bodies, semi-public investigative agencies and civil rights organizations require scholarly research. Only by investigating these widely scattered and virtually untapped sources will it be possible to write the necessary monographs and fill the important gaps in our knowledge of this field.

During the past thirty-five years, an impressive body of information has emerged on the Negro in medicine. Particularly noteworthy have been the special studies of Walter Dyson (1929) on the founding of the Howard Uni-versity Medical School, Charles V. Roman (1934) on the rise and progress of Meharry Medical College, Carter G. Woodson (1934) on the Negro professional man and the community, W. Montague Cobb (1939) on the origin and development of the first Negro medical society, Helen E. Walker (1949) and Dietrich C. Reitzes (1958) on the Negro in medical practice, Mabel K. Staupers (1961) on Negro nurses, and Herbert E. Klarman (1963) on hospital care in New York City. Since the pioneer work of John A. Kenney in *The Negro in Medicine* (1912), and Kelly Miller's article four years later, "The Historical Background of the Negro Physician," Harold E. Farmer (1940) and Midian O. Bousfield (1945) have presented new and additional information on Negro physicians, past and present, in the *Bulletin of the History of Medicine*.

During recent years, our knowledge of the contributions of leading Negro physicians has been greatly enriched. Distinguished autobiographies by John E. Perry (1947), Thomas R. Peyton (1950) and Miles V. Lynk (1951) have cast considerable light on the obstacles facing Negro doctors in a Jim Crow-oriented society. Also helpful have been the vividly written biographies by Helen Buckler

(1954) and Helen K. Branson (1947) on Dr. Daniel H. Williams of Chicago and Dr. Edna L. Griffin of Pasadena, respectively.

Of inestimable value have been the more than a score of biographical sketches of Negro doctors that have come from the productive pen of W. Montague Cobb, pre-eminent in the field of Negro medical history. As editor-in-chief of the *Journal of the National Medical Association* since 1949, he has encouraged many others to contribute to the magazine articles on the lives of leading Negro physicians, hospitals established by Negroes, struggles for integration, and the health care needs of the Negro people. Following the broad lines laid down by the versatile W. E. B. Du Bois in his brilliantly conceived and edited work *The Health and Physique of the Negro American* (1906), Dr. Cobb has written extensively on the retarded health status of the Negro people and their desperate need for adequate medical care. In this connection, two recent books—*A Profile of the Negro American* by Thomas F. Pettigrew and *To Be Equal* by Whitney M. Young, Jr., both published in 1964—contain provocative chapters on the same subject.

This bibliography attempts to bring together the solid contributions that already have been made and to offer as many valuable nuggets as possible from the rich lode of primary source material that is available. The 60 volumes of the *Journal of the National Medical Association,* as well as the more than 70 volumes of the *Crisis,* official organ of the National Association for the Advancement of Colored People, furnished much new and important material, as did the autobiographies of various Negro doctors, official government reports, findings of investigative committees, articles in newspapers, magazines and professional journals, press releases and bulletins of civil rights bodies and the minutes, transactions and resolutions of organizations in the health field. The Arthur A. Schomburg Negro Collection at the Harlem Branch of the New York City Public Library, as well as the excellent collection of books, documents, clippings and manuscripts at the New York Academy of Medicine, was of invaluable assistance.

The bibliography that follows is designed to provide the reader with the most comprehensive compilation of primary sources and secondary accounts that is presently available on the history of the Negro in medicine. The bibliography includes, in addition to the several hundred references the author has used, supplementary items that should prove useful for further research and writing. The author should like to take this opportunity to acknowledge his indebtedness to Lindsay C. Dorney, whose work at the Library of Congress, the National Library of Medicine, the Washington, D.C., Central Public Library and the Howard University Founders Library helped immeasurably to make the bibliography more effective and comprehensive. For the convenience of the reader, the bibliographical guide to the literature listed below has been arranged under five principal headings, even though some of the citations transcend the special categories.

BIOGRAPHICAL REFERENCES

"Aaron McDuffie Moore, M.D.," *Journal of the National Medical Association,* XVI (January–March 1924), 72–74.

"Angels of Saigon: Two Army Nurses," *Ebony,* XXI (August 1966), 44–46.

BELL, HOWARD H. "Benjamin Jesse Covington, M.D., 1869–1961," *Journal of the National Medical Association,* LV (September 1963), 462–63.

BRANSON, H. K. *Let There Be Life: The Contemporary Account of Edna L. Griffin, M.D.* Pasadena, 1947.

BROWN, WILLIAM WELLS. *The Black Man: His Antecedents, His Genius and His Achievements.* New York, 1863.

BUCKLER, H. *Doctor Dan: Pioneer in American Surgery.* Boston, 1954.

BUTTERFIELD, L. H. (ed.). *Letters of Benjamin Rush.* Princeton, N.J., 1951.

"C. O. Dummett Named Dean of Meharry School of Dentistry," *National Negro Health News,* XV (October–December 1947), 18.

CARTER, H. "Long Journey Home of Mathew Page," *Saturday Evening Post,* CCXXXIII (December 17, 1960), 18 ff.

CHAYER, MARY ELLA. "Mary Eliza Mahoney," *American Journal of Nursing,* LIV (April 1954), 29–31.

COBB, WILLIAM MONTAGUE. "Absalom Jones, 1746–1818, and Richard Allen, 1760–1831," *Journal of the National Medical Association,* XLIX (March 1957), 129.

———. "Alexander Thomas Augusta," *ibid.,* XLIV (July 1952), 327–29.

———. "Anderson William Cheatham, 1880–1936," *ibid.,* L (September 1958), 400–401.

———. "Arnold Hamilton Maloney, M.D., 1888–1955," *ibid.,* XLVII (November 1955), 424–26.

———. "Arthur Melvin Townsend, M.D., 1875–1959," *ibid.,* LI (July 1959), 323–24.

———. "Austin Maurice Curtis, M.D., 1868–1939," *ibid.,* XLVI (July 1954), 294–98.

———. "Carl Glennis Roberts, M.D., 1886–1950," *ibid.,* LII (March 1960), 146–47.

———. "Charles Burleigh Purvis, M.D., 1842–1929," *ibid.,* XLV (January 1953), 79–82.

———. "Charles R. Drew, M.D., 1904–1950," *ibid.,* XLII (July 1950), 239–45.

———. "Charles Richard Drew, M.D., 1904–1950," *Journal of Negro History,* XXXV (July 1950), 348–52.

———. "Charles Victor Roman," *Journal of the National Medical Association,* XLV (July 1953), 301–4.

———. "Clarence Sumner Greene, A.B., D.D.S., M.D., 1901–1957," *ibid.,* LX (May 1968), 253–54.

———. "Clyde Donnell, M.D., 1890– ," *ibid.,* LII (September 1960), 382.

———. "Cornelius Nathaniel Dorsette, M.D., 1852–1897," *ibid.,* LII (November 1960), 456–59.

———. "Daniel Hale Williams, M.D., 1858–1931," *ibid.,* XLV (September 1953), 379–85.

———. "Daniel Hale Williams—Pioneer and Innovator," *ibid.,* XXXVI (September 1944), 158–59.

———. "Daniel Smith Lamb, M.D., 1843–1929," *ibid.,* L (January 1958), 62–65.

———. " 'Dr.' James Still, New Jersey Pioneer," *ibid.,* LV (March 1963), 196–99.

———. "Eugene Heriot Dibble, M.D.: Perspective and Profile," *ibid.,* XLVIII (September 1956), 435–37.

———. "Frederick Douglass Stubbs, 1906–1947," *ibid.,* XL (January 1948), 24–26.

———. "Grossi Hamilton Francis, M.D., 1885– ," *ibid.,* LI (November 1959), 489.

———. "Henry Fitzbutler, 1842–1901," *ibid.,* XLIV (September 1952), 403–7.

———. "Henry McKee Minton, M.D., 1870–1946," *ibid.,* XLVII (July 1955), 285–86.

———. "Henry Rutherford Butler, M.D., 1862–1931," *ibid.,* LI (September 1959), 406–8.

———. "John Andrew Kenney, M.D., 1874–1950," *ibid.,* XLII (May 1950), 175–77.

———. "John Edward Perry, M.D., 1870– ," *ibid.,* XLVIII (July 1956), 292–96.

———. "John Henry Hale, M.D., 1878–1944," *ibid.,* XLVI (January 1954), 79–80.

———. "John Patrick Turner, M.D., 1885–1958," *ibid.,* LI (March 1959), 160–61.

———. "John Wesley Anderson, M.D., 1861–1947," *ibid.,* XLV (November 1953), 442–44.

———. "Julian Waldo Ross, M.D., 1884– ," *ibid.,* LII (May 1960), 220–21.

———. "Louis Tompkins Wright, M.D., 1891–1952," *ibid.,* XLV (March 1953), 130–48.

———. "Martin Robison Delany, 1812–1885," *ibid.,* XLIV (May 1952), 232–38.

———. "Monroe Alpheus Majors," *ibid.,* XLVII (March 1955), 139–41.

———. "Nathan Francis Mossell, M.D., 1856–1946," *ibid.,* XLVI (March 1954), 118–30.

———. "Numa P. G. Adams, M.D., 1885–1940," *ibid.,* XLIII (January 1951), 43–52.

———. "Paul Timothy Robinson, M.D., 1898–1966," *ibid.,* LVIII (July 1966), 321–23.

———. "Peter Marshall Murray, M.D., 1888– ," *ibid.,* LIX (January 1967), 71 ff.

———. "Simeon Lewis Carson, M.D., 1882–1954," *ibid.,* XLVI (November 1954), 414–19.

———. "Solomon Carter Fuller, M.D., 1872–1953," *ibid.,* XLVI (September 1954), 370–71.

———. "Solomon Henry Thompson, M.D., 1870–1950," *ibid.,* XLIX (July 1957), 274–78.

————. "Walter Gilbert Alexander, M.D., 1880–1953," *ibid.*, XLV (July 1953), 281–83.

————. "William Alonza Warfield, M.D., 1866–1951," *ibid.*, XLIV (May 1952), 206–19.

————. "William Augustus Hinton," *ibid.*, XLIX (November 1957), 427–28.

————. "William Clarence McNeill, M.D., 1878–   ," *ibid.*, L (July 1958), 314.

————. "William Harry Barnes, 1887–1945," *ibid.*, XLVII (January 1955), 64–66.

COLLIER, FRED C. "Eugene Heriot Dibble, M.D., 1893–1968," *Journal of the National Medical Association*, LX (September 1968), 446.

DAILEY, U. G. "Brigadier General Spencer C. Dickerson, B.S., M.D., 1885–1948," *Journal of the National Medical Association*, XL (July 1948), 165–66.

DALENCOUR, GASTON. "Sketch of Dr. Paul Salomon . . . ," *Journal of the National Medical Association*, XXXVII (November 1945), 204–5.

"Daniel Hale Williams," *Journal of the National Medical Association*, XXIII (October–December 1931), 173–75.

"Dibble Honored at President's Dinner at Cincinnati Convention," *Journal of the National Medical Association*, LVII (September 1965), 436–37.

DIETZ, B. "James Bailey, M.D.," *Look*, XXVIII (December 15, 1964), 29–35.

"Distinguished Americans: Louis T. Wright, M.D., and James Weldon Johnson," *Crisis*, XLI (November 1934), 326.

"Dixon Nominated as Regent of the National Library of Medicine," *Journal of the National Medical Association*, LV (November 1963), 562.

"Dr. A. W. Dumas, Sr.," *Journal of the National Medical Association*, XXXI (September 1939), 191.

"Dr. Clarence Sumner Greene, M.D., 1901–1957," *Journal of the National Medical Association*, L (March 1958), 139–40.

"Dr. Conwell Banton Honored at Edgewood Sanatorium, Delaware," *National Negro Health News*, XV (January–March 1947), 7–8.

"Dr. D. W. Byrd, Our President," *Journal of the National Medical Association*, VIII (October–December 1916), 190–91.

"Dr. Eugene Heriot Dibble, Jr., Distinguished Service Medalist for 1962," *Journal of the National Medical Association*, LIV (November 1962), 711–12.

"Dr. Eugene W. Lomax," *Journal of the National Medical Association*, XIX (October–December 1927), 164–65.

"Dr. Frank S. Hargraves, Our New President," *Journal of the National Medical Association*, VI (October–December 1914), 238–39.

"Dr. George C. Hall," *Journal of the National Medical Association*, XXII (July–September 1930), 170–71.

"Dr. George Hubbard Retires," *Journal of the National Medical Association*, XIII (January–March 1921), 30–31.

"Dr. George W. Cabaniss," *Journal of the National Medical Association*, XII (April–June 1920), 32–33.

"Doctor Gets Call, to Mayor's Chair: Dr. S. F. Monstime," *Ebony*, XX (October 1965), 171 ff.

"Dr. Harold D. West (1904–   ), New President of Meharry," *Journal of the National Medical Association*, XLIV (July 1952), 316–17.

"Dr. Hinton, Now 68, Led Fight on Social Disease," *Boston Daily Globe* (September 15, 1952).

"Dr. Howard Marshall Payne, 1907–1961," *Journal of the National Medical Association*, LIII (November 1961), 653–54.

"Dr. J. W. Jones, Our President," *Journal of the National Medical Association*, XI (July–September 1919), 158.

"Dr. James Malachi Whittico, Jr.," *Journal of the National Medical Association*, LX (January 1968), 50–51.

"Dr. John F. Burton," *Journal of the National Medical Association*, LVIII (May 1966), 223.

"Dr. John Henry Alston," *Journal of the National Medical Association*, XVIII (April–June 1926), 109.

"Dr. Kenneth W. Clement, Distinguished Service Medalist for 1965," *Journal of the National Medical Association*, LVII (November 1965), 505–6.

"Dr. L. L. Burwell," *Journal of the National Medical Association*, XX (April–June 1928), 75.

"Dr. Lionel Fitzroy Swan," *Journal of the National Medical Association*, LVIII (November 1966), 470–71.

"Dr. Louis T. Wright," *Journal of the National Medical Association*, XXVII (February 1935), 32.

"Dr. Pierce S. Moten," *Journal of the National Medical Association*, LIII (July 1961), 432–35.

"Dr. Purvis," *Journal of the National Medical Association*, XXI (July–September 1929), 141.

"Dr. R. H. Brooks," *Journal of the National Medical Association*, XXII (October–December 1930), 206.

"Dr. Turner, a Police Surgeon," *Journal of the National Medical Association*, XXII (October–December 1930), 177.

"Dr. Ulysses Grant Dailey, 1885–1961," *Journal of the National Medical Association*, LIII (July 1961), 432.

"Doctor on Wheels, J. A. Bailey," *Ebony*, XIX (October 1964), 83–84.

"Dr. William McKinley Thomas, M.D., 1903–1958," *Journal of the National Medical Association*, L (May 1958), 221–22.

"Dr. Willis E. Sterrs," *Journal of the National Medical Association*, XIII (April–June 1921), 108–9.

"Dr. Williston," *Journal of the National Medical Association*, XX (October–December 1928), 193–94.

DREW, CHARLES R. "Carl Glennis Roberts, M.D., 1886–1950," *Journal of the National Medical Association,* XLII (March 1950), 109–10.

———. "Negro Scholars in Scientific Research," *Journal of Negro History,* XXXV (April 1950), 135–49.

DU BOIS, W. E. B. "Negro Scientist," *American Scholar,* VIII (July 1939), 309–20.

"E. Mae McCarroll," *Journal of the National Medical Association,* LV (July 1963), 367–68.

"Edith Irby Revisited," *Ebony,* XVIII (July 1963), 52–54.

"Edward Craig Mazique, the President-Elect," *Journal of the National Medical Association,* L (November 1958), 463 ff.

EPPS, CHARLES H. "Leonidas H. Berry, B.S., M.S., M.D.," *Journal of the National Medical Association,* LVI (November 1964), 538–39.

"Eugene Heriot Dibble," *Journal of the National Medical Association,* XXXV (September 1943), 175.

FARMER, H. E. "An Account of the Earliest Colored Gentlemen in Medical Science in the United States," *Bulletin of the History of Medicine,* VIII (April 1940), 599–618.

"First Negro Medical Officer, U.S. Navy," *National Negro Health News,* XII (July–September 1944), 16.

"First Negro Physician Appointed to the District of Columbia Board of Examiners in Medicine and Osteopathy," *Journal of the National Medical Association,* XLVII (May 1955), 201.

FISHMAN, G. M. "Copy of a Letter on Dr. James Still, Which Appeared in the *Courier-Post,* Camden, N.J., May 16, 1961," *Negro History Bulletin,* XXV (April 1962), 154.

FLEMING, G. JAMES, and BURCKEL, CHRISTIAN E. (eds.). *Who's Who in Colored America: An Illustrated Biographical Directory of Notable Living Persons of African Descent in the United States.* Yonkers, N.Y., 1950.

HAUPT, ALMA C. "Pioneer in Negro Nursing," *American Journal of Nursing,* XXXV (September 1935), 857–59.

HENTOFF, NAT. "Doctor Nyswander," *New Yorker,* XLI (June 26, 1965), 32 ff.; XLI (July 3, 1965), 32–34.

"A History in the Making: Adah B. Thoms," *American Journal of Nursing,* XXIX (May 1929), 560.

"James Derham," *Journal of the National Medical Association,* IV (October–December 1912), 50.

"James Lowell Hall, Sr., M.D., 1892–1965," *Journal of the National Medical Association,* LVIII (January 1966), 82–83.

"James McCune Smith, 1811–1865," *Journal of the National Medical Association,* XLIV (March 1952), 160.

"Joseph Gouverneur Gathings, M.D., 1898–1965," *Journal of the National Medical Association,* LVII (September 1965), 427–28.

KENNEY, JOHN A. "Dr. John Henry Hale," *Journal of the National Medical Association,* XXXVI (July 1944), 130–31.

KINGDON, F. "Patriot and Physician," *Crisis,* XLVII (January 1940), 14 ff.

"Lady Doctor to Migrant Workers," *Ebony,* XVII (February 1962), 59–60.

LAWLAH, JOHN W. "Dr. Franklin Chambers McLean," *Journal of the National Medical Association,* LIV (November 1962), 716 ff.

———. "George Cleveland Hall, M.D., 1864–1930," *ibid.,* XLVI (May 1954), 207–10.

———. "The President-Elect: William Montague Cobb," *ibid.,* LV (November 1963), 551–54.

LILLIE, F. R. "Ernest Everett Just," *Science,* XCV (January 2, 1942), 10–11.

"Long, President of Putnam County [Florida] Medical Society," *Journal of the National Medical Association,* LVII (May 1965), 247.

LYNK, M. V. *Sixty Years of Medicine: An Autobiography.* Memphis, 1951.

MCCLEAVE, B. F. "Memphis Honors Dr. Wheelock A. Bisson," *Journal of the National Medical Association,* LVIII (March 1966), 134–36.

"Mary Eliza Mahoney: First Negro Nurse," *Journal of the National Medical Association,* XLVI (July 1954), 299.

MATHER, FRANK L. (comp.). *Who's Who of the Colored Race: A General Dictionary of Men and Women of African Descent.* Chicago, 1915.

"The Mellow Militant [Dr. John L. S. Holloman, Jr.]," *Medical Tribune* [New York] (September 7, 1966).

"Men of the Month [Dr. Algernon B. Jackson]," *Crisis,* III (November 1911), 18–19.

"Men of the Month [Dr. Brown]," *ibid,* VII (December 1913), 65–66.

"Men of the Month [Dr. C. Banton]," *ibid.,* XV (November 1917), 22.

"Men of the Month [Dr. Charles H. Garvin]," *ibid.,* XIX (April 1920), 334.

"Men of the Month [Dr. David N. C. Scott]," *ibid.,* XIX (March 1920), 273–74.

"Men of the Month [Dr. Dibble]," *ibid.,* XII (August 1916), 191.

"Men of the Month [Dr. Humbert]," *ibid.,* XVIII (August 1919), 200.

"Men of the Month [Dr. J. H. Lowery]," *ibid.,* XVI (May 1918), 14.

"Men of the Month [Dr. John R. Francis]," *ibid.,* VI (August 1913), 173.

"Men of the Month [Dr. L. A. Lewis]," *ibid.,* III (January 1912), 103.

"Men of the Month [Dr. S. Marie Steward]," *ibid.,* XVI (May 1918), 15.

"Men of the Month [Dr. Solomon C. Fuller]," *ibid.*, VI (May 1913), 18.

"Men of the Month [Dr. William S. Quinland]," *ibid.*, XIX (December 1919), 65.

"Men of the Month [Nurse Adah Thoms]," *ibid.*, XVI (August 1918), 183.

MOTT, A. *Biographical Sketches and Interesting Anecdotes of Persons of Color.* New York, 1839.

MURRAY, PETER MARSHALL. "Midian O. Bousfield, M.D., 1885–1948," *Journal of the National Medical Association*, XL (May 1948), 120.

"N.A.A.C.P. Mourns Dr. Louis T. Wright," *Crisis*, LIX (November 1952), 548–50.

"Negro Nurses: Captain Mary L. Petty and Captain Della H. Raney," *National Negro Health News*, XII (April–June 1944), 7–8.

"Negroes Distinguished in Science," *Negro History Bulletin*, II (May 1939), 67–70.

"New Dean of Meharry School of Dentistry, Dr. William H. Allen," *National Negro Health News*, XVII (October–December 1949), 27.

"On Dr. Taylor of Philadelphia," *Journal of the National Medical Association*, VII (July–September 1915), 206–8.

PERRY, G. S. "Negro Doctor Wins Over a Southern Town: Dr. J. Dickey, Taylor, Texas," *Saturday Evening Post*, CCXXVI (October 24, 1953), 36 ff.

PERRY, J. E. *Forty Cords of Wood: Memoirs of a Medical Doctor.* Jefferson City, Mo., 1947.

PEYTON, T. R. *Quest for Dignity: An Autobiography of a Negro Doctor.* Los Angeles, 1950.

"Physician of the Eighties: Dr. Henri Jones," *Journal of the National Medical Association*, XLII (November 1950), 403–4.

"Poindexter, 1964 Distinguished Service Medalist," *Journal of the National Medical Association*, LVI (November 1964), 537.

PORTER, DOROTHY B. "David Ruggles: An Apostle of Human Rights," *Journal of Negro History*, XXVIII (January 1943), 23–50.

———. "David Ruggles, 1810–1849: Hydropathic Practitioner," *Journal of the National Medical Association*, XLIX (January 1957), 67–72; XLIX (March 1957), 130–34.

———. "Sarah Parker Remond, Abolitionist . . .," *Journal of Negro History*, XX (April 1935), 287–93.

"Portrait of a Successful Nurse: Latis M. Campbell," *National Negro Health News*, XVI (April–June 1948), 7–9.

"The President-Elect: John L. S. Holloman, M.D.," *Journal of the National Medical Association*, LVII (November 1965), 507–8.

"Race Woman Gets Important U.S.D.A. Post," *National Negro Health News*, XII (April–June 1944), 23.

"Relliford Stillmon Smith, M.D., 1889–1965," *Journal of the National Medical Association*, LVIII (March 1966), 145.

RICHARDSON, C. (ed.). *National Cyclopaedia of the Colored Race.* Montgomery, Ala., 1919.

"Robert Fulton Boyd," *Journal of the National Medical Association*, XLV (May 1953), 233–34.

ROBINSON, HENRY S. "Robert and Roderick Badger, Pioneer Georgia Dentists," *Negro History Bulletin*, XXIV (January 1961), 77–79.

ROY, J. H. "Pinpoint Portrait of Doctor Dorothy Boulding Ferebee," *Negro History Bulletin*, XXV (April 1962), 160.

SCHARLIEB, M. "Medical Women," *19th Century and After*, XCVI (October 1924), 599–607.

SCOTT, C. W. "Biography of a Surgeon," *Crisis*, LVIII (October 1951), 501 ff.

SIMMONS, W. J. *Men of Mark: Eminent, Progressive and Rising.* Cleveland, 1891.

"Some Chicagoans of Note," *Crisis*, X (September 1915), 237–42.

STILL, JAMES. *Early Recollections and Life of Dr. James Still.* Philadelphia, 1877.

THOMS, ADAH B. *Pathfinders.* New York, 1929.

"Top Nurse in Uniform: Highest-Ranking Negro Woman in the U.S. Army Nurses' Corps," *Ebony*, XXI (September 1966), 50.

"Ulysses Grant Dailey," *Journal of the National Medical Association*, XXXV (March 1943), 64.

WATSON, IRVING A. *Physicians and Surgeons of America.* Concord, N.H., 1896.

WELLS, L. "Jungle Doctor: Epic of an American Trained Negro Doctor in Africa," *Reader's Digest*, XL (May 1942), 103–6.

"West Virginia's Director of Mental Health," *Ebony*, XIX (January 1964), 63–68.

WILKERSON, E. L. *Struggling to Climb: A Biography* [Fred D. Sessoms, M.D.]. Cleveland, 1958.

WILKINS, R. "Louis T. Wright: Fighter for Equality and Excellence," *Crisis*, LXX (May 1963), 261–69.

"William Wells Brown, M.D., 1816–1884," *Journal of the National Medical Association*, XLVII (May 1955), 207–11.

WILLIAMS, A. (ed.). "I Joined the Human Race: Negro Surgeon at Memorial Center for Cancer and Allied Diseases," *Saturday Evening Post*, CCXXVI (May 29, 1954), 17 ff.

WOODSON, CARTER G. *Negro Makers of History.* Washington, 1928.

YOUNG, M. WHARTON. "Edward Arthur Ballock, M.D., 1857–1948," *Journal of the National Medical Association*, XL (May 1948), 121.

YOUNGE, S. L. "Toussaint Tourgée Tildon, Sr., M.D., 1893–1964," *Journal of the National Medical Association*, LIV (June 1962), 565–67.

INTEGRATION IN HOSPITALS, MEDICAL SCHOOLS AND PROFESSIONAL ORGANIZATIONS

"A.A.A.S. Will Meet No More in Segregating Cities," *Journal of the National Medical Association,* XLVIII (March 1956), 129.

"Access to a Hospital for Every Race Doctor," *Journal of the National Medical Association,* XXXVIII (January 1946), 35–36.

ALEXANDER, W. G. "The N.M.A. Defense Fund," *Journal of the National Medical Association,* XVIII (January–March 1926), 33–34.

———. "Presidential Address," *ibid.,* XVIII (October–December 1926), 191–97.

"American College of Surgeons Admits Negro Candidates," *Opportunity,* XXV (January 1947), 29.

AMERICAN MEDICAL ASSOCIATION. *Minutes of the House of Delegates.* San Francisco, 1950.

———. *Summary of Actions of the House of Delegates, A.M.A., 117th Annual Convention, June 16–20, 1968, San Francisco, California: From the Office of the Executive Vice-President.* San Francisco, 1968.

AMMON, JOHN D. "The Negro Pharmacist in New York: 'His Growth,'" *Journal of the National Medical Association,* XXXII (March 1940), 87–88.

"Army Taboo on Negro Obstetricians?" *Journal of the National Medical Association,* XLIV (January 1952), 53–54.

"Association of American Medical Colleges Acknowledges Problem," *Journal of the National Medical Association,* XLVII (January 1955), 73–74.

BABOW, I. "Minority Group Integration in Hospitals: A Sample Survey," *Hospitals,* XXXV (February 1964), 47–48.

"Baton Rouge Hospitals Integrate," *Journal of the National Medical Association,* LVI (September 1964), 447.

BERRY, LEONIDAS H. *The Days of Our Year: An Assessment.* Address of the outgoing President of the National Medical Association at the 71st Annual Convention. Chicago, 1966.

"Bexar County [San Antonio, Texas] Admits Third Negro Member: No Negro Applicants for Dental Society," *Journal of the National Medical Association,* XLVIII (January 1956), 68.

BOURNE, GWENDOLYN. "Negro Nurses Need Opportunity To Make the Supply Balance the Demand," *Modern Hospital,* LXIV (March 1945), 76–77.

BOWEN, ELINOR M. "The Nurse's Part in Winning the War," *Journal of the National Medical Association,* XI (July–September 1919), 125–26.

BREWMAN, M. P. "Negro Nurse," *Nation,* CLXXV (August 23, 1952), 160.

"Briefs: National Association of Colored Graduate Nurses Disbands," *Journal of the National Medical Association,* XLIII (January 1951), 59.

"Britons' Lives in Colored Hands," *Ebony,* XVII (November 1961), 111–12.

BROOKS, A. N. D. "Science, U.S.A.," *Negro History Bulletin,* XXI (January 1958), 96 ff.

BROWN, L. G. "Experience with Racial Attitudes of the Medical Profession in New Jersey," *Journal of the National Medical Association,* LV (January 1963), 66–68.

———. "The Hospital Problem of Negro Physicians," *ibid.,* XXXIV (March 1942), 83–85.

CALVET, INIS. "Integration in Hospitals," *Interracial Review,* XXXV (July 1962), 163 ff.

CANNON, GEORGE E. "The Negro Medical Profession and the United States Army," *Journal of the National Medical Association,* XI (January–March 1919), 21–28.

CARNEGIE, M. E. "Impact of Integration on the Nursing Profession: Historical Sketch," *Negro History Bulletin,* XXVIII (April 1965), 55 ff.

———, and OSBORNE, E. M. "Integration in Professional Nursing," *Crisis,* LXIX (January 1962), 5–9.

CARTER, H. "He's Doing Something about the Race Problem," *Saturday Evening Post,* CCXVIII (February 23, 1946), 30 ff.

"Catholic Hospital Association Passes Anti-Discrimination Resolution," *Journal of the National Medical Association,* LV (September 1963), 440.

"A Challenge to Organized Negro Medicine," *Journal of the National Medical Association,* XXVI (January–March 1934), 31.

"Charleston County [South Carolina] Medical Society Admits Negroes," *Journal of the National Medical Association,* XLV (March 1953), 153–54.

"Charlotte Dentist Sues for Admission to North Carolina Dental Society," *Journal of the National Medical Association,* LII (May 1960), 207–10.

"Chicago Activity against Hospital Discrimination Continues," *Journal of the National Medical Association,* XLVII (July 1955), 264–67.

"Chicago Staff Appointments of Negro Physicians," *Journal of the National Medical Association,* LVII (November 1965), 514–15.

CHICAGO URBAN LEAGUE RESEARCH DEPARTMENT. "A Staff Working Paper on Integration in Hospital Appointments and Hospital Care." Report prepared for the workshops of the Second Imhotep National Conference on Hospital Integration, May 23–24, 1958. (Mimeographed MS in the Arthur A. Schomburg Negro Collection, Harlem Branch of the New York Public Library.)

"Children's Hospital, Washington, D.C., Accepts First Colored Physician," *Journal of the National Medical Association,* XLII (May 1950), 183.

CLARKE, S. M. "President's Address, Volunteer State Medical Association," *Journal of the National Medical Association*, XVIII (January–March 1926), 21–23.

COBB, WILLIAM MONTAGUE. "The Future of Negro Medical Organizations," *Journal of the National Medical Association*, XLIII (September 1951), 323–28.

———. "Hospital Integration in the United States: A Progress Report," *ibid.*, LV (July 1963), 333–37.

———. "Medico-Chi and the National Selective Service," *ibid.*, XXXVII (November 1945), 192–97.

———. "Negro Members of Specialty Boards and Fellows of Clinical Colleges," *ibid.*, XLVIII (July 1956), 273–80.

———. "The Negro Physician and Hospital Staffs," *Hospital Management*, LXXXIX (March 1960), 22–24.

———. "New Dawn in Medicine," *Ebony*, XVIII (September 1963), 166–68.

———. *Progress and Portents of the Negro in Medicine*. New York, 1948.

———. "The Pursuit of Excellence," *Journal of the National Medical Association*, LVI (September 1964), 432–44.

———. "Surgery and the Negro Physician: Some Parallels in Background," *ibid.*, XLIII (May 1951), 145–52.

——— (ed.). "Integration in Medicine: A National Need," *ibid.*, XLIX (January 1957), 1–71.

"Color and the A.M.A.," *Newsweek*, XXXII (July 12, 1948), 46.

COMMITTEE TO END DISCRIMINATION IN CHICAGO MEDICAL INSTITUTIONS. "What Color Are Your Germs?" *Journal of the National Medical Association*, XLVII (July 1955), 264–67.

"Cook County Physicians Association's Role in Illinois Hospital Segregation Ban," *Journal of the National Medical Association*, XLVIII (January 1956), 68.

CORNELY, PAUL B. "Segregation and Discrimination in Medical Care in the United States," *American Journal of Public Health*, XLVI (September 1956), 1074–81.

———. "Trend in Racial Integration in Hospitals in the United States," *Journal of the National Medical Association*, XLIX (January 1957), 8–10.

"The Crushing Irony of De Luxe Jim Crow," *Journal of the National Medical Association*, XLIV (September 1952), 386–87.

CUNNINGHAM, R. M., JR. "Jim Crow, M.D.," *Nation*, CLXXIV (June 7, 1952), 548–51.

DAILEY, U. G. "The Future of the Negro in Medicine," *Journal of the National Medical Association*, XXI (July–September 1929), 116–17.

———. "The Negro in Medicine," *ibid.*, XXXIV (May 1942), 118–19.

———. "The New Hospital Era," *ibid.*, XXII (July–September 1930), 167–68.

———. "Proposals with Reference to the Idea of a Negro College of Surgeons," *ibid.*, XXXIV (March 1942), 76.

"Dallas Hospital Admits Five Negro Physicians to Staff," *Journal of the National Medical Association*, XLVI (September 1954), 367 ff.

"The Dawn of a Better Day," *Journal of the National Medical Association*, XVII (October–December 1925), 209–10.

DETROIT COMMISSION ON COMMUNITY RELATIONS. *Racial Factors in Policy and Practice: Hospital and Bed Utilization, 47 Detroit Area General Hospitals*. Detroit, 1956.

"Difficulties in Wilmington, Delaware," *Journal of the National Medical Association*, XLII (March 1950), 117–18.

DINGELL, JOHN D. "Address, Sixth Imhotep Conference," *Journal of the National Medical Association*, LIV (July 1962), 505–7.

"Discrimination in North Carolina Hospitals," *Journal of the National Medical Association*, LV (January 1963), 57–58.

"Discrimination *v.* the Right to an Education," *New Republic*, CXIII (September 10, 1945), 318.

DODSON, DON W. "No Place for Race Prejudice," *American Journal of Nursing*, LIII (February 1953), 164–66.

DOUGLASS, J. H. "Racial Integration in the Psychiatric Field," *Journal of the National Medical Association*, LVII (January 1965), 1–7.

DREW, CHARLES R. "Letters to the Editor of J.A.M.A., January 13 and January 30, 1947," *Journal of the National Medical Association*, XXXIX (September 1947), 222–24.

DUMAS, A. W. "Address of the President," *Journal of the National Medical Association*, XXXII (September 1940), 186–91.

———. "The Negro Physician and National Defense," *ibid.*, XXXIV (January 1942), 36.

DUNSTAN, C. A. "President's Annual Address," *Journal of the National Medical Association*, XIII (April–June 1921), 125–28.

"Flood Tide for the N.M.A.," *Journal of the National Medical Association*, LIV (September 1962), 623–25.

"Fort Lauderdale, Florida, Hospital Controversy," *Journal of the National Medical Association*, LII (May 1960), 210.

"Forward Detroit," *Journal of the National Medical Association*, XLIV (March 1952), 146–47.

"Fourth Imhotep National Conference on Hospital Integration," *Journal of the National Medical Association*, LII (July 1960), 283–85.

FREEMAN, ANDREW A. "Hospital Integration in Columbus, Ohio," *Journal of the National Medical Association*, LI (July 1959), 301–2.

"The Future of the Negro Nurse," *American Journal of Nursing,* XLV (November 1945), 914.

GAGE, NINA D., and HAUPT, ALMA C. "Some Observations on Negro Nursing in the South," *Public Health Nursing,* XXIV (December 1932), 674–82.

GHEE, EUCLID P. "A Plea for the Admittance of Negro Doctors to Municipal Hospital Staffs," *Journal of the National Medical Association,* XXVIII (August 1936), 102–5.

GOLDSTEIN, R. L. "Negro Nurses in Hospitals," *American Journal of Nursing,* LX (February 1960), 215–17.

"Government Taboo on Negro Physicians?" *Journal of the National Medical Association,* XLIV (March 1952), 145.

"A Gratifying Accomplishment," *Journal of the National Medical Association,* XVIII (July–September 1926), 137–38.

GREEN, H. M. "Annual Address," *Journal of the National Medical Association,* XXII (October–December 1930), 191–93.

———. "The Annual Address to the National Hospital Association," *ibid.,* XXI (October–December 1929), 169–74.

———. "Our Hospital Problem," *ibid.,* XXVII (May 1935), 72–74.

———. "President's Address: The National Hospital Association," *ibid.,* XIX (January–March 1927), 16–21.

———. "President's Address to the National Hospital Association," *ibid.,* XXIII (October–December 1931), 154–57.

———. "Some Observations on and Lessons from Experiences of the Past Ten Years," *ibid.,* XXVI (January–March 1934), 21–24.

Guilford County, North Carolina, Medical Society Drops Racial Bars," *Journal of the National Medical Association,* XLVI (May 1954), 201.

GUNTER, L. M. "The Effect of Segregation on Nursing Students," *Nursing Outlook,* IX (February 1961), 74–76.

HADLEY, C. O. "President's Address before the Tennessee State Medical Society at Knoxville, Tennessee, June 21, 1910," *Journal of the National Medical Association,* II (July–September 1910), 176–79.

"H.E.W. Conference on Elimination of Hospital Discrimination," *Journal of the National Medical Association,* LVI (September 1964), 445–46.

"H.E.W. Responds to Demands Made by Poor Rally," *Medical Tribune* [New York] (June 27, 1968).

HIGGINS, W. H. "The President's Annual Address to the National Medical Association," *Journal of the National Medical Association,* XXIII (October–December 1931), 145–48.

HIRSCH, E. F. "The Hospital Care of Negroes and the Appointment of Negro Physicians to Medical Staffs of Hospitals in Chicago," *Proceedings of the Institute of Medicine of Chicago,* XXIII (November 15, 1960), 156–59.

"History of the Imhotep National Conference on Hospital Integration," *Journal of the National Medical Association,* LIV (January 1962), 116–19.

HOLLOMAN, JOHN L. S., JR. "Shalom," *Journal of the National Medical Association,* LIX (September 1967), 369–72.

"Hospital Council of National Capital Area Integration Policy Statement," *Journal of the National Medical Association,* LVII (March 1965), 165.

"Hospital Discrimination Must End!" *Journal of the National Medical Association,* XLV (July 1953), 284–86.

HOWARD, T. R. M. "The Role of the National Medical Association in a Changing Social Order," *Journal of the National Medical Association,* XLVIII (September 1956), 353 ff.

"Imhotep National Conference on Hospital Integration: Proceedings," *Journal of the National Medical Association,* XLIX (May 1957), 189–200.

"Imhotep National Conference on Hospital Integration: Proceedings," *Journal of the National Medical Association,* L (January 1958), 66–76; L (March 1958), 142–44; L (May 1958), 224–33.

"Integrating a Public Health Nursing Staff," *American Journal of Nursing,* LXV (April 1965), 100–102.

"Integration Advances in Veterans' Hospitals," *Journal of the National Medical Association,* XLVI (January 1954), 68.

"Integration Battle-Front," *Journal of the National Medical Association,* XLIV (March 1952), 149–50.

"Integration of Hospital Staffs and Medical Institutions in Louisville, Kentucky," *Journal of the National Medical Association,* LII (July 1960), 286–87.

"The Internist in Medicine among Negroes," *Journal of the National Medical Association,* XL (July 1948), 169.

"The Interracial Way," *Journal of the National Medical Association,* XXIII (April–June 1931), 93–94.

JASON, ROBERT S. "Our Hospitals and the Negro: Keynote Address of Imhotep National Conference on Hospital Integration," *Journal of the National Medical Association,* L (March 1958), 144–45.

JAVITS, JACOB K. "Challenge Hospital Segregation," *Journal of the National Medical Association,* LIV (July 1962), 504–5.

" 'Jim Crowing' Nurses," *Crisis,* XXXVII (April 1930), 123 ff.

"Johns Hopkins Medical School Open to Negro Students," *Journal of the National Medical Association,* LIV (March 1962), 262–63.

JONES, G. A. "A Survey To Determine the Extent of Hospital Discrimination in Pennsylvania: A Preliminary Report," *Journal of the National Medical Association,* LVI (March 1964), 206–7.

KENNEY, JOHN A. "The American College of Surgeons: Breaking Down Barriers," *Journal of the National Medical Association,* XXXVIII (January 1946), 32–33.

———. "The Hospital Idea Essentially Altruistic," *ibid.,* IV (July–September 1912), 193–99.

———. "It Can Be Done," *ibid.,* XXXIII (July 1941), 175.

———. "The Liaison Committee of the N.M.A.," *ibid.,* XXXIII (March 1941), 85–86.

———. "Medical Civil Rights: The Desire for Medical Equality," *ibid.,* LV (September 1963), 430–32.

———. "The Negro Doctor and Organized Medicine," *ibid.,* XXXI (November 1939), 252–53.

———. "The Negro Physician," *ibid.,* XXXI (May 1939), 126. Reprinted from *Bulletin of the Essex County Medical Society* (April 1939).

———. "The Negro's Position in Medicine," *ibid.,* XLI (January 1949), 31–32.

———. "Open Letter to Physicians, Pharmacists, Dentists," *ibid.,* II (January–March 1910), 47–49.

———. "A Plea for Interracial Cooperation," *ibid.,* XXXVII (July 1945), 121–24.

———. "Report of Survey of Hospital Committee, Inter-Racial Committee of Montclair, New Jersey," *ibid.,* XXIII (July–September 1931), 97–109.

KINGDON, F. "Discrimination in Medical Colleges," *American Mercury,* LXI (October 1945), 391–99; LXI (December 1945), 758–59; LXII (March 1946), 123 ff.

LACKEY, L. "The Detroit Medical Society in Civic and Community Activities," *Journal of the National Medical Association,* LV (November 1963), 485–87.

LANGER, E. "Hospital Discrimination: H.E.W. Criticized by Civil Rights Groups," *Science,* CXLIX (September 17, 1965), 355–57.

LEWIS, STEPHEN J. "The Negro in the Field of Dentistry," *Opportunity,* II (July 1924), 207–11.

"A Look at the Negro Physician," *Medical World News,* IX (August 23, 1968), 42–46.

LOTH, D., and FLEMING, H. *Integration, North and South.* New York, 1956.

"Louisiana Medical Association Calls For Dropping of Racial Bars," *Journal of the National Medical Association,* XLV (July 1953), 289.

McLEAN, F. C. "Negroes and Medicine in Chicago," *Proceedings of the Institute of Medicine of Chicago,* XXIII (January 15, 1960), 2–6.

McPHERSON, E. "The Role of the Negro in the Healing Professions in Contemporary America," *Journal of the National Medical Association,* XLVII (September 1955), 316–19.

MARCINICK, EDWARD. "Physicians, Hospitals and the Negro Patient," *Journal of the National Medical Association,* LV (July 1963), 346–49.

MASON, VAUGHAN C. "President's Inaugural Address," *Journal of the National Medical Association,* LIII (September 1961), 516–20.

MAUND, A. "New Day Dawning: Negro and Medicine," *Nation,* CLXXVI (May 9, 1953), 396–97.

MAZIQUE, EDWARD C. "Integration Enters Medicine," *Journal of the National Medical Association,* LI (September 1959), 381–87.

———. "The Negro Physician in a Sick Society," *ibid.,* LII (May 1960), 182–86.

MEAD, JAMES M. "Negro Nurses in Armed Forces," *Journal of the National Medical Association,* XXXVII (September 1945), 163.

MEDICAL COMMITTEE FOR HUMAN RIGHTS. *Health Rights News,* I–IV (1965–1968).

"Medical Society of the District of Columbia To Admit Negro Physicians," *Journal of the National Medical Association,* XLIV (September 1952), 389–90.

"Medico-Chirurgical Society Letter of Protest," *Journal of the National Medical Association,* XXXIX (March 1947), 80–81.

MELTSNER, M. "New Federal Court Decision Advances Desegregation of Professional Societies," *Journal of the National Medical Association,* LVI (March 1964), 204–5.

"Memphis N.A.A.C.P. Branch Rescinds Endorsement of Negro Hospital," *Journal of the National Medical Association,* XLIV (July 1952), 314.

"Milwaukee Hospital Integration Story," *Journal of the National Medical Association,* LI (July 1959), 300–301.

MINOR, NANNIE J. "Status of the Colored Public Health Nurse in Virginia," *Public Health Nurse,* XVI (May 1924), 243–44.

"Minutes of the Twenty-first Annual Meeting of the American Medical Association, Held in the City of Washington, May 3–6, 1870," *Transactions of the American Medical Association,* XXI (1870), 9–67.

MORRIS, H. H., JR., APPEL, K. E., and PROCOPÉ, J. L. "Psychiatric Community and Racial Integration in a General Hospital," *American Journal of Psychiatry,* CXIX (May 1963), 1049–54.

MORRIS, JOHN P. "The Denial of Staff Positions to Negro Physicians: A Violation of the Sherman Act," *Journal of the National Medical Association,* LII (May 1960), 211–15.

MORRIS, R. G., JR. "The Problems in Securing Hospital Staff Appointments for Negro Physicians in Chicago," *Journal of the National Medical Association,* LII (May 1960), 194–97.

MOTLEY, C. B. "Desegregation: What It Means to the Medical Professions and the Responsibilities It Places on the Negro Professional," *Journal of the National Medical Association,* LV (September 1963), 441–43.

MULLOWNEY, JOHN J. "Dentistry and Pharmacy as a Vocation," *Journal of the National Medical Association,* XXVIII (November 1936), 163–65.

————. "What Future Is There for the Negro Pharmacist?" *ibid.*, XXIV (July–September 1932), 127–29.

MURRAY, PETER MARSHALL. "Democracy Advances in Medicine," *Journal of the National Medical Association*, XLIII (November 1951), 396–99.

"N.A.A.C.P. Legal Defense and Educational Fund, Inc., Cases," *Journal of the National Medical Association*, LVII (November 1965), 513–14.

NATIONAL ASSOCIATION FOR THE ADVANCEMENT OF COLORED PEOPLE. *Fifty-eighth Annual Convention Resolutions, July 10–15, 1967, Boston, Mass.* Boston, 1967.

NATIONAL COUNCIL OF ARTS, SCIENCES AND PROFESSIONS, SOUTHERN CALIFORNIA CHAPTER. *A Survey of Discrimination in the Health Field in Los Angeles.* Los Angeles, 1951.

"The National Hospital Association," *Journal of the National Medical Association*, XVII (October–December 1925), 207–8.

"The National Hospital Association," *Journal of the National Medical Association*, XVIII (October–December 1926), 211.

NATIONAL MEDICAL ASSOCIATION BOARD OF TRUSTEES. *Report: Cooperation between A.M.A. and N.M.A. . . . 73rd Annual Convention of the National Medical Association, Houston, Texas, August, 1968.* Houston, 1968.

"The National Medical Association's Contribution to the Selma-Montgomery March," *Journal of the National Medical Association*, LVII (May, 1965), 243–44.

NATIONAL URBAN LEAGUE. *Report of the Hospital Committee.* Washington, 1963.

"Negro Doctors To Serve in Veterans' Hospitals," *National Negro Health News*, XIV (April–June 1946), 24.

"The Negro in Medicine Today," *Medical Tribune* [New York] (October 10, 14, 17, 21, 24, 1968).

"Negro Membership," *Journal of the American Dental Association*, LXXI (August 1965), 384.

"The Negro Nurse in 17 Agencies," *Public Health Nursing*, XXXIII (August 1941), 463–66.

"Negro Nurses in Public Health," *National Negro Health News*, XVII (January–June 1949), 14 ff.

"Negro Physicians and Office Facilities," *Journal of the National Medical Association*, LI (March 1959), 147.

"Negroes in Nursing Schools," *Modern Hospital*, LXIV (February 1945), 10.

"New Jersey Hospital Survey," *Journal of the National Medical Association*, XLII (May 1950), 183–84.

"New York County Medical Society Condemns Discrimination," *Journal of the National Medical Association*, XLIV (March 1952), 149.

"New York Hospital Association Anti-Discrimination Resolution," *Journal of the National Medical Association*, LV (November 1963), 560.

NEW YORK STATE ADVISORY COMMITTEE OF THE UNITED STATES COMMISSION ON CIVIL RIGHTS. *Report on New York City: Health Facilities.* Albany, N.Y., 1964.

"N.M.A. Activities: Interim Meetings," *Journal of the National Medical Association*, LIX (February 1967), 296–97.

"The N.M.A. Defense Fund," *Journal of the National Medical Association*, XIX (January–March 1927), 30.

"The N.M.A.: Review and Forecast," *Journal of the National Medical Association*, II (October–December 1910), 295–96.

"No Negro Nurses Wanted," *Crisis*, LII (February 1945), 40.

"No Time for Prejudice," *Journal of the National Medical Association*, XXXIII (July 1941), 175–76. Reprinted from the *Montgomery Advertiser* [Montgomery, Ala.] (June 18, 1941).

N.O.P.H.N. CONFERENCE ON THE EDUCATION AND EMPLOYMENT OF THE NEGRO PUBLIC HEALTH NURSE. "The Negro Public Health Nurse," *Public Health Nursing*, XXXIV (August 1942), 452–54.

"North Carolina Civil Rights Advisory Committee To Study State Health Programs," *Journal of the National Medical Association*, LIII (May 1961), 303–4.

"North Carolina Physicians Refuse Limited Membership," *Journal of the National Medical Association*, XLIX (March 1957), 115.

"North Carolina Points the Way," *Journal of the National Medical Association*, XVIII (January–March 1926), 26–27.

"Nurse Shortage Eases Color Bar," *Journal of the National Medical Association*, XLIV (November 1952), 469.

OPPENHEIMER, H. C. "Non-Discriminatory Hospital Service," *Mental Hygiene*, XXIV (April 1945), 195–200.

"The Palmetto Medical, Dental, Pharmaceutical Association," *Journal of the National Medical Association*, LV (January 1963), 88–92.

PEYTON, T. R. "The Negro Specialist and the Negro General Practitioner," *Journal of the National Medical Association*, LV (May 1963), 248–50.

PHILLIPS, GEORGE M. "The Public Mental Hospital: An Example of Minority Isolation," *Journal of the National Medical Association*, LVII (January 1965), 47–52.

PITTER, EVELYN. "The Colored Nurse in Public Health," *American Journal of Nursing*, XXVI (September 1926), 719–20.

"Plight of the Black Doctor," *Time*, XCII (August 23, 1968), 46.

POWELL, ADAM CLAYTON, JR. "Hospital Integration and Job Opportunity Equality—Goals for 1963," *Journal of the National Medical Association*, LV (July 1963), 338–41.

"Present Status of Negro Physician and Negro Patient," *Journal of the National Medical Association*, XXVII (May 1935), 79.

PRINGLE, H. F. "Color Line in Medicine," *Saturday Evening Post*, CCXX (January 24, 1948), 15 ff.

"Professional Pariahs," *Journal of the National Medical Association*, VI (April–June 1914), 99–101.

"Professional and Public Focus on Hospital Discrimination," *Journal of the National Medical Association*, LVI (January 1964), 95–96.

"Progress on Integration in Veterans' Hospitals," *Journal of the National Medical Association*, XLV (November 1953), 437–38.

"Progress in Kansas City," *Journal of the National Medical Association*, XLVII (May 1955), 199.

"Progress and Prejudice," *Journal of the National Medical Association*, VII (October–December 1915), 287.

"A Progressive Step," *Bulletin of the Hospital Council of Greater New York*, VIII (1952), 2.

QUIGLEY, JAMES M. "Meeting Challenge with Progress [Reprint of the C. V. Roman Public Health Lecture at the 52nd Annual Meeting of the John A. Andres Clinical Society, Tuskegee Institute, April 1964]," *Journal of the National Medical Association*, LVI (July 1964), 307–11.

"Racism Rules A.M.A. Policies," *Journal of the National Medical Association*, XLI (January 1949), 34–35.

RANN, E. L., and COBB, W. M. "The Imhotep Conference: Why a Conference," *Crisis*, LXX (May 1963), 274–75.

RAVITZ, M. J. "Integration of Nurses: A Latent Function of Hospital Discrimination," *Phylon*, XVI (Fall 1955), 295–301.

RAWLS, W. B. "The Discrimination Question," *New York Medicine*, IV (September 20, 1948), 23 ff.

"Recognition of the Negro Medical Profession in Public Health Work," *Journal of the National Medical Association*, XXVII (January–March 1935), 29.

"Recognition of the N.M.A.," *Journal of the National Medical Association*, XI (April–June 1919), 75.

"Red Cross Nurse Continues," *National Negro Health News*, XIII (October–December 1945), 8.

REID, LUCILLE. "Negro Nurses and Nutritionist Cooperate," *Public Health Nursing*, XXIII (November 1931), 548–50.

"The Relationship between N.M.A. and the A.M.A. and the Federal Government," *Journal of the National Medical Association*, XXXI (July 1939), 150–51.

"Report of the Liaison Committee [N.M.A.]," *Journal of the National Medical Association*, XXXIII (July 1941), 186–90.

"Requirements for Membership in the N.M.A.," *Journal of the National Medical Association*, XI (April–June 1919), 76.

"Resolution concerning Alleged Discrimination against Negro Physicians in Chicago Hospitals," *Journal of the National Medical Association*, L (January 1958), 66.

"Richmond Academy of Medicine Drops Bars," *Journal of the National Medical Association*, LVII (May 1965), 247.

ROMAN, C. V. "After Fifty Years—What and Whither?" *Journal of the National Medical Association*, VI (April–June 1914), 103–10.

RUSK, HOWARD A. "Negro and Medicine," *New York Times* (April 7, 1968).

SCHLEIFER, C. "Desegregation of a State Mental Hospital for Negroes: A Study of Staff Attitudes," *American Journal of Psychology*, CXXI (April 1965), 947–52.

"Scientists Avoid Atlanta as Segregation Protest," *Science News Letter*, LXVII (May 21, 1955), 328.

SCOTT, DORIS BELLE. "Negro Nurse in Industry," *American Journal of Nursing*, LII (February 1952), 170–71.

"The Second Imhotep National Conference on Hospital Integration, May 23, 24, 1958," *Journal of the National Medical Association*, L (September 1958), 381–83.

"Segregated Doctors," *Time*, LXXVIII (August 18, 1961), 36.

SEHAM, M. J. "Discrimination against the Negro in Medicine: A Paradox in the Democracy-Battlefront on Integration," *Journal of the National Medical Association*, LVI (March 1964), 155–59.

———. "Discrimination against Negroes in Hospitals," *New England Journal of Medicine*, CCLXXI (October 29, 1964), 940–43.

SMITH, EARL B. "Medical Justice and Injustice," *Interracial Review*, XXXV (November 1962), 254–55.

———. "Practical Aspects of Hospital Integration," *Journal of the National Medical Association*, LII (September 1960), 367–68.

SMITH, FREDERICK C. "Race Consciousness and the Blood Bank," *Journal of the National Medical Association*, XXXV (May 1943), 102.

SMITH, T. M. "A Half Century Review of the National Medical Association," *Journal of the National Medical Association*, XXXVI (September 1944), 139–42.

SNYDER, J. D. "Race Bias in Hospitals: What the Civil Rights Commission Found," *Hospital Management*, XCVI (November 1963), 52–54.

"Specialty Boards and Colleges," *Journal of the National Medical Association*, XLIV (January 1952), 55–56.

"The Status of the National Medical Association," *Journal of the National Medical Association*, XVI (July–September 1924), 198–201.

STAUPERS, MABEL KEATON. *No Time for Prejudice: A Story of the Integration of Negroes in Nursing in the United States*. New York, 1961.

STEVENS, RUTHERFORD B. "Interracial Practices in Mental Hospitals," *Mental Hygiene*, XXXVI (January 1952), 56–65.

STRITCH, SAMUEL CARDINAL. "Interracial Justice in Hospitals," *Journal of the National Medical Association*, XLVIII (March 1956), 133–34.

"Surgeons' Color Line," *Time*, XLV (June 11, 1945), 61.

SWAN, LIONEL F. "The Exigencies of the American Environment, 1967," *Journal of the National Medical Association*, LIX (September 1967), 373–77.

———. "Meeting the Challenges of Medicine Today," *ibid.*, LX (September 1968), 424 ff.

TAYLOR, HOLMAN. "Cooperation between Races in the Practice of Medicine," *Journal of the National Medical Association*, XXXIII (January 1941), 8–12.

TAYLOR, K. BEATRICE. "Nursing Problems in the South," *Journal of the National Medical Association*, XII (October–December 1920), 77.

"Ten Years of Integration in Nursing," *Nursing Outlook*, IX (September 1961), 533.

"Texas Medical Association and Negro Physicians," *Journal of the National Medical Association*, XLV (September 1953), 369–70.

THOMPSON, W. A. "The Negro in Medicine in Detroit," *Journal of the National Medical Association*, LV (November 1963), 475–81.

THOMS, ADAH B. "President's Address, National Association of Colored Graduate Nurses," *Journal of the National Medical Association*, XII (October–December 1920), 73–74.

"Three Washington Hospitals Open Staffs to Negro Physicians," *Journal of the National Medical Association*, XLVI (November 1954), 431.

TURNER, JOHN P. "The Negro Medical Doctor and Organized Medicine," *Journal of the National Medical Association*, XXXVI (November 1944), 202.

U.S. COMMISSION ON CIVIL RIGHTS. *Equal Opportunity in Hospitals and Health Facilities: Civil Rights Policies under the Hill-Burton Program*. Washington, 1965.

———. *Report of the United States Commission on Civil Rights*. Washington, 1961.

U.S. PRESIDENT'S COMMITTEE ON CIVIL RIGHTS. *To Secure These Rights*. New York, 1947.

WALLING, W. E. "Science and Human Brotherhood," *Independent*, LXVI (June 17, 1909), 1318–27.

WASHINGTON, BOOKER T. "Negro Doctor in the South," *Independent*, LXIII (July 11, 1907), 89–91.

"Washington Urban League Findings on Appointment of Negro Physicians to Hospital Staffs," *Journal of the National Medical Association*, LV (July 1963), 350–53.

WEEKES, LEROY R. "The Negro in the Practice of Medicine in Los Angeles," *Journal of the National Medical Association*, LV (January 1963), 61 ff.

———. "Professional Public Relations," *ibid.*, XLVI (January 1954), 57–62.

"What Color Is Death?" *Time*, XLVII (January 21, 1946), 56 ff.

"What Price Liaison?" *Journal of the National Medical Association*, XLIV (September 1952), 387–88.

WHITTICO, JAMES M., JR. "Close 'the Medical Gap,' " *Journal of the National Medical Association*, LX (September 1968), 427–31.

"Why a National Hospital Association?" *Journal of the National Medical Association*, XVIII (July–September 1926), 138–39.

WIERS, EDGAR SWAN, KENNEY, JOHN A., and PHILLIPS, CHARLES G. "The Inter-Racial Committee of Montclair, New Jersey: Report of Survey of Hospital Committee," *Journal of the National Medical Association*, XXIII (July–September 1931), 97–109.

WILKINS, R. "Nurses Go to War," *Crisis*, L (February 1943), 42–44.

"Wilmington, North Carolina, Physicians Sue for Hospital Privileges," *Journal of the National Medical Association*, XLVIII (May 1956), 201–2.

WOODSON, CARTER G. *The Negro Professional Man and the Community: With Special Emphasis on the Physicians and Lawyers*. Washington, 1934.

WRIGHT, C. H. "Negro Physician in Detroit," *Negro History Bulletin*, XXVII (February 1964), 109–10.

WRIGHT, L. T. "The Negro Doctor and the War," *Journal of the National Medical Association*, XI (October–December 1919), 195–96.

———. "The Negro Physician," *Crisis*, XXXVI (September 1929), 305–6.

GENERAL HEALTH STATUS OF THE NEGRO AND DISTRIBUTION OF DOCTORS AND NURSES

"A.M.A. Assailed on Opposition to Health Needs Mandate [Joint Statement of June 25, 1968, by the national leaders of three medical organizations]," *Health Rights News*, III (August 1967), 1 ff.

ACKARD, H. J. "Tuberculization of the Negro," *Journal of the National Medical Association*, IV (July–September 1912), 224–26.

"An Alarming Condition," *Journal of the National Medical Association*, XVI (January–March 1924), 28–29.

ALEXANDER, W. G. "Birth Control for the Negro . . . : A Fad or a Necessity?" *Journal of the National Medical Association*, XXIV (April–June 1932), 34–39.

———. "The Negro Health Program for New Jersey," *ibid.*, XXXIII (March 1941), 96–98.

ALLEN, KATHLEEN. "Some Medical Social Problems in Hospitals," *Journal of the National Medical Association*, XXVIII (February 1936), 42–45.

ALLEN, L. C. "The Negro Health Problem," *American Journal of Public Health,* V (March 1915), 194–203.

ALTEMUS, L. A. "Comparative Incidence of Birth Defects in Negro and White Children," *Pediatrics,* XXXVI (July 1965), 61–65.

ALTENDORFER, MARION E., and CROWTHER, BEATRICE. "Relationship between Infant Mortality and Socio-Economic Factors in Urban Areas," *Public Health Reports,* LXIV (March 18, 1949), 331–39.

"Anti-Tuberculosis Work among the Negroes of Philadelphia," *Journal of the National Medical Association,* XV (July–September 1923), 94–95.

BANTON, C. "Tuberculosis among Negroes," *Journal of the National Medical Association,* XXXI (May 1939), 105–6.

BENNETT, EMILY W. "The Work of a Rosenwald Nurse," *Public Health Nurse,* XXIII (March 1931), 119–20.

BETHEA, DENNIS A. "Some Significant Negro Movements To Lower Their Mortality," *Journal of the National Medical Association,* XXII (April–June 1930), 85–88.

["Better Health for Negroes"], *Journal of the National Medical Association,* VII (January–March 1915), 51–54.

BIRNIE, C. W. "The Influence of Environment and Race on Diseases," *Journal of the National Medical Association,* II (October–December 1910), 243–51.

BOUSFIELD, M. O. "Reaching the Negro Community," *American Journal of Public Health,* XXIV (March 1934), 209–15.

BOYLE, EDWARD MAYFIELD. "A Comparative Physical Study of the Negro," *Journal of the National Medical Association,* IV (April–June 1912), 134–38.

———. "The Negro and Tuberculosis," *ibid.,* IV (October–December 1912), 344–48.

BRADLEY, E. N. "Health, Hospitals and the Negro," *Modern Hospital,* LXV (August 1945), 43–44.

BRAILEY, M. E. *Tuberculosis in White and Negro Children.* New Haven, Conn., 1958.

BRENNER, JOSEPH, et al. *Children in Mississippi: A Report.* Atlanta, 1967.

BRUNNER, WILLIAM F. "The Negro Health Problem in Southern Cities," *American Journal of Public Health,* V (March 1915), 183–90.

BRYANT, BERTHA. "Five Years in a Negro Health Program," *Public Health Nursing,* XXVII (June 1935), 324–26.

CLAUSEN, J. A. "Drug Addiction," in R. K. MARTIN and R. A. NISBET (eds.), *Contemporary Social Problems.* New York, 1961.

COBB, WILLIAM MONTAGUE. *Fifty Years of Progress in Health.* Pittsburgh, 1950.

———. *Medical Care and the Plight of the Negro.* New York, 1947.

———. "The National Health Program of the N.A.A.C.P.," *Journal of the National Medical Association,* XLV (September 1953), 333–39.

———. "The Negro as a Biological Element in the American Population," *Journal of Negro Education,* VIII (July 1939), 336–48.

———. "The Physical Constitution of the American Negro," *ibid.,* III (July 1934), 340–88.

———. "Removing Our Health Burden," *Crisis,* LIII (September 1946), 268 ff.

COBBS, BESSIE E. "Health on Wheels in Mississippi," *American Journal of Nursing,* XLI (May 1941), 551–54.

COMMISSION ON CHRONIC ILLNESS. *Chronic Illness in a Large City: The Baltimore Study.* (*Chronic Illness in the United States,* Vol. IV.) Cambridge, Mass., 1957.

COMMITTEE ON TUBERCULOSIS AMONG NEGROES. *Tuberculosis among Negroes.* New York, 1937.

CONFERENCE ON MEDICAL CARE. *Report of the Conference on Medical Care, Washington, D.C., December 8–9, 1944.* New York, 1945.

CORNELY, PAUL B. "Distribution of Negro Physicians in the United States in 1942," *Journal of the American Medical Association,* CXXIV (March 25, 1944), 829 ff.

———. "Distribution of Negro Physicians in Urban Communities with Less Than 50,000 Negroes," *Journal of the National Medical Association,* XXXVII (January 1945), 81.

———. "The Economics of Medical Practice and the Negro Physician," *ibid.,* XLIII (March 1951), 84–92.

———. "Problems in Health and Medical Care for Negroes." (Mimeographed.)

———. "Race Relations in Community Health Organization," *American Journal of Public Health,* XXXVI (September 1946), 984–92.

———. "Trends in Public Health Activities among Negroes in 96 Southern Counties during the Period 1930–1939," *ibid.,* XXXII (October 1942), 1117–24.

COWLES, WYLDA, et al. "Health and Communication in a Negro Census Tract," *Social Problems,* X (Winter 1963), 228–36.

CRAWFORD, R. R., HELLINS, G. W., and SUTHERLAND, R. L. "Variations between Negroes and Whites in Concepts of Mental Illness and Its Treatment," *Annals of the New York Academy of Science,* LXXXIV (December 8, 1960), 918–37.

DAVIS, M. M. "Rural Accomplishments of Negro Public Health Nurses," *Public Health Nursing,* XXIII (June 1931), 270–71.

———, and SMYTHE, H. H. "Providing Adequate Health Service to Negroes," *Journal of Negro Education,* XVIII (Summer 1949), 305–17.

DAVIS, W. A. "Some Facts Relative to Negro Mortality in the United States," *Journal of the National Medical Association,* XXII (January–March 1930), 26–29.

"Detroit Reports on Racial Factors in Health Areas," *Journal of the National Medical Association,* XLVIII (September 1956), 258–60.

DORN, HAROLD F. "The Health of the Negro." Memorandum prepared for GUNNAR MYRDAL, *An American Dilemma.* New York, 1944.

DOWNES, JEAN. "A Study of Food Habits of Tuberculous Families in a Harlem Area of New York City," *Milbank Memorial Fund Quarterly,* XXI (April 1945), 16–18.

DRAKE, ST. CLAIR. "The Social and Economic Status of the Negro in the United States," *Daedalus,* XCIV (Fall 1965), 788–800.

DUBLIN, L. I. "Effect of Health Education on Negro Mortality As Shown by Metropolitan Life Insurance Company's Figures," *National Conference on Social Work Proceedings* (1924), 274–79.

———. "The Problem of Negro Health As Revealed by Vital Statistics," *Journal of Negro Education,* VI (July 1937), 268–75.

———, and LOTKA, ALFRED J. *Twenty-five Years of Health Progress.* New York, 1937.

DU BOIS, W. E. B. *The Health and Physique of the Negro American.* Atlanta, 1906.

———. "Postscript: Death Rate," *Crisis,* XXXIV (October 1927), 275.

———. "Postscript: Our Health," *Crisis,* XL (February 1933), 44.

——— (ed.). *Mortality among Negroes in Cities.* Atlanta, 1896.

———. *Social and Physical Condition of Negroes in Cities.* Atlanta, 1897.

DUMAS, A. W. "Address of the President," *Journal of the National Medical Association,* XXXII (September 1940), 186–91.

DUMMETT, C. O. "Dental Health Problems of the Negro Population," *Journal of the American Dental Association,* LXI (September 1960), 308–14.

DUNCAN, C. F. "Negro Health in Jacksonville," *Crisis,* LXIX (January 1942), 29–32.

ELLIS, E. "Tuberculosis among Negroes," *Crisis,* XLVI (April 1939), 112.

EMBREE, EDWIN R. "Negro Illness and Its Effect upon the Nation's Health," *Modern Hospital,* XXX (April 1928), 49–54.

ENGEL, LEONARD. "We Could Save 40,000 Babies a Year," *New York Times Magazine* (November 17, 1963).

ESHLEMAN, FANNIE. "The Negro Nurse in a Tuberculosis Program," *Public Health Nursing,* XXVII (July 1935), 375–78.

EWING, O. R. "Facing the Facts on Negro Health," *Crisis,* LIX (April 1952), 217 ff.

FISCHER, W. A. "Negro Health Week in Texas," *Survey,* XLV (October 16, 1920), 100–101.

FISHER, CONSTANCE. "The Negro Social Worker Evaluates Birth Control," *Birth Control Review,* XVI (June 1932), 174–75.

FIUMARA, N. J., *et al.* "Venereal Diseases Today," *New England Journal of Medicine,* CCLX (April 23, 1960), 863–68.

"For Those Who Need It Most," *Medical World News,* IX (March 8, 1968), 46 ff.

FORT, A. G. "The Negro Health Problem in Rural Communities," *American Journal of Public Health,* V (March 1915), 191–93.

FRANCE, JOSEPH J. "Presidential Address, Old Dominion Medical Society," *Journal of the National Medical Association,* IX (October–December 1917), 181–83.

FRIEDSAM, N. J., WHATLEY, C. D., and RHODES, A. L. "Some Selected Aspects of Judicial Commitments of the Mentally Ill in Texas," *Texas Journal of Science,* VI (January 1954), 27–30.

FRUMKIN, R. M. "Race and Major Mental Disorders: A Research Note," *Journal of Negro Education,* XXIII (January 1954), 97–98.

GARVIN, CHARLES H. "Negro Health," *Opportunity,* II (November 1924), 341–42.

———. "A Post-War Job for Negro Doctors," *Journal of the National Medical Association,* XXXVI (March 1944), 62–63.

"Ghetto Destroyed," *Time,* LXIV (August 23, 1954), 58.

GOLDSTEIN, MARCUS S. "Longevity and Health Status of the Negro American," *Journal of Negro Education,* XXXII (Fall 1963), 337–48.

———. "Longevity and Health Status of Whites and Non-Whites in the United States," *Journal of the National Medical Association,* XLVI (March 1954), 83–104.

GOWER, M. "Physical Defects of White and Negro Families Examined by the Farm Security Administration, 1940," *Journal of Negro Education,* XVIII (Summer 1949), 251–65.

GRANDY, C. R. "Negro Consumptive," *Conference of Charities and Corrections, National Proceedings* (1908), 134–40.

GRANNUM, E. S. "Medical Economics and the Negro Physician," *Journal of the National Medical Association,* LV (September 1963), 426–29.

GROSSACK, MARTIN M. (ed.). *Mental Health and Segregation.* New York, 1963.

GUZMAN, JESSIE PARKHURST (ed.). "Health and Medical Facilities," in *Negro Year Book.* New York, 1952.

HALL, JOHN B. "Negro Death Rate in Boston," *Journal of the National Medical Association,* XVIII (July–September 1926), 133–35.

HANSEN, CARL F. "Mental Health Aspects of Desegregation," *Journal of the National Medical Association,* LI (November 1959), 450–56.

HARRISON, S. W. "President's Address, Arkansas State Medical Association," *Journal of the National Medical Association,* VII (July–September 1915), 197–99.

"Health Campaign among Negroes," *American Journal of Public Health,* VII (May 1917), 510–11.

HERRING, B. D. "Pernicious Anemia and the American Negro," *American Practitioner,* XIII (August 1962), 544–48.

HICKMAN, S. B. "Health," *Journal of the National Medical Association,* VIII (July–September 1916), 142–44.

HIMES, NORMAN. "Clinical Service for the Negro," *Birth Control Review,* XVI (June 1932), 176–77.

HOFFMAN, F. L. "Cancer in the North American Negro," *Crisis,* XLIV (November 1937), 329–31.

HOLLINGSHEAD, A. B., and REDLICH, F. C. *Social Class and Mental Illness: A Community Study.* New York, 1958.

HOWARD UNIVERSITY. DEPARTMENT OF PREVENTIVE MEDICINE AND PUBLIC HEALTH. *Cultural Considerations in Changing Health Attitudes.* Washington, 1961.

HUBBARD, K. "Are There Any Blind Black Babies?" *Survey,* LII (April 15, 1924), 91–93.

"Hygiene among the Negro Population," *American Journal of Public Health,* V (January 1915), 81.

IVINS, S. P. "Psychoses in the Negro: A Preliminary Study," *Delaware State Medical Journal,* XXII (August 1950), 212–13.

JANIFER, CLARENCE S. "The Negro Infant Mortality Rate and What the Well-Baby Clinics Are Doing To Lower It," *Journal of the National Medical Association,* XXIII (October–December 1931), 168–69.

JANSON, DONALD. "Is Health Care a Right or [a] Privilege?" *New York Times* (July 2, 1967).

JOHNSON, C. S. "The Socio-Economic Background of Negro Health Status," *Journal of Negro Education,* XVIII (Summer 1949), 429–35.

JOHNSON, J. L. "The Supply of Negro Health Personnel: Physicians," *Journal of Negro Education,* XVIII (Summer 1949), 346–56.

JOHODA, MARIE. *Race Relations and Mental Health.* New York, 1960.

JONES, E. K. "Negroes Struggle for Health," *National Conference of Social Work Proceedings* (1923), 68–72.

KENNEY, JOHN A. "Health Problems of Negroes," *Journal of the National Medical Association,* III (April–June 1911), 127–35.

———. "Is the Negro More Susceptible to Syphilis Than the White Man?" *ibid.,* XXXVI (January 1944), 28–29.

———. "Shortage of Negro Doctors, with Special Reference to Residents and Interns," *ibid.,* XXXII (May 1940), 112–14.

———. "The Status of the Negro Doctor in the National Health Program," *ibid.,* XXXIII (January 1941), 29–30.

———. "Syphilis and the American Negro: A Medico-Sociologic Study," *ibid.,* II (April–June 1910), 115–17.

KENNEY, JOHN A., JR. "What the N.M.A. Can Do about the Shortage of Physicians," *Journal of the National Medical Association,* LV (January 1963), 46.

KISER, CLYDE V. "Birth Rates and Socio-Economic Attributes in 1935," *Milbank Memorial Fund Quarterly,* XVII (April 1939), 139–41.

KITAGAWA, EVELYN M., and HAUSER, PHILIP M. "Trends in Differential Fertility and Mortality in a Metropolis: Chicago," in E. W. BURGESS and D. J. BOGUE (eds.), *Contributions to Urban Sociology.* Chicago, 1964.

KLINEBERG, O. (ed.). *Characteristics of the American Negro.* New York, 1944.

KNOX, J. H. M., JR., and ZENLAI, J. "Health Problem of the Negro Child [a bibliography]," *American Journal of Public Health,* XVI (August 1926), 805–9.

LANDIS, H. R. M. "The Tuberculosis Problem and the Negro," *Public Health Nurse,* XIX (January 1927), 25–26.

LEWIS, JULIAN H. *The Biology of the Negro.* Chicago, 1942.

———. "Number and Geographic Location of Negro Physicians in the United States," *Journal of the American Medical Association,* CIV (April 6, 1935), 1272–73.

LOVE, A. G., and DAVENPORT, C. B. "A Comparison of White and Colored Troops in Respect to Incidence of Disease," *Proceedings of the National Academy of Sciences,* V (March 1919), 58–67.

LYONS, RICHARD D. "Hunger and Sickness Afflict Mississippi Negro Children," *New York Times* (March 25, 1968).

McGRAW, M. B. *A Comparative Study of a Group of Southern White and Negro Infants.* ("Genetic Psychology Monographs," Vol. X.) Worcester, Mass., 1931.

McKINNEY, GENEVIEVE H. "Comments on the Study of Negro Public Health Nursing," *Public Health Nursing,* XXIII (April 1931), 188.

McLEAN, H. V. "The Emotional Health of Negroes," *Journal of Negro Education,* XVIII (Summer 1949), 283–90.

McPHERSON, E. "The Health Program in Greenville, South Carolina, Negro Schools," *Journal of the National Medical Association,* XLIV (March 1952), 142–44.

MADDOX, G. L. "Drinking Behavior of Negro Collegians: A Study of Selected Men," *Quarterly Journal of Studies on Alcoholism,* XXV (December 1964), 651–68.

MALZBERG, BENJAMIN. "Mental Disease among Negroes in New York State," *Human Biology,* VII (December 1935), 417–513.

———. "Migration and Mental Disease among Negroes in New York State," *American Journal of Physical Anthropology,* XII (January 1936), 107–13.

"Maryland Commission Report Cites Negro Health Needs," *Journal of the National Medical Association,* LIV (March 1962), 259–62.

MAXCY, K. F. (ed.). *Rosenau Preventive Medicine and Public Health.* New York, 1956.

MAY, J. M. *The Ecology of Human Disease.* New York, 1958.

MAYER, J. "Food Habits and Nutritional Status of American Negroes," *Postgraduate Medicine,* XXXVII (January 1965), A110 ff.

———. "The Nutritional Status of American Negroes," *Nutrition Review,* XXIII (June 1965), 161–64.

MAYOR'S COMMISSION ON CONDITIONS IN HARLEM. "The Negro in Harlem." Unpublished report, New York, 1936.

MAZIQUE, EDWARD C. "Health Services and the Poor People's Campaign," *Journal of the National Medical Association,* LX (July 1968), 332–33.

MEDICAL COMMITTEE FOR HUMAN RIGHTS. *The American Health Care Crisis: Statement to the American Medical Association, Presented at the 117th A.M.A. Annual Convention in San Francisco, June 1968.* San Francisco, 1968.

MEDICAL TRIBUNE. *Health Manpower: Factors of Crisis.* New York, 1968.

"Medicine for the Mob," *Outlook,* LXXXV (February 2, 1907), 249–50.

MELTON, MARLI SCHENCK. "Health Manpower and Negro Health: The Negro Physician," *Journal of Medical Education,* XLIII (July 1968), 798–814.

"More Negro Doctors Needed," *World Tomorrow,* XVII (February 15, 1934), 85.

MOSELEY, J. E. "Cancer and the Negro," *Crisis,* LVI (May 1949), 138–39.

MOUNTIN, JOSEPH W. "Participation by State and Local Health Departments in Current Medical Care Programs," *American Journal of Public Health,* XXXVI (December 1946), 1387–93.

MYRDAL, GUNNAR. *An American Dilemma.* New York, 1964.

"N.A.A.C.P. Resolutions in Health Area," *Journal of the National Medical Association,* XLIII (September 1951), 342–43.

NATIONAL ADVISORY COMMISSION ON CIVIL DISORDERS. *Report: With a Special Introduction by Tom Wicker, of the* New York Times. New York, 1968.

NATIONAL ASSOCIATION FOR THE ADVANCEMENT OF COLORED PEOPLE. "Resolutions on Health," *Journal of the National Medical Association,* LI (September 1959), 401 ff.

NATIONAL HEALTH ASSEMBLY. *America's Health: A Report to the Nation.* New York, 1949.

"The National Medical Association Foundation, Inc.: A Comprehensive Health Plan Program for the Inner City," *Journal of the National Medical Association,* LX (March 1968), 138–44.

"The National Medical Association's Official Position on the Implementation of Comprehensive Care Units," *Journal of the National Medical Association,* LX (January 1968), 77–78.

"Need for Medics," *Ebony,* XVIII (November 1962), 98–99.

"Negro in Florida," *Time,* LIX (January 14, 1952), 71–72.

"Negro Health," *Journal of the National Medical Association,* XI (July–September 1919), 107–8.

"The Negro Menace to the Public Health," *American Journal of Public Health,* VI (June 1916), 607.

"The Negro and Public Health," *American Journal of Public Health,* IV (July 1914), 624–25. Reprinted from *Southern Workman* (May 1914).

"Negroes in the United States," *American Journal of Public Health,* V (April 1915), 378–79.

"Negro's Health," *Survey,* XLV (January 29, 1921), 637–38.

NELSON, HARRY. "Idea of Health Centers May Help All One Day," *Los Angeles Times* (May 19, 1968).

NICHOLS, FRANKLIN. "Opportunities and Problems of Public Health Nursing among Negroes," *Public Health Nurse,* XVI (March 1924), 121–23.

"N.M.A. President's Testimony in Support of H.R. 6675, Medicare for the Aged . . . before the Committee on Finance of the United States Senate, Tuesday, May 4, 1965," *Journal of the National Medical Association,* LVII (July 1965), 335–37.

"Our Preventable Death Rate," *Journal of the National Medical Association,* IX (January–March 1917), 28–29.

PARRAN, THOMAS. "Hospitals and the Health of the People," *Journal of the American Medical Association,* CXXXIII (April 12, 1947), 1047–50.

PASAMANICK, BENJAMIN. "Myths regarding Prevalence of Mental Disease in Negroes," *Journal of the National Medical Association,* LVI (January 1964), 6–17.

———. "Some Misconceptions concerning Differences in the Racial Prevalence of Mental Disease," *American Journal of Orthopsychiatry,* XXXIII (January 1963), 72–86.

PAYNE, H. M. "Leading Causes of Death among Negroes: Tuberculosis," *Journal of Negro Education,* XVIII (Summer 1949), 225–34.

PERKINS, J. E. "The Stage Is Set: A Program for More Effective Control of Tuberculosis in the United States," *Tuberculosis Abstracts,* XXVII (October 1954), 13.

PETTIGREW, ANN HALLMAN, and PETTIGREW, THOMAS F. "Race, Disease and Desegregation: A New Look," *Phylon*, XXIV (Winter 1963), 315–33.

PHILLIPS, J. H., and BURCH, G. E. "Cardiovascular Diseases in the White and Negro Races," *American Journal of the Medical Sciences*, CCXXVIII (July 1959), 97–124.

PINDERHUGES, CHARLES A. "Effects of Ethnic Group Concentration upon Educational Process, Personality Formation and Mental Health," *Journal of the National Medical Association*, LVI (September 1964), 407–14.

POINDEXTER, HILDRUS. "Handicaps in the Normal Growth and Development of Rural Negro Children," *American Journal of Public Health*, XXVIII (September 1938), 1048–52.

———. "A Morbidity Study of 271 Rural Negro Families in the Mississippi Delta," *Journal of the National Medical Association*, XXXI (March 1939), 59–66.

———. "Special Health Problems of Negroes in Rural Areas," *Journal of Negro Education*, VI (July 1937), 399–412.

"Poll of New Orleans Doctors Challenges Statements That School Integration Will Be Psychiatrically Dangerous," *Journal of the National Medical Association*, XLVIII (September 1956), 358.

POSTELL, W. D. "Mental Health among the Slave Population of Southern Plantations," *American Journal of Psychiatry*, CX (July 1953), 52–55.

PROCOPÉ, JOHN L. "The Colored Man and the Blue Cross," *Modern Hospital*, LXII (April 1944), 59.

"Public Health and the Negro," *Journal of the National Medical Association*, XV (October–December 1923), 271–72.

"Race and Disease," *Journal of the National Medical Association*, XL (November 1948), 259.

RAYFIELD, STANLEY, STIMSON, MARJORY, and TATTERSHALL, LOUISE M. "A Study of Negro Public Health Nursing," *Public Health Nurse*, XXII (October 1930), 525–36.

"Recognition of the Negro Medical Profession in Public Health Work," *Journal of the National Medical Association*, XXVII (January–March 1935), 29.

"Recommendations of a Special Committee of the National Medical Association to the Technical Committee on Medical Care, in Conference, U.S. Public Health Service Building, Washington, D.C., November 22, 1938," *Journal of the National Medical Association*, XXXI (January 1939), 35–36.

"Report on the Subcommittee To Co-ordinate Health Work among Negroes with the Activities of National Defense," *Journal of the National Medical Association*, XXXIII (January 1941), 37–38.

"Responsibility of the Negro Suffering with Syphilis and Gonorrhea," *Journal of the National Medical Association*, XXXIV (November 1942), 250.

RIDDLE, E. M. "Nurse Shortage: A Concern of the Negro Public," *Opportunity*, XXV (January 1947), 22–23.

RIVERS, EUNICE. "Health Work with a Movable School," *Public Health Nurse*, XVIII (November 1926), 575–77.

ROMAN, C. V. "Fifty Years' Progress of the American Negro in Health and Sanitation," *Journal of the National Medical Association*, IX (April–June 1917), 61–67.

———. "The Medical Phase of the South's Ethnic Problem," *ibid.*, VIII (July–September 1916), 150–52.

———. "The Negro Woman and the Health Problem," *ibid.*, VII (July–September 1915), 182–91.

———. "Racial Interdependence in Maintaining Public Health," *ibid.*, VI (July–September 1914), 153–57.

———. "Vitality of the Negroes: Comparison of Death Rate with That of the Whites," *ibid.*, II (July–September 1910), 180–81.

ROSE, G. "Cardiovascular Mortality among American Negroes," *Archives of Environmental Health*, V (November 1962), 412–14.

ROSS, M. "Health Hazards of Being a Negro," *Survey*, L (September 15, 1923), 617–19.

RUTLEDGE, A. "Wanted, a Grenfell: Medical Needs of the Southern Negro," *Outlook*, CLIV (April 2, 1930), 522–25.

SCHERMERHORN, R. A. "Psychiatric Disorders among Negroes: A Sociological Note," *American Journal of Psychiatry*, CXII (May 1956), 878–82.

SCHOLZ, B. W. "Medicine in the Slums," *New York State Journal of Medicine*, LXIII (July 15, 1963), 2132–38.

SEHAM, MAX. *Poverty, Illness and the Negro Child.* [Read by the Hon. Donald M. Fraser, of Minnesota, in the House of Representatives, March 25, 1968.] *Congressional Record*, 90th Cong., 2nd sess.

SEIBELS, ROBERT. "A Rural Project in Negro Maternal Health," *Human Fertility*, VI (April 1941), 42–44.

SHEPARD, C. H. "Reducing the Mortality of the Negro," *Modern Hospital*, XXVII (July 1926), 55–57.

SLEET, J. C. "In the Day's Work of a Visiting Nurse," *Charities and Commons*, XV (October 7, 1905), 73–74.

SLOAN, RAYMOND P. "Five Years of Negro Health Activities," *Modern Hospital*, XLVIII (April 1937), 47–52.

SMITH, ALAN P. "Mental Hygiene and the American Negro," *Journal of the National Medical Association*, XXIII (January–March 1931), 1–10.

SMITH, D. ALONZO, HOBDAY, SADIE S., and REID, E. LUCILLE. "Health Service in a Negro District," *Journal of the National Medical Association*, XXII (April–June 1930), 68–74.

SMITH, EARL B. "The Disappearing Pittsburgh Physician," *Journal of the National Medical Association,* LVII (May 1965), 229–30.

———, and FALK, LESLIE A. "Medical Care and the Negro in Allegheny County [Pennsylvania]," *Journal of the National Medical Association,* LV (July 1963), 322–25.

SPINGARN, ARTHUR B. "The War and Venereal Diseases among Negroes," *Journal of the National Medical Association,* XI (April–June 1919), 47–52.

STAMLER, J., *et al.* "Racial Patterns of Coronary Heart Disease," *Geriatrics,* XVI (August 1961), 382–96.

STUART, J. EARLE. "New Jersey State Health Program for Negroes," *Journal of the National Medical Association,* XXXIII (January 1941), 29–31.

SYDNOR, C. S. "Life Span of Mississippi Slaves," *American Historical Review,* XXXV (April 1930), 566–74.

"Syphilis and the Negro," *Journal of the National Medical Association,* XVIII (January–March 1926), 24–26.

TAYBACK, MATTHEW. "Demographic Trends in the South: Implications for Public Health Administration," *American Journal of Public Health,* XLVI (October 1956), 1297–1305.

TAYLOR, J. MADISON. "Remarks on the Health of the Colored People," *Journal of the National Medical Association,* VII (July–September 1915), 160–63.

TIPTON, F. "The Negro Problem from a Medical Standpoint," *New York Medical Journal,* XLIII (May 22, 1886), 569–72.

TRASK, JOHN W. "The Significance of the Mortality Rates of the Colored Population of the United States," *American Journal of Public Health,* VI (March 1916), 254–60.

TURNER, JOHN P. "National Negro Health Week: A Radio Broadcast," *Journal of the National Medical Association,* XXXVI (July 1944), 118–19.

TYSON, W. GEORGE. "The Incidence of Syphilis in Negroes," *Journal of the National Medical Association,* XXVII (February 1935), 8–10.

U.S. BUREAU OF THE CENSUS. *Current Population Reports.* ("Negro Statistics Series," November 14, 1949.) Washington, 1949.

———. *Historical Statistics of the United States: From Colonial Times to 1957.* Washington, 1960.

———. *Statistical Abstract of the United States, 1966.* Washington, 1966.

U.S. CHILDREN'S BUREAU. *The Health Situation of Negro Mothers and Babies in the United States,* by E. C. TANDY. Washington, 1940.

U.S. DEPARTMENT OF LABOR. *Technology and Manpower in the Health Service Industry, 1965–1975.* Washington, 1967.

U.S. HEALTH SERVICE. *The National Health Survey: 1935–1936.* Washington, 1938.

U.S. NATIONAL OFFICE OF VITAL STATISTICS. *Death Rates for Selected Causes by Age, Color and Sex: United States and Each State, 1949–1951.* Washington, 1959.

U.S. OFFICE OF ECONOMIC OPPORTUNITY. *Comprehensive Health Services Programs: Status Report, July 1, 1968.* Washington, 1968.

U.S. SELECTIVE SERVICE SYSTEM. *Physical Examinations of Selective Service Registrants during Wartime.* Washington, 1944.

U.S. SENATE. COMMITTEE ON FINANCE. "Statement of W. Montague Cobb, M.D., President of the National Medical Association, before the Committee on Finance of the United States Senate, Tuesday, May 4, 1965," in *Hearings before the Committee on Finance, United States Senate, on H.R. 6675.* 89th Cong., 1st sess., April 29–30, May 3–7, 1965.

VAN DER ZANDEN, J. W. "The Minority Group Patient," *Nursing Outlook,* XII (February 1964), 57–59.

"The Venereal Situation," *Journal of the National Medical Association,* XI (April–June 1919), 72–74.

WAGNER, PHILLIP S. "A Comparative Study of Negro and White Admissions to the Psychiatric Pavilion of Cincinnati General Hospital," *American Journal of Psychiatry,* XCV (July 1938), 167–83.

WALKER, JOHN W. "Tuberculosis in the Negro," *Journal of the National Medical Association,* XXII (January–March 1930), 19–21.

WASHINGTON, F. B. "Health Work for Negro Children," *National Conference of Social Work Proceedings* (1925), 226–31.

WEBSTER, THOMAS A. "Work, Wages and Welfare in Kansas City: Negro Health Status Improved in Ten Years," *Journal of the National Medical Association,* XLVII (September 1955), 353–54.

"Where Negroes Are Immune," *Literary Digest,* LXXII (February 18, 1922), 62.

WHITTED, HAROLD H. "Problems of the Negro in the Venereal Disease Control Program," *Journal of the National Medical Association,* XXXIII (July 1941), 168–70.

"Why Negro Veterans Lack Negro Doctors," *Outlook,* CXXXIV (July 18, 1923), 396–98.

WILLIAMS, E. Y., and CARMICHAEL, C. P. "The Incidence of Mental Disease in the Negro," *Journal of Negro Education,* XXVIII (Summer 1949), 276–82.

WILSON, R., JR. "Tuberculosis among Negroes," *Charities and Commons,* XXI (November 7, 1908), 248–49.

WITCHEN, E. *Tuberculosis and the Negro in Pittsburgh: A Report of the Negro Health Survey.* Pittsburgh, 1934.

WOODWARD, G. N. "Racial Health," *Journal of the National Medical Association,* XVI (July–September 1924), 177–79.

WOOFTER, T. J., JR. "Organization of Rural Negroes for Public Health Work," *National Conference of Social Work Proceedings* (1923), 72–75.

WORTIS, JOSEPH. "Psychiatric Problems of Minorities," *Journal of the National Medical Association,* XLIV (September 1952), 364–69.

YANKAUER, ALFRED, JR. "The Relationship of Fetal and Infant Mortality to Residential Segregation," *American Social Review,* XV (October 1950), 644–48.

YERBY, A. S. "The Role of the Public Health Physician in Social Welfare," *Health News* [New York State Department of Health], XXXVIII (February 1961), 4–11.

YOUNG, WHITNEY M., JR. *To Be Equal.* New York, 1964.

ZANTAI, PAUL. "The Health Problem of the Negro Child," *American Journal of Public Health,* XVI (August 1926), 805–9.

MEDICAL EDUCATION AND HOSPITAL FACILITIES

ADAMS, NUMA P. G. "The Fifth Year Training of the Negro Medical Student," *Journal of the National Medical Association,* XXIV (April–June 1932), 25–30.

——. "An Interpretation of the Significance of the Homer G. Phillips Hospital," *ibid.,* XXVI (January–March 1934), 13–17.

ALEXANDER, LESLIE L. "Provident Clinical Society of Brooklyn, New York: Historical Notes," *Journal of the National Medical Association,* LII (May 1960), 200–201.

ALEXANDER, W. G. "An Appeal to Teachers," *Journal of the National Medical Association,* XVI (April–June 1924), 115.

——. "Our Hospital Number," *ibid.,* XXII (July–September 1930), 165–67.

"Army Nurses," *National Negro Health News,* XII (January–March 1944), 7.

ASHFORD, MAHLON. "Medical Education for Minority Groups," *Journal of the National Medical Association,* XL (July 1948), 167–69.

BARRETT, W. H. A. "Hospital Symposium: The Missouri Hospital Situation," *Journal of the National Medical Association,* XXII (July–September 1930), 140–41.

BARTKER, N. "Medical Practice by the Unqualified," *Contemporary,* CXXIX (April 1926), 469–74.

BENT, MICHAEL J. "Negro Medical Students in the United States," *Journal of the National Medical Association,* XLIII (July 1951), 275–77.

"Better Mousetrap: Good Samaritan Hospital," *Time,* LII (July 26, 1948), 60.

"Better Preparation for the Practitioners of Medicine," *Journal of the National Medical Association,* XI (July–September 1919), 108–9.

BOUSFIELD, M. O. "Internships, Residencies and Post-graduate Training," *Journal of the National Medical Association,* XXXII (January 1940), 24–30.

BOWERS, JOHN Z., COGAN, LEE, and BECKER, E. LOVELL. "Negroes for Medicine: Report of a Conference," *Journal of the American Medical Association,* CCII (October 16, 1967), 213–14.

BRIGHT, M. H. "Hospital Symposium: The Houston Negro Hospital," *Journal of the National Medical Association,* XXII (July–September 1930), 148.

BROWN, CHARLES A. P. "The Health Careers Program of the Manhattan Central Medical Society," *Journal of the National Medical Association,* LVI (July 1964), 353.

BROWNE, H. A. "A Brief History of McRae Memorial Sanatorium," *Journal of the National Medical Association,* LIV (July 1962), 517–19.

BRYANT, CAROLYN. "The Cincinnati Clinic," *Birth Control Review,* XVI (June 1932), 177.

BUTTS, HUGH F. "Organization of the Psychiatric Day Hospital," *Journal of the National Medical Association,* LVI (September 1964), 381–89.

CALLIS, H. A. "Hospital Symposium: The Hospital in Modern Communities," *Journal of the National Medical Association,* XXII (July–September 1930), 145.

CALLOWAY, N. O. "A Medical Viewpoint on the Proposal To Place a Branch of Cook County Hospital on the South Side of Chicago," *Journal of the National Medical Association,* XLVII (March 1955), 128–31.

CARNEGIE, M. E. "Are Negro Schools of Nursing Needed Today?" *Nursing Outlook,* XII (February 1964), 52–56.

——. "The Path We Tread," *International Nursing Review,* IX (September–October 1962), 25–33.

CARY, J. J. "The Hospital Unit, Knoxville, Tenn.," *Journal of the National Medical Association,* XXXIV (May 1942), 131.

CASEY, ALBERT E. "Research Activity and Quality of Teaching in Medical Schools," *Science,* XCVI (July 31, 1942), 110–11.

CHESNEY, ALAN M. "Baltimore's Stake in Provident Hospital," *Journal of the National Medical Association,* XLVIII (March 1956), 130–32.

CLARKE, S. M. "President's Address, Volunteer State Medical Association," *Journal of the National Medical Association,* XVIII (January–March 1926), 21–33.

COBB, WILLIAM MONTAGUE. "Burrell Memorial Hospital, Roanoke, Virginia," *Journal of the National Medical Association,* LV (May 1963), 256–57.

——. "The Establishment, the Negro and Education," *Journal of the National Medical Association,* LX (July 1968), 320–31.

——. "St. Agnes Hospital, Raleigh, North Carolina, 1896–1961," *ibid.,* LIII (September 1961), 439–46.

——. "A Short History of Freedmen's Hospital," *ibid.,* LIV (May 1962), 271–87.

"Colored Hospitals," *Commonweal*, XXXVIII (October 1, 1943), 593.

COMMISSION ON HOSPITAL CARE. *Hospital Care in the United States*. New York, 1947.

COOPER, CHAUNCEY I. "Present and Future Prospects of Pharmaceutical Education," *Journal of the National Medical Association*, XXXII (January 1940), 6–10.

COOPER, EDWARD S. "The Mercy-Douglass Hospital," *Journal of the National Medical Association*, LIII (January 1961), 1–7.

———. "Report of the Council on Talent Recruitment," *Journal of the National Medical Association*, LX (January 1968), 74–75.

CORNELY, PAUL B. "Negro Students in Medical Schools in the U.S., 1955–56," *Journal of the National Medical Association*, XLVIII (July 1956), 264–66.

———. "Opportunities for Postgraduate Study for Negro Physicians in the South," *Journal of the American Medical Association*, CXVIII (February 14, 1942), 524–28.

CORWIN, EDWARD H. L., and STURGES, GERTRUDE E. *Opportunities for the Medical Education of Negroes*. New York, 1936.

COUNCIL ON MEDICAL EDUCATION AND HOSPITALS. "Hospitals and Medical Care in Mississippi," *Journal of the American Medical Association*, XII (June 3, 1939), 2317–32.

CROSS, R. J. "Hospital Symposium: Provident Hospital (Baltimore, Maryland)," *Journal of the National Medical Association*, XXII (July–September 1930), 144–45.

DAVIDSON, ARTHUR T. "A History of Harlem Hospital," *Journal of the National Medical Association*, LVI (September 1964), 373–80.

DAVIS, M. M. "Three Negro Hospitals: Their Growth and Service," *Modern Hospital*, XXXIX (September 1932), 55–60.

DELANEY, LEMUEL T. "Hospital Symposium: St. Agnes Hospital," *Journal of the National Medical Association*, XXII (July–September 1930), 135–36.

DELILLY, MAYO R. "The Julian W. Ross Medical Center," *Journal of the National Medical Association*, LV (July 1963), 261–67.

"Developing Specialists," *Journal of the National Medical Association*, XVII (January–March 1925), 34.

DIBBLE, EUGENE H. "Hospital Symposium: The John A. Andrew Memorial Hospital," *Journal of the National Medical Association*, XXII (July–September 1930), 137–39.

———, ROTH, LOUIS A., and BALLARD, RUTH B. "John A. Andrew Memorial Hospital," *Journal of the National Medical Association*, LIII (March 1961), 103–18.

DODD, R. A. "Training Negro Nurses," *Survey*, XLV (March 26, 1921), 926–27.

"The Douglass Hospital of Philadelphia," *Crisis*, III (January 1912), 118–20.

DOWNING, L. C. "Early Negro Hospitals," *Journal of the National Medical Association*, XXXIII (January 1941), 13–18.

———. "Hospital Symposium: Burrell Memorial Hospital," *ibid.*, XXII (July–September 1930), 158–59.

———. "The Small Hospital," *ibid.*, XVI (January–March 1924), 20–22.

———. "Some Points on Developing a Hospital," *ibid.*, XI (July–September 1919), 95–98.

DU BOIS, W. E. B. "Opinion: The Tuskegee Hospital," *Crisis*, XXVI (July 1923), 106–7.

———. "Opinion: Tuskegee and Moton," *ibid.*, XXVIII (September 1924), 200–202.

———. "Opinion: The Woman's Medical College," *ibid.*, XXVI (August 1923), 154.

DUMAS, A. W. "Address of the President," *Journal of the National Medical Association*, XXXII (September 1940), 186–91.

DUMMETT, C. O., and DIBBLE, EUGENE H. "Historical Notes on the Tuskegee Veterans Hospital," *Journal of the National Medical Association*, LIV (March 1962), 133–38.

DYSON, W. *Founding of the School of Medicine of Howard University, 1868–1873*. ("Howard University Studies in History," No. 10.) Washington, 1929.

"Educational Facilities for Colored Nurses," *American Journal of Nursing*, XXV (April 1925), 299–300.

"Educational Facilities for Colored Nurses, and Their Employment," *Public Health Nurse*, XVII (April 1925), 203–4.

ELDREDGE, ADDA. "The Need of a Sound Professional Preparation for Colored Nurses," *Journal of the National Medical Association*, XXIII (July–September 1931), 123–28.

"Fair Haven Infirmary," *Journal of the National Medical Association*, V (April–June 1913), 107.

FLEXNER, ABRAHAM. *Medical Education: A Comparative Study*. New York, 1925.

"For Negroes Only: Atlanta's Grady Memorial Hospital," *Time*, LIX (June 30, 1952), 64.

"For the Training of Negro Doctors," *Outlook*, CXXXVI (March 19, 1924), 462–64.

FRANKLIN, J. M. "Hospital Symposium: Prairie View Hospital," *Journal of the National Medical Association*, XXII (July–September 1930), 161–62.

FREEMAN, C. V. "Presidential Address: National Medical Association," *Journal of the National Medical Association*, XX (October–December 1928), 165–69.

GAMBLE, H. F. "Report of the Committee on Medical Education and Negro Medical Schools," *Journal of the National Medical Association*, I (October–December 1909), 257–58.

———. "Report on Medical Education," *ibid.*, II (January–March 1910), 23–29.

GARVIN, CHARLES H. "Hospital Symposium: The Negro Physicians and Hospitals of Cleveland," *Journal of the National Medical Association,* XXII (July–September 1930), 124–27.

————. "Post-War Planning for 'Negro' Hospitals," *ibid.,* XXXVII (January 1945), 28–29.

GOLDSTEIN, MOISE H., and MACLEAN, B. C. "A Hospital That Serves as a Center of Negro Medical Education," *Modern Hospital,* XXXIX (November 1932), 65–70.

GRANNUM, E. S. "Whittaker Memorial Hospital, Newport News, Virginia," *Journal of the National Medical Association,* LVI (March 1964), 119–23.

GREEN, H. M. "Annual Address of the President of the National Hospital Association," *Journal of the National Medical Association,* XX (April–June 1928), 90–93.

————. "Hospital Symposium: A Brief Study of the Hospital Situation among Negroes," *ibid.,* XXII (July–September 1930), 112–14.

————. "Hospital Symposium: Mercy Hospital," *ibid.,* XXII (July–September 1930), 147–48.

————. "President's Address: The National Hospital Association," *ibid.,* XIX (January–March 1927), 16–21.

"A Half Million Endowment for Meharry," *Journal of the National Medical Association,* XI (April–June 1919), 77.

HALL, OSWALD. "The Stages of a Medical Career," *American Journal of Sociology,* LIII (March 1948), 327–36.

HAMILTON, LUCILLE. "Hospital Symposium: Dunbar Memorial Hospital," *Journal of the National Medical Association,* XXII (July–September 1930), 151–52.

HANSEN, AXEL. "George W. Hubbard Hospital, 1910–1961," *Journal of the National Medical Association,* LIV (January 1962), 1–16.

HARNEY, B. C. H. "Provision for Training Colored Medical Students," *Journal of the National Medical Association,* XXII (October–December 1930), 186–90.

HEDRICK, ROBERT L. "Hospital Symposium: St. John Hospital," *Journal of the National Medical Association,* XXII (July–September 1930), 163.

HELSON, J. THOMAS. "Hospital Symposium: The New Provident Hospital and Training School," *Journal of the National Medical Association,* XXII (July–September 1930), 128–30.

HIGGINS, W. H. "The Necessity for Rural Hospitals," *Journal of the National Medical Association,* XXII (July–September 1930), 169–70.

HOFFLER, OSWALD. "Norfolk Community Hospital," *Journal of the National Medical Association,* LVIII (April 1966), 151–54.

HOGE, VANE M. "The National Hospital Construction Program," *Journal of the National Medical Association,* XL (May 1948), 102–6.

HOLIDAY, SADIE STEWART. "How the Negro Health Center in Tulsa Came To Be Built," *Public Health Nurse,* XXI (October 1929), 526–28.

HOLMES, M. R. "Hospital Symposium: Whittaker Memorial Hospital and School for Nurses," *Journal of the National Medical Association,* XXII (July–September 1930), 153.

"Hospital Symposium: Carson's Private Hospital," *Journal of the National Medical Association,* XXII (July–September 1930), 148–51.

"Hospital Symposium: The Home Infirmary," *Journal of the National Medical Association,* XXII (July–September 1930), 162.

"Hospital Symposium: Three Hospitals—Frederick Douglass Memorial Hospital and Training School; Wheatley Provident Hospital; General Hospital No. 2," *Journal of the National Medical Association,* XXII (July–September 1930), 155.

"Hospital Symposium: The Van Buren Sanitarium and Training School for Nurses," *Journal of the National Medical Association,* XXII (July–September 1930), 156.

"Hospital and Training-School Items," *American Journal of Nursing,* I (February 1901), 369.

"How the Shoemaker Clinic Is Serving Cincinnati's Negro Quarter," *Modern Hospital,* XXX (January 1928), 142.

"Howard and Meharry Internship Appointments, 1965–66," *Journal of the National Medical Association,* LVII (July 1965), 321–23.

"Howard and Meharry Internship Appointments, 1966–67," *ibid.,* LVIII (September 1966), 384–86.

"Howard and Meharry Internship Appointments, 1967–68," *ibid.,* LIX (September 1967), 380–82.

"Howard and Meharry Internship Appointments, 1968–69," *ibid.,* LX (July 1968), 337–39.

HUBBARD, GEORGE W. "Yesterday, Today and Tomorrow," *Journal of the National Medical Association,* I (July–September 1909), 133.

JACKSON, ALGERNON BRASHEAR. "Hospital Symposium: Hospitals and Health," *Journal of the National Medical Association,* XXII (July–September 1930), 115–19.

JACKSON, E. A. "The Need of Better Hospital Facilities among Our People," *Journal of the National Medical Association,* XIII (January–March 1921), 57–58.

"John A. Andrew Memorial Hospital," *Journal of the National Medical Association,* V (April–June 1913), 89–94.

JOHNSON, LEONARD W. "History of the Education of Negro Physicians," *Journal of Medical Education,* XLII (May 1967), 439–46.

JOHNSON, WAVERLY B. "Red Cross Hospital, Louisville, Kentucky," *Journal of the National Medical Association,* LVII (July 1965), 332–34.

JOSIAH MACY, JR., FOUNDATION. *Preparation for Medical Education in the Traditionally Negro College Recruitment-Guidance-Curriculum: Summary Report of a Macy Conference, Atlanta, Georgia, February 25–27, 1968.* New York, 1968.

KANE, FRANCIS FISHER. "How Success Was Achieved in [a] Drive for [a] Negro Hospital," *Modern Hospital,* XXXII (February 1929), 73–78.

KENNEY, HOWARD W. "Tuskegee Veterans Administration Hospital: Present and Future," *Journal of the National Medical Association,* LIV (March 1962), 139–45.

KENNEY, JOHN A. "The First Graduating Class of the Tuskegee School of Midwifery," *Journal of the National Medical Association,* XXXIV (May 1942), 107–9.

———. "Fort Huachuca Is Tops," *ibid.,* XXXVI (July 1944), 130.

———. "Hospital Symposium: Kenney Memorial Hospital," *ibid.,* XXII (July–September 1930), 156–57.

———. "Hospital Symposium: The Negro Hospital Renaissance," *ibid.,* XXII (July–September 1930), 109–12.

———. "The Proposed Development of Teaching for Negro Personnel in Psychiatry," *ibid.,* XXXII (January 1940), 34.

———. "A Reasonable Program for Our Hospitalization Movement," *ibid.,* XXIII (October–December 1931), 158–60.

———. "Some Facts concerning the Medical Education of the Negro," *National Conference on Social Work Proceedings* (1928), 180–83.

———. "Some Facts concerning Negro Nurses' Training Schools and Their Graduates," *Journal of the National Medical Association,* XI (April–June 1919), 53–68.

KLARMAN, H. E. *Hospital Care in New York City: The Role of Voluntary and Municipal Hospitals.* New York, 1963.

KNIGHT, H. W. "Hospital Symposium: Flint-Goodrich Hospital," *Journal of the National Medical Association,* XXII (July–September 1930), 130–31.

LAWLAH, JOHN W. "How the Facilities of Our Medical Schools Could Be Enlarged To Meet the Prospective Shortage of Negro Doctors," *Journal of the National Medical Association,* XXXV (January 1943), 27–29.

"Leonard Hospital," *Journal of the National Medical Association,* V (April–June 1913), 86–89.

LYNCH, C. MAUD H. "The Negro College and Nursing," *American Journal of Nursing,* XLV (April 1945), 307–8.

LYTTLE, HULDA M. "A School for Negro Nurses at the George W. Hubbard Hospital and Meharry Medical College, Nashville, Tennessee," *American Journal of Nursing,* XXXIX (February 1939), 133–38.

McBRAYER, L. B. "Health Training in North Carolina with a Touch of Color," *Hygeia,* IV (June 1926), 309–12.

McCUISTION, FRED. *Graduate Instruction for the Negroes in the United States.* Nashville, Tenn., 1939.

McFALL, T. CARR. "Needs for Hospital Facilities and Physicians in Thirteen Southern States," *Journal of the National Medical Association,* XLII (July 1950), 235–36.

MANLEY, FLOSSIE. "Training and Opportunities for Colored Nurses," *American Journal of Nursing,* XXIII (June 1923), 784–85.

MARIA, SISTER. "History of St. Martin de Porres Hospital, Mobile, Alabama," *Journal of the National Medical Association,* LVI (July 1964), 303–6.

MASSEY, G. ESTELLE. "The Negro Nurse Student," *American Journal of Nursing,* XXXIV (August 1934), 806–10.

MATHEWS, HENRY B. "Provident Hospital: Then and Now," *Journal of the National Medical Association,* LIII (May 1961), 209–24.

"Meharry, Hartshorn and Walden," *Crisis,* XXVI (July 1923), 122–24.

"Mercy Hospital," *Journal of the National Medical Association,* I (January–March 1909), 43.

"Merited Recognition," *Modern Hospital,* LVII (September 1941), 50.

MINTON, HENRY M. "Hospital Symposium: Mercy Hospital," *Journal of the National Medical Association,* XXII (July–September 1930), 119–21.

MINTON, RUSSELL F. "History of Mercy-Douglass Hospital," *Journal of the National Medical Association,* XLIII (May 1951), 153–59.

MULLOWNEY, JOHN J. "First Formal Instruction in Dentistry in America," *Journal of the National Medical Association,* XXVIII (November 1936), 165–68.

———. "Hospital Symposium: The New Meharry Medical College Plant," *ibid.,* XXII (July–September 1930), 146–47.

MURRAY, PETER MARSHALL. "Hospital Symposium: The Hospitals in New York State and Harlem," *Journal of the National Medical Association,* XXII (July–September 1930), 132–33.

NATIONAL MEDICAL FELLOWSHIPS, INC. *New Opportunities for Negroes in Medicine.* Chicago, 1962.

———. *Newsletter* [Downer's Grove, Ill.] (January 1968).

———. *Opportunities for Negroes in Medicine.* Chicago, 1959.

"Negro Hospital Fund," *Literary Digest,* CXVIII (February 2, 1935), 22.

"Negro Hospital Needs and How They Should Be Met," *Modern Hospital,* XXXV (September 1930), 86.

"The New Community Hospital of Evanston, Illinois," *Journal of the National Medical Association,* XLV (January 1953), 74–75; XLV (March 1953), 154–56.

"New Hospital for Howard," *Journal of the National Medical Association*, L (July 1958), 295–96.

"New Hospital Opened Today," *Journal of the National Medical Association*, III (January–March 1911), 105–7.

"A New York Hospital," *Journal of the National Medical Association*, IV (April–June 1912), 143–44.

N.M.A. COMMISSION ON MEDICAL EDUCATION. *Final Report of the Commission on Medical Education*. New York, 1932.

"N.M.A. Commission on Medical Education: Sixth Annual Report of the Commission on Medical Education of the National Medical Association," *Journal of the National Medical Association*, XV (January–March 1923), 53–58.

OLESEN, ROBERT. "Better Training for Negroes," *Modern Hospital*, LIII (August 1939), 61.

"An Open Letter to the Members of the Medical Profession," *Journal of the National Medical Association*, XVIII (April–June 1926), 109.

"Opening of State Hospital for Colored Insane in West Virginia," *Journal of the National Medical Association*, XVIII (July–September 1926), 136–37.

"Our Hospital Problem," *Journal of the National Medical Association*, XXI (July–September 1929), 114–16.

"Our Medical Schools Again," *Journal of the National Medical Association*, XVI (January–March 1924), 29–30.

"Out of the Basement," *Time*, LIX (June 16, 1952), 78 ff.

"Out of the Mud," *Time*, XXXVII (January 20, 1941), 56–57.

PERRY, E. P. "Riverside General Hospital," *Journal of the National Medical Association*, LVII (May 1965), 258–63.

PERRY, J. E. "Hospital Symposium: Kansas City [Missouri] Hospital," *Journal of the National Medical Association*, XXII (July–September 1930), 127.

PINN, PETRA. "Hospital Symposium: Working Benevolent Society Hospital," *Journal of the National Medical Association*, XXII (July–September 1930), 147.

PITTMAN, J. H. "Education and Organization," *Journal of the National Medical Association*, XXXIV (September 1942), 216.

"A Plea for More Hospitals for Negroes," *Modern Hospital*, XXV (August 1925), 126.

"A Plea for Support of Our Medical Schools," *Journal of the National Medical Association*, XV (October–December 1923), 273–74.

PROCOPÉ, JOHN L. "Mercy-Douglass Hospital Today," *Journal of the National Medical Association*, LIII (January 1961), 8–11.

QUIMBY, JENNIE. "A School for White and Colored Students," *American Journal of Nursing*, XXVII (May 1927), 359–60.

"A Recommended Hospital Program," *Journal of the National Medical Association*, XXIII (July–September 1931), 140–43.

REID, J. L. "Hospital Symposium: People's Hospital," *Journal of the National Medical Association*, XXII (July–September 1930), 164.

"Report of Committee on Medical Education in Colored Hospitals," *Journal of the National Medical Association*, II (October 1910), 283–91.

RIDDLE, E. M. "Our Staff Goes to College," *American Journal of Nursing*, XLI (July 1941), 764.

ROBERTS, A. "Nursing Education and Opportunities for the Colored Nurse," *National Conference on Social Work Proceedings* (1928), 183–85.

ROBERTS, CARL GLENNIS. "Hospital Symposium: Hospitals in Chicago," *Journal of the National Medical Association*, XXII (July–September 1930), 122–24.

ROBERTSON, A. W. "Where Federal Money Aids a Private School: Freedmen's Hospital," *U.S. News and World Report*, XLV (July 4, 1958), 83–85.

RODGERS, SAMUEL U. "Kansas City General Hospital No. 2," *Journal of the National Medical Association*, LIV (September 1962), 525–44.

ROMAN, C. V. "An Appeal to Meharry Alumni," *Journal of the National Medical Association*, III (January–March 1911), 21–24.

——. "Hospital Symposium: The Hospital Situation in Nashville, Tenn.," *ibid.*, XXII (July–September 1930), 131.

——. *Meharry Medical College: A History*. Nashville, Tenn., 1934.

ROSS, M. "Improved Negro Hospital Facilities Is Hopeful Sign for the South," *Modern Hospital*, XXXIX (October 1932), 53–60.

"Rotary-Started Hospital for Negroes: Asheville Colored Hospital," *Rotarian*, LXV (August 1944), 20–21.

"Sarah Goodridge Hospital, New Orleans, Louisiana," *Journal of the National Medical Association*, V (April–June 1913), 94–95.

"Scholarships for Negro Medical Students," *School and Society*, X (September 20, 1919), 344–45.

SEBASTIAN, S. P. "Hospital Symposium: The L. Richardson Memorial Hospital," *Journal of the National Medical Association*, XXII (July–September 1930), 142–44.

SHANAHAN, T. J. "Negroes in Nursing Education: A Report on Catholic Hospitals," *Hospital Progress*, XLII (July 1961), 100–102.

SHEPARD, C. H. "Hospital Symposium: The Lincoln Hospital," *Journal of the National Medical Association*, XXII (July–September 1930), 139–40.

SLOAN, RAYMOND P. "Parkside Teaches—Learns, Too," *Modern Hospital*, LII (April 1939), 57–59.

"Southern Hospital Facilities for Negroes," *Survey*, LXXXVIII (April 1952), 178–79.

"A Spark—a Flame—a Beacon Light: The Holy Family Hospital, Ensley, Alabama," *Journal of the National Medical Association,* LV (January 1963), 86–88.

STEPTO, ROBERT C. "Recruitment for Medicine by National Medical Fellowships, Inc.," *Journal of the National Medical Association,* LVII (November 1965), 444–46.

TAYLOR, A. W. "Meharry Ponders Offers," *Christian Century,* LXV (May 5, 1948), 429.

"Trends in Characteristics of M.C.A.T. Examinee Population, 1962–1967," *Journal of the National Medical Association,* LX (July 1968), 317.

TURNER, JOHN A. "Hospital Symposium: The Dentist in the Hospital," *Journal of the National Medical Association,* XXII (July–September 1930), 157–58.

UNITED COMMUNITY SERVICES: SOCIAL PLANNING COUNCIL. *A Study of Negro Hospital Facilities and Service.* Charlotte, N.C., 1954.

U.S. OFFICE OF EDUCATION. *Nurses' Training Schools, 1917–1918.* Washington, 1919.

"The U.S. Veterans Hospital, Tuskegee, Ala.: Colonel Joseph Henry Ward," *Journal of the National Medical Association,* XXI (April–June 1929), 65–67.

VAN DE VREDE, JANE. "The Need for Negro Public Health Nurses and the Provision Being Made To Meet It," *Journal of the National Medical Association,* XIII (January–March 1921), 55–57.

VENABLE, H. PHILIP. "The History of Homer G. Phillips Hospital," *Journal of the National Medical Association,* LIII (November 1961), 541–55.

"The Veterans Hospital," *Journal of the National Medical Association,* XV (July–September 1923), 203–4.

WALLACE, WILLIAM. "Hospital Symposium: Mercy Sanitarium," *Journal of the National Medical Association,* XXII (July–September 1930), 153–54.

"Wanted: A Hospital in New York," *Journal of the National Medical Association,* I (April–June 1909), 104–5.

WARD, J. H. "Hospital Symposium: U.S. Veterans Hospital," *Journal of the National Medical Association,* XXII (July–September 1930), 133–34.

WARFIELD, W. A. "Hospital Symposium: Some Educational Advantages of the Freedmen's Hospital and Asylum, Now a Prime Factor in Training Physicians and Nurses," *Journal of the National Medical Association,* XXII (July–September 1930), 141–42.

WARLICK, LULA G. "Hospital Symposium: New Nurses' Home of Mercy Hospital and School for Nurses," *Journal of the National Medical Association,* XXII (July–September 1930), 121.

WATTS, CHARLES D. "Lincoln Hospital of Durham, North Carolina: A Short History," *Journal of the National Medical Association,* LVII (March 1965), 177–82.

WESLEY, CHARLES H. "The First Commencement of the School of Medicine," *Howard Alumnus,* V (March 1927), 135 ff.

"The West Virginia State Colored Tuberculosis Sanatorium," *Journal of the National Medical Association,* XI (January–March 1919), 19.

WILLIS, FLOYD W. "Hospital Symposium: The Willis Physiotherapeutic Sanitarium," *Journal of the National Medical Association,* XXII (July–September 1930), 159–61.

"Women Physicians Graduated from Howard University, 1872–1967," *Journal of the National Medical Association,* LX (March 1968), 152–54.

"Women Physicians Graduated from Meharry Medical College, 1891–1967," *ibid.,* LX (March 1968), 154–55.

YERBY, A. S., and YURCHENCO, B. "Blueprint for Group Medical Centers," *Modern Hospital,* LXXXIII (December 1954), 88–96.

HISTORICAL REFERENCES

APTHEKER, HERBERT. *To Be Free: Studies in Negro History.* New York, 1948.

———. *Toward Negro Freedom.* New York, 1956.

——— (ed.). *A Documentary History of the Negro People in the United States.* New York, 1951.

ASHBURN, P. M. *The Ranks of Death: A Medical History of the Conquest of America.* New York, 1947.

BARBER, J. MAX. "The Philadelphia Negro Dentist," *Crisis,* VII (February 1914), 179–80.

BLANTON, W. B. *Medicine in Virginia in the Eighteenth Century.* Richmond, Va., 1931.

———. *Medicine in Virginia in the Nineteenth Century.* Richmond, Va., 1933.

BOTKIN, B. A. (ed.). *Lay My Burden Down: A Folk History of Slavery.* Chicago, 1945.

BOUSFIELD, M. O. "An Account of Physicians of Color in the United States," *Bulletin of the History of Medicine,* XVII (January 1945), 61–84.

BRASFIELD, EGBERT HAYWOOD. "The History and Problems of the Dental Profession," *Journal of the National Medical Association,* XI (January 1919), 103–4.

BRAWLEY, B. *A Short History of the American Negro.* New York, 1919.

BROUGH, C. H. "Work on the Commission of Southern Universities on the Race Question," *Annals of the American Academy of Political and Social Science,* XLIX (September 1913), 47–57.

BROWN, SARA W. "Colored Women Physicians," *Journal of the National Medical Association,* XVI (July–September 1924), 229.

CALDWELL, A. B. (ed.). *History of the American Negro.* Vol. III. Atlanta, 1919.

"Can a Colored Woman Be a Physician?" *Crisis,* XL (February 1933), 33–34.

CHAMBERS, L. A. (ed.). *America's Tenth Man: A Pictorial Review of One-Tenth of a Nation.* New York, 1957.

COBB, WILLIAM MONTAGUE. *The First Negro Medical Society: A History of the Medico-Chirurgical Society of the District of Columbia, 1884–1939.* Washington, 1939.

"Colored Doctors," *Commonweal,* XIX (January 12, 1934), 284.

"The Colored Specialist," *Journal of the National Medical Association,* XVII (April–June 1925), 72–73.

"David Ruggles' Water Cure Establishment," *North Star* [Rochester, N.Y.] (January 28, 1848). (Advertisement.)

DELANY, MARTIN R. *The Condition, Elevation, Emigration and Destiny of the Colored People of the United States, Politically Considered.* Philadelphia, 1852.

DEUTSCH, A. "The First U.S. Census of the Insane . . . and Its Use as Proslavery Propaganda," *Bulletin of the History of Medicine,* XV (May 1944), 469–82.

"Dr. Jackson and the Tulsa, Oklahoma, Riots," *Journal of the National Medical Association,* XIII (July–September 1921), 202–3.

DUMMETT, C. O. *The Growth and Development of the Negro in Dentistry in the United States.* Chicago, 1952.

DUMOND, D. L. *Antislavery: The Crusade for Freedom in America.* Ann Arbor, Mich., 1961.

EDWARDS, G. F. *The Negro Professional Class.* Glencoe, Ill., 1959.

FILLER, L. *The Crusade against Slavery, 1830–1860.* New York, 1960.

FLEXNER, J. T. *Doctors on Horseback: Pioneers of American Medicine.* New York, 1937.

FONER, P. S. *The Life and Writings of Frederick Douglass.* New York, 1950.

FORTUNE, F. W. "The Negro Physician," *Journal of the National Medical Association,* XXXI (May 1939), 107–10.

FRANKLIN, J. H. *From Slavery to Freedom: A History of the American Negro.* New York, 1947.

FRAZIER, E. FRANKLIN. *The Negro in the United States.* New York, 1965.

GUTHRIE, DOUGLAS. *A History of Medicine.* Philadelphia, 1946.

HAGGARD, HOWARD W. *The Doctor in History.* New Haven, Conn., 1934.

HOGAN, W. R., and DAVIS, E. H. (eds.). *William Johnson's Natchez: The Antebellum Diary of a Free Negro.* Baton Rouge, 1951.

HUBERMAN, L. *We, the People.* New York, 1947.

JOHNSON, CHARLES S. *Growing Up in the Black Belt.* Washington, 1941.

———. *Into the Main Stream.* Chapel Hill, N.C., 1947.

———. *The Negro College Graduate.* Chapel Hill, N.C., 1938.

KENNEY, JOHN A. *The Negro in Medicine.* Tuskegee, Ala., 1912.

———. "Specific Racial Contributions," *Journal of the National Medical Association,* XXXIII (March 1941), 83–85.

KRAUS, M. "American and European Medicine in the 18th Century," *Bulletin of the History of Medicine,* VIII (May 1940), 679–95.

LAMB, DAVID SMITH. *History of the Medical Society of the District of Columbia: 1817–1909.* Washington, 1909.

LEWIS, JULIAN H. "Contribution of an Unknown Negro to Anesthesia," *Journal of the National Medical Association,* XXIII (January–March 1931), 23–24.

LITWACK, L. F. *North of Slavery: The Negro in the Free States, 1790–1860.* Chicago, 1961.

LLOYD, WYNDHAM, and HAAGENSEN, C. D. *A Hundred Years of Medicine.* New York, 1943.

McMURDY, R. "Negro Women as Trained Nurses in Chicago," *Survey,* XXXI (November 8, 1913), 159–80.

McPHERSON, J. M. *The Negro's Civil War: How American Negroes Felt and Acted during the War for the Union.* New York, 1965.

———. *The Struggle for Equality: Abolitionists and the Negro in the Civil War and Reconstruction.* Princeton, N.J., 1964.

MANGUM, CHARLES STAPLES, JR. *The Legal Status of the Negro.* Chapel Hill, N.C., 1940.

MEDICAL SOCIETY OF THE DISTRICT OF COLUMBIA. *Constitution and By-Laws of the Medical Society of the District of Columbia.* Washington, 1924.

MEIER, A. "Booker T. Washington and the Rise of the N.A.A.C.P.," *Crisis,* LXI (February 1954), 69 ff.

"The Memorial of 1844 to the United States Senate," *Liberator* [Boston] (May 31, 1844).

MILLER, ELIZABETH W. *The Negro in America: A Bibliography.* Cambridge, Mass., 1966.

MILLER, K. "The Historical Background of the Negro Physician," *Journal of Negro History,* I (April 1916), 99–109.

MUMFORD, J. G. *A Narrative of Medicine in America.* Philadelphia, 1903.

NABRIT, S. M. "Negro in Science," *Negro History Bulletin,* XX (January 1957), 184–86.

"National Association of Colored Graduate Nurses Organized," *American Journal of Nursing,* IX (November 1908), 144–45.

"The Negro Cesar's Cure for Poison," *Massachusetts Magazine,* IV (1792), 103–4.

"Negro Nurses and Physicians," *Modern Hospital,* LXIII (October 1944), 41–42.

NORWOOD, WILLIAM F. *Medical Education in the United States before the Civil War.* Philadelphia, 1944.

PACKARD, F. R. *History of Medicine in the United States.* 2 vols. New York, 1931.

PETTIGREW, THOMAS F. *A Profile of the Negro American.* Princeton, N.J., 1964.

PHILLIPS, U. B. *American Negro Slavery.* New York, 1918.

REDDING, J. SAUNDERS. *They Came in Chains: Americans from Africa.* Philadelphia, 1950.

REITZES, DIETRICH C. *Negroes and Medicine.* Cambridge, Mass., 1958.

RIESMAN, DAVID. *Medicine in Modern Society.* Princeton, N.J., 1938.

ROSE, A. (ed.). *Race Prejudice and Discrimination.* New York, 1951.

RUGGLES, D. *An Antidote for a Poisonous Combination Recently Prepared by a "Citizen of New York" Alias Dr. Reese.* New York, 1838.

———. *The "Extinguisher" Extinguished! Or D. M. Reese, M.D. "Used Up!"* New York, 1834.

SEELIG, M. G. *Medicine: An Historical Outline.* Baltimore, 1925.

SHEPPARD, G. B. "Early Medical and Health Progress in Maryland," *Journal of the National Medical Association,* LIII (November 1961), 627–32.

SHRYOCK, R. H. *The Development of Modern Medicine.* New York, 1947.

SILBERMAN, C. E. *Crisis in Black and White.* New York, 1964.

SPENCER, G. A. *Medical Symphony: A Study of the Contributions of the Negro to Medical Progress in New York.* New York, 1947.

STAMPP, K. M. *The Peculiar Institution: Slavery in the Antebellum South.* New York, 1956.

STANTON, W. *The Leopard's Spots: Scientific Attitudes toward Race in America, 1815–1859.* Chicago, 1960.

STAUDENRAUS, P. J. *The African Colonization Movement, 1816–1865.* New York, 1961.

STEWARD, S. M. "Women in Medicine." Paper read before the National Association of Colored Women's Clubs at Wilberforce, Ohio, August 6, 1914.

TOKUNAGE, M. "Contribution of the Negro to Science and Invention," *Negro History Bulletin,* XVIII (April 1955), 172 ff.

WALKER, H. E. *The Negro in the Medical Profession.* Charlottesville, Va., 1949.

WASHINGTON, BOOKER T. "University Education for Negroes," *Independent,* LXVIII (March 24, 1910), 613–18.

WELLS, A. O. "Journey to Understanding: Four Witnesses to a Mississippi Summer: The Doctor," *Nation,* CXCIX (December 28, 1964), 515–16.

WERTENBAKER, T. J. *The Old South: The Founding of American Civilization.* New York, 1942.

WILLIAMS, GEORGE W. *History of the Negro Race in America.* New York, 1883.

WILLIAMS, R. F. *Negroes with Guns.* New York, 1962.

WOODS, L. D. "Negro in Chemistry," *School and Society,* LII (July 6, 1940), 11–12.

WOODWARD, C. V. *The Strange Career of Jim Crow.* New York, 1957.

WRIGHT, C. W. "Negro Pioneers in Chemistry," *School and Society,* LXV (February 1, 1947), 86–88.

Picture Credits

The author is grateful to the many libraries and special collections whose personnel aided in the search for unusual and interesting photographs. Those pictures which have not been listed are in the private collection of United Publishing Corporation, Washington, D.C.

Key: T: Top; B: Bottom; L: Left; R: Right; C: Center

Fabian Bachrach, Washington: 173, 198
Dr. Joe Brown, Cleveland: 61T
Dr. Eugene H. Dibble, Tuskegee, Alabama: 72BL, BR, 83, 98, 113
District of Columbia General Hospital: 153
Dr. Hubert A. Eaton, Wilmington, North Carolina: 143B, 247–253
Freedmen's Hospital, Washington: 96
Historical Society of Pennsylvania–Edward Carey Gardiner Collection, Philadelphia: 33
Dr. Theodore R. M. Howard, Chicago: 150T
Howard University, Washington: 90B
James Lewis, Washington: 190
Library of Congress: 14, 17, 123
Medical Committee for Human Rights, Washington: 167B, 264, 266, 267
Medical Tribune, New York: iiBL, 163, 164, 165B, 191, 203
Merkle Press, Washington: 3
National Association of Colored Graduate Nurses, New York: 73T, 129T, 258
National Library of Medicine, Bethesda, Maryland: iiTC, TR, 8L, 9, 11, 13, 18, 30, 32, 40, 43, 44, 46BR, 47, 48T, 51, 54–56, 60, 61B, 63, 64, 65T, 69–71, 72T, 73B, 74, 77B, 78, 82, 84L, 85, 87T, 91, 95, 114R, 118, 145, 221–223, 230–234, 236, 237
National Urban League, New York: 157
New York City Department of Hospitals: iiC, 107, 117
New York Public Library: 11, 19B, 49
New York Public Library–Schomburg Collection: iiTL, 10, 22, 28, 29, 31B, 35, 38, 44R, 47B, 68, 86, 102, 109, 143T, 199
Office of Economic Opportunity–Day Walters, Washington: 205BR
Office of Economic Opportunity–Paul Conklin, Washington: 205BL
PHS World, Department of Health, Education and Welfare, Washington: 183, 205T

Index

Page numbers in *italic type* refer to illustrations.